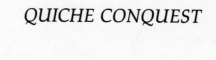

QUICHE CONQUEST

Quiche Conquest

Centralism and Regionalism in
Highland Guatemalan State Development

JOHN W. FOX

UNIVERSITY OF NEW MEXICO PRESS

Albuquerque

Library of Congress Cataloging in Publication Data

Fox, John W.   1946–
    Quiche conquest.

    Bibliography: p. 305
    Includes index.
    1. Quichés—History.   2. Quichés—Antiquities.
3. Indians of Central America—Guatemala—History.
4. Indians of Central America—Guatemala—Tribal
government.   5. Guatemala—Antiquities.   I. Title.
F1465.2.Q5F68   970'.004'97   77-89437
ISBN 0-8263-0461-3

CONTENTS

TABLES

MAPS

FIGURES

PREFACE

This is a study of the cultural effects of the conquest and political domination of the Guatemalan Highlands by the Quiche people in the Late Postclassic Period (A.D. 1250–1524). It is based on my analysis of the region's abundant, well-preserved archaeological remains in conjunction with the rich ethnohistory of pre-Hispanic Guatemala.

In order to assess degrees of Quiche influence on subjugated peoples, I have analyzed the remains of some 110 settlements of the conquered ethnic groups before and after Quiche domination. These settlements constitute the majority of elite communities once within the Quiche state. Because settlement patterns spatially reflect sociocultural organization, their analysis is particularly appropriate for this kind of study. I have correlated Quiche influences in settlement remains with the political relationships reflected in ethnohistory. The dynastic chronology worked out by Carmack (n.d.a) provides a temporal framework for the political events described in the native documents (see also Wauchope 1948b, 1949). In addition, ethnohistory provides data on specific acts of political domination by the Quiche, such as levies of tribute in goods or military service, as well as military occupation by Quiche royalty.

One of my purposes in locating the elite centers of the Quiche state and identifying them ethnohistorically is to examine the territorial organization and ecological underpinnings of an archaic state system (see Fox 1977). I also infer economic relationships by viewing the information on tribute payments gleaned from ethnohistory alongside the material and agricultural production of different regions.

Finally, a significant portion of this book is descriptive, adding to the archaeological record many Postclassic sites in Highland Guatemala. The new data I present here address three hitherto "unanswered criticisms" recently voiced by Crumley (1976:59, 62–63) of the usefulness of settlement-pattern analysis in understanding the development of the state. Specifically, my data, in this one case, correct the "lack of detailed settlement data and lack of close chronological control for periods in the development of the state"; they pinpoint the territorial boundaries of the state as well as those of its provincial subsystems; and they identify hierarchies of urban centers.

A brief description of my archaeological field research is in order. I collected only data that bore directly on elite settlement pattern variability; hence I did little test pitting or systematic ceramic collection, since these were largely incidental to my research design. Data collection involved five procedures: (1) mapping configurations of monumental architecture with a Brunton Pocket Transit; (2) measuring the site; (3) recording ecological data that might have influenced the site's location or size; (4) obtaining small ceramic and lithic collections; and (5) identifying the site with an aboriginal community. Late Postclassic civic centers were located by examining detailed Instituto Geográfico Nacional (IGN) maps for Quiche place names. For example, such toponyms as Ojertinamit, Xetinamit, and Chuitinamit contain the Quiche word *tinamit*, which translates roughly as "fortified town." Also, the Spanish term *pueblo viejo* commonly designates a Late Postclassic civic center. Finally, Robert Carmack often obtained the locations and aboriginal names of sites by questioning local officials and Maya farmers. His fluency in Quiche was invaluable.

Sites varied widely in preservation, but the large number of intact and excavated structures allowed me to develop a typology of Quichean buildings on which I based interpretive site diagrams of poorly preserved civic centers. Although few house platforms were exposed on the surface, the size of residential areas could be approximated from the extent of occupational debris. Eastern sites, on the whole, were better preserved than western ones, perhaps because the latter, which often overlook modern cities and towns, have been altered by reuse of the building materials in post-Hispanic construction. All of the sites were abandoned, although many were used as shrines as well as for milpa (agricultural plots).

Each of the five substantive chapters in this book covers one major ethnic subsystem or province of the Quiche state. Mention is also made of the Sajcabaja region, where a French team has recently located a number of Late Postclassic sites (Ichon 1975, n.d.), and the Uspantec region, where I did a limited amount of

surveying; full treatment of these areas must await further research. Although the Tzutuhil and the Pokoman, located respectively on the southern and eastern borders of the Quiche state, will
also be mentioned only tangentially, they were undoubtedly influenced by the Quiche. To the west, the Jacalteca and the Tzotzil and
Tzeltal of Chiapas were beyond Quiche control and, seemingly,
influence and will not be discussed; nor will the small Kekchi and
Pokomchi sites in the northeastern highlands.

In accordance with current practice, I have not used Spanish
accents in aboriginal words. Citations of native documents follow
the format used by Carmack (1968, 1973, n.d.d), giving the lineage
names of the authors of the documents (Xajil of the Cakchiquel, for
example) rather than their lengthy Spanish titles. Maps are drawn
according to magnetic north rather than true north.

The comparative analysis of Late Postclassic highland settlement
patterns in this study is a continuation of work begun by A.
Ledyard Smith and Robert M. Carmack. Indeed, a significant
number of the data used here come from Smith's maps and
descriptions of Late Postclassic sites (Smith 1955, 1961; Smith and
Kidder 1943, 1951). When resurveying a number of the sites
treated in Smith's *Archaeological Reconnaissance in Central
Guatemala* (1955), I found his maps faultless. I used his correlation
of Late Postclassic settlement features with Mexican architectural
derivations (1955: Table 2), as well as some of his other architectural comparisons (1961, 1965), as a beginning point in the
analysis of conquest settlement systems, especially regarding an
ultimate Mexican-influenced cultural base.

Robert Carmack has undertaken a comprehensive study of the
Late Postclassic Quichean cultures. This book relies primarily on
two of his works. First, in "Toltec Influence on the Postclassic Culture History of Highland Guatemala" (1968), Carmack describes the
Gulf Coast and Epi-Toltec origins of the Late Postclassic conquest-
based sociocultural systems of Highland Guatemala. I try to add an
archaeological dimension to his largely ethnohistoric and linguistic
evidence for Gulf Coast origins of the highland groups. Second,
Carmack's unpublished "Quichean Political History" (n.d.a) is a
highly detailed account of political interaction among the various
highland peoples, compiling events recorded in the native chronicles. I use Carmack's syntheses of historical events to test cultural
processes of Quiche domination in the archaeological record.

The data for this study are drawn largely from my dissertation (Fox 1975). For their guidance I would like to acknowledge the members of my graduate committee, Drs. Dwight T. Wallace, Robert M. Carmack, and Dean R. Snow. Both Carmack and Wallace also collaborated with me in fieldwork as well as generously providing me with data from their own research. The new data presented herein were gathered in the survey effort of the Quiche Project, sponsored by the State University of New York at Albany, which has given rise to the Institute of Mesoamerican Studies there, and the Instituto de Antropología e Historia de Guatemala. Luis Lujan Muñoz, the Director of the Instituto, has provided invaluable direction, assistance and encouragement to the Quiche Project since its inception. The survey spanned the summer field seasons of 1970 through 1974 and was aided by some forty graduate and undergraduate students altogether. We thank the many descendants of the pre-Hispanic Quiche who aided us in locating and identifying sites; we hope this study will add to the general recognition of their rich heritage. I wish finally to thank my wife, Naomi Thorp Fox, for continuous support and for efforts expended on this study both in the field and in its writing.

The site diagrams appearing herein were drawn from the work of others, who are cited within the text, and from my own field notes (Figs. 3, 4, 6–10, 22, 23, 27–30, 32–34, 37, 39–41). John M. Weeks, of the State University of New York at Albany, generously traced into ink my 43 pencil site diagrams and 19 topographic maps. Mark Miller of Baylor University traced Map 11.

Munro S. Edmonson, of Tulane University, carefully critiqued the manuscript with his thorough knowledge of Quichean ethnohistory. Elizabeth Hadas Heist, of the University of New Mexico Press, made this work possible by thorough editing. For Paulette Edwards of Baylor University, special thanks for finding time in a busy schedule to type the final chapter.

1

INTRODUCTION

The Development of the Conquest State

The Quiche and a number of related groups left written political histories that were transcribed into a Latin alphabet shortly after the Spanish conquest. The first event these documents describe with historical accuracy is a movement into the highlands by small groups of warriors from the Gulf Coast, following the collapse of Chichen Itza (called Tulan in the *Annals of the Cakchiquels;* see Xajil 1953:47–51). These warriors eventually became the Quichean dynasties—the Quiche, the Cakchiquel, the Tzutuhil, the Pokoman, and so forth—that ruled across the highlands. Ethnohistoric accounts of these first communities established in the highlands are corroborated by archaeological remains (see Carmack, Fox, and Stewart 1975). The historicity of the documents progresses with time from rather vague legendary accounts, corresponding to the transition from the Early to Late Postclassic periods, to accounts specific in detail on events, persons, and places during the later part of the Late Postclassic (Carmack n.d.d).[1]

The Late Postclassic Period begins in Mesoamerica about A.D. 1200 to 1250 with the emergence of new political systems following the approximately simultaneous collapse of Chichen Itza in the Yucatan and Tula in Highland Mexico. Chichen Itza was a crucial part of a trading network encompassing most of southern Meso-

1

america (see Sabloff and Rathje 1975:25–26); as I will argue in this study, Chichen Itza was linked to the Guatemalan Highlands prior to the ascent of the Quiche. In the Yucatan and along the Gulf Coast a number of ruling dynasties arose, claiming Toltec ancestry, who initiated conquest- and commerce-based systems (Scholes and Roys 1968; Thompson 1970). Like other Late Postclassic ruling dynasties across Mesoamerica, the Quichean rulers also claimed Toltec descent (Carmack 1968, 1974).

The elite strata of the Quiche state, who lived in the civic centers analyzed in this study, were descended from Epigonal Toltec warriors who migrated into the highlands following the collapse of Chichen Itza. The Quichean chronicles assert that 13 separate groups (13 is an ideologically symbolic Maya number; probably there were more groups) entered the Guatemalan Highlands some ten generations prior to the Spanish conquest—about A.D. 1250 according to Carmack's calculations (n.d.a). The identification of Gulf Coast place names in the Quichean documents (Carmack 1968:66–70) suggests that these migratory groups originated along the Veracruz-Tabasco Gulf Coast, the frontier between Mexican and Maya culture areas.[2] A "Mexicanized" culture introduced by these small migratory groups was the basis for the eventual development of the Quiche conquest state.[3]

Different Epigonal Toltec groups (henceforth abbreviated as Epi-Toltec) settled in different parts of the highlands. It is clear from ethnohistory that these small groups of warriors took local highland women as wives and soon lost their Gulf Coast language. Their descendants became known by the different languages they adopted, such as Quiche, Rabinal, Cakchiquel, and Aguacatec, which were long established in the various regions they settled.[4] The Quiche, the most successful of the Mexicanized militarily expansive systems introduced by the Epi-Toltec forefathers, eventually came to dominate the descendants of the other Epi-Toltec groups as well as neighboring indigenous Highland Maya[5] groups (the Vukamak, Mam, Ixil).[6]

The "conquest" sociocultural system of the Quiche exhibits Mexican features that may be traced to the Gulf region of Mexinayan frontier culture. Nahua loan words in Quiche, such as *tinamit* ("fortified town"), *tecpan* ("palace"), and *calpul* ("ward"), as well as terms for altar-temple, pyramid, and adobe brick, reflect settlement features of the Mexican conquest system (Carmack

1968:72). Campbell's general comments on Nahua loan words in Quiche are pertinent here:

> Much has been made of the fact that many of these loans involve religious and military terms, reflecting the post-classic militarism of the Toltecs. . . . This kind of contact is certainly confirmed by the content of the loans, but in our emphasis of religious and militaristic content we should not forget that many of these loans reflect prestigious domestic and household terms, parallel to the Norman French prestige culture words borrowed into English. (1976:16)

Some time ago, A. L. Smith (1955) recognized that certain features of Quichean architecture, such as round structures, enclosed I-shaped ball courts, and colonnaded long buildings (known hereafter as long structures), were also Mexican in derivation. The conquest orientation of Quiche culture is readily evident in other basic aspects, such as an economic system based on tribute supplied by conquered peoples, a social organization in which warfare was a means of social mobility and government offices related directly to conquest politics, and a religion centered around human sacrifice for which victims were obtained in battle.

Quichean settlements were located around centers established at the beginning of the Late Postclassic Period, but each of the Quichean groups gradually expanded its territories. A number of the regional groups abandoned their earliest centers and established new ones in the mid-to-late 1300s, about the same time as the expansion of the Quiche state. To refer to this temporal and evolutionary point of demarcation, the Late Postclassic Period is divided into Early (c. 1200–1350) and Late (c. 1350–1524) phases (Carmack, Fox, and Stewart 1975).

After subjugating neighboring indigenous Maya peoples, known as the Vukamak in the chronicles, and incorporating them as peasant agriculturalists, the Quiche conquered much of the highlands and Pacific piedmont and coast within a span of only two generations (between the late 1300s and c. 1460). During the first series of conquests, under the Quiche ruler Gucumatz (whose name translates as Quetzalcoatl), the Quiche subjugated the Cakchiquel, Rabinal, Akahal, Agaab (who probably included the Sacapulas Quiche), Aguacatec, Uspantec, Northern Mam, and perhaps the Ixil.[7] During the second generation of expansion, under the ruler Quicab, the Quiche extended their control to the rich areas to the west and southwest and along the Pacific coast, conquering the Western Quiche and much of the Southern Mam during this period. According to Carmack (1968:77), "At its maximum extent, during the reign of Quicab (ca. A.D. 1450), the Quiche state stretched from Soconusco at its southwest border to the northern reaches of Alta Verapaz . . . and included approximately 1,000,000 inhabitants." By 1470, however, the Quiche state became too large in area for effective administration, and a number of subject groups (the Cakchiquel, the Rabinal, and the Aguacatec) revolted and initiated rival systems. In the half-century prior to the Spanish conquest, the Quiche were involved in a number of protracted wars with their former subject groups.

Settlement Pattern Analysis

Distinct communities with individual territories have probably existed in the segmented Guatemalan highlands since the beginning of the Preclassic Period.[8] The Quiche civic centers whose remains I analyze in this study were the loci for the elite ruling stratum and associated functionaries (such as artisans) of larger communities. Ethnohistory tells us that the elite lived in civic centers. As an example, elite groups from specific civic centers identified archaeologically are said in a number of documents to have been subjugated by the Quiche (e.g., C'oyoi 1973; Xpantzay II 1957). As in most archaic states, the elite dwelled in "urbanized" civic centers, known as *tinamit* in Quiche, while peasants were dispersed around the countryside in hamlets known as *amak*. The surface remains of civic centers are generally characterized by monumental architecture, such as temples and long structures arranged around civic plazas as well as in other configurations. Adjacent activity areas on level ground, without monumental architecture, and containing such occupational debris as ceramics, obsidian tools, and other lithics are lumped under the general classification of "residential area." In the few such areas that have been excavated, small, dwellinglike foundations and associated domestic artifacts predominate (Guillemin, personal communication; Weeks 1975; Ichon 1975:97; Lehmann 1968:41). Concentrations of specialized artifacts have also been noted, however, in different segments of a single residential area. These may represent occupation by distinct social segments, such as metal workers or soldiers, who are referred to in the native chronicles and early dictionaries. Most of the surface remains in these areas have been significantly altered by hoe cultivation practices in the four centuries since abandonment. The classification of such areas as "residential," though perhaps too general, is justified in this study, I believe, since such units are only considered in determining the overall size of the occupied areas of a site outside the civic complexes of monumental architecture.

Settlement pattern analyses traditionally have taken one of two approaches: the ecological approach, which views settlement remains as manifestations of a community's adaptation to a particular environment, and the functionalist approach, in which settlement remains allow inferences about social, political, and religious organization (Trigger 1968:54; Hole and Heizer 1973:355). This study utilizes both approaches. I employ the ecological approach primarily in locational analysis, focusing on the relationship of site location and size to such environmental variables as proximity to water, amount of nearby arable land, nearby resources worthy of interregional circulation (for example, obsidian, clay, salt), and defensible topography. We know from the chronicles (e.g., Alvarado 1924) that lands near Quiche centers were used for cultivation to support the elite community and that tribute was often paid in specialty products from different regions. In a broader perspective, viewing the network of microenvironments from each community allows us to see the ecological organization of a conquest state system. A major purpose of this study, however, is to examine various sociocultural changes in component communities of a conquest state; hence the functionalist approach is the more important one in my settlement pattern analysis. (In this study, *architecture* refers to individual buildings or constructions; *settlement pattern* refers to the actual arrangement of architecture.)

In examining sociocultural change, three levels of settlement pattern analysis are useful. The individual building or structure may be analyzed, as well as the arrangements of structures within single civic centers, and the distribution of civic centers within each region. As Trigger points out, "The patterns displayed at each of these levels can be viewed as being functionally related in some way to all aspects of a culture and therefore able to shed light on a variety of problems. But in fact, each level displays tendencies especially appropriate to the study of particular aspects of society" (1968:73-74). Thus variation in size and location of special purpose constructions, such as temples, altars, walls, palaces, and long buildings (lineage houses), allows inference about associated social segments of the community (priests, rulers, lineage organizations). In addition, architectural styles (varieties of balustrades, wall motifs, numbers of platforms), particularly of buildings used for religious activities, reflect cultural values specific to communities and, usually, ethnic groups. Occasionally, variability in architectural style is related to the cosmological ordering of individual groups, as known from ethnohistoric studies (see, for example, Thompson 1970).

In conjunction with ethnohistoric mention of locations of specific groups and distributions of language groups (see Campbell 1971, 1976), the layout of structures within a site is the basis for defining ethnicity. In essence, I am stipulating, in the sense of Schiffer (1976:16–17), that arrangements of buildings reflect spatially, to some degree, the sociocultural organization (government, religion, social stratification) of individual elite communities. When particular settlement patterns tend to cluster in separate geographic regions that can be correlated with distinct linguistic patterns, I speak of ethnicity.

In short I am proposing that there is a direct relationship between the differences in the arrangement of buildings and architectural styles in civic centers and the differences in ethnicity of elite communities. Furthermore, the buildings grouped around civic plazas, such as temples, long structures, altars, skull racks, ball courts, and palaces, reflect spatially the relationships among some governmental institutions. For example, the relationships among elite lineages, priests who related the "commands" of principal deities, and supreme office holders, such as the Quiche "king" (*ahpop*) are reflected in the spatial relationships among long structures, temples, and palaces. This stipulation is supported by ethnohistoric references to government functionaries associated with spatial segments of the civic plaza. For example, Las Casas (1958:151–52) states that only the Quiche ruling group could play at the ball game or eat the flesh of humans sacrificed at the temples. Also, only members of the ruling group attended to the idols in the temples. Only the principal Quiche lineages maintained lineage houses within the civic centers. A sixteenth-century native rendering of Utatlan recently examined by Carmack associates what are believed to be long structures in the civic plaza with specific kinship groups. Finally, the monumental architecture was built by artisans apparently under the direction of members of the ruling stratum. Terms designating occupations that would have been involved in building construction, such as Quichean words for architect, mason, sculptor, stonecutter, and quarry worker, have survived in the native texts and early dictionaries (see Weeks 1975:18–19).

Conquest Sociocultural Change: A Model of Centralism and Regionalism

Carneiro's environmental circumscription hypothesis (1970), according to which conquest states evolve in areas of highly segmented topography, is instructive in viewing the emergence and dominance of the Quiche in the rugged highland terrain. According to Carneiro, when population expands to the limit of arable land, warfare ensues between communities competing for space to continue growth. Since the arable land is circumscribed by mountains or desert inappropriate for agriculture, defeated communities cannot flee. They become peasant agriculturalists supporting the victors, who emerge as a nonagrarian elite stratum maintaining their superiority by military rule. As this process continues, the most militarily viable group eventually welds "an assorted collection of petty states into a single integrated and centralized political unit," the conquest state (Carneiro 1970:736).[9]

My assessment of the acculturative influences resulting from the Quiche conquest, both on subject ethnic groups and on the Quiche themselves, will make use of the concepts of centralism and regionalism. *Regionalism* refers to a centrifugal process, the tendency by various geographically separated highland peoples to maintain ethnic continuity. Thus regional ethnic groups existed before and after the Quiche conquest, later withstood the Spanish conquest, and, indeed, exist today. *Centralism* refers to the centripetal process by which one group dominates other groups.

> In a fully centralized relationship political power resides in
> one system and is not shared with others with which it has
> ties. In other words, this kind of political system is char-
> acterized by the exclusive right to political power among
> articulating political systems. . . . A completely decentralized
> relationship is apportioned out equally among related sys-
> tems. (Gorenstein 1973:6)

Since individual communities always exercise some local rule,
centralism may vary in degree. However, the dominating group
grows in proportion to the degree of control and size of groups
subjugated, as seen in the urban communities of the Quiche at
Utatlan and the colonial Spanish at sixteenth-to eighteenth-century
Guatemala City (Antigua). "In centralization," to quote Hole and
Heizer (1973:446, after Hall and Fagen 1956:22), "one element
becomes dominant in the system to the point that a change in this
part greatly affects the whole system." This study of the Quiche
and their subject groups addresses itself to changes within the
system resultant from centralized growth.

I examine Quiche influence on subject regional systems on two
levels. First I discuss the adoption of specific elements of Quiche
culture; since distinct regional settlement patterns can be defined
for ethnic groups once within the Quiche state, items of Quiche
culture can then be seen in the settlement record after Quiche
domination. At the second level, I trace the continued political
adaptation of regional systems to this conquest. It should be
possible to correlate various forms of Quiche political domination
known from ethnohistory—enclaves of aristocratic administrators,
large Quiche colonies, and tributary relationships in material goods
or military service—with various kinds of Quiche influence evident
in the settlement record. Thus, complete Quiche settlement
patterns in other ethnic regions may indicate Quiche colonies,
whereas single Quiche plazas in non-Quiche civic centers are
theorized to correspond to enclaves of Quiche administrators. (See
Carmack and Fox n.d. and Fox 1977 for an application of this idea
to Cakchiquel expansion processes.) In assessing methods of
control of entire ethnic groups, is there evidence of direct Quiche
influence at a centrally located civic center, rather than many
centers in each region? More diffuse Quiche influence in the
settlement record, such as a few buildings in Quiche style, a

change in orientations of buildings, or a Quiche architectural "veneer" over earlier non-Quiche construction, may reflect less direct mechanisms of Quiche control. For example, ethnohistory suggests that groups defeated in battle had to adopt the Quiche deities Tohil and Awilix. In fact, Carmack (1968:78) argues from ethnohistory and by analogy with the better documented Aztecs that statues of the gods were "carried into battle on the backs of priests, and once the enemy had been conquered" they were required to place statues of the Quiche deities "along with their local deities." Does religious architecture at subject sites manifest a corresponding degree of Quiche influence (see Sloane 1974)? Alternatively, can less direct Quiche influence be seen as a function of the prestige the Quiche had throughout the highlands? An association with the Quiche is a constant undercurrent in chronicles written by regional peoples. Such "prestige" influence may be reflected in general stylistic changes of architecture toward Quiche forms.

The various regional ethnohistoric documents clearly reflect regionalism and centralism. Such regional documents as, for example, those of the Western Quiche (i.e., Totonicapan 1953; C'oyoi 1973; Nijaib I–II 1957) or the Cakchiquel (Xajil 1953; Xpantzay I–III 1957) justify their rights to enjoy special privileges and to maintain rule over various regional communities by their close relationship with the Central Quiche. One way of establishing aristocratic standing, which led to preferential treatment by the Spanish, was to recount the precontact relationships between the ruling regional lineages and the Quiche lineages of Greater Utatlan (see Carmack 1973:20).

A well-established principle of general systems theory, briefly referred to above, is that growth of a central component will necessitate change in articulating components (see, for example, Maruyama 1963). As a corollary in evolutionary theory, Service (1960, 1971) argues that subordinate provincial systems will successfully adapt to and eventually surpass the central, dominant system by incorporating the basis for its success more efficiently in their own systems (this is Service's "Law of Evolutionary Potential"). On a general level, then, it may be possible to test less obvious Quiche influence, resultant from the success of the conquest system, by examining change in centralism and militarism reflected in regional settlement remains. In an important study focusing on military specialization in a Late Postclassic Mixtec community in Highland Mexico, Gorenstein (1973:6) writes that

> specialization in the military system and centralization of power in the political system are related variables. The greater the military specialization, the greater the political centralization. . . .

To provide a framework for "measuring" change in centralization of regional systems, we can establish several dimensions of centralization: fortification, growth, and territorial organization.

1. *Fortification.* The interaction of competing systems within a conquest polity necessitates both offensive military actions—for example, to procure tributary communities or sacrificial victims—and defensive actions to withstand the adversary's offense (see R. M. Adams 1966:160–64). Rather than constructing large-scale fortifications like these used for defense in areas of undifferentiated topography (such as walled communities in Mesopotamia), an elite community in the highlands could attain the same goal with less energy expenditure by utilizing naturally defensible locations (see Smith 1955; Borhegyi 1965; Rowlands 1972:447). Is there an increase in defensive use of natural topography after interaction with the Quiche? Is there a corresponding increase in artificial defenses, such as moats (drý ditches), terraces (vertical masonry retaining walls set into hillslopes), and the contouring of hilltops? And does this apparent lack of fortifications in peasant communities indicate that they were pawns in warfare among the elite, paying tribute regardless of the outcome of war?

2. *Growth.* Increasingly more bellicose systems require larger elite populations and greater specialization in military-related activities—full-time militarists, administrators of tribute, a priesthood to attend to the deities, which, as we have seen, were sometimes forced on subject peoples, artisans to manufacture weapons and sumptuary symbols for class and office distinction—to maintain a competitive position (see Carneiro 1970:736; Service 1975:313; Gorenstein 1973). High population density, which is characteristic of the Late Postclassic Period across Mesoamerica (see Armillas 1951), is related to militaristically oriented elite communities forced to dwell together for mutual defense (see Service 1975:299–300). For a well-documented case, see the

account of the siege of the Quiche in which the entire community, including women, were pressed into military service (*Popol Vuh* 1950:200–204; *Totonicapan* 1953:173–74; cf. Brundage 1975:36; Fox 1977). Elite communities of conquest polities were restricted in growth by the confines of defensible landforms, such as mountaintops or islands (e.g., Tenochtitlan, Topoxte).

Growth may be measured by population increase as well as by increase in social differentiation and integration (see Plog 1974:56–58; Sanders and Price 1968:96–97). Population increase is evident in the size of occupied space at civic centers, as well as in numbers of houses, when such data are available. However, except in a few instances where population size may be fairly securely approximated from ethnohistoric sources, I refrain from making population estimates. Social differentiation can be seen in an increase in the number of distinct settlement components (i.e., building types, or functionally distinct clusters of buildings). Increased integration through centralization of power should be evident in the distribution of government buildings, such as one central governmental focus, a single civic plaza, in contrast to a number of such plazas within a single civic center.

An important question in regard to growth is, in general, do regional centers emulate Quiche settlement organization in the arrangement of newly evolved sectors of society, such as full-time militarists?

3. *Territorial organization.* Geographers have long theorized that as political and economic cohesiveness increases within a bounded system, a centrally located community will emerge to serve as a coordinating center for the surrounding region (see Haggett 1966; Crumley 1976). In response to Quiche expansion, did a single civic center emerge as a political-economic coordinating center for the various regional groups?

Central-place theory (Christaller 1966) further maintains that, given an undifferentiated physiography, systems united by a principal center should have hexagonal shaped perimeters since "the hexagon provides the most economical geometrical form for the equal division of an area between a number of points" (Haggett 1966:88). However, since the boundaries of regional ethnic systems in the rugged highlands, as revealed by ethnohistory (see, *Título Sacapulas* and *Título C'oyoi* in Carmack 1973), tend to be determined by topographic features, particularly mountain ranges, this model does apply. C. Smith's (1972) findings, delineating spheres of post-Hispanic economic interaction in the highlands, also negate the hexagonal model. Nonetheless, applying the economic premises of central-place theory to the segmented highland physiography, we may pose questions such as, Are regional centers situated approximately in the geographic centers of ethnic regions on natural passageways—such as river valleys or mountain passes—to principal hinterland areas? In other words, are they located on the lines of least resistance? Are regional centers located on or near broad ecological boundaries, thereby serving as exchange points for symbiotic areas of differing ecology?

A final way of viewing change resulting from centralism is to examine the central group itself. It should grow at "a constant fraction of the growth of the entire system . . ." (Berry 1967:76). Thus we should expect a slightly earlier growth for the Quiche in fortification, population growth, specialization, and centralization of government. What, however, was the Quiche pattern of expansion in acquiring and settling ecologically diverse territories?

Environmental Diversity

Highland Guatemala is a region of ecological contrast, with cool, upland mesas and mountains over 3,000 meters in elevation often separated by only a day's walk from hot, arid valleys less than 1,000 meters above sea level. During the Late Postclassic Period, generally speaking, different ethnic groups inhabited environmentally different regions. Thus broad ecological sectioning can be seen as one basis for regionalism, pre-Hispanic as well as modern. By the same token, the politics of conquest is related to these sharply circumscribed ecological regions, for the relatively short-lived Quiche conquest state as well as for the Spanish regime.

As a centralized political system, the Quiche state derived strength from uniting ecologically diverse territories. At its maximum it extended in the highlands from about the present Mexican border on the west to near the Valley of Guatemala on the east, where Guatemala City sprawls today, and to the foothills forming the northern edge of the highlands just above the Peten rain forest. Although the Quiche conquest system reached out of the highlands to the piedmont and Pacific coast, no Late Postclassic civic centers have been found in the latter regions, so they will only be touched upon briefly in this study.

In addition to the sketch of environmental variability for broad highland zones provided here, ecological differentiation within each region is discussed below in the appropriate chapters, on a fairly general level. Specific data about Late Postclassic paleoenvironments are beyond the research design. I hold that the Late Postclassic environment was essentially the same as it is today, and that cultivation systems of the Maya peasants in the various regions today are relatively unchanged (with a few notable exceptions, such as Momostenango, and where European-introduced crops are grown). The few available data, such as descriptions of cultivation and cultigens in the native and Spanish documents (Carmack n.d.c), as well as limited archaeological work in this regard (pollen sampling by the Kaminaljuyu Project, maize ears excavated by Guillemin at Iximche), support my point of view.

The exceedingly rugged highlands are characterized generally by hilly to mountainous terrain, interspersed with relatively level basins. This topography, in addition to abundant rainfall, has resulted in abrupt gullies called barrancas, which are often 100 meters deep. There are several minor mountain chains; two principal east-west-running mountain ranges; a geologically recent volcanic axis, forming the southern rim of the highlands; and the older, more eroded Cuchumatanes massif, marking the northern limit of Quiche speakers along the northern third of the highlands. The most fertile agricultural lands are in the relatively level intermontane basins immediately north of the volcanic axis. In contrast, the northern half of the highlands is generally eroded hilly country, underlain by limestone bedrock, with less fertile karst soils.

This "vertical" highland physiography supports a series of closely juxtaposed environmental zones spanning the highlands. To designate these mutually exclusive broad zones with varying altitudes, I use the traditional Mesoamerican ecological classification of the *tierra caliente* habitat (generally below 1,200 meters elevation), the mid-highland *tierra templada* (1,200–2,000 meters), and the *tierra fria* zone (above 2,000 meters). However, I have raised the *tierra caliente-templada* cutoff to 1,200 meters, rather than the traditional 1,000 meters, to match changes in flora. Most of the highlands is subject, in varying degrees, to a "rainy" season in the spring and summer and a "dry" season during the fall and winter.

Within the Quiche conquest state, in the middle of the highlands, were two regions of the *tierra caliente* zone—the narrow, east-west-running Rio Motagua and Rio Negro basins. Both basins are quite dry, supporting only xerophytic vegetation. The rain clouds that sweep up daily from the Pacific Ocean invariably dissipate before they reach these basins. A variety of fruit trees and tropical crops are cultivated on the basin floors, sometimes with irrigation.

The southern highlands comprise upper-range *tierra templada* and *tierra fria* habitats. The remaining forests are largely pine, with lesser stands of oak and cypress. Dryland farming on rich volcanic alluvium, watered by almost daily rains, supports the dense populations today, as it did pre-Hispanically. The land is almost continuously cultivated, with relatively short seasonal fallow periods, in these intermontane regions. In contrast, slash-and-burn cultivation predominates in the less fertile *tierra templada* northern third of the highlands and on the steeper basin walls of the southern highlands, supporting far more scattered populations (cf. Colby and Van Den Berghe 1969:29). Both cultivation systems utilize the hoe, machete, and digging stick, and produce for the most part the native Mesoamerican staples of maize and beans.

Notes

Chapter 1

1. I use the temporal designation Late Postclassic rather than Protohistoric because the prefix *proto* is vague.

2. Thompson's study of this general area (1970) provides a good background for understanding the "Mexicanized-Maya" frontier cultural milieu.

3. I use the term *Mexican* to refer to the general area and elements of culture extending throughout Mexico to the Tabasco region in the south, and into the Guatemalan Highlands, during the Late Postclassic Period (Carmack 1968:57). *Toltec* refers to a complex of interrelated elements such as the cult of Quetzalcoatl and to certain architectural features first evident at Chichen Itza.

4. The term *Quichean* is applied by Carmack (1973:6) to the culturally related Quiche, Cakchiquel, Tzutuhil, Rabinal, and Uspantec peoples, who also had closely related languages. I would expand this category to include the Aguacatec, whose Early-phase Late Postclassic Period material culture remains demonstrate a similar tradition. Indeed, the

documents mention that the Aguacatec, known as the Balamiha, migrated into the highlands with the other Quichean groups (*Popol Vuh* 1950:171). The native chronicles also mention that the languages of these migratory groups were lost soon after settlement in the highlands. Thus, the linguistic distance apparent in glottochronology between the Aguacatec and the other Quichean peoples merely reflects a language distribution of long antiquity in the highlands, one that surely predates the Epi-Toltec migration. The Late-phase Eastern Mam at Zaculeu and the Western Pokoman (at Chinautla Viejo) also appear to have been heavily influenced by Quiche peoples, and thus may be considered part of the culturally related Quichean group. The homogeneity in language (Campbell, personal communication) and in settlement pattern and architectural style (Los Cimientos Tulumajillo and Pueblo Viejo in San Pedro Pinula) of the Eastern Pokoman, who were spread over a wide geographical area, suggests a possible Late-phase expansion. This seems to have been influenced by Quiche and Cakchiquel expansion to the east.

5. In this study I will use the term *Maya* to refer to regional ethnic groups in the highlands who spoke Mayan languages. Quiche was spoken in a number of separate regions within the Quiche state, and I will designate the Quiche speakers of the Quiche Basin, who controlled the conquest state, as the Central Quiche. I call their close linguistic affiliates in the western highlands the Western Quiche. The Eastern Quiche, with sharper dialectical differences, are sometimes classified as speaking Achi, and the dialect of the Sacapulas Quiche may be idiosyncratic enough to warrant its classification as a separate language known as Sacapultec (Campbell 1971).

6. The Quiche confederates first settled in the western reaches of the Sierra de Chuacus, now within the Departmento El Quiche. Since the centrally situated civic center of the Quiche, known ethnohistorically as Hacawitz, is today situated in the aldea of Santa Rosa Chujuyub, I refer to this general area of early settlement as simply the Chujuyub area. Chujuyub is also spelled Chujuyup.

7. There is a good possibility that the single long reign attributed to Gucumatz by Carmack (1968, n.a) actually covered the reign of Cotuha as well (or Qotuha; see *Totonicapan* 1953:184–88). Carmack argues that Gucumatz and Cotuha are the same person. For our purposes, however, it makes little difference whether a single leader ruled the Quiche for some fifty years or two rulers reigned for about twenty-five years each, so we can simply refer to the early expansion as having been accomplished under the leadership of Gucumatz.

8. Murdock (1949:79) defines a community as "the maximal group of persons who normally reside in face-to-face association," which corresponds in archaeology to a single component.

9. The archaic state level of sociocultural organization is characterized by large, often multiethnic populations, numbering at least in the tens of thousands, and stratified into social classes. States are ruled by formal governments, legitimized by laws and backed by force which is supported by taxation (Service 1962:166–69, 1975:14–15).

2

CENTRAL QUICHE

Before their major expansion, the Quiche inhabited Chujuyub, a mountain range directly north of the Quiche Basin. Chujuyub sites were first settled by the Epi-Toltec ancestors of the Quiche at the time of their initial entry into the highlands, probably in the early 1200s A.D.. The descendants of the Epi-Toltec, the Central Quiche, conquered local groups in the Quiche Basin and established their capital city, Utatlan (Gumarcaaj, ethnohistorically), in the western corner of the basin during the Late phase of the Late Postclassic Period. Tied to the elite center of Utatlan were the peasant communities that surrounded it. From this core area the Quiche not only controlled other highland groups but also obtained colonists to settle subjugated provinces (see Fox 1977).

In this chapter I will first describe the Central Quiche settlement pattern and architectural style at Greater Utatlan and at the Early-phase centers in the Chujuyub area, and then compare the settlement remains of the Early- and Late-phase central Quiche communities to assess sociocultural changes resultant from the growth of the conquest state system. I will also briefly describe the small satellite or "ward" sites that ringed Utatlan for a distance of two to perhaps twenty-five kilometers, forming a still larger community with Greater Utatlan, designated as the Central Quiche heartland. Finally, I will describe the communities with which the Early-phase Central Quiche interacted in the initial development of a conquest state.

16

Greater Utatlan

The ruins of Utatlan lie two kilometers west of the modern department capital of Santa Cruz del Quiche (Map 1.) The site is roughly in the center of the highlands that run east-west from the Mexican border to the Valley of Guatemala. Utatlan, the elite center of the Nima Quiche, is the central plateau in an extended settlement comprising six contiguous plateaus with ruins. We will refer to the larger settlement of six plateaus as Greater Utatlan. Today the central plateau is a national park.

The importance of Greater Utatlan, the last Quiche capital, is attested by the long list of investigators who have commented upon the ruins in the four and one-half centuries since its abandonment. With a few notable exceptions, their investigations have been limited in scope, probably because of the large size of site, its poor preservation, and, in many cases, the limits on the time they spent there. Most of the investigations were centered at the central plateau, the most celebrated of the architectural remains.

Francisco Antonio Fuentes y Guzmán (1932–33) provides a rich, although exaggerated, description of the civic complex at Resguardo and some of the notable buildings within Utatlan, apparently based on a visit to the ruins in the late seventeenth century and on early documents that he cites, which are not known to have survived. Soon after national independence, Miguel Rivera Maestre (1832) published a map and several drawings of the temples in the civic plaza, showing architectural features that were soon thereafter destroyed. The notable explorer of Maya sites John L. Stephens (1841) briefly visited the site in 1839 and commented on the ruins. César Daly, a French architect, also made some maps and a few drawings near midcentury, accompanied by a brief description of Utatlan (1857). Because of the architectural destruction that continued throughout the nineteenth century as local inhabitants removed stones for construction elsewhere, these various glimpses of building, showing many now-destroyed features, are indeed valuable in reconstructing architectural detail.

Toward the close of the nineteenth century, Alfred P. Maudslay sketched a rough topographic map of Utatlan and surrounding plateaus, including the principal causeway that runs past Resguardo to Utatlan (1899–1902). At about the same time, Karl

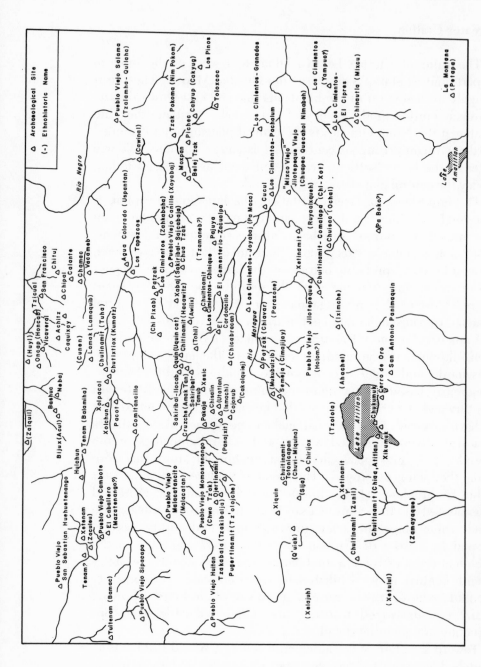

MAP 1   Late Postclassic Settlements

Sapper (1896) provided a sketch of the plateau of Utatlan and several descriptions of buildings. In 1916 Samuel Lothrop (1933) took valuable photographs of the civic plaza at Utatlan, showing structures that have since disappeared. Also during this period J. Antonio Villacorta (Villacorta and Villacorta 1930) excavated briefly at Utatlan.

Over the past three decades investigations have been increasingly intensive. In 1947 Robert Wauchope (1948b, 1970) test pitted Utatlan, amassing a ceramic sample from stratigraphic contexts, and in the process uncovered a mural. He provides a description of several structures at Utatlan, notably one elite residential structure. Ten years later Jorge F. Guillemín spent a season making a topographic map that included the principal civic groups of Greater Utatlan. Guillemin also made a sketch map of the civic plaza at Chisalin. Excavations during the summers of 1972, 1973, and 1974 were carried out at the civic complexes of Utatlan, Chisalin, Pakaman, and Resguardo (see Map 2), under the direction of Dwight T. Wallace and Robert M. Carmack. At this time, Wallace uncovered the mural discovered earlier by Wauchope. The site diagram of Utatlan (Fig. 1) was made by Dwight T. Wallace, John Weeks, and Jan Townsend of the Quiche Project. I spent the field season of 1972 mapping the various groups of civic architecture and plotting concentrations of occupational debris within Greater Utatlan.

Topography and Ecology

Greater Utatlan is situated in the western portion of the rolling Quiche Basin at a point where the topography is increasingly chopped into small plateaus by 100-meter-deep precipitous barrancas. The barrancas drop from each of the six plateaus down nearly vertical cliffs, revealing the hard-packed talpetate (volcanic ejecta) subsoil. These canyon walls are impassable except where paths have been cut through the cliffs. Varying between 1,980 and 2,000 meters in elevation, the six plateau tops are generally flat and are about the same height. The remainder of the basin, to the east, including the municipalities of Santa Cruz, Chinche, Chinique, and Zacualpa, is for the most part characterized by rolling to level terrain.

The key local resource is the land itself, totaling some 750 sq

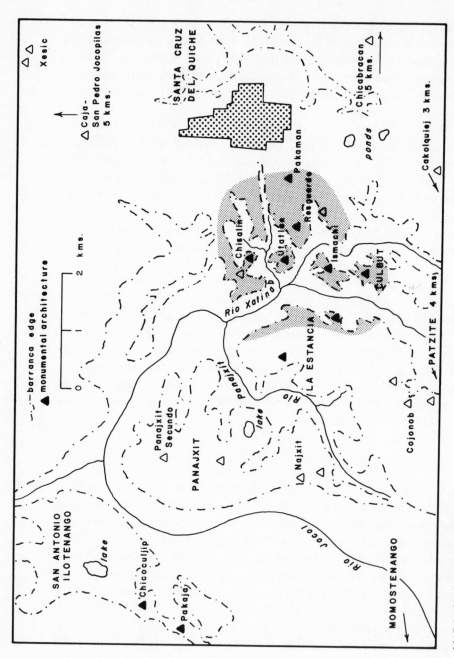

MAP 2 Nuclear Utatlan and Environs

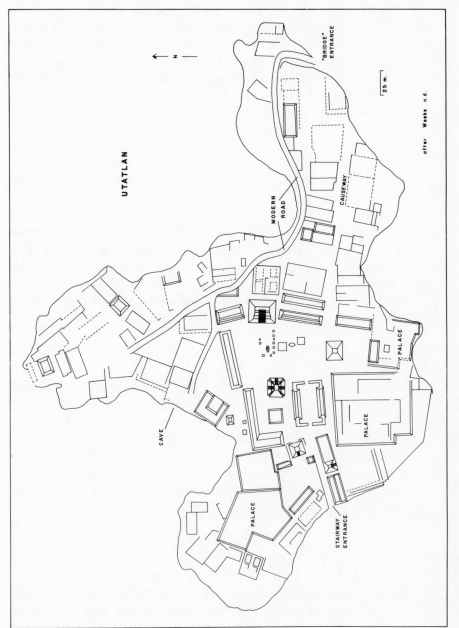

UTATLAN

N

25 m.

after Weeks n.d.

"BRIDGE" ENTRANCE

CAUSEWAY

MODERN ROAD

CAVE

PALACE

PALACE

PALACE

PALACE

STAIRWAY ENTRANCE

FIG. 1 Utatlan

kms of relatively level terrain (Simmons, Tarano, and Pinto 1959:589, 613). The soils are well drained and are composed largely of older volcanic ash. Much of the relatively dense population today is engaged in milpa cultivation, primarily of maize and beans.

At the foot of the plateaus are streams that feed into the Rio Xatinab. The Rio Xatinab runs west past Ilotenango and Momostenango and eventually feeds into the Rio Negro to the north (Map 1). Drinking water was probably brought up to the plateau settlement as it is today by the modern Quiche. The steep 100-meter drop to the watercourses precludes hydraulic agriculture. There are several wet-season shallow ponds on the east and west borders of the nucleated settlement.

At its 2,000-meter elevation, Greater Utatlan is situated near the *tierra templada–tierra fria* ecological boundary. The Quiche Basin lies within the upper limits of *tierra templada* while the bordering mountains to the north and west, beginning around Santa Maria Chiquimula, are firmly *tierra fria*. Moreover, the *tierra caliente* Rio Negro Basin at Sacapulas is only about twenty kilometers north of Greater Utatlan by a fairly straight valley route.

Settlement Description

Civic architecture at Greater Utatlan occurs in three principal large clusterings, known as civic complexes, and several smaller clusters. On the plateaus of Utatlan, Chisalin, and Ismachi (Map 2) each civic complex features one civic plaza surrounded by monumental architecture. Civic architecture also occurs in three single plazas outside the principal civic complexes, at Resguardo, Pakaman, and outside Chisalin. The remaining civic architecture consists of isolated structures removed from these clusters.

Utatlan

Utatlan is the largest civic group, with at least 70 structures literally covering the plateau surface. The plateau is accessible only over a causeway and bridge from the east and a steep stairway ascending the barranca on the west side (Fig. 1). The causeway and stairway are connected by a fairly straight main "avenue," bisecting the plateau (Fig. 1). Although the facades of many of the structures have been looted over the years, the structure shapes, for the most part, can still be distinguished. Moreover, within this heavy concentration of monumental architecture, one can still distinguish a central civic plaza, three complexes which I will term elite residential complexes, and several additional court groups yet to be defined.

The causeway runs directly from the entrance bridge to the civic plaza in the center of the plateau. The civic plaza consists of two temples, on the east and west sides, oriented about 279° west and 85° east respectively; a long structure on the north plaza side, facing 172° south; flanking rectangular structures on either side of the west-facing temple, with orientations of 287° and 296° west; and an I-shaped ball court oriented to the east-west cardinal points in the southwest corner of the plaza. There is a possibility that the as yet unexcavated long structure may be in fact two rectangular structures. Architectural details of the two temples can be discerned from illustrations drawn by Rivera and copied by Stephens, both in the 1830s. The temples' differences in form and secondary features are reflected in their rubble cores today. The temple of Tohil seemingly rises at a sharper angle, with correspondingly steep *talud-tablero* balustraded stairways on all but its posterior side, and has four terraces inset into the core. Painted figures, including, apparently, a jaguar, adorned its plaster surface. The west-facing temple is presently about a third larger across the front base than the east-facing temple, and the Rivera lithograph suggests a comparable size difference when the temples were intact. Also the west-facing temple has two substructure levels; a small level is set back on the massive bottom level. A broad front stairway spans the two levels, with one set of heavy *talud-tablero* balustrades on each level. Its two levels can be distinguished today, while the east-facing temple is largely a rubble core. A third temple stands on the south plaza side, but this structure seems to be associated with an elite residential complex adjacent to the civic plaza. The rectangular structure flanking the west-facing temple to the south was partially excavated in 1972, revealing a single long superstructure room with a bench and altar against the back wall (Wallace, personal communication). The court has a plaster floor, with three separate layers (Lothrop 1933:109), and a number of geometric shapes clearly outlined that no doubt once were small structures (cf. Lothrop 1933, photographs of 1916). Also in the plaster plaza floor, a round imprint, two larger square imprints, an elliptically shaped impression, and eight small squares, six of which are in a row, suggest small altarlike structures. Finally, there is a man-made cave in the west cliff side just below the plateau surface, extending for about 90 meters and ending in the vicinity of the civic plaza. Interestingly, the cave is hewn in the shape of a corbeled arch, and has several "dead end" side passages, each projecting a short distance from the main tunnel.

At least four other smaller courts with surrounding structures exist in other portions of the densely packed plateau. One or possibly two courts are evident on the northern spur (Fig. 1). Structures here are not as distinct as in the other sections of Utatlan, so we will have to await further exploration to determine their patterning.

Three additional courts, referred to as elite residential complexes, but not yet thoroughly enough excavated to identify them as such securely, are situated directly west and south of the main civic plaza. Each of these three court groups has one temple, at least one rectangular structure, and a large multiroomed apartmentlike structure known as a palace (Stewart 1973). The centrally situated elite residential complex, directly south of the ball court, contains the largest palace. It is approximately ninety meters square, and has a number of interior patios. Excavations by Wallace in 1972 and 1974 revealed masonry wall foundations, adobe walls, murals, and some plaster sculpture clearly of a Mixteca-Puebla art style. The elite residential complex on the west side of the plateau contains a curiously shaped palace also with interior patios. This structure, however, apparently is divided into halves by a wall, with each half facing a slightly different southerly direction onto the court. Stewart (1973) contends that the two rectangular structures in this complex are respectively aligned with the two palace halves.

There are numerous structures at Utatlan not associated with the elite residential complexes and the civic plaza. Along the long and fairly narrow eastern spur of the plateau, rectangular structures of various sizes line both sides of the causeway. Three moderate-sized, square, multiroomed structures in a row immediately behind the civic structures form the eastern side of the civic plaza, and similar square and rectangular structures are found on the extremity of the western spur (Fig. 1).

Chisalin

On a spur of an adjacent plateau some 250 meters north of Utatlan is a large concentration of buildings. This spur is connected to a larger plateau also called Chisalin by a narrow causeway bridging a steep moat. High cliffs surround its three other sides. Although the monumental architecture has lost its outer facade, this destruction apparently took place in fairly recent times, for many architectural details, particularly structure shapes, are still readily evident. Test excavations by Wallace in 1972 showed masonry to be comprised largely of finely dressed pumice blocks. My rough map (Fig. 2) uses measurements taken hastily in 1971.

Although unexcavated, some 50 structures are readily visible which, like Utatlan, consume much of the flat mesatop. A single civic plaza is situated in the center of the complex (Fig. 2). It has two temples on the east and west sides, both with two flanking short rectangular structures; a long structure on the north side; and a sunken I-shaped ball court in the southwest corner. The plaza is oriented between 20 and 25 degrees off an east-west magnetic alignment. According to J. M. Weeks, the larger temple, manifesting two tiers like the corresponding structure at Utatlan, is oriented some 290°W, whereas the east-facing structure is oriented 115°E. Like the west-facing temple at Utatlan, the temple at Chisalin is about a third longer at the base than the temple on the opposite side of the court. In the plaza center are variously shaped low geometric constructions.

There are numerous square and rectangular low platforms outside the civic plaza. To the south, facing on the plaza, is a low platform with some raised construction, suggesting walls. Sunken patios are discernible in three other relatively large square platforms on the periphery of the Chisalin complex, perhaps suggesting elite residences.

Ismachi

On the plateau immediately south of Utatlan is a third major grouping of structures, called Ismachi today as well as ethnohistorically. The plateau is most accessible by a causeway from the south, although a narrow passageway climbs its northwestern side,

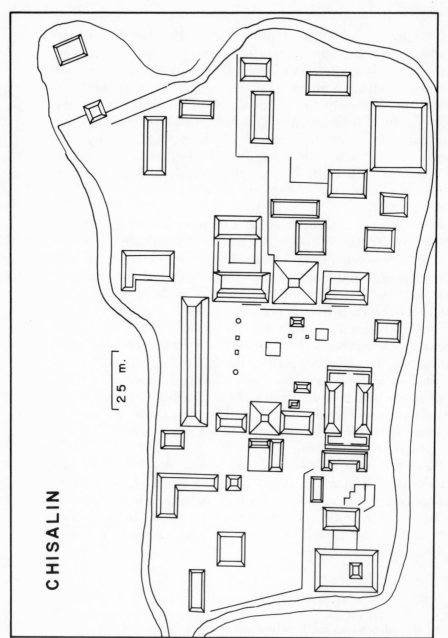

FIG. 2   Chisalin

just across a small stream from the rear stairway to Utatlan. The site diagram of Ismachi (Fig. 3) was made from my survey of 1972.

Unfortunately, the structures here have been badly ravaged over the years. All that now stands is a large civic plaza and traces of an additional court group on a parallel small spur northwest of the main civic plaza. The present-day inhabitants of Ismachi remember dismantling structures in the area where the small spur is connected to the main plaza area. The plateau is rich in occupational debris, suggesting a once extensive complex. The civic plaza, situated on a crest of the plateau that might once have been a broad platform, contains two temples on opposite ends of the plaza, oriented about 52° northeast and 230° southwest, a long structure oriented 335° north, a short rectangular structure forming the eastern side of the plaza, and a ball court roughly perpendicular to the northeast-facing temple. Like the west-facing temples at Chisalin and Utatlan, the southwest-facing temple is significantly broader than the opposite temple. There are two basic alignments, seemingly dividing the plaza in half. The temple, flanking structure, and long structure on the northern plaza form one unit aligned at a right angle, while the northeast-facing temple and the perpendicularly aligned short rectangular structure and ball court seem to form a second unit. Curiously, however, the two ball-court walls are aligned to noticeably different angles, whereas most I-shaped ball courts are symmetrical (see A. L. Smith 1961). Immediately behind the southern temple are traces of another court enclosed by structures. The remains are too far destroyed to show the structure forms, although there are heavy concentrations of plaster. Similarly, traces of another court group, also beyond the point of recognition, can be seen on the spur parallel to the civic plaza.

Pakaman

Near the eastern boundary of Greater Utatlan, a little over one kilometer east of Utatlan, is an isolated single plaza on the leveled rectangular summit of a small hill. Near the top of its moderate northwestern slope is a series of small terraces. The plaza comprises a single temple, a short rectangular flanking structure, a large square platform and perhaps another short rectangular

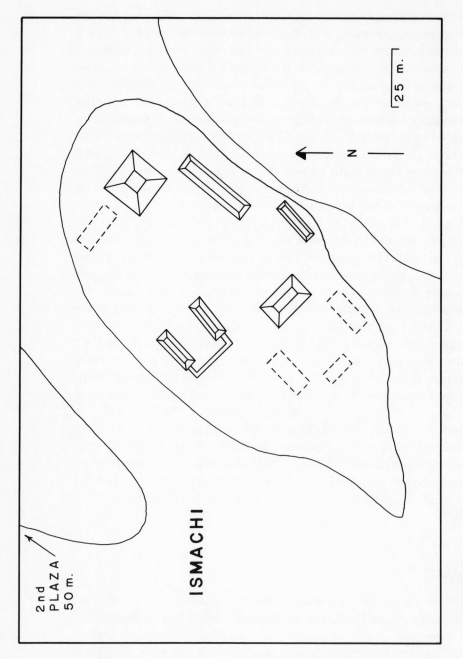

FIG. 3 Ismachi

structure forming the east plaza side, a long structure running the entire west plaza side, and what may have been short rectangular structures on the north and south plaza sides (Fig. 4). The plaza configuration conforms to the cardinal points of the compass. Construction is primarily of dressed pumice blocks. There is also a heavy concentration of plaster fragments within the plaza. The structures are in very poor condition, primarily because of their use in hoe cultivation over the years, and some, particularly the temple, have been all but obliterated by pot hunters in recent years.

Resguardo

Situated on the same plateau as Pakaman, some 250 meters east of Utatlan, Resguardo lies on a hill that has been contoured into a steep terrace, thus rising as a five-meter-high platform. The plaza consists of two temples, one flanked by short rectangular structures, facing each other across the plaza, oriented 81° east and 261° west; a long structure on the north side; one short rectangular structure on the south; and a small I-shaped ball court in the southwest corner (Fig. 5). Today two mounds separated by 50 meters stand in the small area between Resguardo and Utatlan. Weeks (1975) has excavated in this area, exposing several foundations. Immediately east of the civic plaza is a disproportionately heavy deposition of obsidian cores, blades, and projectile points. Indeed, Stephens (1841:(2) 171) commented over a century ago on the numerous projectile points there.

Chisalin Entrance Plaza

Just outside the man-made "moat" at Chisalin, adjacent to the entrance causeway, is situated a single plaza, almost completely obliterated. All that can be made out today are amorphous mounds and several foundation lines of cut stones, grouped around a court.

Peripheral to the three civic complexes in the center of Greater Utatlan are at least ten poorly preserved, small, rectangular, altarlike platforms. These single structures occur on small, widely

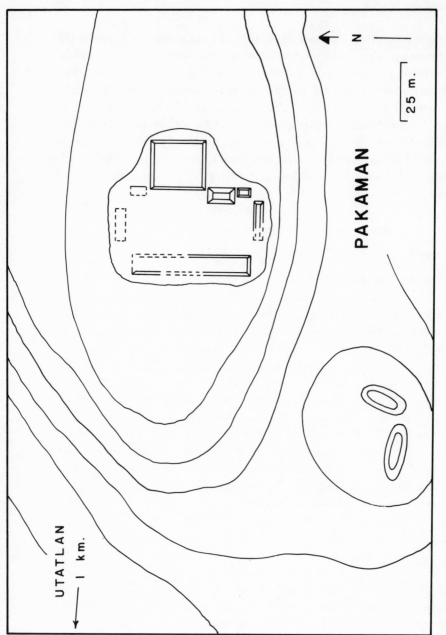

FIG. 4 Pakaman

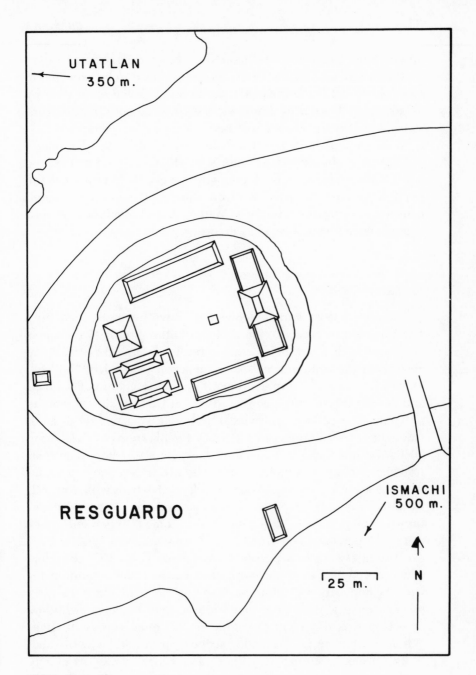

FIG. 5   Resguardo

spaced hills. Today no house mounds or house terraces are evident on the surface outside the civic complexes; this is to be expected in view of hoe cultivation over the centuries. Limited excavation by Weeks near Resguardo, however, has revealed considerable construction below the ground surface.

In an attempt to comprehend the extent of Greater Utatlan, I plotted areas of occupational debris, mostly delineated by ceramic and obsidian remains, on topographic maps. To summarize the results, an area comprising seven square kilometers contained continuous occupational debris. Within these boundaries are four square kilometers of level plateau top.

Artifacts

Although several ceramic collections have been obtained from Utatlan, such as those of Villacorta and Lothrop, only Wauchope's 1947 sample has yet been systematically described (1970). The analysis of the immense collection amassed by Dwight Wallace, including stratified samples from Chisalin, Resguardo, Pakaman, and the civic plaza and palace complexes at Utatlan, should soon be available. This collection also includes burial artifacts, such as gold, jade, and amber jewelry, in a Mixteca-Puebla style (see Nicholson 1960; Marqusee 1974). At present, however, Wauchope's analysis provides the most complete data. His major ceramic types and frequencies (when available) are as follows: Fortress white-on-red, white-on-brown (12.5 percent), monochrome red, orange-brown, brown (62.9 percent), "dull paint" polychrome (1.6 percent), mica ware (4.1 percent), red-on-white (1.6 percent), censers (1.3 percent), crude ware (5.4 percent). Wauchope (1970:103) considers white-on-red and monochrome red to be the same ceramic type, with the application of white paint as the only distinction. He sees no chronological distinctions for white-on-red, however, while he detects increased percentages of the monochrome wares with time. White painted designs include "stripes, spots, circles with small spots attached, scrolls or spirals, and other crude, carelessly applied, bands and curvilinear lines" (Wauchope 1970:186). Slipped sherds are for the most part fairly thin-walled, often decorated with horizontal grooves and ridges on the rims and less often on the bodies of jars. Double-groove rims on in-curving bowls and tall-necked jars are common (Carmack, Fox, and Stewart 1975). The "dull paint" polychrome, consisting of "red and black or dark brown on smoky white, creamy white, or tan" is apparently a late ware, occuring in the highest stratigraphic levels (Wauchope 1970:193–94).

In my survey of Greater Utatlan, I collected numerous obsidian projectile points, primarily from the Resguardo area. They conform for the most part to two types—a side-notched point and an indented-base triangular point. Both types average 3.7 cm in length, ranging from 3.5 to 4 cm. Interestingly, only one large "lance" point was recovered, from Ismachi, and no such points were recovered in the Greater Utatlan excavations.

Architecture and Settlement Pattern Interpretations

A comparison of the four relatively intact civic plazas within Greater Utatlan reveals that the Late-phase Central Quiche utilized a number of distinct types of buildings. These structures carry functional names of long-standing use, such as *temple, altar,* and *ball court,* and descriptive names such as *long structure, short rectangular structure,* and the like. The following structure types occur in at least two civic plazas within Greater Utatlan:

Temple Two temple types have been distinguished at Utatlan.

I-shaped enclosed ball court Described by Sapper (1896) and A. L. Smith (1961). Between 33 and 50 meters long.

Round structure Between 1 and 2 meters in diameter.

Long structure Between 45 and 56 meters long; has two tiers at Utatlan and Chisalin. Maudslay (1899–1902:69) observes that "the sides of the long mounds . . . are perpendicular," implying that they do not have broad *talud-tablero* bordered stairways spanning much of the front facade.

Short rectangular structure Generally between 15 and 20 meters long. Often flank a temple's sides; then called "flanking structures." Excavated short rectangular structures have one-room superstructures with a long bench against the back and side walls and square pillars across the court side.

Altar Small square or rectangular structures, less than 5

meters on a side. Occur generally in front of temples or
rectangular structures.

  Low square platforms   About 30 cm high at Chisalin;
occur in pairs at Chisalin and Utatlan.

Only one cave has so far been discovered within Greater Utatlan.
Nevertheless, caves may have been functional components of civic
precincts.

  Within the civic plazas at Utatlan, Chisalin, Ismachi, and
Resguardo, these specific structures are arranged in consistent
positions with respect to other structures. This suggests that the
Late-phase Central Quiche of Greater Utatlan had a uniform
spatial organizational scheme, which can be seen as a common
"cultural style." The traits that characterize the Late-phase plaza
are two temples on east and west sides; east-west oriented I-shaped
ball court in the west corner; long structure spanning north side;
two low square platforms in center; small, round structure in
center; short, rectangular "flanking structures." Interestingly,
while the temples at Ismachi and Chisalin are too far destroyed to
distinguish architectural features, the sizes of their (roughly)
square mounds are parallel to the size relationship between
Utatlan's two main plaza temples, where the west-facing temple is
considerably larger than the east-facing temple. Structures at
Utatlan are the largest, Ismachi's are next in size, and buildings at
Chisalin and Resguardo are about the same size.

  While generally similar to the three other civic plazas, the plaza
at Ismachi stands apart in certain organizational aspects. First,
Ismachi is oriented northeast-southwest, ranging nearly 40° from
the east-west cardinal (magnetic) points, while Resguardo is
aligned 10° off the marks, Utatlan's structures range between 5° off
and directly on the cardinal points, and Chisalin varies 20–25°
from the east-west points. The ball court at Ismachi occupies a west
corner of the plaza, which, if Ismachi were aligned like the other
plazas, would be the northwest corner, rather than the southwest
corner where the ball courts stand at the three other plazas.
Moreover, the ball court ranges are aligned at slightly different
angles. The plaza is also laid out on two slightly variant axes. The
entire civic plaza is on a platformlike rise, forming the crest of the
narrow plateau and differing from the flat, mesalike situations of
Utatlan and Chisalin. Finally, unlike the other complexes, except

perhaps Utatlan, Ismachi has an additional plaza of some sort on a narrow spur parallel to the main plaza.

The cluster at Pakaman, located on the periphery of the nucleated settlement, differs fundamentally from the four intact civic plazas discussed above. It contains a single considerably smaller temple, rather than two temples opposite each other; a long structure opposite the temple, rather than perpendicular to it; and a broad square platform on plaza side, flanking the temple. It lacks a ball court, and is situated on a square contoured hilltop with terraced slopes. Pakaman is, however, oriented to the east-west cardinal points and does have a plaster plaza floor. Its single temple, flanking structure, long structure, and, notably, the broad square platform, which may be an elite residence, are the same components seen in the elite residential complexes at Utatlan.

Ethnohistory

A great many sixteenth-century documents refer to the nucleated settlement of Greater Utatlan. Quiche lords—many of whom, such as the authors of the *Popol Vuh*, lived within Utatlan—make reference to distinct social groups, and, to a lesser degree, to specific buildings. The conquistador Pedro de Alvarado briefly described some parts of the city when he burned it in 1524. Quiche chronicles refer to the central plateau as Gumarcaaj, which translates as "place of the rotten reeds." However, its Nahuatl translation, Utatlan, apparently was in common use before the conquest. Ismachi, the first Central Quiche capital in the Quiche Basin, was founded about 1370 after the abandonment of the Early-phase Chujuyub centers. After living at Ismachi for about a generation, the Quiche moved across the barranca around 1400 and established Utatlan. Indeed, the proximity of the two sites is indicated by their single hyphenated name Gumarcaaj-Ismachi (e.g. Nijaib I 1957: 77, 78, 83; C'oyoi 1973:295).

The Central Quiche comprised three closely related confederate groups—the Nima Quiche (often called simply the Quiche), the Ilocab, and the Tamub. The Nima Quiche, the most powerful, provided the supreme rulers of the alliance. In fact, *Nima* translates as "big." These three groups intermarried and generally considered themselves as "brothers of the same great 'clan' (*chinamit*), and this ideology of kinship was never entirely

replaced" (Carmack n.d.b:4). At the conquest the three groups
may have been respectively located on the three adjacent central
plateaus of Utatlan, Chisalin, and Ismachi. This particular distribution is suggested by the fact that the entrance causeways to
the centers lead from the directions of lands respectively controlled
by each of these groups. Utatlan's supportive lands were largely to
the east, in the Quiche Basin proper; there are also numerous
references to the Nima Quiche dwelling at Utatlan (*Popol Vuh*
1950; Alvarado 1924). The causeway running into Ismachi comes
from the south, the traditional Tamub area of control. Moreover, a
passage in the Tamub document (1957:43) suggests that the Tamub
took over Ismachi when the Nima Quiche moved to Utatlan. The
causeway to the civic precinct of Chisalin comes from the west, but
it may eventually lead from the northwest, where the larger
plateau is connected to a main section of the Quiche Basin. The
Ilocab held territory north and northwest of Greater Utatlan
(Ilotenango and San Pedro Jocopilas) (Carmack, personal communication). Chisalin apparently was still called PaIlocab into this
century (Carmack, personal communication).

At the conquest, the Nima Quiche were organized into 24 main
patrilineages, forming four larger divisions of

> 9 (*Cawek*), 9 (*Nijaib*), 4 (*Ajaw Quiche*), and 2 (*Zaquic*). The
> Tamub had 22 patrilineage divisions, grouped into moieties of
> 9 (*Ekoamak*) and 12 (*Kakoj*). The Ilocab had 18 patrilineages,
> apparently grouped into 4 sections (*Chivatuj, Chivatziquin,
> Yolchitun, Yolchiamak*). (Carmack 1974 n.d.b:4)

Insofar as the identification of Utatlan as the Nima Quiche locus
is certain, perhaps the four or so court groups situated around the
edge of the plateau, including the three elite residential complexes
so far identified, pertain to the four Nima Quiche divisions. The
civic plaza, located in the center of the plateau and connected to
these various groups by "streets," may have been used by all four
divisions. In a schematized rendering of Utatlan found by Carmack
in the sixteenth-century Totonicapan manuscript, four Quiche
divisions (Cawek, Nijaib, Ajaw, and Achij) are each represented by
a single structure in each of four corners of a square, perhaps
representing Utatlan. Moreover, the four structures shown may be
profiles of long structures, which were the loci for these kinship
"long house" divisions, called *nim ja* (Carmack n.d.b:5).

Several buildings at Utatlan mentioned in the sixteenth-century documents may be identified with specific structures. Two temples are described in the Xpantzay II chronicle (1957:137–39) as the house of Tojil and the house of Awilix (Carmack n.d.b). Since the only place at Utatlan with two temples is the main plaza, the chronicle probably refers to them. The east-facing temple here was called Tojil by local people in the seventeenth century and in the nineteenth century (Fuentes y Guzman 1932; Stephens 1841). Since the proportional difference in size as well as the locations of these temples with respect to each other is repeated at Chisalin, Ismachi, and Resguardo, we may speculate that temples at these plazas pertain to the same deities. In all these plazas, interestingly, the two temples are not directly opposite but slightly off center from one another. This arrangement may have been created so that sunset and sunrise would not be blocked by temples. Tojil, facing the sunrise, is associated with the "morning star," Venus (*Popol Vuh* 1950: 173, 180, 185), whereas Awilix is associated with the sunset or evening and perhaps has affinity with the "moon goddess" (Carmack n.d.b; cf. Edmonson 1971). Similarly, the placement of the east-west-aligned ball court in the west plaza corner seems to relate to the association of the ball court with the underworld, which is in the west, where the sun sets. Perhaps the flanking short rectangular structures, associated with temples in the civic plazas as well as in the elite residential complexes, were loci for attendants of the temples (cf. Landa 1941; Pollock et al. 1962). The Totonicapan pictorial referred to above, portraying a profile of a *tzompantli* or skull rack (*waetzumpan*) in the center of Utatlan, may pertain to the two low platforms in the plaza center, which apparently are associated with the two temples. Finally, we may note that Alvarado's (1924) brief description of Utatlan's two entrances, a bridge causeway and a steep stairway, correlates well with the actual remains of a front causeway passing over the narrow ravine and running across the plateau, terminating at the stairway.

The two civic areas at Ismachi—the main civic plaza and the barely distinguishable civic group on the parallel spur—may pertain to the Tamub moieties delineated in the documents.

The two single plazas and once-adjacent structures located on the opposite side of the moats at Utatlan and Chisalin may have had defensive functions. Around Resguardo, the dense occupation revealed by test excavations and the heavy surface occupational debris, particularly obsidian, suggest a military ward. Apparently warriors dwelled in such wards, "whose function was to guard the fortified centers. In one source, the occupants of such settlements are described as 'defensive blockers of the ramparts of the fortress' " (Carmack n.d.b:5). Resguardo's fortified situation by the entrance to Utatlan might well be called a "blocker," for anyone desiring to enter Utatlan would first have to deal with it. Moreover, in a conquest-based state dependent upon forced tribute payments, the military would need a prominent location adjacent to the main center, where the rulers and nobility dwelled. The Totonicapan manuscript mentions the *achij*, which translates as "warriors," as one of the four major political divisions at Utatlan. In fact, the military were an increasingly powerful force within Quiche society. The Xajil document (1953:94–97) records a coup d'état at Utatlan by the military.

The Nima Quiche maintained a separate fortified group of buildings, including a palace, referred to as Panpetak (Nijaib I 1957:83; Carmack n.d. b). Panpetak is also the place where the Quiche ruler was imprisoned during the military revolt just mentioned (Xajil 1953:95). Pakaman is situated on the periphery of the nucleated settlement, adjacent to the causeway leading to Utatlan, and apparently is a fortified elite residential complex. Perhaps it is Panpetak.

The native chronicles tell us that the Quiche nobility held numerous administrative offices, as required in a large, centralized sociopolitical system. Perhaps the numerous smaller, square, often multiroom structures peripheral to the civic plaza and four courts at Utatlan and Chisalin housed nobility.

The *Popol Vuh* (1950:88) and the Xajil (1953:103–4) document mention a number of skilled craftsmen, notably silversmiths, lapidaries (working jade, polished obsidian, turquoise, and other substances), workers in gourds, and wood and stone sculptors. Jewels and precious metals were associated with the nobility (*Rabinal Achi* 1955; C'oyoi 1973:297), as indicated by burial goods excavated at Utatlan; perhaps, then, these artisans dwelled within the civic precincts and were supported by various aristocratic households (Carmack 1974). Much occupied space within the nucleated settlement peripheral to the three civic precincts has not yet been identified with a segment of Quiche society, however. Alvarado (1924:62, 65) describes "neighborhoods" on the plains outside Utatlan, and we shall now turn our attention to these "suburbs."

The Outlying Wards of Greater Utatlan

Greater Utatlan controlled a considerable portion of the surrounding Quiche Basin. Thus far, five small Late Postclassic sites have been surveyed in this Central Quiche area. Ranging from some two kilometers outside Greater Utatlan to about ten kilometers, the sites correspond to the outlying communities, or wards, that sustained the capital. The conquistador Alvarado (1924:65) mentions subject towns and cornfields in the vicinity of Utatlan, apparently referring to the wards. Evidently the ruling confederates maintained separate wards, for the Tamub document (1957:55–61) lists 13 Nima Quiche and 12 Tamub ward centers; these are mentioned as well in the Nijaib I (1957:71–73) and Nijaib II (1957:105) documents, which also refer to Ilocab wards. The following sites are thought to have been wards.

Cakolquiej

Five kilometers south of Greater Utatlan near the southern end of the rolling plateau of Resguardo and Pakaman is the small site still called Cakolquiej. It lies on a bluff north of the Quiche-Patzite road, about five kilometers east of Patzite. This bluff rises about 40 meters above the road and a more acute 120 meters above its south and west sides.

The only standing structure is a temple, built of finely dressed pumice blocks, whose base measures 6 meters on a side and rises 4 meters in height. No secondary architectural features are discernible. In addition, however, there is evidence of a leveled rectangular structure nearby. There is also a moderate distribution of ceramics and obsidian over an area measuring approximately 100 by 50 meters, suggesting a small adjacent activity area of some sort. The pumice blocks, "double groove" red-slipped rim sherds, and side-notched "arrow" obsidian projectile points all suggest the Late-phase Central Quiche.

Cakolquiej apparently was the Nima Quiche ward center of Cakolqueh (Nijaib I 1957:72; Nijaib II 1957:105; C'oyoi 1973:302).

Its identification as a Nima center is supported by its location on the same plateau as Pakaman, also thought to be a Nima Quiche outpost.

Panajxit

The broad plateau of Panajxit, covering at least six square kilometers, begins just two kilometers west of Greater Utatlan (Map 2). The plateau is ringed by cliffs rising about 100 meters. There are also several ridges on the plateau, rising an additional 40 meters, which contain two Early Postclassic centers. These Early Postclassic sites, situated in the center and northern parts of the plateau, also apparently were occupied into the Early phase of the Late Postclassic Period (Carmack, Fox, and Stewart 1975).

On the ridge overlooking the east edge of the plateau, closest to Greater Utatlan, are several leveled structures, a foundation line of dressed blocks, piles of dressed pumice blocks, and three separate concentrations of Late-phase ceramics. This construction may relate to the Late-phase Tamub ward settlement Nacxit (Tamub 1957:59–60; Nijaib II 1957:105). The documents also tell of a large Mexicanized site occupied before the Late-phase Quiche movement into the basin. With such "Mexican" features as a long structure and a chacmoollike sculpture, perhaps the large Early Postclassic settlement at Panajxit pertains to an early Mexicanized horizon, probably contemporaneous in its latter part with the Early phase of the Late Postclassic Period. The Late-phase remains seemingly pertain to the Late-phase Tamub Quiche administrative outpost (Carmack, Fox, and Stewart 1975).

Ilotenango

Ilotenango is the next plateau west of Panajxit, about six kilometers northwest of Greater Utatlan (Map 2.). As is true at neighboring Panajxit, there are at least three separate concentrations of civic architecture on the broad cliff-line plateau (see Carmack, Fox, and Stewart 1975; Stewart n.d.). Two sites on the southern extremity of the plateau, Chicoculjip and Pakaja, are Late Postclassic settlements, whereas the center of the plateau and its ridges contain Early Postclassic remains.

On the southern plateau edge is a badly ruined enclosed plaza, known as Chicoculjip. Unfortunately, all that can now be discerned is a temple on the east side, a long structure on the north side, cut-stone construction material, and probable residential terraces on its south side. Ceramics show Early Postclassic and Late-phase Late Postclassic occupations. A west-facing temple perpendicular to a long structure on the north side of the plaza is a settlement pattern feature characteristic of Greater Utatlan.

About 250 meters directly south of Chicoculjip is a larger site, Pakaja, which manifests only Late-phase ceramics. Pakaja is situated on the crest of a narrow plateau surrounded by 100-meter-high cliffs on all but the north side, which is connected to Chicoculjip and the principal Ilotenango plateau by a narrow land bridge. The only architecture now discernible within the plaza is a large temple on the north side and a long structure on the west side. Construction is of dressed blocks and plaster. The remainder of the plateau spur is strewn with occupational debris, and several leveled mounds can be made out. We may infer that Pakaja was a sizable Late-phase settlement.

Pakaja and Chicoculjip are separated only by a 250-meter causeway and have contemporaneous Late-phase ceramics, suggesting that they may have been components of a single settlement, largest of the wards. Chicoculjip, situated immediately adjacent to the narrow causeway leading from the main Ilotenango plateau, may have been a defensive plaza like those occurring about the same distance outside Utatlan and Chisalin. Moreover, the temple at Pakaja is comparable in size to the ·two main plaza temples at Utatlan. Thus there is a possibility that Pakaja and Chicoculjip constituted the main Ilocab locus Mukuis Ilocab (C'oyoi 1973:293, 295), rather than Chisalin, as its modern name Ilotenango suggests (Stewart 1973). However, the principal plateau of Ilotenango, just north of the Chicoculjip ruins, may have been the prominent ward Amak Mes, controlled by the Ilocab apparently from Early-phase times (Tamub 1957:39; Nijaib II 1957:73) through the Late phase (C'oyoi 1973:302) and long thought to have been at Ilotenango (Recinos 1957:73 n.; Carmack, Fox, and Stewart 1975).

Xesic

About five kilometers north of Greater Utatlan, in an area of rolling hills on the edge of the Quiche Basin, is the Late Postclassic

site Xesic (Map 2). The site lies on a knoll at the western foot of the
rugged Chujuyub Range, overlooking to the west the strategic
narrow pass running from Greater Utatlan north to Jocopilas and
eventually to Sacapulas. The hilltop has moderately steep slopes
and is potentially defensive.

At the present, two small areas of construction are discernible on
two separate crests of this small knoll, separated by about a
hundred meters. One is a small temple; the other is simply a
foundation line of dressed stone blocks flush with the ground
surface. Late-phase ceramics were noted as well as several typically
small-notched "arrow" projectile points made of obsidian.

Chicabracan

In the canton of Chicabracan, nine kilometers directly east of
Greater Utatlan in the midst of the Quiche Basin, is an small
templelike structure in the center of a narrow 100-meter-long spur.
This spur, projecting from the rolling Quiche Basin floor, is
surrounded on all sides but the northeast by 80-meter-high cliffs.
Several hundred meters to the northeast, on the main basin floor,
is an enclosed plaza of an earlier date.

The solitary "temple," built of dressed masonry blocks, is
surrounded by a moderate concentration of red-slipped thin-walled
sherds, suggesting a small Late-phase activity area. This apparently
was the Nima Quiche ward center Cakbrakan (Tamub 1957:57;
Nijaib I 1957:72; Nijaib II 1957:105; C'oyoi 1973:302).

Chujuyub Settlements

Commencing some ten kilometers northeast of Greater Utatlan
is a group of seven small Late Postclassic sites on neighboring
ridgetops. A high mountain range, four to eight kilometers wide,
separates this group of sites from the broad Quiche Basin. The sites
occupy high ridges and mountains of this range that form, for the
most part, a high rim around an open, highly eroded, basinlike
area. Near the center of this depression is a small village called
Santa Rosa Chujuyub. Modern occupation is dispersed over about
six square kilometers of rolling hills, the only inhabitable portion of
the area. Since the floor here is exceedingly rugged, comprised

almost entirely of steep barrancas and lacking the level space characteristic of basins, it will simply be called the Chujuyub Depression. This eroded and sparsely populated depression is slightly lower in elevation than the Quiche Basin, although firmly *tierra templada*, and its soils are considerably less productive (cf. Simmons, Tarano, and Pinto 1959). The region is underlain by an older crystalline bedrock, often seen as schistose outcrops.

The seven Chujuyub sites were the first Central Quiche centers in the Guatemalan Highlands, established soon after the Epi-Toltec migration from the Tabasco Gulf Coast area around 1250 (Carmack 1968). The Early phase of the Late Postclassic, c. 1250–1350, when the Chujuyub area was the administrative nucleus, is delineated by distinctive Central Quiche archaeological remains. The Late phase, running from about 1370 to 1524, coincided with the abandonment of the Chujuyub area as the principal nucleus and the movement into the Quiche Basin to Ismachi and then Greater Utatlan.

Since the seven Chujuyub sites are situated on adjacent ridges, within view of each other, and are all small, I will analyze them collectively to determine Early-phase Central Quiche settlement characteristics.

Settlement Description

Oquin

The archaeological remains of Oquin are situated along a long, narrow ridge descending from Cerro Telecuch and projecting into the low Chujuyub Depression (Map 3). Oquin can most easily be reached by the road over Cerro Telecuch eight kilometers east of San Pedro Jocopilas, which ends about two kilometers west of the ruins. The Jocopilas municipal boundaries terminate just beyond Oquin. The site is strung along 300 meters of this exceedingly narrow ridgetop, varying from 30 to 35 meters in width. Although its sides drop a precipitous 400 meters, they are not the cliffs characteristic of many Late-phase sites. In some places the ridge slope can be climbed, but the site is nevertheless quite appropriate for defense. From Oquin the nearby sites of Chitinamit and Cruzche can be distinquished (Map 3). We surveyed Oquin in 1973.

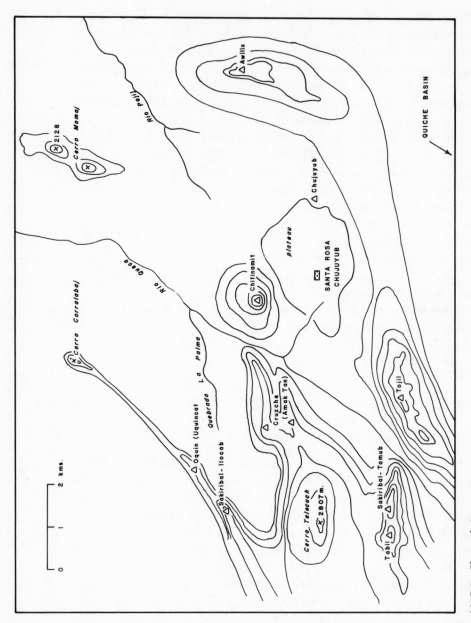

MAP 3   Chujuyub Area

Four small groups of poorly preserved structures can be discerned at various intervals along the narrow ridge. Two of these groups, with temples, are rectilinear civic plazas. The remaining two groups, lying adjacent to each other, have small, rectangular house platforms and small foundation lines that may have constituted residential courts. The main civic plaza consists of a temple facing 200° south, a perpendicularly positioned long structure on the west side, and a short rectangular structure on the south side (Fig. 6). A second civic plaza, immediately to the southwest, about 40 meters higher, consists of a temple associated with two short, perpendicular rectangular structures on either side of it placed together on a large rectangular platform. One of the rectangular structures, most of the temple itself, and all of the base platform have been hewn from a natural schistose outcrop. In addition, the facade of the temple combines masonry *talud-tablero* balustrades with a staircase carved from the bedrock. Still intact, this masonry is mostly of roughly shaped schistose slabs. A gently sloping area on a spurlike projection extending 200 meters north of the main plaza contains apparent residential terraces.

Cruzche

Just two kilometers south of Oquin is a parallel ridgetop site in the municipality of Santa Cruz del Quiche (Map 3). Indeed, the main plazas at Cruzche and Oquin differ only 10 meters in elevation and are clearly visible from each other. The ruins of Chitinamit to the east can also be seen from Cruzche. Cruzche consists of a main ridge group and a secondary adjoining ridge group. Carmack and I surveyed the main group in 1973, and Carmack and Wallace surveyed the smaller group in 1974.

Settlement remains on the main ridge stretch for nearly a kilometer of the exceedingly narrow ridge (5 to 20 meters wide except at the places where monumental architecture is situated). The ridge sides drop nearly vertically 300 meters to streams on its north and south. Three slightly wider areas along the ridge seem to contain pre-Hispanic construction, but only the largest has structures whose arrangement is discernible. At the point where the ridge makes an abrupt 90° turn to the east there is a well-delineated plaza on an elevated 3.5-meter-high rectangular platform (Fig. 7). Three rectangular structures and a temple form a

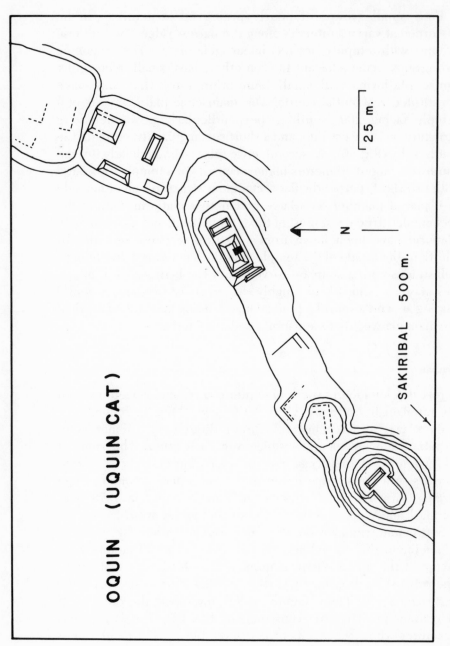

OQUIN (UQUIN CAT)

25 m.

N

SAKIRIBAL 500 m.

FIG. 6 Oquin

four-sided enclosed plaza oriented to the east-west cardinal points. The three rectangular structures are now mostly earthen mounds. A small quantity of unworked basalt stone and a lesser amount of shaped schistose slabs protrude from the 3-meter-high temple. One interesting cone-shaped piece of tuft, with a 22 cm diameter, was noted at the foot of the temple. Immediately below this elevated plaza to the west is a 100-meter-wide level area containing a number of leveled structures and several sloping possible residential terraces to the north.

On the small ridge parallel to and several hundred meters southeast of this main ridge, and a little over 100 meters lower in elevation, is a small single plaza (Map 3), east-west aligned and situated on a squared elevation. It comprises a rectilinear arrangement of a low temple in the plaza center with rectangular platforms, varying from 10 to 20 meters long, on its east and west sides. Ceramics are both Early- and Late-phase Late Postclassic.

Chitinamit

In the center of the Chujuyub Depression is a cone-shaped hill with the ruins of Chitinamit on its leveled summit. Santa Rosa Chujuyub, the only modern settlement of any size within the depression, is situated one kilometer south of Chitinamit. Differently shaped on each side, the Chitinamit hill is most accessible from the heavily terraced south side, although it still is a steep 100-meter ascent to the ruins. The west slope descends an incredible two kilometers to the Rio Queca. We mapped and test pitted the ruins in 1971, 1972, and 1973.

The architectural remains are poorly preserved but structure forms and arrangements can still be distinguished. The facades of the buildings have been removed by cultivators in fairly recent times, exposing the mostly earthen fill. The leveled summit is occupied by two back-to-back civic plazas on a long rectangular platform, three meters high at its steepest point. The two plazas are aligned to the north-south cardinal points, with the single temple of each plaza facing south (Fig. 8).

The higher plaza contains a temple on its north side, two perpendicular rectangular structures each on its east and west sides, and an altar in the plaza center in front of the temple. The south side of the plaza is formed by an I-shaped ball court oriented

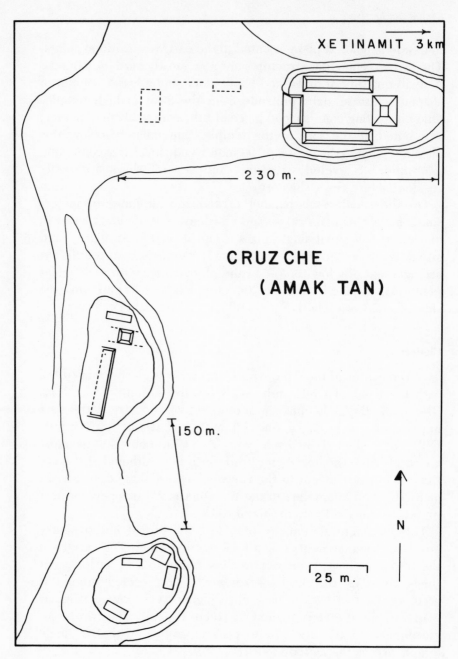

FIG. 7   Cruzche

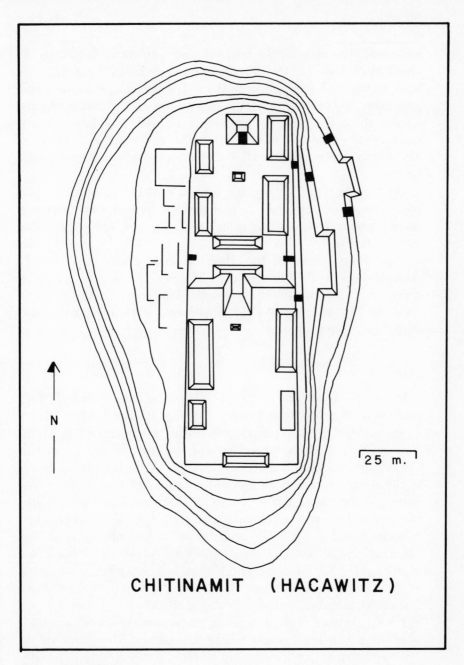

N

25 m.

CHITINAMIT (HACAWITZ)

FIG. 8   Chitinamit

east-west. The temple, the best preserved structure at the site, is about two meters high with a single stairway facing the court. It is built mostly of shaped schistose slabs. The four long structures and altar range in height from 20 cm to a meter. Many fired bricks are strewn about the plaza, suggesting that brick may have been a primary construction material for the rectangular structures. The bricks are porous, with reddish exteriors and gray-to-black interiors.

The temple of the lower plaza projects from the center of the ball court's south outside wall, so that the two buildings are part of a single structure. The plaza sides are formed by low rectangular structures (Fig. 8).

Immediately west of the elevated civic plazas is a slightly down-sloping area containing rows of upward-projecting schistose slabs, about fifteen centimeters high. This area and the terraces connected by stairways to the upper east slope may have once contained residences.

Tohil

There is a small site on the wooded mountaintop called Tohil southwest of Santa Rosa Chujuyub (Map 3). The modern Santa Cruz–San Andrés road passes only about 100 meters south of the ruins. The mountain forms part of the rim of the Chujuyub Depression, dividing the depression from the broad Quiche Basin to the south. At 2,589 meters elevation, Tohil rises at least 500 meters above much of the Chujuyub Depression and is well into the *tierra fria* ecological zone. In fact, few of its slopes are cultivated and the terrain at its peak is virtually uninhabited hardwood forest. From Tohil one can look down upon the three centers of Oquin, Cruzche, and Chitinamit, as well as a panorama of the Chujuyub Depression including the far-off twin peaks of Mamaj (Map 3). We visited the ruins in 1973.

The single plaza is on the apex of the narrow elongated mountain summit, which here is not unlike a ridgetop. The ruins are in disarray because pot hunters have recently dug through virtually every structure. This is indeed unfortunate since Tohil was the only Early-phase site with much masonry. Nevertheless, we were able to distinguish a small temple in the center of a square plaza enclosed on four sides by rectangular structures (Fig. 9). There was little space in the court except perhaps for a small altar. Construction material was largely of basaltic slabs, with some shaped schistose slabs. Among this large amount of recently exposed masonry, however, lime plaster was noticeably absent.

Several interesting sculptured pieces of cream-colored volcanic tuff were recovered from the temple rubble. Four were cone-shaped, with diameters of about 20 cm and lengths of 35 to 40 cm. Two of these cones had square projecting bases and apparently were the tenons for the attachment of an outer facade of thin blocks (as at Zaculeu [Smith 1955] or Tula in Mexico). In addition, we recovered a fragment of a stylized skull or face in relief, on a once square slab about 30 cm on a side and 5 cm thick. Square eyes with a round pupil, a nose hole, prominent teeth in a horizontal, rectangular mouth, and a border of consecutive squares, which may be stylized braided hair, can be made out. A second sculpture consists of a curved line of consecutive squares in the same geometric style as the skull sculpture.

Awilix

Awilix is a small, single-plaza site, 700 meters high, on the northeastern extreme of the elongated crest of a mountain forming an eastern rim of the Chujuyub Depression (Map 3). The municipal center of San Andres Sajacabaja can be so clearly seen from Awilix that one is quite surprised to learn that it is almost 15 km distant. To the west the northern half of the Chujuyub Depression is visible. I visited Awilix in 1972.

Although the site is covered with brush and trees, I did note several low rectangular structures and a square "temple" a meter and one-half high. This temple had recently been dug into, exposing schistose slab masonry laid in mud mortar.

Sakiribal-Ilocab

Sakiribal is a small site on the same ridge as Oquin, about two-thirds of a kilometer southwest of Oquin and 170 meters higher in elevation (Map 3). It is distinguished as a separate site because of the sharp topographic difference and, perhaps more important, because local inhabitants make the distinction between the two sites with two separate names. I have added the suffix Ilocab to Sakiribal because it lies within the Ilocab municipality of

TOHIL

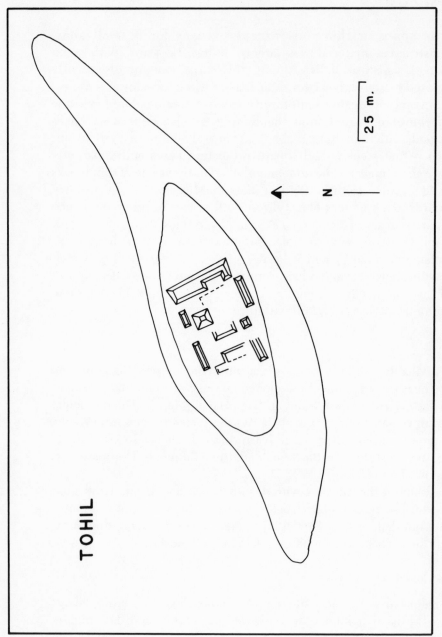

25 m.

N

FIG. 9 Tohil

San Pedro Jocopilas, and to dintinguish it from the site above Cruzche also called Sakiribal (see below). From its lofty position, every group at Oquin can be distinguished as well as much of the Chujuyub Depression. The precipitous ridge slopes are 600 meters on its north and south sides. The ruins at Sakiribal occupy two areas along 140 meters of the 25-30-meter-wide ridgetop. We visited the ruins in 1973.

The main ruins on the western edge of Sakiribal are heavily wooded. One small group of structures can be distinguished, however, as well as an adjoining small area of amorphous rises that may once have been low structures. The discernible structures comprise a low temple, oriented 54° east, and two short rectangular structures on opposite sides from the temple, all of which are situated on an elevated platform (Fig. 10).

About 90 meters east of this group, just before the rapid descent to Oquin, is a short rectangular structure and perhaps an additional short rectangular platform. In the area between the first group and these additional structures is a modern athletic field, whose recent construction may have destroyed pre-Hispanic settlement features.

Construction material at Sakiribal consists of a basaltlike rock and a lesser amount of schistose slabs. One construction block was observed with a one-centimeter-thick facing of plaster on one side.

Sakiribal-Tamub

This hilltop site, also known as Sakiribal, is three kilometers southwest of Cruzche and 300 meters higher (Map 3). Moreover, the site is connected to Cruzche by a pass. Sakiribal forms the east peak of a ridge one kilometer long with a second site, Tabil, on its west end. The ridge's north and south sides each rise only about 100 meters. We have not yet visited Sakiribal, although local inhabitants describe it as containing small ruins. However, a team from the Quiche Project did visit the single mound site Tabil, which was controlled by the Tamub (Tamub 1957:57). This implies that the entire ridge, and thus Sakiribal, were also Tamub controlled.

Artifacts

Except for Chitinamit and Tohil, the Chujuyub sites yielded only a few sherds each. Chitinamit, however, produced a large surface sample of highly eroded ceramics, lacking slip, paint, or

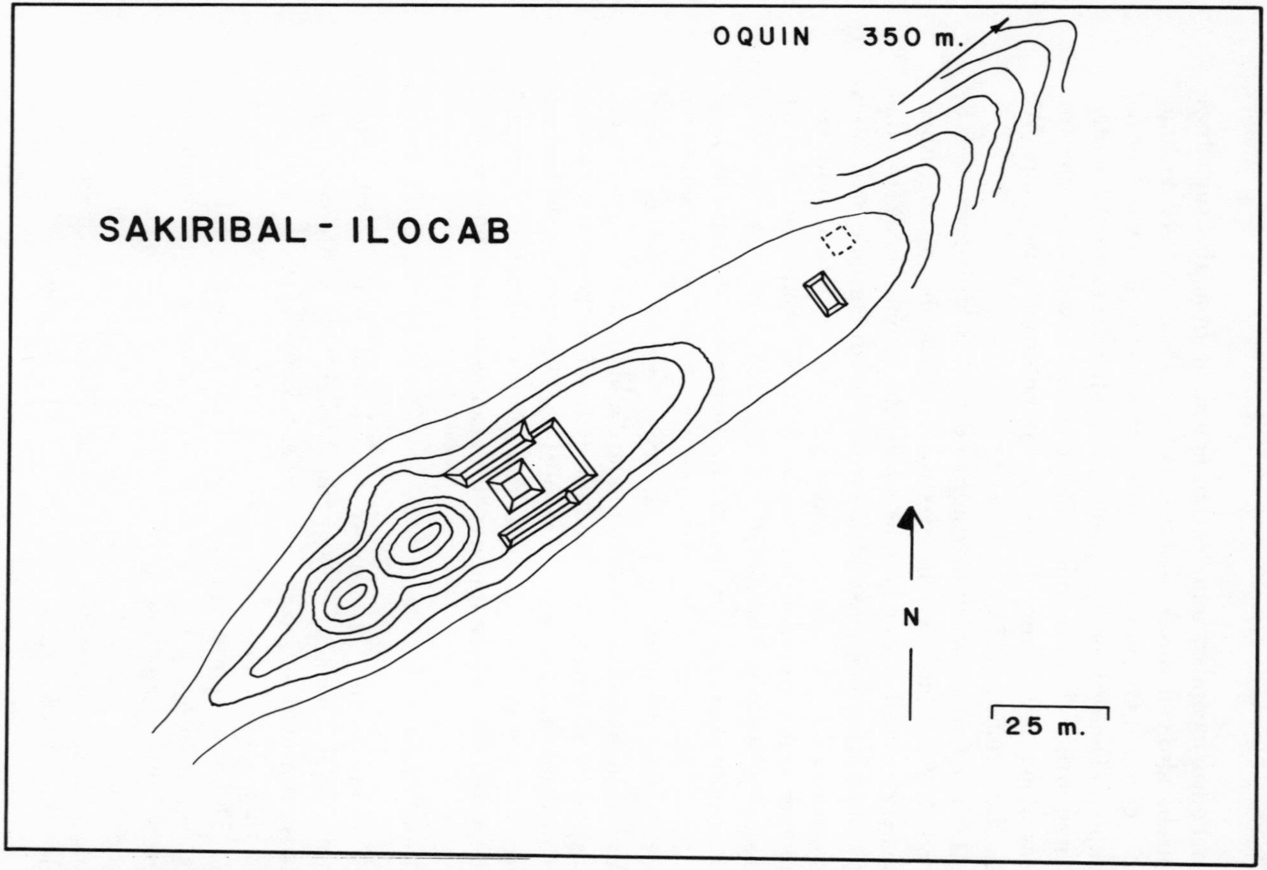

SAKIRIBAL - ILOCAB

OQUIN 350 m.

25 m.

N

FIG. 10   Sakiribal-Ilocab

surface decoration. Many of the plentiful rim sherds, nevertheless, manifest the thick outflaring lip common during the Early Postclassic Period. The temper contains bits of quartz and mica. Since the local bedrock is schistose and the soil contains much mica and quartz, we may infer that ceramics at Chitinamit were locally made.

Ceramics from nearby Tohil contrast markedly with those from Chitinamit. First, sherds are often slipped, particularly red, and a few have thick white lines painted over a red slip, not to be confused with the Late-phase Fortress white-on-red. Thick-walled red-slipped sherds were also noted at Awilix. However, since the Tohil sherds were unearthed recently, rather than lying on the surface like those at Chitinamit, the lack of slip and paint on the latter may partially reflect exposure to the elements. Nevertheless, the Tohil sample is also distinguished by plastic decoration, notably punctate and wavy-line incision in addition to finer temper. Such decorative modes also occur at Sakiribal-Ilocab and on the ridgetop sites in the Quiche Basin with the three-mound linear pattern (see in the next section Cojonob, Panajxit Secundo) (Carmack, Fox, and Stewart 1975).

Broad, leaf-shaped obsidian "lance" projectile points were noted at Chitinamit and Oquin. Two unusually long and quite narrow points were recovered from Tohil. At none of these Early-phase Chujuyub sites, however, have we found the small, side-notched "arrow" projectile points common in Greater Utatlan and at many other Late-phase sites. Only one "lance" point was recovered within Greater Utatlan, at the earlier center of Ismachi. Their total absence in both surface and excavated contexts within the remainder of Greater Utatlan suggests that the lance was replaced as the primary weapon by the bow. The small "arrow" points are absent at the Early-phase Chujuyub sites, thought to have been abandoned about 1350, and the "lance" points are absent at the Late-phase sites built after 1400, so perhaps the bow was introduced into the Guatemalan Highlands in the 1300s and came into common use in the late 1300s. This would be slightly later than its introduction into the Gulf Lowlands (cf. Thompson 1970; Landa 1941).

Architecture and Settlement Pattern Interpretations

Two fundamental topographic and building patterns can be seen among the seven Chujuyub sites, breaking down into the three "low" sites of Oquin, Cruzche, and Chitinamit and the four "high" sites of Tohil, Awilix, Sakiribal-Ilocab, and Sakiribal-Tamub. While all the sites are situated on high, steep ridges, Cruzche, Chitinamit, and Oquin are situated on long and narrow ridgetops rising about 300 meters in the midst of *tierra templada* agricultural lands, whereas Tohil and Awilix are on elongated mountaintops rising 500 and 700 meters respectively in uninhabited *tierra fria* forest. Like Tohil and Awilix, Sakiribal-Ilocab and Sakiribal-Tamub are situated in the mountain chain overlooking the low sites. Oquin, Cruzche, and Chitinamit are about the same elevation, with Oquin and Cruzche differing by only 10 meters. Moreover, these three lower sites are also considerably larger, with at least two civic plazas each, a main plaza typified by a temple and long structures on the plaza sides, and large adjacent residential areas. The more lofty sites, Tohil, Awilix, Sakiribal-Ilocab, and Sakiribal-Tamub, share a pattern of a low temple in the plaza center enclosed by short rectangular structures. While exhibiting the same base measurements, temples within the low sites are 2 or 3 meters high, whereas temples in the high sites are only about 1 meter high. The differences between the two groups point to possible different functions. The larger low sites, with long structures and residential terraces on the upper slopes below the civic plazas and above the agricultural lands, may have had administrative functions like the Late-phase *tinamit* sites (e.g. Utatlan, Chisalin). The lofty, far-removed "high" sites, with a truncated temple as the central feature, were perhaps dedicated to specialized religious activities. In fact, taking Chitinamit as the geographic center of the Chujuyub Depression, two of these higher sites, Tohil and Awilix, form directional points; Awilix is east, Tohil is south (Cerro Telecuch is west and Cerro Mamaj is north) (Map 3). Finally, ceramics also conform to this dichotomy. Ceramics from Tohil and Awilix are highly ornate luxury wares, with fine pastes, whereas ceramics from Chitinamit appear to be locally made, largely crude wares. (Too few sherds were recovered from Oquin and Cruzche to generalize.)

Considering the principal civic plazas at the low sites, Oquin, Cruzche, and Chitinamit, we may designate as Early-phase Central Quiche settlement pattern features rectilinear plazas; temple at "head" of plaza (the short side); long structure at right angle to temple; I-shaped ball court oriented east-west; two civic plazas; at least one plaza on a broad elevated rectangular platform;

orientations to the cardinal points (Chitinamit, Cruzche); and high ridgetop locations. Moreover, the smaller civic plaza at Oquin and the secondary plaza on the south spur at Cruzche share features. Both comprise a single temple with two perpendicular short rectangular ("flanking") structures together on an elevated platform.

Ethnohistory

Fortunately, references to the seven Chujuyub sites in various colonial documents and the retention today of some pre-Hispanic names allow their ethnohistoric identification.

Oquin is *Uquin cat*, the first Ilocab center (Carmack, Fox, and Stewart 1975). This identification is supported by its associations with the Ilocab municipality San Pedro Jocopilas. Immediately behind the temple in its main plaza is a trench marking the municipal boundary between San Pedro and San Bartolomé Jocotenango. The boundary of San Pedro extends just far enough—literally not a meter more than necessary—to include the site within the municipality. Furthermore, local tradition has it that the patron saint, San Pedro, originally came from Oquin.

Cruzche is identified as the early Tamub center Amak tan in an early colonial document (1717) as well as by one modern inhabitant (Carmack, Fox, and Stewart 1975). The Tamub were split into moieties from their earliest times in the highlands. Perhaps the two parallel ridge groups at Cruzche represent these moieties. The smaller and lower group is the only Chujuyub site to yield Late-phase as well as Early-phase ceramics. It may therefore have been the small Late-phase ward center Ah Mactan (Tamub 1957:57). Ceramics and ethnohistory suggest, however, that the main portion of Amak tan was abandoned by the Tamub near the end of the Early phase (C'oyoi 1973:288–89).

The third large *tinamit* site in the Chujuyub Depression, Chitinamit, may be Hacawitz, the center for the Nima Quiche. Chitinamit is situated in the center of the Chujuyub Depression on a lofty peak from which each of the six other sites can be seen. Hacawitz is described as a fortified town on a round mountain above the great "red" river (*Popol Vuh* 1971:175; Carmack 1968:62). Chitinamit has an elaborate terrace system, with its upper terraces containing residences, and is clearly fortified.

Moreover, it overlooks the Rio Queca, by far the largest and most central river in the Chujuyub Depression. The municipal boundaries of Santa Cruz del Quiche extend northeastward in an oddly shaped narrow corridor to include Chitinamit. Thus, just as the municipality boundary from San Pedro Jocopilas extends far enough east to include the sacred site Uquin Cat, so, too, municipal boundaries of Santa Cruz were seemingly established to include the sacred Nima Quiche site Hacawitz. From the native histories, we know that the three principal Nima Quiche deities, Hacawitz, Tohil, and Awilix, were placed on separate mountains; one of the two temples at Chitinamit probably contained the idol Hacawitz (Carmack, Fox, and Stewart 1975), the others being respectively located on the isolated peaks of Tohil and Awilix (*Popol Vuh* 1971:176n, 178). Finally, the deity Hacawitz, who was called the "messenger" and may be a manifestation of the merchant god (Carmack, Fox, and Stewart 1975), was represented by bees (e.g. *Popol Vuh* 1971:199). Apparently in an allegorical sense, the fortress town Hacawitz was saved from destruction by use of bees as a weapon. Much of the highlands are too cold for apiculture, but bees are still raised in the Chujuyub region. Beekeeping has traditionally been associated with the Gulf Coast, where the Quiche originated.

The mountaintop site still called Tohil is obviously the mountain where the idol Tohil was kept (e.g. *Popol Vuh* 1971:175; Carmack, Fox, and Stewart 1975). Moreover, there are several references to "air plants" and "mosses" in the high forest on Tohil (*Popol Vuh* 1971:175, 177, 185). Within this *tierra fria* forest today are numerous aerophytic plants resembling small pineapple plants, often ensconced in the branches of a tall orange-bark hardwood tree, as well as hanging Spanish moss. As the mountain Hacawitz is associated with bees, the mountain Tohil is associated with numerous varieties of snakes (e.g. *Popul Vuh* 1971:175, 1950:184). This should not be surprising insofar as the Quiche called Tohil Quetzalcoat (*Popol Vuh* 1971:183), the Mexican feathered serpent deity, often represented as a snake. Indeed, perhaps the stylized relief found in the temple here was similar in concept to stylized reliefs on the temple of Quetzalcoatl at Tula. Stone-tenoned cones similar to those recovered from the Tohil temple can be seen today projecting from the temple at Tula, specifically for the attachment of thin rectangular relief carvings. We are told that non-Quiche peoples were sacrificed on Tohil (*Popol Vuh* 1950:189, 191). To summarize, the specialized religious functions of the small complex on Tohil as the keeping place for the idol, as a "dawning" place, and as a locus for sacrifice of Quiche enemies as well as autosacrifice by Quiche priests (*Popol Vuh* 1971:171, 190) are well documented. Perhaps, then, the short rectangular structures enclosing the temple on Tohil were employed in temple or religious activities, as suggested above for similar structures at Utatlan. Finally, there also may have been a long structure at Tohil, which may relate to one Quiche *nim ja* (lineage house) (Carmack, Fox, and Stewart 1975).

The three administrative-residential centers for the three Central Quiche confederates, Oquin, Cruzche, and Chitinamit, are literally in the shadow of Tohil. Tohil was the principal deity of all three Quiche divisions, although each had its own idol (*Popol Vuh* 1971:162–63). The Tohil site was abandoned during fairly early times (Totonicapan 1953:180), perhaps contemporary with the abandonment of Hacawitz. Ceramics support an Early-phase abandonment, although it is listed as a Late-phase ward (Nijaib I 1957:77).

The lofty mountaintop site still called Awilix was the locus for the Nima Quiche idol Awilix. The Quiche took victims to be sacrificed on the forested summit of Awilix (*Popol Vuh* 1971:175, 192–93). In legends, both the deity Awilix and the mountaintop sanctuary are symbolized by the jaguar.

The Ilocab saw the mythological "dawn" at Uquin cat, where they kept their god Tohil (*Popol Vuh* 1971:176, 163). The documents, however, do not distinguish between Uquin and Sakiribal, as do the modern inhabitants of the area. *Sakiribal* translates as "place of the dawning" (Recinos 1957:37 n.; Edmonson 1971:178). The architectural remains of lofty Sakiribal, comprising a truncated temple in the center of a small complex, overlooking Oquin on the same ridge, seem to fit the description of a removed spot where Ilocab priests could observe the heavens and attend their god. In fact, the low, truncated temple here, as well as temples at the other mountaintop complexes at Tohil, Awilix, and Sakiribal-Tamub, may have been the actual loci for statuary representations of deities.

Like Oquin and Sakiribal-Ilocab, the site known as Sakiribal-Tamub, high above Cruzche to the west, may have been the "dawning" place for the Tamub Quiche and a shrine for their deity Tohil (*Popol Vuh* 1971:176, 183–84). Sakiribal-Tamub is named in the Tamub (1957:39) document. To reiterate, the Tamub were divided into moieties but maintained a symmetrical four-part community comprising two high and two low complexes, with the two Tamub peaks of Sakiribal and Tabil situated together on the same mountain and the two parallel spurs of Cruzche similarly separated by only a few hundred meters.

The spatial positioning of the Early-phase Central Quiche sites with respect to each other allows inference about some aspects of their political alliance. First, the three confederates are situated on high, extremely defensible locations that are at least two kilometers apart but are nevertheless at the same elevation and mutually visible. Indeed, the fires of Amak tan were said to be visible from Uquin cat (Carmack, personal communication). These highly defensible locations, their spatial proximity, and the fact that each *tinamit* had a separate mountaintop shrine for its own idols representing the same god suggest cultural and political affinity along with definite individuality. The Tamub (1957:39) document tells us that the three confederates were equal in the Chujuyub area.

Early Postclassic Period

In order to gain a perspective on the local culture immediately preceding the Epi-Toltec immigration, which doubtless lasted into the Early phase, we shall summarize the settlement config-urations of the Early Postclassic sites in the Quiche Basin. Two distinct settlement patterns are evident—a linear group of three mounds in a roughly east-west line on a ridgetop, and an enclosed plaza group of larger structures, often in more open locations. These two settlement types apparently were in use at the same time, since both patterns occur within Panajxit and Caja San Pedro with similar ceramics. Many ceramic types also correspond to those found in the Early-phase Chujuyub area, especially the punctate and wavy-line incised ware, although there is an additional bi-chrome type of orange and brown on buff that is absent in the Chujuyub area. However, these diagnostic sherds have not been recovered for Caja San Pedro.

Cojonob

On the southeast edge of La Estancia plateau, about two kilometers southwest of Greater Utatlan, are three low hills containing contemporary earth mounds. The largest group comprises three small structures at about 40-meter intervals stretched along a 60-meter-high ridgetop.

La Estancia

Near the center of La Estancia plateau is an elevated square platform with a small temple on one side and a long structure perpendicular to it. Its platform, the right-angle relationship between the temple and long structure, and structure sizes as well as the wavy-line and punctate wares indicate relationship with the Chujuyub Quiche.

Panajxit

The Late-phase occupation at Panajxit is described above. Two sections of the plateau reflect Early Postclassic civic arrangements. On the northern third of the plateau is a ridge with two and possibly three earth mounds in a line. An interesting chacmoollike sculpture, rendered in a different style from the Toltec statues, was unearthed here (Carmack, Fox, and Stewart 1975). Near the plateau is an enclosed plaza of badly destroyed earth mounds at the foot of a knoll, crested by a massive pyramidal structure.

Caja San Pedro

On three different levels of a sloping ridge from Cerro Telecuch, overlooking the small San Pedro Jocopilas side valley, is the large site of Caja San Pedro. Its steep, terraced sides are quite defensible. The lowest group consists of four large, templelike structures on four sides of a square court. The intermediate level has a semienclosed rectilinear group, while the highest ridgetop group has three mounds in a row running exactly east-west.

Pakaja and Aldea Lemoa

Two large neighboring sites on the Lemoa Plateau in the Quiche Basin proper reveal similar patterns. Both have one large rectilinear court with four structures, like the first group at Caja San Pedro, and an additional semienclosed court with a long structure (Carmack, Fox, and Stewart 1975; Stewart, personal communication).

Conclusions

A comparison of the Early-phase Central Quiche centers grouped together in the Chujuyub area and the Late-phase centers within Greater Utatlan reveals both changes and continuities in Central Quiche settlement organization. First, the three *tinamit* within Greater Utatlan are spatially closer together, with Chisalin and Ismachi separated from Utatlan by only 300 meters each. In contrast, Cruzche, the central site in the Chujuyub depression, is two kilometers from Oquin and three kilometers in a straight line from Chitinamit. The closer grouping of allied groups within Greater Utatlan may point to an increase in centralization from the Early to Late phases.

Moreover, there was a shift from the Tamub site, Cruzche, as the geographic center, to the Nima Quiche site, Utatlan, as the center. But the areas controlled by each of the three Quiche confederates remained the same. That is, the Nima Quiche controlled the eastern portion of the Chujuyub Depression at Chitinamit, Awilix, and Tohil, and the eastern portion of Greater Utatlan at Utatlan and Pakaman and the eastern Quiche Basin. The Ilocab controlled the northwest Chujuyub Depression at Oquin and Sakiribal-Ilocab as well as the northwest Quiche Basin (Ilotenango and Jocopilas areas); the Tamub controlled the southwest Chujuyub Depression at Cruzche, Sakiribal-Tamub, and Tabil, and the southwest Quiche Basin (Patzite area).

The central sites in both nucleated communities, Cruzche and Utatlan, are oriented east-west. In contrast, the Early-phase Nima Quiche center, Chitinamit, is oriented directly south, whereas the Late-phase Tamub center, Ismachi, is oriented northeast-southwest. These orientations can be understood with a simple ethnohistoric explanation. The Early-phase Nima center Chitinamit or Hacawitz is dedicated to the deity Hacawitz, whose direction may have been south. The primary deities at Utatlan were Tohil and Awilix, facing east and west respectively. Significantly, orientations to the cardinal points persisted with the Nima Quiche over three centuries. While absolute correlation between orientations at the Tamub Early-phase and late-phase centers of Cruzche and Ismachi is lacking, there is a continuity between the large and small civic precincts on parallel spurs at each site, suggesting a continuity of two-part social organization among the Tamub. Ismachi was also the intermediate Central Quiche capital, between 1350 and 1370, where the three Quiche allies seemingly dwelled together, and it manifests orientations intermediate between the Early-phase and Late-phase sites. Its topographic situation also has both Early and Late features. The mesatop is narrow, and the main plaza is situated on an elevation, like the elevated platforms on the narrow Chujuyub ridgetops.

There is a lack of correlation between Oquin, the Early-phase Ilocab center oriented sightly west of south, and Chisalin, perhaps their Late-phase center, variously oriented east-west. There is however, a positive correlation between Ilocab Oquin and Pakaja in Ilotenango, whose orientation is also basically south. Moreover, the Nima Quiche and Tamub Late-phase centers are situated within the sixteenth-century municipal boundaries of Santa Cruz del Quiche, as are their thirteenth-century centers, Chitinamit and Cruzche. Similarly, both Pakaja-Chicoculjip and Oquin lie just outside these municipal boundaries to the west. These locations suggest spatial and, probably, political distance between the Ilocab and the Nima Quiche and Tamub. Indeed, at one time the Ilocab tried to take over the leadership of the Central Quiche alliance and were nearly annihilated (*Popol Vuh* 1950:213). If Ilotenango was the Late-phase Ilocab locus, then the degree of political centralization, reflected by spatial proximity, among the Ilocab and the two other confederates would actually be less than during the Early-phase Chujuyub alliance. Alternatively, after their defeat, the Ilocab may have been forced to relocate at Chisalin from Pakaja. If this was the case, they may have had to adopt Nima plaza organization, particularly temples. A community often defeated by the Quiche had to adopt its ideological structure and patron deity (cf. Xajil 1953).

Two of the three Early-phase residential-administrative centers, Sakiribal-Ilocab and Sakiribal-Tamub, have one religious satellite site situated high above them; Chitinamit has two such sites, Tohil and Awilix. In contrast, the single satellite site associated with each of the Late-phase residential-administrative centers probably had military functions (i.e., Resguardo; the plaza outside Chisalin; the small ruins on Culbut outside Ismachi; and Chicoculjip outside Pakaja). Like its Early-phase counterpart Chitinamit, Utatlan also had two satellite sites, Resguardo and Pakaman. The function of the satellite site appears, then, to have changed, no doubt reflecting fundamental changes in Quiche society. Parallelling this changed settlement component, the leaders during the Early phase were priests, whereas leaders during the Late phase were noted for their military prowess (e.g., *Popol Vuh* 1950; Totonicapan 1953). Late-phase Quiche society is also characterized by the emergence of a powerful military sector, which challenged the traditional authority of the aristocratic elite lineages (Carmack 1974). Therefore, the change in the satellite component associated with each *tinamit* probably represents an increased militarization of Quiche society, with a military sector gaining at the expense of the priests and the nobility.

This societal change also seems to parallel the shift at the Nima residential-administrative centers from the worship of Hacawitz at Chitinamit to the worship of Tohil and Awilix at Utatlan. To reiterate, this would also account for the change from south to east-west orientations at these centers. Thus, Hacawitz, the merchant god, was of critical importance to the first Quiche, newly arrived from the Gulf Coast "port of trade" area, where commerce was a medium of interaction (cf. Chapman 1957; Thompson 1970). In contrast, the war gods Tohil and Awilix gained in prominence with the expansion of the conquest-based Quiche (*Popol Vuh* 1950; Xajil 1953). The adoption of Awilix and Tohil as the deities for the *tinamit* also accounts for the change from one temple at the plaza head at Chitinamit and Cruzche to the two temples on opposite plaza sides at Utatlan and Ismachi.

Changes in size of settlement components also bespeak evolutionary changes in Quiche society. Thus, there is a dramatic growth in the size of both residence areas—judging from the limited available space on the narrow ridgetops and upper terraces at Oquin, Cruzche, and Chitinamit and the wide mesas at Greater

Utatlan—and residence structures, comparing the small foundations at Oquin and Cruzche with the large, multiroom residences
within the densely packed plateaus of Greater Utatlan. There is a
corresponding size increase in civic structures, such as long structures, ball courts, and temples. The change in construction material from roughly shaped schistose slabs to finely dressed pumice
and limestone blocks implies the advent of specialized masons as
well as a procurement system for the latter materials, which do not
exist within the Quiche Basin.

Several changes in civic pattern between the Early and Late
phases are noteworthy. First, the Late-phase civic plazas are not
situated on broad, elevated rectangular platforms. Second, instead
of the two temples on opposite plaza sides characteristic of the Late
phase, the Early-phase centers of Oquin, Chitinamit, and probably
Cruzche had two "back-to-back" civic plazas with one temple each.
These two plazas seem to have evolved with time into the single
civic plaza of the Late phase, with two temples. Forerunners of the
two short, rectangular structures flanking the Late-phase temples
may have been the two short, rectangular structures on opposite,
although perpendicular, sides at Sakiribal-Ilocab and Oquin. There
are, however, continuities in pattern, such as the perpendicular
relationship between the temple and long structure and the overall
rectilinear shape of the plaza.

Greater Utatlan and its ward centers formed an extended
community. The ward centers are characterized in general by
small civic complexes in semidefensive situations on some of the
larger plateau segments within the Quiche Basin. Their limited
remains—construction, ceramics, projectile points—are of the
same types found in Greater Utatlan, supporting the documentary
references to small enclaves of Central Quiche in these locations.
Interestingly, these small Quiche outposts often occur near large
Early Postclassic centers, such as Panajxit, Lemoa, and Caja San
Pedro (Xesic). The Early Postclassic autochthonous populations
eventually subjugated by the immigrant Central Quiche were
thought to have been incorporated into the larger Quiche society
by Late-phase times, serving largely as peasant agriculturalists
(Carmack, Fox, and Stewart 1975; Carmack 1974). Thus the small
Quiche ward centers may have functioned as administrative
outposts overseeing agrarian populations whose leaders were
probably forced to abandon the large Early Postclassic centers

nearby sometime during the Early phase of the Late Postclassic Period.

The sixteenth-century Quiche documents differentiate between the administrative-residential centers like Utatlan, known as the *tinamit*, where the nobility and their retainers dwelled, and the outlying small wards, called the *amak*. *Tinamit* translates as "within the walls," whereas *amak* translates as "spider's legs" (Carmack 1975, n.d.b).

> The Quiche saw this type of settlement in analogy to the many legs of the spider, for it was a scattered population living in hamlets. We are given to understand that they generally correspond to patrilineal descent groups. . . . The word also connotes permanency . . . apparently because they were the basic landholding units from time immemorial. (Carmack n.d.b:5)

In selecting the Chujuyub area for their first settlements, the newly arrived Central Quiche, apparently few in number, seemed to be conscious of existing local sociocultural groups, particularly the large Quiche Basin Early Postclassic centers and the already established power centers in the Rio Negro Basin. The Chujuyub area, mountainous and highly eroded, is much less fertile than the neighboring Quiche Basin to the south and the rolling Jocotenango plains to the northwest. Thus it was an out-of-the-way locale of little agricultural value that the first Quiche selected for settlement, but one ideal for defense. Many of the neighboring Early Postclassic settlements—such as Cojonob, Panajxit Secundo, and Caja San Pedro—were also located on ridgetops, suggesting that the highland political climate, like that of much of Mesoamerica, was already militaristically oriented. The Chujuyub centers, however, were even more fortified—and far higher and steeper—than those in the Quiche Basin, which would indicate that the Epi-Toltec forefathers of the Quiche introduced an even more militaristic system.

The small Early-phase Chujuyub civic centers manifest architectural features that first occur in Mexico, including, apparently, the Tabasco Gulf Coast. The Mexican features discernible among the poorly preserved Chujuyub remains are the I-shaped ball court; the *talud-tablero* balustrades on temples; long structures; rectilinear plazas; and cone-shaped tenons for temple reliefs. In addition, what may be fired bricks are common at Chitinamit and noticeable at Oquin. Indeed, the heavy use of bricks at Chitinamit seems anomalous with such abundant rock outcrops on its slopes. Bricks are rare in Late-phase Quiche construction and quite unusual throughout Mesoamerica. They are, however, a major construction material on the Tabasco Gulf Coast and the adjacent alluvial plain, where building stone is scarce (Berlin 1956:102; Scholes and Roys 1968). This is the precise region that Carmack (1968) argues, from ethnohistoric and linguistic data, to be the Quiche homeland. Moreover, unfamiliarity with highland construction material by the newly arrived Quiche can be seen in other Chujuyub building techniques. At Oquin, the early Ilocab carved a temple, and the platform upon which it is situated, largely from bedrock. The conspicuous dearth of plaster contrasts with Late-phase architecture, which is typified by thick plaster coats (cf. Smith 1955). Apparently, it took the early Quiche some time to begin to utilize the highland lime plaster (reduced from limestone, in contrast to the shell lime plaster of the Gulf Coast).

One area in the general Laguna de Términos region, about fifty kilometers inland along the Rio Candelaria, reveals settlement patterns strikingly similar to the Chujuyub sites. Andrews (1943:45–47) briefly characterizes this area as containing a number of sites on neighboring leveled hilltops. Like the Chujuyub sites, they are characterized by small plazas, usually in groups of four or five mounds, and by an absence of faced stone. From Andrews's (1943: Fig. 11) illustration of a typical site there, Pozas de Ventura, a number of features can be seen that are shared with the Chujuyub sites, namely the single temple; the temple at the head of the plaza; long structures perpendicular to the temple; ball court opposite the temple, with its ranges perpendicular to the front of the temple; rectilinear plaza; plaza resting on a rectangular platform; and nucleation of neighboring hilltop sites. In sum, it can be argued that the Quiche brought with them Mexican architecture and settlement patterns from the Laguna de Terminos–Usumacinta alluvial plain region.

Unlike architecture, however, few ceramic wares characteristic of the Gulf Coast were perpetuated by the Quiche. Only a few fine paste sherds, notably fine orange, were recovered from Tohil. Instead, the predominant ceramic types at the Chujuyub sites are local wares (punctate, wavy-line incised, outflaring rims).

Furthermore, judging from temper and overall crudity, ceramics from Chitinamit appear to have been made in the immediate area. The Quiche would then appear to have lost their ceramic traditions, perhaps as they lost their Gulf Coast Chontal language soon after their arrival in the highlands (Carmack 1968). The small groups of warriors who entered the region married local highland Maya (Quiche)-speaking women. If women were the potters then, as they are today, then lowland pottery styles would soon have gone the way of the lowland language. The Nahuat terms that persisted were associated with warfare, architecture, and government, that is, male-dominated activities (Carmack 1968). As we have seen, Gulf Coast architecture also persisted. Men may also have been the "Toltec" artisans (*Popol Vuh* 1950:88), for there is a persistence of the highly geometric Mixteca-Puebla art style from the Tohil sculptures to the burial goods and murals at Utatlan.

Finally, let us note the Gulf Coast associations of the three principal Quiche gods, Tohil, Awilix, and Hacawitz. Tohil is the highland manifestation of Quetzalcoatl or Kukulcan, the principal Toltec deity of the ancestral home of the Toltecs, Tulan (i.e., Chichen Itza, see Carmack 1968). Tohil is also the principal deity of all Quiche peoples. In fact, Tohil is the "morning star," a prelude to the dawn. The dawn, the arrival of the sun, is the essence of the conquest ideology of the Quiche, for the sun (also personified by Tohil, and by Awilix) had to be fed blood to make its daily journey. Awilix may have been originally an aspect of the lowland moon goddess (Carmack n.d.b), which was of utmost importance to the Gulf Coast Chontal "warrior-merchants" (Thompson 1970). Hacawitz is associated with bees, which have long been kept in the Gulf Coast area and are in turn connected with merchant association of the lowland gods, the Bacabs (Thompson 1970).

3

SACAPULAS QUICHE, IXIL, AND AGUACATEC

This chapter will discuss the peoples to the north of the Central Quiche who were brought within the Quiche state during the first expansion outside the Quiche Basin, perhaps beginning in the early 1400s A.D., or slightly before. In what is now the northern two thirds of the Department of Quiche were located the Sacapulas Quiche (i.e., Sacapultec) and the Ixil during the Late Postclassic Period. In addition, the Aguacatec, who border the Sacapulas Quiche and Ixil to the west, were also subjugated during this early expansion. The six known Sacapulas civic centers will be described and analyzed in order to appraise Central Quiche influence and define the local settlement pattern and architectural style. The basic pattern characterizing most of the twenty Ixil sites will be defined and Central Quiche influence, where present in settlement remains, will be discussed. The Aguacatec, with a culture and habitat apparently similar to those of the Sacapulas Quiche, will also be compared to them. A final section will briefly describe the Early Postclassic patterns in the western Rio Negro Basin, examining earlier cultures possibly ancestral to the Mexicanized river basin groups (the Sacapulas Quiche and the Aguacatec) during the Late Postclassic Period.

The Sacapulas Quiche

Four of the six Sacapulas Quiche sites are closely spaced along bluffs of the Rio Negro, within a span of just nine kilometers (Map 4). The other two Sacapulas sites overlook small side valleys a short

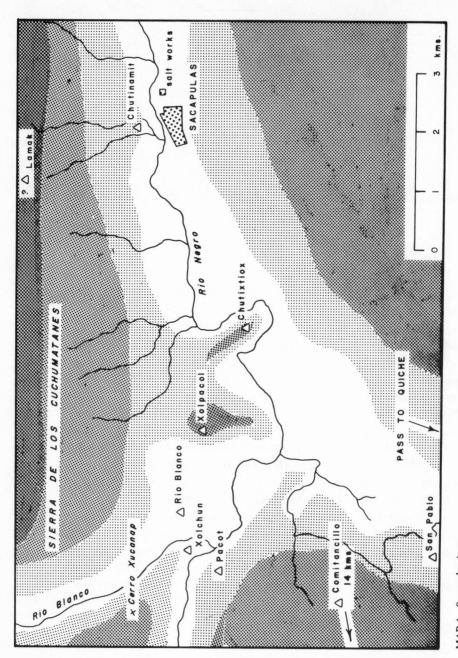

MAP 4 Sacapulas Area

distance back from the Rio Negro Basin. There is an abrupt descent into the Rio Negro Basin from Aguacatan to the west, Nebaj to the north, and Cunen to the east (Map 4). Entry from the south, however, is less dramatic, since the Santa Cruz del Quiche road follows a narrow natural corridor about thirty kilometers from the Quiche Basin. The four sites situated on the intersection of this north-south corridor and the east-west Rio Negro Basin form a strategic crossroads.

The Rio Negro Basin is an area of sharp geographic contrast. The Sierra de Cuchumatanes, the north wall of the basin, rise 1,000 meters, almost vertically. The basin is also a geological boundary, separating the ancient crystalline beds to the south from the limestone of the Cuchumatanes to the north (McBryde 1945:131). Highly contrastive zones of vegetation reflect the dramatic phys-. iography. The basin walls are stark in their dryness; the river bottomland is green with intensive cultivation. The land divides into these two zones as soon as it rises beyond reach of water from the river. Indeed, cactus and other thorny vegetation often predominate only 200 meters from the river. About 1,100 meters above sea level, the basin floor lies within the *tierra caliente* habitat. The steep hills in the basin, descending near the water's edge, divide the bottomland into three distinct agricultural tracts (Map 4).

The salt springs and copper deposits along this narrow stretch at Sacapulas were, no doubt, critical resources before the conquest. Indeed, there are only two salt-producing areas in the highlands of Guatemala and Chiapas (see McBryde 1945).

A. L. Smith (1955) mapped and described five of the Sacapulas sites in 1945. I have used his maps, redrawing them to the same scale as the other maps; I have made some additions to his maps of Chutinamit and Chutixtiox. We visited Chutixtiox, Chutinamit, Xolpacol, and Early Postclassic Xolchun in July 1973.

Chutixtiox

Chutixtiox is situated approximately in the center of the Sacapulas group, in the middle of the narrow basin at Sacapulas. The settlement can be observed from the bluffs on the opposite side of the Rio Negro, which also mark the terminus for the corridor running from the Quiche Basin to the south.

Topography and Ecology

Chutixtiox is connected to a ridge one and one-half kilometers long by a "neck" of land five meters wide. The sheer cliffs of the river surround the site on the other three sides.

> It is ideally situated for defense and commands a wonderful view up and down the valley. The hill, over 100 m. above the river, drops off almost vertically except in two places: on the northern part of the west side, where it slopes gently down to the river, a defense wall about 4 m. high extends from the crest of the hill down to the river; on the northern part of the east side . . . the slope, already very steep, is cut away at the upper edge to leave a vertical drop of about 3 or 4 m. The only entrace lies at the northwest end of the hill near the upper end of the defense wall. Here a narrow neck of land originally joined another hill, but a deep gap was cut through it so that approach was cut off from this side. (A. L. Smith 1955:17)

The site overlooks two of the three agricultural segments of the Sacapulas Basin. The larger is immediately across the river, while the second floodplain tract follows the river to the east (Map 4). The cultivable land below contrasts with the aridity of the site itself, which is covered with cacti and thorny acacias.

Settlement Description

All but two of the civic structures àre associated with a civic plaza on top of an acropolis (Fig. 11). The acropolis, four meters above the next main level, has inset masonry walls and five stairways. The well-preserved masonry (cf. Woodbury and Trik 1953:3) is for the most part composed of thin cut schistose slabs covered with plaster, although a second building stage uses some dressed limestone blocks.

The civic plaza consists of one temple and two identical flanking structures on the east side, three rectangular altars and a minuscule stucco round structure in a line across the plaza, centered on the temple, and two long structures on the north and south sides, oriented 200°S and 343°N respectively. The temple is situated in the center of the acropolis and, with one stairway on each of its four sides, is oriented to the four cardinal points. The flanking structures are about three meters high with a single stairway on

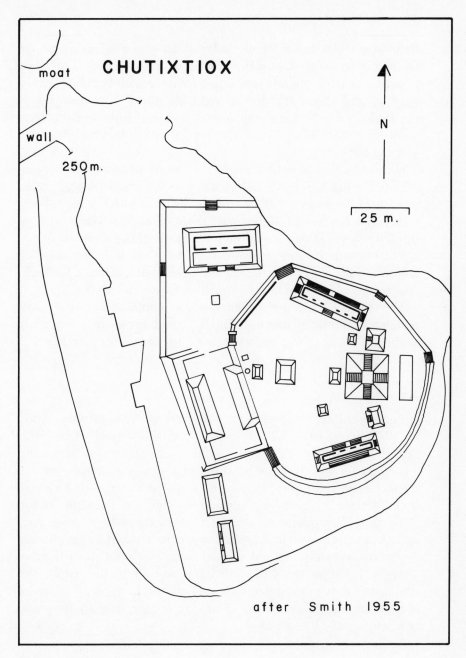

CHUTIXTIOX

moat

wall

250 m.

N

25 m.

after Smith 1955

FIG. 11   Chutixtiox

their west sides. Interestingly, a life-sized stucco jaguar decorated the foot of this stairway on the north flanking structure. Both long structures have a single-room superstructure with benches against the back and side walls. A tomb excavated by A. L. Smith, under the back bench in the north long structure, contained the fragments of a second large stucco jaguar, as well as human bones and grave goods.

On the level below the acropolis is a sunken I-shaped ball court, oriented roughly north-south, with nearly vertical playing walls. The top of the eastern ball court range is level with the plaza floor, so perhaps it was considered part of the close-knit plaza. Also on this lower level is an unusual long structure. It has a sunken court, and a one-room superstructure with benches and free-standing masonry walls. A. L. Smith calls the holes near the top of the walls "unquestionably beam holes," probably for a wooden roof.

The terraces on the western slope contain numerous low rectangular house platforms. Finally, a subterranean passageway leading to the river was reported, but Smith could not locate it.

Artifacts

Large ceramic samples were collected by A. L. Smith (1955), by Wauchope (1970:153–59) in 1947, and by ourselves in 1973. Wauchope's analysis revealed typically Late-phase Quiche ceramics, characterized by large amounts of Fortress white-on-red and monochrome red types surprisingly close to his excavated sample from Utatlan. We recovered a small but significant quantity of the distinctive Early-phase carved ware characterized by heavy geometric designs carved and incised in a narrow panel, often painted white, on an otherwise red-slipped vessel. While this distinctive ware is absent in the Chujuyub area, not far to the south, the similarities in types and percentages between Late-phase ceramics at Chutixtiox and those found at Utatlan suggest strong Late-phase ties between the two areas.

Architecture and Settlement Pattern Interpretations

The general structure types found in civic plazas at Greater Utatlan also occur at Chutixtiox. Moreover, they are similarly arranged with principal temple facing west; two flanking structures associated with temples; temple on plaza side, though in acropolis center; long structures perpendicular to temple; round structure in court; plaster plaza floor; moat at entrance; and cave (reported by Smith, but neither he nor we could find it). The exceptional preservation at Chutixtiox shows some additional architectural traits shared with Greater Utatlan, notably long structures with single-room superstructures containing benches against the back and side walls; chamber tombs under the center of the rear bench in long structures; recessed corners of rectangular structures and altars; and, rarely, dressed stone blocks in the last building stage. A number of architectural and settlement pattern features, however, are distinct from those seen at Greater Utatlan. Chutixtiox has an acropolis, with a steeped masonry retaining wall; its plaza is not enclosed or rectilinear; its ball court is north-south rather than east-west. There is a low, rectangular structure immediately behind the temple, and stairways are found on all four sides of the temple. The plaza contains two long structures rather than one, and on the long balustraded structure there is a large *tablero* over a slight inset *talud*. Buildings at Chutixtiox are generally smaller than corresponding types in Greater Utatlan. The temple and ball court, however, are comparable in size to similar structures at Chisalin, Ismachi, and Resguardo.

The similarities and discrepancies of this pattern to that of the Central Quiche may correlate with Late-phase and Early-phase ceramic complexes, respectively, at Chutixtiox. The similarities, in other words, may be a Central Quiche–influenced veneer over an earlier non–Central Quiche pattern. The nature of this influence, however, remains to be determined. Chutixtiox lacks the hallmark of Central Quiche plazas, that is, two temples perpendicular to one long structure. Thus, Central Quiche influence seems to be stylistic and organizational, but, apparently, it does not represent a pattern transplanted from Greater Utatlan. An underlying Early-phase pattern at Chutixtiox may account for such discrepancies as an acropolis, a temple with one stairway on four sides in the acropolis center, stairways on four sides of the long structures, and a north-south ball court. The stepped acropolis retaining wall is unusual in the Guatemalan Highlands, but this may simply be a reflection of preservation. This style does occur in the Mixteca Alta region of Highland Mexico (cf. Gorenstein 1973:24, fig. 12).

The Late-phase plaza at Chutixtiox has symmetrical halves, each containing one long structure, a flanking structure, and an altar, at slightly offset orientations. The plaza is bisected by the perfect east-west alignment of the temple, with the low rectangular structure behind it, the three altars, and the round structure that together span the acropolis.

This central east-west alignment may have been an ideological axis, for at the east end of the temple projects toward the sky, perhaps symbolizing the rising of the sun, and the sunken ball court descends at the western terminus, perhaps symbolizing the setting of the sun.

The two symmetrical sections, in contrast, may have had more secular functions. Indeed, a dualistic scheme of organization pervades Toltec-derived organization. The Late-phase Central Quiche civic plazas, for example, also have symmetrical halves, but each half contains its own temple. Interestingly, the north symmetrical section at Chutixtiox has similar-sized stucco jaguars associated with both the long structure and flanking structure. Perhaps the jaguar served as a symbol for a social group that occupied this section. Among the better-known Central Quiche, the Cawec lineage, for example, was represented by a jaguar (see Edmonson 1971:189–90), and there is evidence of a jaguar military order in Quiche society (*Rabinal Achi;* C'oyoi 1973; Carmack 1968:57, 80).

Ethnohistory

Four of the thirteen or so lowland groups mentioned in the migration epic—the Lamakib, the Kumatz, the Tuhal Haa, and the Uch'aba Haa—settled near Sacapulas (Brasseur de Bourbourg 1861, cited in Recinos, Goetz, and Morley 1950:171n.). For this early time, however, we cannot distinguish exact dates of arrival into the highlands. There is some evidence to suggest that the Sacapulas comunities were established prior to the Epi-Toltec Quiche. Kumatz is associated today with the western portion of the narrow basin on the river's north side (Carmack, personal communication), so Chutixtiox may have been Kumatz. Kumatz was burned and subjugated by the Central Quiche in the early decades of the fifteenth century (Xajil 1953:93; Xpantzay II 1957:141). The Late-phase Central Quiche influence seen in architecture and ceramics can thus be correlated with actual military takeover recorded ethnohistorically.

Chutinamit

The ruins of Chutinamit lie on a low bluff on the opposite side of the Rio Negro from Santo Domingo Sacapulas. The modern bridge from the town ends at the foot of Chutinamit.

Topography and Ecology

The site is on a narrow tongue half a kilometer long. The civic precinct is concentrated on the southernmost tip of this tongue, immediately overlooking the Rio Negro 100 meters below. Its terraced slopes, 100 meters high, are steep but are not the cliffs typical of Late-phase sites. Apparently the main entrance was over a narrow neck from the north, which was fortified with a moat and three walls (A. L. Smith 1955:20).

A broad segment of bottomland runs west from Chutinamit to Chutixtiox; a narrow stretch of riverbank runs east. Significantly, the principal salt springs are located across the river from Chutinamit, on the outskirts of the modern town.

Settlement Description

In 1973 the ruins were little more than earth and rubble mounds, used in cultivation, as they were when Smith observed them 28 years earlier. Proximity and easy access from the modern cabecera seemingly was a major factor in the loss of the masonry facades.

There are three groups of monumental architecture: the acropolis group, the terrace complex, and the main plaza, situated near the southern border of the settlement. In the center of the main plaza is a pyramidal temple oriented to the four cardinal points. There are two short, or intermediate-sized, rectangular platforms on the east and north plaza sides, a curious large "altar" in the northwest corner, and two altars centered on the temple to the west (Fig. 12). The plaza is bounded to the south by an oddly shaped sunken ball court, oriented 102°E–282°W, whose end zones are shaped differently. Smith detected a stairway on the west

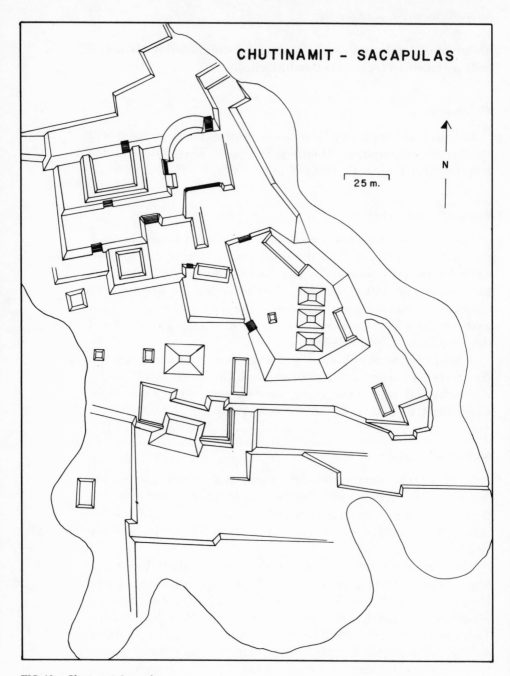

CHUTINAMIT – SACAPULAS

25 m.

N

FIG. 12.   Chutinamit-Sacapulas

side of the temple, facing the altars. However, this may have been simply the last building phase; an earlier structure may have had stairways on all four sides. With the same orientations and west-facing altars, the temple at Chutixtiox has four such stairways. The present owner of Chutinamit claims that the plaza's floor is so thick that it cannot be broken with metal hoes.

An irregularly shaped acropolis rises 12 meters above the main plaza to the east. The two are connected by a broad stairway (Fig. 12). The acropolis plaza consists of equal-sized triple temples facing west and spanning the width of the acropolis; a long structure following the acropolis edge, oriented 222°SW; and a short, rectangular structure immediately behind the triple temples. A second stairway leads from the acropolis to the first tier of the terrace complex to the north.

Rising above the acropolis and main plaza are four narrow successive levels, linked by stairways, that rise to the level of the remainder of the land tongue to the north (see A. L. Smith 1955: Fig. 66). This terrace complex faces the acropolis and main plaza, as well as the river valley and salt springs below, in much the same manner as an amphitheater. On the first and third levels of the complex are single square, sunken courts, delineated by what may be collapsed walls (Fig. 12). The first level also contains an intermediate rectangular structure. A long narrow bench, projecting from the back wall, spans the length of the second level. Set apart, on an eastern portion of the second tier, is an unusual "chamber" of courts. This centrally situated section is directly linked to each of three other levels by single stairways and by a passageway to the main part of the second level. A long curved bench is set against its back wall. From surface remains we could detect neither columns nor signs of walls, so we could not determine whether the chamber once had a roof.

Artifacts

Both Smith's moderate-sized sample (Wauchope 1970:159–66) and our small sample revealed largely Late-phase Quiche ceramic types, notably Fortress white-on-red and monochrome red, tan, and brown. In addition, there are ceramic types generally assigned to the Early Postclassic Period, as well as the distinctive carved ware thought to pertain to the Early-phase Late Postclassic.

Chutinamit thus seems to have been occupied at least through the Late Postclassic Period.

Architecture and Settlement Pattern Interpretations

Chutinamit has several unusual settlement pattern features. First, it appears to be a large *tinamit*, with its long "residential" zone (half a kilometer) on higher ground than the civic precinct. The civic precinct is separated from the residential sector by an unusual four-terrace complex. On the first and third levels of this complex are sunken courts similar in size to sunken patios in the palaces at Utatlan. Against the back wall of the second tier is a 50-meter-long bench which is within the size range for benches against the back walls of long structures in Greater Utatlan. The curved chamber, connected to each of the four levels within this multistoried edifice, is of particular interest. Its central location and its bench imply a gathering or council locus, so it may have been a central nucleus of some sort. This four-story complex faces the two plazas as well as commanding a panoramic view of the river valley and salt works. Its long benches suggest administrative activities, while its sunken patios, like those in the palaces at Utatlan, suggest the possibility of an elite residence.

The settlement patterns of both Chutinamit and Greater Utatlan include temples facing west, ball court oriented east-west, the plaster plaza floor, and the elite residence adjacent to the civic plaza. The single pyramidal temple and the triple temples are comparable in size to temples at Chisalin, Ismachi, and Resguardo. Finally, the multitiered administrative-elite-residential complex roughly compares in area to the combined area of the two palaces adjacent to the civic plaza at Utatlan.

Considerably more settlement pattern features, however, are not found in Greater Utatlan, among them the acropolis, the triple temple, the temple in the center of the court, the rectangular platform behind the temple(s), the ball court with irregular end zones, and the four-tiered administrative-elite residential complex. At Chutinamit, finally, the plazas are not rectilinear and enclosed. In sum, settlement patterning at Chutinamit is apparently independent of Central Quiche influence. The architectural facades are too poorly preserved to reveal a possible Central Quiche overlay, which has been suggested for Chutixtiox.

Ethnohistory

Several early land documents provide substantial clues as to which of the four immigrant Toltec-associated groups at Sacapulas dwelt at Chutinamit. The *Titulo Sacapulas* (1551) states that the ruling lines at Sacapulas were the Canil and Toltecat, who apparently controlled the valuable mineral springs (Carmack 1973:207, 358–59). Inasmuch as Chutinamit overlooks the principal salt springs, with the next closest site, Chutixtiox, four kilometers upriver, it seems likely that Chutinamit was the calpul Tuha and thus the locus of the Tuhal Haa. If this is the case, either the Toltecat or the Canil or both dwelled at Chutinamit, since they jointly claimed ownership of the springs. Perhaps the two civic plazas at Chutinamit correspond to two such social divisions.

Tuha fell under Central Quiche control during the Late-phase Late Postclassic (Xajil 1953:93; Xpantzay II 1957:141, 143; Uchabaja 1973:370–71).

Xolpacol

Xolpacol is a small site above the Sacapulas-Aguacatan road, about two kilometers west of Chutixtiox (Map 4). Both Chutixtiox and Pacot can be distinctly seen from Xolpacol.

Topography and Ecology

Xolpacol sits on top of a small, narrow, U-shaped mesa, rising just 50 meters above the road and 80 meters above the bottom-land to the west (see A. L. Smith 1955: fig. 74). It is surrounded by nearly vertical barrancas, with a stone terrace just below the top of the mesa. The entrance, in the northeast corner, is a more gradual incline, blocked by a moat. Smith (1955:25) suggests that a wooden bridge could easily have been withdrawn here in times of stress.

A bone-white fine-grained soil, incapable of cultivation, surrounds the plateau on all except its west side. In fact, *Xolpacol* translates as "among the white earth" (A. L. Smith 1955:25). At the foot of the site to the west, however, is rich bottomland (Map 4).

Settlement Description

Upon first seeing Xolpacol one is immediately struck by how small and compact the ruins are (Fig. 13). The crowding of the structures into the single plaza is understandable, since it is situated on the widest point on the exceedingly narrow mesa.

The rectilinear plaza is completely enclosed, with its structures aligned to the four cardinal points. The plaza sides are formed by twin temples on a common platform to the east, a sunken I-shaped ball court to the west, and intermediate-sized rectangular platforms on the north and south sides, with a low, short, rectangular structure in the northwest corner. A low, round structure is situated just off the southwest corner. A two-chambered tomb was reported by A. L. Smith near the top of the main temple. This is, to my knowledge, the only Late Postclassic temple to contain a burial. The temples here were covered with earth and vegetation, obscuring architectural details. The intermediate rectangular structure on the north plaza side has two major building phases. The small, round structure once supported a round superstructure, with four doorways and, apparently, a wooden roof (Smith 1955:26). The playing walls of the well-preserved ball court are nearly vertical. Some green and blue paint can still be seen on its plaster finish, and on the benches and their bases. Finally, the intermediate rectangular structure on the south plaza side spans the width of the mesa, seemingly blocking access from the south plateau prong.

Excavation by A. L. Smith revealed the plaster plaza floor to have four layers. These layers can be correlated with structures to determine relative age. The ball court apparently was part of the first complex, inasmuch as its four plaster layers correspond to the plaza floor. The two altars, in contrast, are later additions; the first two plaza floors lie beneath them, and the later two plaza layers turn up on the altar's sides.

Construction is primarily of schistose slabs, with a few dressed pumice blocks.

Artifacts

Smith's fairly large ceramic sample resembles those taken at nearby Chutixtiox and Chutinamit, with a large percentage of Late-phase ceramics (e.g., Fortress white-on-red, double-groove red-slipped rims) typical of the Central Quiche, and a smaller amount of Early-phase carved ware.

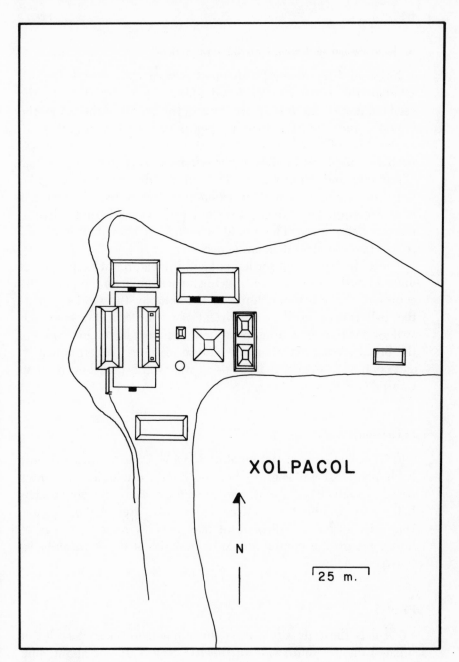

XOLPACOL

N

25 m.

FIG. 13   Xolpacol

Architecture and Settlement Pattern Interpretations

Xolpacol shares several settlement pattern features with Greater Utatlan: the rectilinear enclosed plaza; the orientations to the cardinal points; the round structure in the center of the court; the "moat"; and the structure perpendicular to the temples. In explanation of this last point, we should note that Xolpacol was perhaps one of the smallest Quiche *tinamit*, certainly smaller than Chutixtiox and Chutinamit. The intermediate-size rectangular structure, then, may have functioned in this reduced space as a long structure. The ball court is similar in style and size to Central Quiche ball courts. The round structure, a later addition, may reflect Late-phase Quiche influence.

The architecture and settlement pattern features at Xolpacol that differ from those of the Central Quiche are the main temple in the center of the court; the tomb in the temple; the twin temples; the ball court's north-south orientation; the broad rectangular structure with two parallel rooms; and the stairways on four sides of the broad rectangular structure. These features, like ethnohistory and ceramics, suggest that Xolpacol was well established prior to Central Quiche ascendancy.

Ethnohistory

If Chutixtiox was in fact inhabited by the Kumatz, then the only Early-phase Sacapulas group not yet identified with a civic center is the Uch'aba Haa. Pacot, the remaining site at Sacapulas, has Late-phase architecture and ceramics only. Hence the Uch'aba Haa may pertain to Xolpacol, or may possibly refer to an earlier center where the community who built Pacot dwelt prior to its construction.

Pacot

Pacot is the only site within the immediate Sacapulas cluster situated on the south side of the Rio Negro. It lies about nine kilometers west of Sacapulas, directly across the river from Early Postclassic Xolchun (see Proskouriakoff's reconstruction drawing in A. L. Smith 1955: fig. 17; or Wauchope 1970: Fig. 31). Ledyard Smith spent just a few hours there, and we did not visit it.

Topography and Ecology

Pacot covers the summit of a small terraced hill, rising 130 meters above the Rio Negro. This small site is accessible only by a narrow neck, which is fortified with a moat and a large masonry wall.

Unlike its neighboring sites, Pacot does not border on a broad segment of bottomland. In fact, the terrain here is rugged and dry.

Settlement Description

Pacot has a single plaza on what is either an elevated platform or a squared hilltop (Fig. 14). Except for the ball court, oriented 0°N–180°S, the structures lie on a single axis, 284°W–104°E. The plaza structures are curiously grouped in pairs—twin temples in the center court, aligned with two identical altars, each with stairways on all four sides, two identical short rectangular platforms behind the twin temples, and two intermediate-sized rectangular platforms, forming the north and west plaza sides. A low, round structure, similar in size to the one at Chutixtiox, is centered on the twin temples and altars in the plaza center. The plaza floor is of plaster. The ball court, two levels below the plaza, has steep playing walls in a *talud-tablero* profile. Masonry at the site consists of shaped schistose slabs and a few roughly faced blocks, covered with a thick single layer of plaster (A. L. Smith 1955:22).

Artifacts

Ceramics from Pacot thus far known are entirely Late-phase Late Postclassic styles typical of the Central Quiche (cf. Wauchope 1970:140–42).

Architecture and Settlement Pattern Interpretations

The restricted space within the defenses at Pacot precludes a residential area of any size. This absence is reflected in the lack of agricultural lands on the south side of the river.

Similarities to Greater Utatlan are few. Both have a round structure in the center of the court, a plaster plaza floor, and a

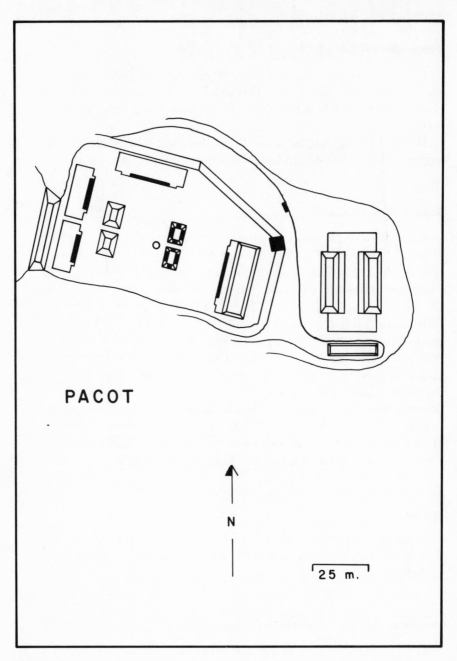

PACOT

N

25 m.

FIG. 14   Pacot

moat. In both, the longest rectangular structure is on a side of the plaza perpendicular to the temples. The dissimilarities to Greater Utatlan are much more noticeable. They include twin temples, low platform behind temple, north-south oriented ball court, and low rectangular platform associated with ball court. Moreover, except for the ball court, which is similar in size, structures at Pacot are significantly smaller than structures within Greater Utatlan. In sum, although Pacot seems to be Late phase, the lack of Central Quiche influence suggests that it was built prior to control by Utatlan (thought to have taken effect in the early 1400s or late 1300s). Alternatively, Pacot being a small, somewhat peripheral center, direct Central Quiche influence may simply have been directed to the larger nearby centers.

Situated on the opposite riverbank, within full view of Pacot, Xolchun may have been occupied by the same people who built Pacot. Xolchun also has Late-phase Late Postclassic ceramics as well as large amounts of Late Classic and Early Postclassic ceramics. Its settlement pattern, the "open-end *a* assemblage" type, will be discussed in the Early Postclassic section later in this chapter. Xolchun is still called Pueblo Viejo (Pollock n.d.) and has the same orientation (284°W–104°E) as Pacot. Finally, its semidefensive location, with room for residences, in the rich bottomland, complements Pacot, which has little space for a resident population. Rather than building an acropolislike civic center, then, the early migratory community that in later generations seems to have built Pacot may simply have taken over the already established center of Xolchun.

Comitancillo

Comitancillo lies about fifteen kilometers southeast of Pacot, back from the Rio Negro Basin (IGN, Sacapulas). Sacapulas is still the closest group of Late Postclassic sites, with Greater Utatlan, the next closest group, about twenty-five kilometers distant. Sapper (1895), Villacorta and Villacorta (1930), Pollock (n.d.), Shook (n.d.), and A. L. Smith (1955), as well as a crew from the Quiche Project in 1972, have visited the finely preserved ruins. I did not visit Comitancillo. Again, my analysis relies heavily on Smith (1955:21–22).

Topography and Ecology

The settlement is situated in a small valley on a tributary of the Rio Negro. It occupies the sides of the plateau, which are nearly vertical but rise only 10 or 20 meters. The small tract of *tierra templada* tableland here (3.5 sq. km) is surrounded by rugged terrain on three sides.

Settlement Description

In the center of the plateau is a small plaza, whose structures are aligned exactly to the four cardinal points (Fig. 15). The plaza comprises two identical small temples facing east, two identical broad rectangular platforms, a short, intermediate-sized rectangular structure forming the north plaza side and a sunken I-shaped ball court forming the south plaza side. Despite the site's excellent preservation, there are no altars in the plaza center. The twin temples apparently are not on a single platform as elsewhere in the highlands. They have double stairways on the front, single stairways on the sides, single-room superstructures, and three inset terraces against the core. One temple may have been completely painted red (A. L. Smith 1955:22). The broad, rectangular platforms on the east plaza side have stairways on all four sides. Masonry consists of schistose slabs covered with two thick plaster layers (A. L. Smith 1955; Pollock n.d.). The isolated low rectangular structures on the principal plateau level and the small foundations on lower terraces (cf. A. L. Smith 1955: fig. 67) respectively suggest larger elite residences and smaller "commoner" residences. The Quiche Project group reported large refuse deposits over the plateau sides.

Artifacts

The ceramic samples gathered by A. L. Smith (Wauchope 1970:142–49) and the Quiche Project group showed typically Late-phase Quiche types, such as Fortress white-on-red and monochrome red. Significantly, no Early-phase types were present.

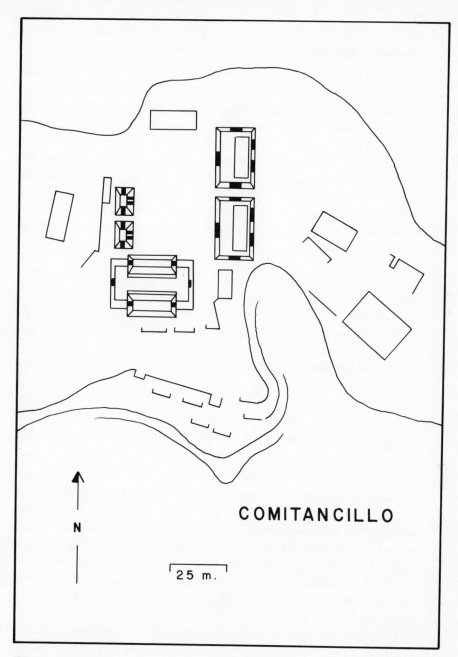

COMITANCILLO

N

25 m.

FIG. 15   Comitancillo

Architecture and Settlement Pattern Interpretations

Considering its size and occupational debris, Comitancillo seems to have been a moderate-sized Late-phase Quiche settlement.

Comitancillo shares the following architectural and settlement pattern features with Greater Utatlan: plateau settlement, temples with stairways on three sides facing east (like the temple of Tohil at Utatlan), enclosed rectilinear plaza, orientations to the cardinal points, longest rectangular structure forming the north plaza side, ball court oriented 90°E–270°W, ball court on south plaza side. The red-painted temple faces east, where the sun rises, an event traditionally associated with the color red. Moreover, like the east-facing temple of Tohil at Utatlan, it has stairways on its front and rear sides. Possibly it too was associated with Tohil.

Several of Comitancillo's architecture and settlement pattern features differ from those at Greater Utatlan. Comitancillo has low plateau slopes, twin temples, double stairways on temples, temple core with three terraces (Utatlan's temples have four terraces), low rectangular platform behind the temple, stairways on four sides of the broad rectangular structures, and it lacks altars in the plaza court (perhaps they were destroyed in post-Hispanic times). These traits, however, do occur in the Sacapulas area. It is evident, then, that Comitancillo had ties of some sort with the Central Quiche, but apparently stronger cultural affinity with the Sacapulas Quiche.

Lamak

The remaining ethnohistorically known migratory group from the lowlands to settle in Sacapulas, the Lamaquib, apparently dwelt at the ruins called Lamak. "Lamak-Zacapulas," which has not yet been surveyed, is situated "four leagues west of Cunen and 5 leagues north of Sacapulas" (Villacorta and Villacorta 1930:94). Carmack (personal communication) was told that such a site existed in the *aldea* of Salinas Magdalena, which fits the Villacortas' directions.

This general area is high above the Rio Negro Basin in the Cuchumatanes Mountains. Salinas Magdalena is a narrow inter-montane trough, with peaks rising 400 and 800 meters respectively on its north and south sides. In addition to the salt springs below Chutinamit, Salinas Magdalena is the second major saltworks in Sacapulas. This trough is also arid, like the Rio Negro Basin at

Sacapulas. Indeed, Carmack was told of an elaborate upland irrigation network on the trough floor.

Lamak would have been a strategic regional border settlement for the Sacapulas Quiche as well as for the separate provinces within the Quiche state during the Late-phase. On the north mountain slope, about three kilometers north of Salinas Magdalena, begin the Late Postclassic Ixil sites as well as the modern Ixil population.

The Ixil

The region occupied by Ixil speakers is bounded on the south by the Sierra de Cuchumatanes and on the north by the foothills just above the Peten rain forest (Maps 1, 5). This large territory constitutes the north half of the Department of Quiche. Twenty remarkably small and uniform Late Postclassic sites here have been reported in the literature (i.e., A. L. Smith 1955; Becquelin 1966, 1969; Smith and Kidder 1951; R. E. W. Adams 1966, 1972; Burkitt 1930; Butler 1959), of which I have visited none.

The nature of Quiche-Ixil relations cannot yet be fully reconstructed from ethnohistory. However, one ethnohistoric reference in the *Rabinal Achi* describes a Quiche prince as ruler of the Ixil, implying Central Quiche political dominance (Smith and Kidder 1951:7; Becquelin 1969:17; Colby and Van Den Berghe 1969:40; Carmack n.d.a:19). Hence an examination of architecture and settlement pattern may add to our scanty understanding of the Quiche-Ixil relationship.

The Ixil, who live at the edge of the highlands, have been considered remote and conservative through the years (Colby and Van Den Berghe 1969). Along with Mam and Aguacatec, Ixil is classified as a Mamean language. Of the highland language families, Mamean is furthest removed in form and, theoretically, in time from the Quichean languages (Campbell 1971; Swadesh 1960; Mayers 1966).

Environmental factors played an important role in Ixil settlement and indicate ecological ties between the Ixil and the northern lowlands. The landscape steadily descends from the Ixil region to the lowlands, as, of course, do the river systems. The prevailing winds come from the lowlands, whereas they come from

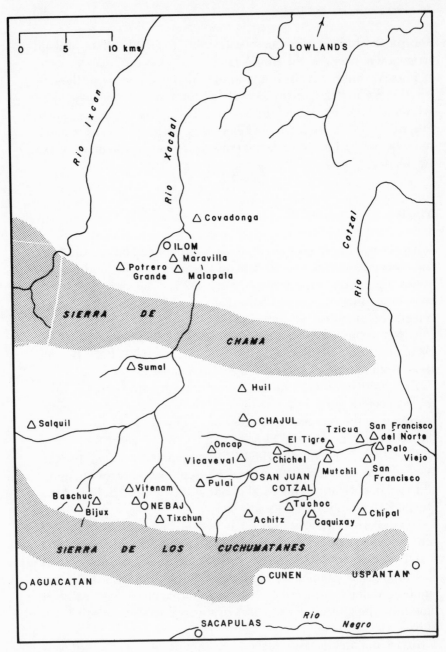

MAP 5 Ixil Area

the south coast in the Quichean areas. The daily rains, rugged
terrain, and karst soil, considered some of the poorest in Guatemala,
make cultivation conditions substandard to those in much of the
highlands (see R. E. W. Adams 1972:5; Colby and Van Den Berghe
1969:25–28; McBryde 1945: Map 5). Much of the highly dispersed
Ixil population today, as well as the Late Postclassic Ixil sites, is
found in a *tierra templada* intermontane trough sheltered between
the Cuchumatanes and the Chamas mountains.

Of the 20 Late Postclassic Ixil civic centers, 8 were occupied only
during the Late Postclassic Period, while 7 had earlier occupations
as well. At 5 remaining sites, which lack ceramics (i.e. Huil, El
Tigre, Mutchill, Potorero Grande, and Tzicuay), Late Postclassic
occupation is suspected on architectural and ethnohistoric grounds
(cf. Remesal 1932(5):245; Becquelin 1969:18–19). The 20 sites are
uniformly small. Each contains one plaza, and they average just 6
structures apiece. Indeed, the largest site, Sumal, contains only 13
civic structures.

The six sites occupied during earlier periods as well as during the
Late Postclassic Period (Tixchun, Achitz, Caquixay, Nebaj–Group
B, Baschuc, and Sumal) exhibit striking similarities. First, they
share a single plaza pattern, called by Smith and Kidder (1951:11)
the "open-end *a* ball court assemblage" and defined in part as "an
assemblage in which a ball court with open ends occupies an
important position at one side of a little plaza in whose center is a
small altar platform." In addition, a broad rectangular temple,
often with double stairways, occupies the plaza side opposite the
ball court and is centered on the altar and the ball court's playing
alley. However, the few well-preserved central altars face the ball
court rather than the temple. There is often a rectangular platform
perpendicular to the temple. The structures on the various sides of
this square plaza are aligned on a central axis (see Figs. 16, 17).
These central axes vary within 25° of the east-west cardinal points.
Indeed, Tixchun and Sumal are aligned exactly to the cardinal
points. The six centers are situated on low, nondefensive or, at
best, potentially defensive hills near valley floors. Each was
occupied during the Late Classic as well as the Late Postclassic
Period. Four sites were also inhabited during the interim Early
Postclassic Period, while only one dates from the Early Classic.
The persistence of the same civic pattern at least from Late Classic
times and perhaps from the Early Classic suggests a stable

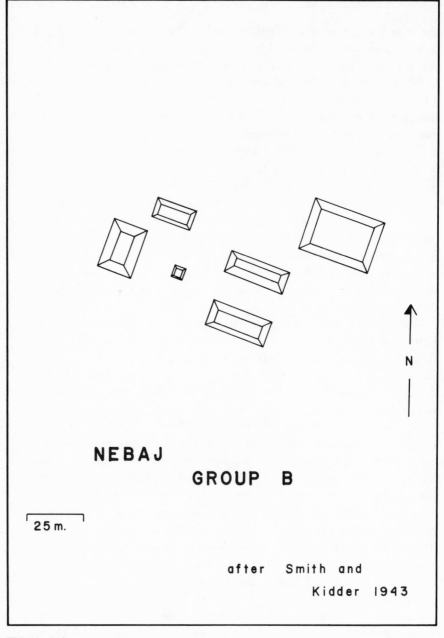

NEBAJ

GROUP B

25 m.

N

after Smith and
Kidder 1943

FIG. 16   Nebaj

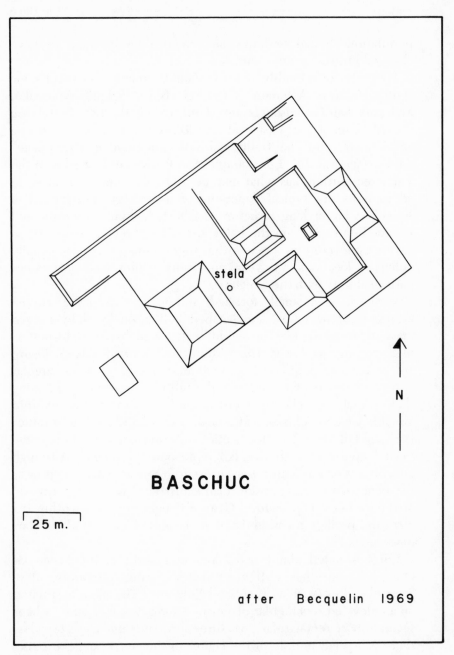

stela

N

BASCHUC

25 m.

after   Becquelin   1969

FIG. 17   Baschuc

population. Social organization can also be inferred to have changed little over nine centuries.

There is considerably more variability among the eight civic centers (Oncap, Vitenam, Vicaveval, Bijux, Salquil, Maravilla, Malapala, San Francisco) occupied only during the Late Postclassic Period. Except for Vicaveval and Bijux, there are also strong continuities with the traditional Ixil "open-end *a* assemblage" pattern (see Fig. 18). For example, San Francisco, located near the Uspantec border, has what may be a Quiche veneer. That is, in addition to the typical "open-end *a* assemblage" pattern, San Francisco has a long structure, a short flanking structure, and I-shaped end zones on the ball court. Excepting Vicaveval, these seven civic centers have either nondefensive or potentially defensive locations. Vicaveval and Bijux exhibit some settlement pattern affinity with the Quiche.

Vicaveval is a small, fortified, hilltop site. It has a unique arrangement of a horseshoe-shaped hollow enclosed by curved masonry terraces, like an amphitheater, and by an eight-meter-high masonry wall (Fig. 19). Within the centers of this enclosure are an I-shaped ball court, a small altar, and a short rectangular structure. Just over the edge of the hill is a large cave containing skeletal material. The ball court is similar in form to these within Greater Utatlan. This area still bears a Quiche place name, rather than an Ixil one. The Rio Xetinamit, translated as "below the town," contrasts with the Ixil equivalent, *Xetenam*. Although Quiche settlement features are present in this unusual site, it lacks the civic plaza configuration characteristic of *tinamit*. Vicaveval may have been a specialized Central Quiche site deep within Ixil territory, perhaps an administrative outpost of some kind (cf. Carmack n.d.a:19).

Bijux, situated about five kilometers north of the Sacapulas Quiche border, has settlement pattern features reminiscent of Sacapulas sites (such as Pacot and Xolpacol). The plaza is situated on an elevated rectangular platform. A long structure and perhaps several short rectangular structures form rectilinear plaza sides, there is a small temple in the center of the court, and the structures are aligned to the cardinal points (Fig. 20). Bijux has a nondefensive location and, interestingly, a stela. Given the proximity of earlier-period sites (see Becquelin 1966, 1969), however, the stela may well be a relic of earlier manufacture.

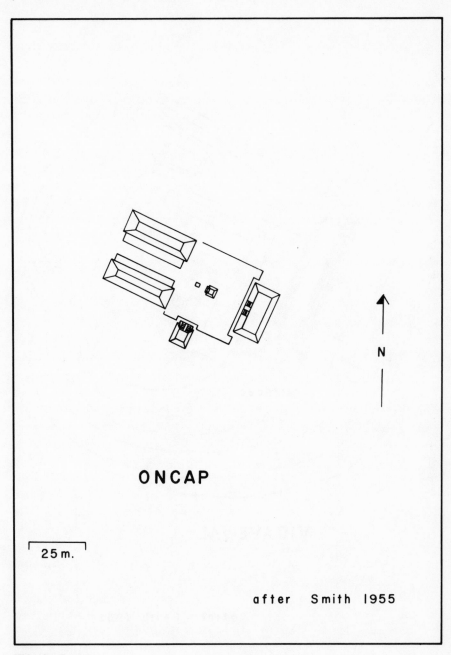

ONCAP

25 m.

N

after Smith 1955

FIG. 18 Oncap

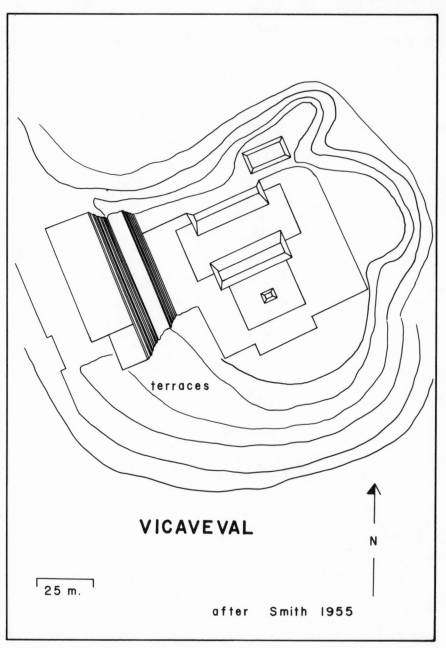

terraces

VICAVEVAL

N

25 m.

after   Smith   1955

FIG. 19   Vicaveval

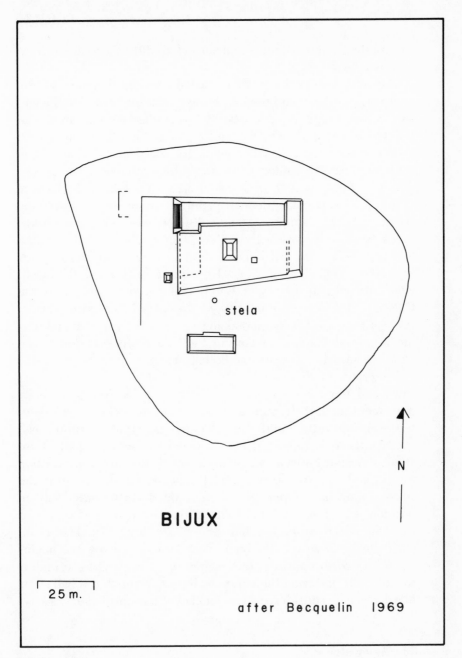

stela

BIJUX

N

25 m.

after Becquelin 1969

FIG. 20   Bijux

Alternatively, it may represent an old tradition among the conservative Ixil.

The small size of the single-plaza Ixil sites, the large number of actual civic centers, and their fairly close distribution and nondefensive locations suggest a dramatically less political centralization than that found among the Quiche. In fact, these essentially equal-sized civic centers suggest small segmentary social units. Rather than settlement pattern homogeneity arising from influence from a more powerful group or even from colonization, like that of the Central Quiche, perhaps Ixil settlement pattern homogeneity is simply the result of a fairly uniform, static culture entrenched since Classic times. Thus, the east-west oriented "open-end *a* assemblage" pattern may reflect an Ixil belief system seemingly unchanged over nine centuries prior to the Spanish conquest. Analyzing Ixil religion, which undoubtedly corresponds to building arrangements, from the Classic period to the present day, Colby (1976:74) describes it as "a survival from the Classic period and . . . relatively unchanged during a possible period of control by Tula ["Mexican"-influenced Quiche leaders] . . . during the Postclassic."

The east-west alignment of the ceremonial centers, with the ball court and temple on opposite ends, may reflect the sun's daily movement, with the temple and ball court directed respectively to the rising and setting of the sun. The movement of the rubber ball used in the ball game has been likened to the sun's path (Caso 1966). Located between the temple and ball court, representing the sky and underworld respectively, the altar in the center of the square plaza may represent the four-sided earth's intermediate position (cf. Thompson 1970:196, 276). The plaza entrance was through the open-ended ball court (see Fig. 17). Thompson (1970:296, 300) writes that birth, both human and vegetal, begins below the earth's surface, in the uppermost region of the underworld. Thus, entering the ceremonial plaza through the ball court may have been considered a special kind of transformation.

The Aguacatec

Approximately twenty kilometers northwest of Sacapulas and about ten kilometers directly west of the Ixil is a small enclave of Aguacatec speakers in the river basin at Aguacatan in the

Department of Huehuetenango. This small basin, an ecological extension of Sacapulas, contains the Rio Blanco, a primary headwater river of the Rio Negro. The Aguacatan Valley is a fairly level floodplain of rich volcanic alluvium (Recinos 1954:51; Simmons, Tarano, and Pinto 1959:129), about a kilometer wide, extending along five kilometers of the Rio Blanco (Map 6). The *tierra caliente–tierra templada* habitat of the valley floor contrasts sharply with the surrounding steep arid hills. The valley is bounded on the north by the 1,500-meter-high Cuchumatanes massif and on the south by the rugged interior hilly country. The bottomland, rising only a few meters above the river, is irrigated today (Recinos 1954:293), as it was in pre-Hispanic times. In fact, Aguacatan is one of three highland centers of garden cultivation (McBryde 1945:30, 33), in addition to its developed arboriculture. The name *Aguacatan* translates as "place of the avocados," so presumably its avocado cultivation, if not arboriculture in general, was important pre-Hispanically (Recinos 1954:293–94).

The Aguacatec are a small ethnic enclave whose closest linguistic affiliates are the Ixil, bordering to the east, and the Mam, bordering to the north and west. We know from ethnohistory, however, that the Central Quiche controlled this valley during much of the fifteenth century.

There are three pre-Hispanic civic centers within the valley —Tenam, Huitchun, and Chalchitan (Map 6). Tenam, a Late Postclassic center, is described below. Huitchun and Chalchitan will be briefly described in the Early Postclassic section of this chapter.

Tenam

Tenam lies four kilometers east of the cabecera Aguacatan, on the edge of the valley (Map 6). I use the name *Tenam*, used by our guides, rather than *Xolchun*, used by Recinos (1954:439) and by A. L. Smith (1955:15), to avoid confusion with the Early Postclassic Xolchun in Sacapulas. We spent perhaps an hour at the site on July 3, 1974, examining the ruins with Smith's report.

Topography and Ecology

The site occupies a roughly square plateau a tenth of a square kilometer in area. Its slopes drop sharply 100 meters to the Rio

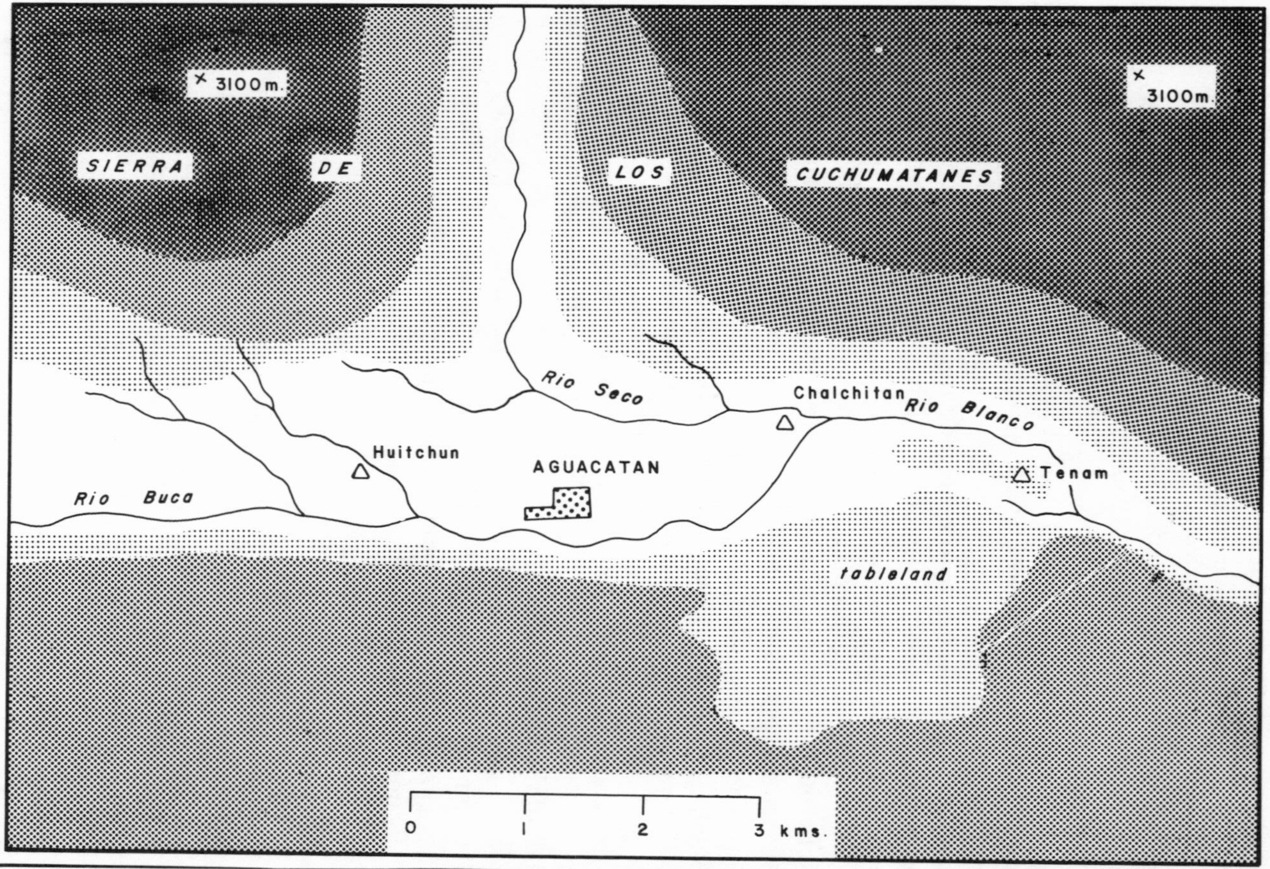

MAP 6   Aguacatan Area

Blanco on the north and east, and 60 meters to a ravine on the south. The entire west side is separated from a larger plateau by a long ditch, between 4 and 5 meters deep, and by several masonry terraces. The narrow entrance on the west side passes before a massive bulwarklike structure (Fig. 21).

The east edge of the Aguacatan Valley terminates in a narrow, 300-meter-deep gorge that runs the twenty or so kilometers from Tenam to Sacapulas. Outside Tenam's defenses to the west is a kilometer-long plateau; to the south are about seven square kilometers of rolling tableland (Map 6). The settlement is also within easy reach of the rich bottomlands of the Aguacatan Valley.

Settlement Description

Tenam has two large clusters of monumental architecture—a lower main group and an acropolis group. Buildings within both groups are aligned to the four cardinal points. Because of darkness we had time to investigate only the lower group, which has a main plaza and what may be two additional groups bordering the plaza on its east and west sides. Today these two groups consist of just a single temple each (Fig. 21). The entire site is under cultivation, however, and numerous structures have been leveled. The main plaza consists of a temple each on the east and west sides, altars in the center, a long structure on the north side, and a sunken I-shaped ball court on the south side. The top of the ball court is level with the plaster plaza floor. At a height of 5.75 meters, the temple oriented west is the largest structure at the site. It has two distinct tiers, joined by a single broad front stairway (Fig. 21). The temple facing east has a single substructure level. The well-preserved ball court, built of dressed blocks, has steep playing walls, and plaster painted in red, blue, green, yellow, and black (A. L. Smith 1955:16). The huge long structure, set into the embankment, is built of dressed blocks with two stairways spanning its two levels.

The remainder of monumental construction rises above the main plaza on two broad terraces and an acropolis (Fig. 21). "In several instances terraces have stairways with balustrades and central ramps" (A. L. Smith 1955:15). The terraces are built of dressed stone masonry and, like the buildings, are covered with two coats of plaster. There are schistose slabs just before the acropolis, but

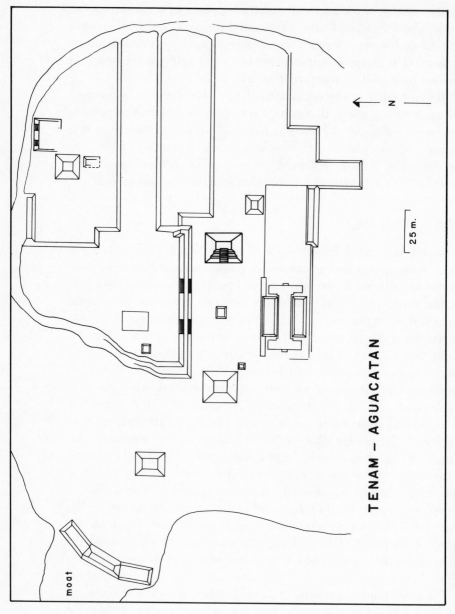

N

25 m.

TENAM – AGUACATAN

moat

FIG. 21 Tenam-Aguacatan

Smith does not comment on whether the acropolis structures employ schistose masonry. The acropolis plaza consists of a pyramidal temple in the center with a short rectangular structure flanking it to the south and an intermediate rectangular structure on the north plaza side. There is a low square platform immediately behind the temple.

Artifacts

Ceramics collected by Smith reveal typical Late-phase Quiche types. One mold-made sherd may in fact represent the Early-phase carved ware.

Architecture and Settlement Pattern Interpretations

The size of the plateau, strewn with occupational debris, and the amount of monumental architecture indicate that Tenam was a significant *tinamit*. Occupational debris suggests a large resident population, which could have dwelt on the terraces between the plazas and the large area outside the plazas.

The main plaza at Tenam reveals striking similarities with the civic plaza at Utatlan. They share the following features: civic plaza located in center of plateau; close orientations for the same structure types; one temple on both the east and west plaza sides; long structure, with two levels, spanning the north plaza side; I-shaped ball court in southwest plaza corner, oriented 90°E–270°W; plaster plaza floor; and construction of dressed blocks. The west-facing temple at Tenam, like that at Utatlan, is the largest at the site; it has two tiers and a single front stairway like the Temple of Awilix at Utatlan. The east-facing temple has a single substructure level like that at Utatlan's Temple of Tohil. Tenam is also about the same size as Utatlan, has a large moat over which the causeway passes, and lies adjacent to open tableland country. Tenam lacks a "military" plaza, like Resguardo, outside the *tinamit*. However, the large "bulwark" just inside the moat may be a temple and flanking structures, the remains of a fortified plaza not unlike part of the complex at Resguardo. A notable incongruity between Tenam and Utatlan is the lack of flanking structures in Tenam's main civic plaza. However, there is little available space for such flanking structures on the east plaza side, with its location on the narrow shelf. Perhaps the largely leveled groups immediately behind the east and west temples were once palace complexes. Each of these groups has a single temple, as do the palace complexes adjacent to the civic plaza at Utatlan.

Similarities between Utatlan and Tenam appear strong enough to suggest that Tenam was constructed by architects from the Central Quiche capital. Tenam may thus have been a Central Quiche elite colony. Since Utatlan was first built about 1400 (Carmack, n.d.a) the main plaza at Tenam was probably built sometime later. The principal route from Greater Utatlan to Aguacatan is by way of Sacapulas. Thus, the Central Quiche may have had to control Sacapulas, as they did by the early 1400s, before they could effectively exploit Aguacatan.

The acropolis bears no resemblance to Greater Utatlan but does share several features with the Sacapultec sites Chutinamit and Chutixtiox, namely, the temple in the acropolis center; the temple oriented to the four cardinal points; the terrace complex; probable schistose construction; and location 100 meters above a *tierra caliente* riverine habitat. The acropolis complex, as at Sacapulas, may correspond to the Early phase of the Late Postclassic, prior to Central Quiche ascendancy. The difference in construction material between the acropolis, which may employ schistose slabs, and the main plaza, which utilizes finely dressed blocks, may point to chronological as well as cultural differences.

Ethnohistory

The Aguacatec are clearly identified as the Balamiha ("jaguar house") in a 1739 land-dispute document (Carmack 1973:207). The Balamiha were one of the thirteen or so groups who migrated from the "east" into the highlands (*Popol Vuh* 1950:171 etc.). The acropolis, dating to the Early phase and probably before, may thus have been the Balamiha locus.

The Balamiha were conquered by the Central Quiche in the same campaign as the Sacapulas communities, apparently in the early decades of the fifteenth century (Totonicapan 1953:188; Xpantzay III 1957:145; Carmack n.d.a:19). The apparent copying of Utatlan in Tenam's main plaza suggests that the Central Quiche were probably located here in the mid fifteenth century. Prior to the Spanish conquest, however, the Central Quiche were expelled by the Balamiha (*Santa Clara* 1957:179; Carmack n.d. a:43).

However, if the acropolis plaza does prove to be a local Aguacatec governmental center predating occupation from Utatlan, then the orientations to the cardinal points, shared by the acropolis and the Utatlan-like plazas, may suggest some cultural syncretism between the Aguacatec and the Central Quiche.

Tenam lies within the post-Hispanic ward of Aguacatan known as Chalchitan (Burkitt 1930; Recinos 1954). There is some possibility that Tenam was known as Chalchitan prior to the conquest, as Utatlan was known by its Nahuatl name. *Chalchitan* is Nahuatl for "place of the jade," and precious metals, such as silver and gold, and gemstones, have traditional associations with this general area (Recinos 1954:76–75).

Early Postclassic Period

There are six Early Postclassic civic centers within the western Rio Negro Basin, spanning the municipalities of Sacapulas, San Andrés Sajcabaja to the east, and Aguacatan to the west (Map 1). Their settlement patterns are described below. However, each of these sites is described more fully and illustrated by A. L. Smith (1955).

Xolchun

Xolchun, as pointed out earlier, lies directly across the Rio Negro from Pacot in Sacapulas. The ruins are situated on a low basin shelf defensible on three sides. The single plaza at Xolchun is an "open-end *a* assemblage" pattern with several additional structures, all of which are aligned on a 104°E–284°W axis (see A. L. Smith 1955: Fig. 7). Four broad, rectangular structures, one low, broad temple with double front stairways, and an open-ended ball court enclose the plaza. The ball court has an enclosed I-shaped end zone on the end farthest from the plaza and its associated altar. Smith unearthed a tomb in the central altar, revealing a carved stela used as a capstone. Immediately behind the temple is an unusual oval temple, the highest structure at the site. It has seven inset battered terraces and a single offset stairway. Ceramics indicate Late Classic and Early Postclassic occupations, as well as a Late Postclassic occupation.

Pantzac

Pantzac is about fifteen kilometers due east of Sacapulas, on a low plateau, in the Sajcabaja cluster (Map 1). With at least 40 civic structures, Pantzac, along with the equal-sized Chalchitan in Aguacatan, is the largest Early Postclassic center in the western Rio Negro Basin. Four enclosed courts, including two distinct plazas, run in an east-west line (see A. L. Smith 1955: Fig. 93). The plaza on the east end of the configuration is a typical "open end *a* assemblage" pattern. The 14-meter-high temple is the highest at Pantzac. Interestingly, near the base of the temple, apparently from its balustrades, were recovered two tenoned "carved serpent heads with human faces between their open jaws." The remainder of the civic precinct consists of typically "Mexican" architecture, such as long structures, a temple with flanking structures, and an enclosed I-shaped ball court.

La Iglesia

La Iglesia was inhabited from Preclassic times into the Post-classic (Ichon, personal communication). It is situated in a non-defensive location near the basin floor in Sajcabaja. The site has two distinct plaza patterns. One comprises four altar mounds in a line on a square platform, like the Early Postclassic ridgetop sites in the Quiche Basin. In fact, nearby Xabaj in Sajcabaja (Map 1) has the altar mound pattern (A. L. Smith 1955: Fig. 92), and is thought to pertain to the Early-phase Late Postclassic Period. Xabaj is known locally as Sakiribal, or "place of the dawning," and may be related to the neighboring Chujuyub sites (Carmack, personal communication).

The second plaza at La Iglesia consists of three mounds on three separate sides of a square court. This pattern is also seen at Early Postclassic sites in the Quiche Basin.

La Lagunita

La Lagunita lies on the eroded basin floor at Sajcabaja. The settlement is made up of two distinct plazas (A. L. Smith 1955: Figs. 89, 90). The west group has a linear arrangement with a small court in the center, containing three uncarved stelae. The east group is enclosed, with a pattern and *palangana* ball court quite similar to the numerous Late Classic sites in and around the Valley of Guatemala, particularly at Kaminaljuyu (Shook and Proskouriakoff 1956:99, Fig. 1; Shook n.d.; A. L. Smith 1961:117; Borhegyi 1965:31) and at Early Postclassic Zacualpa (Wauchope 1948a, east end of group A and group B). Recent investigations in the Valley of Guatemala indicate a persistence of Late Classic cultural traditions into what would be chronologically classified as the Early Postclassic Period (Michels 1971; Sanders n.d.:2). This *"palangana"* group at La Lagunita is also similar to Late Classic Llano Grande (A. L. Smith 1955: Fig. 92), just two kilometers away.

Huitchun

Huitchun is situated in a nondefensive location on the Aguacatan Valley Floor (Map 6). The site has a single "open-end *a* assemblage" plaza, oriented to the cardinal points (Smith 1955: Fig. 52). The temple has two building phases, with double front stairways and four inset terraces on the last facade. Ceramics reveal Late Classic, Early Postclassic, and Late Postclassic occupations. However, its essentially nondefensive location and its architecture suggest that Huitchun may have been a small wardlike center serving a local population culturally related in some manner to the Ixil. They may have been dominated by the Balamiha during the Early phase, if not before, as well as by the Central Quiche during part of the Late phase.

Chalchitan

Chalchitan is an immense site situated at the juncture of the two main rivers in the Aguacatan Valley (Map 6). Among the forty or so civic structures extant are three plazas: a large "Mexican" main plaza and two "open-end *a* assemblage" groups (see Burkitt 1930: Plate XXX; A. L. Smith 1955: Fig. 56). Our efforts in 1973 were directed to the Mexican plaza. Briefly, the plaza is rectilinear and enclosed, with an immense pyramidal structure and a temple on the west and east sides respectively, each with a flanking rectangular structure; a long structure on the south side; and an altar in the center, with four large, round pillars. The pyramid has seven distinct inset terraces and contained a tomb with corbeled arches. Orientations for Chalchitan vary from the cardinal points (Burkitt 1930) to 7° east of north (A. L. Smith 1955). Neighboring Huitchun and Late Postclassic Tenam have orientations to the cardinal points, suggesting a continuity in successive centers at Aguacatan regarding sacred directions from the Late Classic to the Spanish conquest.

Conclusions

The varying ecology of the three adjoining regions covered in this chapter—the Rio Negro Basin habitat at Sacapulas and Aguacatan, and the mountainous Ixil habitat—allows inference about such distinctions in settlement patterning as the size and distribution of sites in each area, as well as variability of Central Quiche influence in the archaeological record. Each of these regions also experienced influences from "Mexicanized" cultures during the preceding Early Postclassic and probably Late Classic periods. Hence political dominance by the Central Quiche may simply be seen as one of the last waves of outside influence in these regions.

Except for Lamak and Comitancillo, the Sacapulas sites are clustered along a nine-kilometer stretch of the Rio Negro, and are quite low, rising only 40–100 meters above the surrounding territory. They are not thus situated for lack of defensible mountainous terrain, for the rugged Cuchumatanes rise 1,000 meters abruptly above these sites. Moreover, it is unusual for four sites occupied by four different ethnic groups to be placed together. However, the nucleation and low topographic settlements are quite natural in view of the location of life-sustaining resources here; cultivable land, water, and salt are all concentrated on the basin floor within this narrow nine-kilometer stretch, which is surrounded by arid, rugged terrain.

Except for Chutinamit, which has two large plazas and a residential zone half a kilometer long, the Sacapulas sites are uniformly small, containing a single plaza each. Adjacent to each of these sites is a small segment of bottomland, which could be useful for sustaining small separate populations. Comitancillo, south of the Rio Negro Basin in a small valley, also has a single plaza and a low topographic situation, and is also surrounded by rugged hills. Chutinamit, however, immediately overlooks the principal Sacapulas salt springs—a strategic location which may have enabled Chutinamit to be a regional capital, at least prior to Central Quiche hegemony.

The distinctiveness of each site within the Sacapulas architectural style and settlement pattern suggests some individual cultural and perhaps political autonomy for elite communities here. The distances between sites as well as the fortifications of each site bring to mind the spatial distribution of the Early-phase Quiche confederates at Chujuyub, who also appear to have had more political autonomy than they did under the Late-phase alliance of the conquest state. The terraced administrative complex at Chutinamit does, however, support the idea of some political centralization at Sacapulas, probably during the Early phase, if not before.

The success of the Central Quiche conquest system over the Sacapulas Quiche can perhaps be seen in the close positioning of the three Quiche confederates, the Nima Quiche, Tamub, and Ilocab, at Greater Utatlan, in comparison with the distribution of the elite groups at Sacapulas. Bear in mind that the Central Quiche moved against Sacapulas only a few decades after the establishment of the conquest system at Greater Utatlan. There is little indication of population growth among the Sacapulas Quiche between the Early and the Late phases, as there is for the Central Quiche. Thus while there is architectural change during these time periods, there does not appear to have been a major reorganization of elite communities at Sacapulas.

The conquest of Sacapulas was desirable for the Central Quiche, for Sacapulas produced such valuable commodities as salt, copper, small fish, and a wide variety of *tierra caliente* agricultural produce, all of which were lacking in the Quiche Basin. The Central Quiche were linked to Sacapulas by a natural corridor as well as speaking a dialect of the same language (see Campbell 1976 for an evaluation of present-day Sacapultec). As a crossroads, Sacapulas would have been strategic to control. At the north terminus of the natural corridor from Greater Utatlan, the Late-phase pattern at Chutixtiox bears the strongest resemblance of the Sacapulas sites to Utatlan.

The Late-phase ceramic sample at Chutixtiox is also strikingly similar in percentages to samples from Utatlan. If the Central Quiche
were established in Sacapulas, they may well have been situated at
Chutixtiox. Chutinamit, however, with its large size and administrative complex, may have been a regional capital of sorts.

In contrast to the nucleated communities at Sacapulas, the numerous small Ixil civic centers were dispersed over a relatively mountainous, infertile landscape. The large number of small similar-sized
civic centers suggests commensurate segmentary political units,
contrasting with the centralistic tendencies of the Quiche and other
"Mexicanized" Epi-Toltec groups. The lack of either natural or artificial fortifications, such as moats, walls, and terraces, at Ixil sites,
further indicates that the Ixil were culturally removed from the
militaristic milieu and the trend toward urbanism and militarism
characteristic of much of Postclassic Mesoamerica.

The Ixil centers, however, do resemble the Sacapulas centers of
Chutixtiox, Xolpacol, Pacot, and Comitancillo in their small size
and single plazas. Although the Sacapulas sites are also in low
topographic situations, they are considerably more fortified than
Ixil sites.

In contrast to the Sacapulas region to the south, the Ixil region
lacks strategic mineral and agricultural resources and is generally
rugged and inaccessible. Apparently there was little value for the
Central Quiche in the Ixil region, for there is little evidence of
occupation other than perhaps military outposts (e.g., Vicaveval).
In this regard, the highly dispersed Ixil would have been difficult
to control by the more "town"-oriented Central Quiche. Also the
Ixil, being of an autochthonous highland cultural tradition rather
than the Toltec-influenced tradition of the Sacapulas Quiche,
spoke a language unintelligible by the Central Quiche.

Apparently Aguacatan was a desirable region for the Central
Quiche, since they seem to have established a colony at Tenam.
The Aguacatan Valley could have supplied the upland Central
Quiche with tropical produce, as well as gems and precious metals,
as suggested by ethnohistory and local tradition. Tenam also marks
the northwestern border of the Central Quiche state (Carmack
n.d.a) during a time when the Central Quiche controlled the entire
Rio Negro Basin to the east. As the westernmost extension of the
Rio Negro Basin habitat, Tenam may have been of importance as a
"border" settlement in securing the basin.

The heterogeneity of the Sacapulas sites and the two distinct plaza patterns evident at Tenam-Aguacatan may correspond to evolutionary changes in settlement patterns during the Late Postclassic Period. When the settlement pattern traits of the five Sacapulas sites, which occur in at least two sites each, are charted in order of their geographic locations, running east to west, two basic trait clusters are evident (see Table 1). The cluster comprising Chutixtiox and Chutinamit belongs to what we will call the acropolis pattern, whereas the cluster comprising Pacot, Comitancillo, and Xolpacol belongs to what we will call the twin temple pattern. Predictably, there is a certain amount of overlap between these two patterns.

The two exclusively twin temple sites, Pacot and Comitancillo, have only Late-phase Late Postclassic ceramics. Since the Central Quiche took over Sacapulas some time after 1400, and the twin temple is not a Central Quiche trait, the twin temple sites here probably date from the beginning of the Late phase, sometime in the fourteenth century. And since the acropolis sites, Chutinamit, Chutixtiox, and, in some respects, Xolpacol, have Early-phase ceramics as well as Late-phase ceramics, the acropolis pattern probably dates from the Early phase. The overlap of the two patterns at Xolpacol and Chutixtiox seems to be the result of a Late-phase overlying an acropolis pattern at both sites.

In summary, the Sacapulas Quiche had architectural styles independent of the Central Quiche prior to their subjugation and inclusion within the Quiche state. The Late-phase twin-temple pattern (triple temples in the case of Chutinamit) is also characterized by rectangular platforms, often with stairways on four sides (Comitancillo, Chutixtiox), round structures (Pacot, Xolpacol, Chutixtiox), and pairs of identical rectangular platforms (Pacot, Comitancillo, Xolpacol, Chutixtiox). The round structure at Xolpacol provides a clear case of a late addition, with two earlier plaster plaza layers lying underneath it. The distinctive twin-temple pattern seemingly developed from the earlier acropolis pattern. This hypothesis is supported by the apparent derivation of Late-phase rectangular platforms with four stairways on four sides from the Early-phase acropolis temples with stairways on four sides.

The acropolis plaza at Tenam, as suggested earlier, seems to date in construction to the Early phase, if not the Early Postclassic Period. It shares with Chutinamit and Chutixtiox such features as a

TABLE 1. Settlement patterns at five Sacapulas sites.

Settlement Pattern Feature	Comitancillo	Pacot	Xolpacol	Chutixtiox	Chutinamit
Acropolis				x	x
Temple in center			x	x	x
Temple oriented to cardinal points, although primary orientation is west			x	x	x
Alignment of at least two altars centered on temple to the west				x	x
Plaza not enclosed on west side				x	x
Long structure on plaza side perpendicular to temple(s)	x	/	/	x	x
Ball court oriented east-west					x
Ball court oriented north-south		x	x	x	
Ball court forms south border of civic complex	x		x	x	x
Ball court playing walls with steep *talud* slightly overhanging *tablero* profile	x	x	x	x	
Massive defensive wall at entrance		x		x	x
Moat at entrance		x	x	x	x
Plaster plaza floor		x	x	x	x
Low short rectangular structure behind temple(s)		x		x	x
Stairways on four sides of some rectangular structures	x	x	x	x	
Pairs of identical rectangular platforms	x	x	x	x	
Broad rectangular structure with a single narrow superstructure on rear half of platform	x	x	x	x	
Small round structure		x	x	x	
Twin temples	x	x	x		
Twin temples face east		x	x		
Twin temples face west				x	
Rectilinear plaza sides	x	x	x	x	

x = trait present

/ = not certain if trait is present

temple oriented to the cardinal points, a temple in the acropolis center, and a plaza open on at least one side. The twin-temple complex apparently did not develop among the Balamiha of Tenam. Rather the Late phase there is a replica of Utatlan.

The acropolis pattern occurs elsewhere in the highlands—in the warm eastern Rio Negro Basin, the Rio Motagua Basin and the Lake Atitlan Basin. At this point, it is appropriate to compare Chutinamit, and to a lesser degree Chutixtiox and the acropolis plaza at Tenam, with two important acropolis sites, Chuitinamit-Atitlan and Chamac in Uspantan (Map 1), which otherwise lie outside the bounds of the present study. Chuitinamit-Atitlan was the Late Postclassic Tzutuhil capital, which apparently was never controlled by the Quiche. The Uspantec territory in the northern Rio Negro Drainage north of Sajcabaja, where Chamac is situated, was fully within the bounds of the Quiche conquest state. Since, as mentioned earlier, the Late-phase Uspantec center (i.e., Agua Colorado, IGN-Sajcabaja) has not yet been surveyed, the development of the Uspantec cannot yet be appraised for Central Quiche influences. We surveyed Chuitinamit-Atitlan in 1972 and Chamac in 1973.

The main plaza at Chuitinamit-Atitlan is the lower of the two plazas, as at Chutinamit-Sacapulas. Again like Chutinamit-Sacapulas, this plaza features an immense pyramidal temple in the center of the court, enclosed by various-sized square and rectangular platforms on the plaza sides (Fig. 22). At Chuitina-mit-Atitlan, the acropolis has, in addition, a second massive pyramidal structure and what may be a palace complex on top of an adjoining terrace system with broad stairways. This terrace complex lacks the benches and the general complexity of the four-tiered administrative complex at Chutinamit-Sacapulas. Furthermore, Chuitinamit-Atitlan lacks a ball court and the unusual triple temples. The two sites also have sightly differing orientations. Thus, Chuitinamit-Atitlan is aligned on the axis running about 25° east of north, whereas the temples at Chutinamit-Sacapulas are aligned to the cardinal points, and the ball court runs 12° west of north.

Chamac also consists of two civic plazas, which are connected by a broad stairway spanning the 80-meter difference in elevation between the two groups. Unlike Chutinamit-Sacapulas and Chuitinamit-Atitlan, however, the main plaza is on the acropolis.

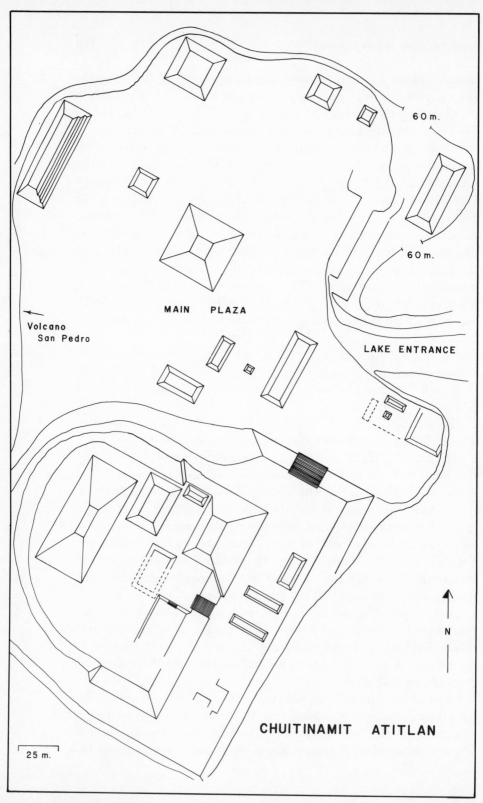

60 m.

60 m.

MAIN   PLAZA

Volcano
San Pedro

LAKE ENTRANCE

N

CHUITINAMIT   ATITLAN

25 m.

FIG. 22   Chuitinamit Atitlan

Nevertheless, the acropolis configuration consists of a temple in the center of the court, several various-sized rectangular platforms on the plaza sides, and a large elite residential complex adjacent to the plaza. The temple, oriented 5° west of north, is well preserved, showing one stairway on each of its four sides, four inset terraces on its core, and construction of large shaped-limestone blocks. An earlier building phase can be distinguished in the temple through large holes recently made by pot hunters. It is of the same style as the outer facade, with one stairway on each side, but it is constructed of smaller, more finely dressed limestone blocks covered with a thick plaster layer. The lower plaza at Chamac, situated on a narrow shelf, has a linear arrangement running 15° west of north. It comprises a high broad platform on the east end, a large east-west-running ball court in the center, and a small temple, about the same size as the interior temple on the acropolis, adjacent to the west ball court end zone facing north. The I-shaped ball court is significantly wider than the generally standard-sized Late-phase ball courts. Moreover, its playing walls slope at a more acute angle, reminiscent of the ball-court walls at Tula, compared with the nearly vertical *talud-tablero* Late-phase playing walls.

The distinctive carved ware occurs at Chutinamit-Sacapulas, Chuitinamit-Atitlan, and Chamac. Carved ware is characterized by red to orange slip, with a panel around the vessel containing heavy-line incised or carved decoration, often painted white (see Lothrop 1933:81–83; Wauchope 1970:230–33). These are geometric "straight line" designs in the Mixteca-Puebla style, such as, for example, the step fret, the interlocking fret, and square "eyes" (a square within a square). Outflaring rims, the predominant type, are a common Early Postclassic form. Chamac also has such Early Postclassic ceramic features as the "reptilian" censer covers (cf. Wauchope 1943a: Fig. 37) and several fragments of Tohil plumbate ware, as does Chutinamit-Sacapulas. This acropolis ceramic assemblage thus contains numerous Early Postclassic ceramic modes.

Carved-ware styles among the Tzutuhil persisted into the Late-phase Late Postclassic, apparently independent of Central Quiche ceramic influences. However, the carved ware at Sacapulas seems to have been replaced, or at least overshadowed, by Late-phase Central Quiche wares. Chamac seems to have been abandoned before or at the time of the control of the Uspantec by the Central Quiche, since Central Quiche influences are absent in the settlement record. Correlating with Early-phase ceramic modes, Chuitinamit-Atitlan and Chamac both have the obsidian leaf-shaped and tapering-base "lance" (dart) points, while lacking the later side-notched and basal-indented "arrow" points.

Chutinamit-Sacapulas, Chuitinamit-Atitlan, and Chamac, as well as the smaller acropolis sites of Chutixtiox and Tenam, occupy similar habitats. That is, each is situated in a warm basin containing either a large river or a lake. Moreover, they share similar low topographic locations, which rise, with the exception of Chamac, no more than 100 meters above the basin floors.

Synthesizing settlement pattern attributes from Chutinamit-Sacapulas, Chuitinamit-Atitlan and Chamac, the acropolis center can be defined by some of the following attributes:

two plazas, one of which is on an acropolis;
pyramidal temple in the center of the main plaza;
pyramidal temple lacking the abrupt *talud-tablero* balustrades of Late-phase central Quiche temples;
pyramidal temple with one stairway on each of its four sides;
pyramidal temple rising in four inset terraces;
main plaza sides consisting of intermediate-sized rectangular platforms;
an elite administrative-residential compount adjacent to main plaza; and
orientations basically north-south (Chamac is oriented 5° and 15° west of north, Chuitinamit-Atatlan is oriented 25° east of north, while the temples at Chutinamit-Sacapulas, Chutixtiox, Xolpacol, and Tenam are oriented to the cardinal points).

As suggested earlier, the west orientation of the Sacapulas temples appears to be a Late-phase adaptation, correlated in time with the ascendancy of the Central Quiche. The long structure, characteristic of "Mexican" Postclassic architecture, may prove not to be present in the main plaza. However, there may be a long structure within the administrative-residential complex north of the main plaza at Chutinamit-Sacapulas, and there is an unusual long building, rising in three or four levels, on the north plaza side at Chuitinamit-Atitlan. Finally, the ball courts, at Chutinamit-Sacapulas and at Chamac, are situated on the lowest level of the civic precinct, perhaps suggesting a relationship between the sunken ball court and the underworld (cf. *Popol Vuh* 1950:143–45, 150–53).

The main plazas at the three acropolis centers are quite similar to the main plaza at Chichen Itza in the Yucatecan Peninsula. The main plaza at Chichen Itza and the plazas at Chutinamit-Sacapulas, Chuitinamit-Atitlan, and Chamac all have a pyramidal temple in the plaza center, lacking abrupt *talud-tablero* balustrades, and with one stairway on each of its four sides. In all four an elaborate administrative-residential complex is adjacent to the main plaza (Group of the "Thousand Columns"), an I-shaped ball court is found on the plaza side opposite the administrative-residential complex, and that complex contains a colonnaded long building. Finally, all share construction of finely dressed limestone blocks (similar to the earliest-building-phase temple at Chamac) and slightly off-north orientation (17° east of north at Chichen Itza). The ball courts at Chamac and Chutinamit are oriented 15° and 12° respectively off the east-west cardinal points, whereas the ball court at Chichen Itza is aligned 17° off the north-south cardinal points.

At Chichen Itza, on the other hand, there is no acropolis, there are two temples in the main plaza, the pyramidal temple in the plaza center (the Castillo) has nine inset terraces rather than four, and the administrative-residential complex is adjacent to two small additional ball courts. Predominant ceramic types at Chichen Itza are the Gulf Coast fine paste and slate wares and the Tohil plumbate trade ware. To reiterate, Tohil plumbate sherds were recovered at both Chamac and Chutinamit-Sacapulas.

The pyramidal temple in the plaza center, with a single stairway on each of the four sides, is fairly rare in Mesoamerica (Kubler 1958:517), and appears to be Lowland Maya in inception. Indeed, to my knowledge, it only occurs in the Yucatan, in the neighboring northern Peten (at Uaxactun and Tikal), and at the acropolis sites in the Guatemalan Highlands. The pyramidal temple with four stairways at Chichen Itza, the Castillo, combines Toltec architectural features—feathered serpent and jaguar friezes, feathered serpent balustrades, and chacmool sculptures—with a basic Puuc temple structure, with nine inset terraces, lacking the pronounced *talud-tablero* balustrades characteristic of Highland Mexico. In contrast, the other temple in the main plaza at Chichen Itza has a "pure Toltec" form, with one stairway, pronounced *talud-tablero* balustrades, four inset terraces, and feathered serpent iconography. A Toltec entourage from Mexico took over Chichen Itza in the late 900s; their presence is symbolized by the deity Quetzalcoatl, the feathered serpent (Nicholson 1957; Thompson 1970).

The founders of the highland acropolis sites had names suggestive of the feathered serpent and the Toltecs. Thus, the occupants of Chutinamit-Sacapulas were called the Toltecat and Canil. *Toltecat* obviously refers to the Toltecs whereas *Canil* translates from the Quiche as "serpent." Neighboring Chutixtiox was inhabited by the *Kumatz*, or, again, "serpents." Finally the Tzutuhil inhabitants of Chutinamit-Atitlan were known as the Tz'ikina, or the "bird" people (*Popol Vuh* 1971:156). It is not yet known who founded Chamac. Significantly, the *Relación de Yucatan* mentions that the Guatemalan Highlands were linked to Chichen Itza (Roys 1966:157). Perhaps, then, the acropolis sites were established by peoples in some way under the tutelage of Chichen Itza.

Chichen Itza apparently was abandoned in the second decade of the thirteenth century at the latest, and probably earlier (Thompson 1970). Judging from ceramics, the acropolis sites seem to date from the Early Phase as well as the Early Postclassic, when Chichen held power in the lowlands. Quichean documents, however, indicate that the founders of these sites arrived with the Central Quiche. These early ethnohistoric documents have simply lumped together the movements of different groups which may actually have taken place at slight intervals, during the reign of Chichen Itza as well as immediately after its demise. In fact, the Tzutuhil acropolis builders were said to be the first peoples in Tulan (Chichen Itza) (Xajil 1953:49) and thus the first migratory group. There seems, then, to be some documentary evidence that the acropolis builders preceded the Central Quiche during what would be the Early Postclassic Period.

Similarities between Chichen Itza and the acropolis sites are of a general nature, such as plaza pattern and general orientation. For example, the acropolis sites are oriented north, but not the Toltec 17° east of north. Sculptured chacmools, feathered serpents, warriors, and the like, the hallmarks of the Toltec proper, are not found at the acropolis sites, as would be expected of emigres from Chichen Itza. It is clear, nonetheless, that the acropolis builders were in some manner influenced by Chichen Itza or a related people. Significantly, south of Chichen Itza in the Puuc Hills of eastern Campeche, sites built on acropolises are commonplace, but their resemblance to Chichen has not been discerned (Andrews 1943:34, 38). Moreover, Puuc Hills ceramics are characterized by red slip and incision, bringing to mind the red-slipped carved ware of the highland acropolis sites. There is thus a possibility that the homeland for the Toltecized acropolis builders was in this intermediate area between Chichen Itza to the north and the Laguna de Términos backwater area to the south. To reiterate, there is also the possibility that the acropolis builders preceded the Central Quiche into the highlands, during the Early Postclassic, since the acropolis sites occupy the favorable warm basins, which are more like the Gulf area than the mountainous infertile Chujuyub area first occupied by the Central Quiche. This idea is supported by the earlier ceramics at the acropolis sites, and their contrasting settlement patterns, which resemble a still viable Chichen Itza. As a third possibility, the builders of the acropolis sites may have moved into the highlands during the Late Classic Period, and come under the political domination of Chichen Itza later.

In contrast with the Toltec-associated architecture at Sacapulas and Aguacatan, the conservative Ixil style, which changed little from the Late Classic Period onward, seems to have been influenced in a general way by the neighboring Lowland Classic Maya. As pointed out earlier, the Ixil area not only blends into the lowland rainforest to the north but is environmentally tied to the lowlands, in hydrography, wind systems, and so forth. Both the Ixil and the Peten Maya relied on slash-and-burn horticulture on karst soils. The "open-end *a* assemblage" occurs only within the Ixil area and just outside its borders to the south. In the Guatemalan Highlands, open-ended ball courts generally occur only in the northernmost zone from the Ixil-Mam area to Verapaz (A. L. Smith 1961:104). Elsewhere in Mesoamerica, open-ended ball courts occur throughout the Lowland Maya area and long the Mexican Gulf coast, while not occurring in Highland Mexico. Only the Lowland Classic Maya, however, have ball courts with sloping walls, like the Ixil, in contrast to the vertical-walled Gulf Coast courts (such as that at El Tajin). Stelae known at some Ixil sites (e.g., Baschuc) may be a conservative trait showing lowland relationship. Stelae are also known in the conservative neighboring Mam area and in the Early Postclassic Rio Negro Basin (at, for example, Xolchun). In the Maya Lowlands, stelae persist at the Epi-Toltec sites of Topoxte (Bullard 1970:269) and Mayapan (Pollock et al. 1962). The Ixil area is also characterized by significant numbers of Peten artifacts in Classic Period contexts (A. L. Smith and Kidder 1951). The Ixil "open-end *a* assemblage" pattern was first established during this period of strong lowland influence.

The five distinct Early Postclassic settlement patterns evident in the western Rio Negro Basin indicate that a number of separate cultures converged here within a short time span. Indeed, the Rio Negro region may have experienced the cultural flux of successive migratory groups characteristic of much of Mesoamerica during this period. The distinctive patterns evident in the western Rio Negro Basin are the open-end *a* assemblage (Xolchun, Pantzac, Huitchun, Chalchitan); the rectilinear *palangana* group (Llano Grande); the linear altar mound (La Iglesia); three temples in a rectilinear court (La Iglesia); and the "Mexican rectilinear plaza" (Pantzac, Chalchitan). Interestingly, all these sites share essentially nondefensive riverine locations.

The open-end *a* assemblage plazas, identical to the Ixil plazas from the Late Classic to the Spanish conquest, lie within 15 kilometers of the current Ixil ethnic border. Huitchun and Xolchun have Late Classic and Early Postclassic occupations, while Chalchitan and Pantzac appear to be only Early Postclassic in date. These sites, then, may pertain to local peoples who were close cultural affiliates of the Ixil.

The rectilinear *palangana* pattern at Llano Grande, and seemingly La Lagunita, on the eastern fringe of this region, may be contempary with the open-end *a* assemblage sites, dating from the Late or Terminal Classic and the beginning of the Early Postclassic Period. Llano Grande dates ceramically to the Classic (A. L. Smith 1955). As pointed out earlier, this pattern is quite common in the eastern highlands during the Late Classic and the beginning of the Early Postclassic and seems related to the waning of Kaminaljuyu there.

The three temples in a rectilinear court and the linear altar mound pattern occur together at Panajxit and Caja San Pedro Jocopilas in the Quiche Basin, as well as at La Iglesia. The linear altar mound pattern occurs at a number of late Early Postclassic as well as sites that persisted into the Early phase of the Late

Postclassic, such as Cojonob, Semeja, and Xabaj-Sajcabaja. Thus this manifestation in the Rio Negro Basin may pertain to the later part of the Early Postclassic Period and may reflect influences from the rich upland basins. This movement may have been a highland development, rather than reflecting immediate influences from the lowlands, as exemplified by the Early Postclassic "Mexican" sites.

Both the equally large Mexican rectilinear plaza sites, Pantzac and Chalchitan, integrate the apparently earlier open-end *a* assemblage plazas into a larger configuration, surrounded by distinctly "Mexican" architecture (long structures, I-shaped ball courts, pillars, human face–serpent jaws sculpture). The Mexican components may reflect domination of an earlier group by foreigners. Xolchun also has a Mexican veneer over an open-end *a* assemblage plaza, with an enclosed end zone on the ball court, double stairways on the temple, and a large oval temple outside in the plaza in a linear alignment. In fact, to judge from the linear nature of the Mexican rectilinear plazas and the linear altar mound groups, linear organization seems to have been widely accepted in the highlands during the latter part of the Early Postclassic Period.

However, the mixture of Lowland Maya with other architectural features—such as corbeled arches at Chalchitan in a Mexicanized complex—suggests a hybrid culture. Indeed, tombs occur in Classic Lowland Maya temples (e.g., at Palenque), but not in temples within Mexico proper. A hybrid culture is also suggested by the seven inset terraces on the pyramid at Chalchitan and the oval temple at Xolchun, which contrast with four inset terraces typical of Highland Mexican temples and Ixil temples as well as the nine inset terraces characteristic of Lowland Classic Maya temples. Such hybrid Mexican-Mayan cultures existed along the Tabasco-Campeche Gulf Coast from the Late Classic on (Carmack 1968; Thompson 1970). Indeed, these commercially motivated militaristic groups expanded greatly during the Early Postclassic Period (Webb 1973a,b), and it seems natural for them to have moved into the highlands along the Usumacinta and Negro rivers (Carmack 1968:60). These Gulf Coast peoples thus simply preceded the Gulf Coast Quichean peoples by one to three centuries. There are, in fact, settlement pattern correspondences between the Early Postclassic Mexican rectilinear plaza sites and the Early-phase Late Postclassic acropolis sites (double stairways on temples, for example, and north-south oriented I-shaped ball courts). Moreover, the only known Late Postclassic example of a tomb in a temple, at Xolpacol, is reminiscent of the tomb in the pyramidal temple at Chalchitan.

As an alternative hypothesis to Early Postclassic movements into the highlands under the influence of Chichen Itza, the acropolis sites may simply represent the descendant communities of the Late Classic emigres from the Gulf Lowlands, who came under the control of Chichen Itza during the Early Postclassic Period and of the Central Quiche during the Late phase of the Late Postclassic Period. If this was the case, then the same community may have occupied the successive centers of Chalchitan and the acropolis component of Tenam at Aguacatan. This may account for the continuity of building orientations at the two sites as well as at Huitchun. At Sacapulas, similarly, Xolchun may have been a Late Classic and Early Postclassic center for the same community that constructed Pacot during the Late Postclassic Period; these two sites manifest identical orientations. At Aguacatan and Sacapulas, these communities may have thus changed locations from the basin floors to fortified positions only 100 meters above the floors with the shift from the Classic to the more bellicose Postclassic times.

4

WESTERN QUICHE AND MAM

After the Central Quiche subjugated the acropolis-dwelling groups of the *tierra caliente* basins to the north in the early fifteenth or late fourteenth century under the Quiche ruler Gucumatz, they turned their expansionistic campaigns against the Western Quiche and Mam, who occupied the highlands and Pacific lowlands west of the Quiche Basin. Gucumatz was slain in an attempt to conquer the Mam of Coha (Xpantzay II 1957). His son, Quicab, the new Quiche ruler, simply resumed the conquest of the western highlands and Pacific lowlands, which was to mark the maximum extent of the Quiche state by the end of the third quarter of the fifteenth century. This chapter will cover the immense territory in the highlands lying west of the Central Quiche that today comprises most of the departments of Huehuetenango, Totonicapan, Quezaltenango, and the eastern fringe of San Marcos. Nineteen sites are analyzed, as well as a number of communities known from ethnohistory whose archaeological remains have not yet been located. The few archaeological data available to date pertaining to the Quiche expansion onto the Pacific piedmont and coast will also be briefly discussed.

Mam speakers controlled much of the western highlands and piedmont. The Mam were an indigenous Highland Maya ethnic group whose material culture contrasted dramatically with that of the Epi-Toltec-derived Quichean (i.e., "Mexicanized") groups. The political interaction of the Mam and Quiche will be viewed within the framework of broad settlement features of habitat and geographic positioning, in addition to the traditional settlement patterning of the various civic centers.

The western highlands are divided into two broad physiographic zones that extend roughly east-west and parallel each other. The zones are separated by an older, eroded volcanic range called by McBryde (1945) the Old Cordillera and the Continental Divide Range and by West (1964a:74) the Old Antillean Range (see Map 8). The first physiographic zone to be considered, to the north, is the rugged hill country containing such municipalities as Santa María Chiquimula, Momostenango, Chiantla, Huehuetenango, Comitancillo, Sipacapa, and San Miguel Ixtahuacan. With the exception of the municipality Huehuetenango, there are no basins to speak of. The soils in this region are only moderately fertile (Simmons, Tarano, and Pinto 1959). Most of the landscape is well into the *tierra fria* ecological zone, although the Huehuetenango Basin, bordered on the north by the high Cuchumatanes, is clearly *tierra templada*. The rivers flow north, either to the Rio Negro to the northeast or the Rio Chiapas to the northwest, eventually draining into the Gulf of Mexico.

The southern physiographic zone is distinguished by a series of connected intermontane basins. These basins lie directly north of the geologically recent and still active volcanic axis, which is in turn the southernmost extension of the highlands. The northern border of these basins, as already pointed out, is the Old Cordillera. Lying in the shadows of volcanos, the basins are further distinguished by some of the richest highland soils (see West 1964a:74, 1964b:373; Stevens 1964:306). Consequently, the region supports some of the largest Guatemalan cities with Indian populations, such as Quezaltenango, Totonicapan, San Cristóbal Totonicapan, and Nahuala. Rivers on this side of the Old Cordillera meander through the basins and then tumble to the piedmont.

Northern Hilly Country

Pugertinamit, Pueblo Viejo Momostenango, Tzakabala, Ojertinamit

Within the immediate vicinity—a radius of no more than seven kilometers—of the cabecera Momostenango are four poorly preserved Late Postclassic sites (Map 7). Since there is little ar-

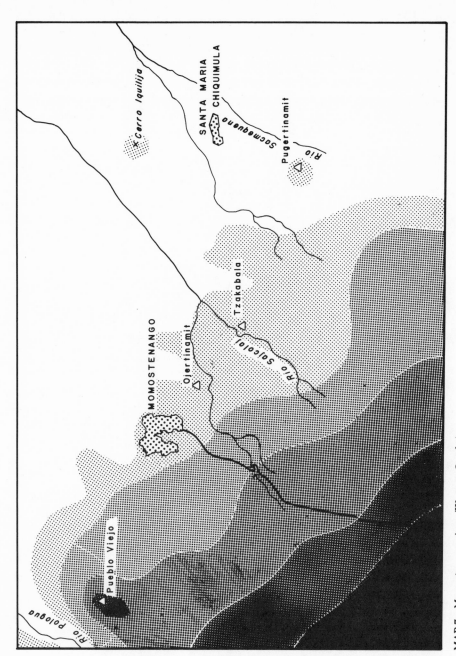

MAP 7   Momostenango Area (Western Quiche)

TABLE 2. Settlement description of four Late Postclassic sites near Momostenango

Site	Location	Topographic Classification	Settlement Description	Ceramics	Water Resources
Pugertinamit	3 km SW Chiquimula	Side ridge, steep sides on 3 sides, same elevation as surrounding landscape (2,100 m)	Signs of enclosed plaza; defensive structure near entrance of site; large settlement	Late phase	Rio Sacmequena at site's foot
Pueblo Viejo Momostenango	7 km W Momostenango	Mountaintop, high above countryside (2,400 m)	One mound observable; dressed stone; once a large settlement	Late phase	Rio Pologua 1 km
Tzakabala	3½ km SE Momostenango	Ridgetop, steep hillslopes on 3 sides, same elevation as surrounding lands (2,240 m)	Small enclosed plaza, long structure, and small temple on adjacent plaza sides; slab rock construction	Early phase, Late phase	Rio Sajcoclaj on 3 sides of site
Ojertinamit	1½ km SE Momostenango	Hilltop, fairly steep cliff sides, elevation similar to surrounding lands (2,280 m)	Only 2 mounds visible plus a "defensive structure" at site's entrance; small settlement	Late phase	Rio Chonima at site's foot

chitecture at these sites, they will be described briefly in Table 2. Pugertinamit, Pueblo Viejo Momostenango, and Ojertinamit were examined by the Quiche Project survey in 1970, (Carmack et al. 1972; Sloane and Stewart n.d.). Tzakabala was located by Carmack (personal communication) in June 1974. I did not visit them. This region today is inhabited by Quiche speakers.

Ecology

The Momostenango area is characterized by rugged topography with soil conditions among the poorest in the highlands. It is underlain by crystalline bedrock, as is most of the hilly altiplane region (McBryde 1945). Most of the area at 2,200–2,800 meters' elevation, is well within the limits of *tierra fria,* although northern parts of the municipality dip into *tierra templada.* The unfavorable situation is compounded today by severe soil erosion. Currently much maize has to be imported from the neighboring Quiche Basin to the east (McBryde 1945:75).

The agricultural situation in Santa Maria Chiquimula, just eight kilometers east of Momostenango, is much the same. The Chiquimultecos rely on the export of pottery, incense, and lime to supplement local subsistence agriculture, as the Momostecos depend on trade in woolen products. Chiquimula is one of just fifteen pottery-producing areas in the highlands (McBryde 1945:54–55) and one of just six lime-producing centers in the highlands south of the Cuchumatanes.

Ethnohistory

While archaeological evidence is scanty, ethnohistoric documentation of Late Postclassic communities is relatively abundant and has been systematically investigated (Carmack ,1967, 1971, 1973; Carmack et al. 1972).

The aboriginal elite center abandoned to form the cabecera of Santa Maria Chiquimula after Spanish takeover has long been known to have been Tzoloj che (*Popul Vuh* 1950:221). Inasmuch as Pugertinamit apparently was a moderate-sized Late-phase settlement and is located near Santa Maria Chiquimula, it probably was Tzoloj che (Carmack et al. 1972). Tzoloj che was forced into submission by the Central Quiche about the mid fifteenth century (*Popol Vuh* 1950:221; C'oyoi 1973:291; Nijaib I–II 1957).

The prominent preconquest *tinamit* Chwa Tz'ak has long been associated with Momostenango (*Popul Vuh* 1950:221 n.) and is still known by its aboriginal name (Carmack et al. 1972:10). The significance of Chwa Tz'ak is attested by its listing in the major Quiche documents (e.g., *Popol Vuh;* Nijaib II). A probable sixteenth-century native drawing, the Buenabaj Pictorial, from a *cantón* adjacent to Pueblo Viejo, shows Chwa Tz'ak and Utatlan connected by a river valley. This illustration is interpreted by Carmack (1973:62) as portraying strong political relations between the two settlements. Chwa Tz'ak was subsumed under the authority of Utatlan during the fifteenth-century western and southwestern Quiche expansion (e.g. *Popol Vuh* 1950:221).

The site name Tzakabala, used by the Quiche-speaking peasants in the vicinity, is probably a perpetuation of the preconquest settlement name Tzakibalja. The *Titulo C'oyoi* (1973:297) locates Tzakibalja, as well as the Momostenango area settlements of Tena and Lotz, and places their subjugation by the Central Quiche in the mid fifteenth century.

> . . . (they arrived) in front of the mountains at Iquiya and Iquilaja; (these places) were abandoned from before the arrow and shield; then they left there in front of Tena, Lotz, and Tzakibalja.

Iquilaja is a mountain (still called by that name today) just north of the cabecera Santa Maria Chiquimula, that is, about six kilometers northeast of Tzakabala and Ojertinamit (IGN, Momostenango; Carmack 1973:329).

Tzakabala appears to have been occupied from Early-phase times, and, judging from ethnohistory and from typically Late-phase ceramics generally associated with the Quiche, such as red-slipped double-groove rims, it was occupied during the Late phase as well. Tzakabala contains diagnostic Early-phase ceramic modes like wavy-line incised and punctate, and it shares with the Early-phase Central Quiche in the Chujuyub area such settlement pattern features as a ridgetop location, a rectangular plaza with a temple at its head, and a long structure forming a plaza side, as well as about the same size of corresponding structures. Tzakabala, then, seems to have had cultural affinity with the Central Quiche prior to actual control by the Late-phase Central Quiche.

Of the four Late Postclassic sites in the vicinity of Momostenango, only Ojertinamit cannot yet be firmly associated with an ethnohistoric community. However, there are numerous references in the Nijaib documents to a settlement called Lotz, and this place is continually associated with Tzakibalja—e.g., *Palotz-Utzaquibala, Chuchilotz Utzakibalha, ahupalotz-utzakibala,* and *Ahpalotz-Utzakibalha.* Inasmuch as Tzakabala (Tzakibalja) and Ojertinamit are neighbors, separated by a hill just two kilometers across and situated along the same Sajcolaj-Chonima river channel (Map 7), then Ojertinamit may be Lotz. There also remains the possibility that two Quiche sociopolitical divisions lived as neighbors, as within Greater Utatlan. In this connection, the Nijaib and Ilocab were the two principal ruling groups prior to the Spanish conquest, with the Nijaib apparently maintaining the upper hand after the Ilocab lost power following their unsuccessful revolt (see *Titulos Nijaib* 1957; Carmack n.d.a:23). The association of the smaller center Tzakabala, manifesting both Early- and Late-phase ceramics, on the same topographic unit as a larger center, Ojertinamit, with just Late-phase ceramics, brings to mind the relationship of the Ilocab sites of Pakaja and Chicoculjip in Ilotenango, just a short distance to the east (see Map 1).

Pueblo Viejo Malacatancito

Pueblo Viejo Malacatancito is located 8 kilometers directly north of San Bartolomé Aguas Calientes and 15 kilometers southeast of Malacatancito (Map 1). It can be most easily reached by a bumpy drive to *cantón* Chocanuleu of San Bartolo, then a 5-km walk to Pueblo Viejo. An *aldea* of the municipality of Santa Ana Malacatancito, it is situated along the departmental border between Quiche-speaking Totonicapan and Mam-speaking Huehuetenango. Recinos (1954:272, 274) mentions the ruins as the ancient population center for the municipality Malacatancito. The site was first examined during the 1970 Quiche Project survey (Sloane and Stewart n.d.), when limited excavations were conducted for three days. I spent five days at Pueblo Viejo in 1971.

Topography and Ecology

The ruins lie near the end of a long, narrow ridgetop that projects, at 1,900 meters elevation, into lower, though rugged, trough country. This ridge winds gradually down from eroded rolling tableland. Just before the entrance of the settlement, on the west, is a moderate-sized depression followed by two successive moats spanning the width of the ridgetop. Its entrance is also marked by a massive defensive structure. The other three sides of the site are rock-faced precipices, dropping 140 meters to the Rio El Aguacate on the north and west. Well-carved stairs are hewn from the limestone cliff descending to the river on the north. A masonry terrace about 3 meters high, around the edge of the ridgetop, functions as a retaining wall for the artificially leveled and filled narrow surface, particularly near the curved edge bordering the civic complex. There is also a series of broad masonry terraces on the more gently declining southern slope before its sudden drop-off.

Pueblo Viejo commands a magnificent view of the *tierra templada* Huehuetenango trough area that begins to its north. The surrounding landscape is corrugated by steep, eroded barrancas; soil conditions are poor. Cultivation is thus largely restricted to mesa tops, and consequently, much of the highly dispersed local population cannot eke out a living from agriculture alone. *Malacatan* translates from Nahuatl as "land of the spindle whorls" (Recinos 1954:272). Although the region is considered dry, and ideal for maguey, we did not see any spindle whorls at the ruins.

The municipality is one of three highland production centers for manos and metates, which are distributed primarily in the Huehuetenango-Quezaltenango area (McBryde 1945:61, 72).

The relatively large Rio El Aguacate, at the foot of the site, has carved a curious U-shaped tunnel through the limestone bedrock just north of the site. The river flows northeast and is one of the principal feeder streams that form the Rio Negro, fifteen or so kms away (Map 1).

Settlement Description

Architecture at Pueblo Viejo Malacatancito is almost entirely concentrated in one complex oriented 107°east–287° west (Fig. 23). Overall architectural preservation is quite good. Most structures

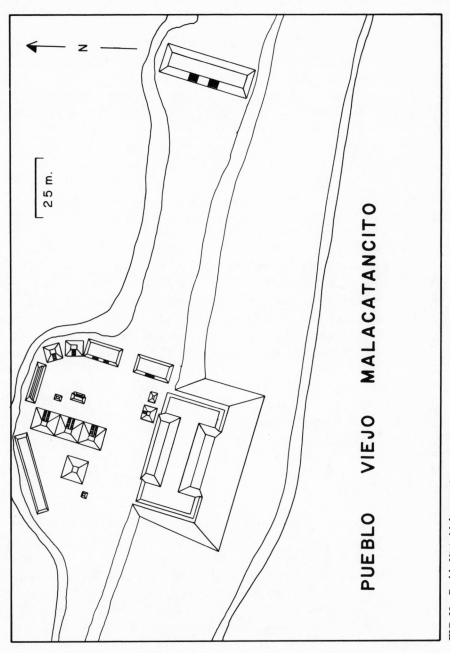

PUEBLO VIEJO MALACATANCITO

25 m.

N

FIG. 23   Pueblo Viejo Malacatancito

are obscured to some degree by weeds and grass, but most features can be distinguished. Often plaster still covers dressed stone and slab construction, with the latter predominating.

The civic complex contains six temples altogether, of which five are in the main plaza. The tallest structures, 5–6 meters high, are identical triple temples which divide the complex into two enclosed plazas. These three steep temples have base dimensions of just 10 meters each, are oriented 17° east south of east, and have double stairways with barely defined *talud-tablero* balustrades. A curiously shaped altar in the plaza center, aligned with the central triple temple, contained a rich burial excavated in 1970 (to be described in the artifact section below). Also within this plaza are twin temples set at slightly different angles, forming the northeast plaza corner. Each has a single stairway bordered by *talud-tablero* balustrades, and there is evidence of a single-room superstructure with pillars in its entrance. An intermediate-sized rectangular structure with two tiers forms a north plaza side. There are two broad rectangular platforms, with one and two front stairways respectively, forming the remainder of the east plaza side. There are also two poorly preserved structures on the south side. The sunken I-shaped ball court, forming a southern flank of the civic complex, has steep playing walls with a slight inset *talud,* covered with a thick plaster coating. On the eastern end wall of the northern range are several short lines painted red and blue. The south and east outside walls drop vertically 5 or 6 meters to a lower terraced level. In this respect, the ball court may have had defensive functions as well.

On the narrow ridgetop immediately west of the triple temples is a triangular plaza. Little space is available here, and the structures are tightly spaced. In the center is a poorly preserved temple whose outside masonry facade has been removed. Its dimensions are about the same as those of the triple temples. The causeway entering the civic group from the west passes just south of this central temple and its altar. A northwestern perimeter is formed by a long structure running along the escarpment top. A burial was excavated in 1971 between the existing facade and an earlier building phase near its front center, lying under the *talud-tablero* balustraded stairway of the last facade.

About 100 meters east of the civic complex is a monumental platform, over 4 meters high, spanning the narrow width of the ridgetop. Two building phases are visible on different portions of its front. The last phase has two broad stairways spanning almost the entire front; the earlier phase is seen in two smaller stairways about 2 meters wide. I spent three days excavating and test pitting this structure. Excavation of its northwest corner top revealed an interesting trough-shaped plaster gutter and the base of a square pillar. A test pit in the center of the structure showed three floor levels almost a meter from the surface, suggesting a room. Scorched soil with numerous charcoal bits after the first and last floors attest to a conflagration of some sort. The length of this platform, stretching the entire width of the ridge and allowing a passage less than a meter wide, suggests that it may have had defensive functions.

South of the ridgetop and east of the civic complex are three broad levels of masonry terraces. Ceramics are distributed in this area as well as within the 150 meters between the civic complex and the entrance to the site. Pueblo Viejo thus appears to have been a sizable settlement, about one-third of a kilometer in length and 100 meters wide at its widest point, in the zone between the entrance and the civic precinct.

Artifacts

Ceramics recovered during two trips to Pueblo Viejo Malacatancito are concisely summarized by Sloane and Stewart (n.d.:25–26), who list

> jaguar, serpent, and bird effigy head supports, effigy ladle handles, Fortress white-on-red, red ware, and jaguar head adornos. . . . Whole pieces uncovered from two burials included a Fortress white-on-red bowl, a narrow necked, globular bodied Fortress white-on-red jar, and a white-on-brown effigy support bowl.

The "brown" ware bowl with large white painted squares, the last item mentioned above, is unlike any style thus far seen at Quiche centers, but resembles ceramics from Zaculeu, which was occupied by the Mam.

A wide variety of artifacts was recovered from a tomb burial within the altar centered on the middle triple temple.

The goods contained in the tomb included two copper rings; 23 copper discs; two copper tweezers similar to those from Zaculeu . . . ; a large number of jade and green-stone beads; three flanked obsidian pieces, either knife blades or projectile points; a pair of ground green obsidian ear spools probably from the Valley of Mexico; two tripod metates, one with a serpent-head support, and two manos; . . . and small pieces of turquoise, probably part of a mosaic plaque. (Sloane and Stewart n.d.:27)

Manos and metates are fairly rare in Late Postclassic burials. The community of Malacatancito, however, today as, apparently, in the past, has been associated with manos and metates. Half a dozen projectile points collected on the surface are leaf shaped, and made of a basaltic substance. They differ in both form and material from the obsidian side-notched "arrow" projectile points characteristic of Late-phase Quiche sites.

Architecture and Settlement Pattern Interpretations

While the total area of the settlement at Pueblo Viejo is fairly large, the civic precinct is highly compact, with very small structures. The civic precinct is located directly in the center of the settlement, which is its highest point.

Good preservation at Pueblo Viejo Malacatancito allows a number of settlement pattern comparisons with the two Quiche groups thus far encountered, the Central Quiche and the Sacapulas Quiche. Pueblo Viejo shares with the Central Quiche its ridgetop settlement (like Chujuyub); its basic east-west orientation (like Greater Utatlan); its rectilinear (for the most part) main plaza; and its "bulwark" and moats. The east-facing temples at Pueblo Viejo have steep dimensions, and *talud-tablero* form, like the east-facing Temple of Tojil at Utatlan, and the ball court forms the southern border of the civic plaza (as at Utatlan, Chisalin). Differences with the Central Quiche, however—the lack of single temples on opposite plaza sides; the lack of a long structure in the main plaza; and, most notably, the size discrepancy of structures—seem to overshadow the similarities. Moreover, triple temples like those at Pueblo Viejo are unusual in the highlands, occurring only at Chutinamit in Sacapulas, and at Xetenam. Other features that Pueblo Viejo Malacatancito shares with Sacapulas are double stairways on temples; twin temples (lacking a single platform, e.g. Comitancillo); single temple in center of court (acropolis sites); I-shaped sunken ball court, on lower terrace; intermediate rectangular structure on north plaza side; broad rectangular platforms opposite temples (Pacot, Comitancillo); large "defensive structure" and moat at site's entrance; 107°–287° axis (3° difference from Pacot and Xolchun).

Settlement pattern features relating to both the Early-phase acropolis pattern and the fourteenth- and fifteenth-century twin temple pattern at Sacapulas suggest that Pueblo Viejo may have spanned at least parts of both the Early and Late phases of the Late Postclassic Period. Indeed, its 17° east of south orientation may be a part of an earlier "Toltec"-influenced acropolis pattern. Moreover, its narrow ridgetop location brings to mind the Early-phase Chujuyub sites, as well as the conservative Mam sites to the west, to be discussed shortly. Dressed block masonry often overlays schistose slab masonry, also suggesting the two phases as seen at Sacapulas and Aguacatan. Architectural similarity with the Rio Negro Basin Quichean cultures should not be entirely surprising, since Pueblo Viejo is situated on one of the primary headwater rivers of the Rio Negro (Map 1).

There are also a number of features at Pueblo Viejo Malacatancito independent of the Quiche, both at Sacapulas and in the Quiche Basin. First, to my knowledge the presence of five temples in a single plaza is unique in the highlands, although at least this number may occur in one plaza at Tenochtitlan, in Mexico (Marquina 1964:185). Moreover, structures at Pueblo Viejo are considerably smaller than those at Quiche sites, while similar in size to those from Mam sites farther west. Ceramics exhibit both Mam and Quiche influence. Burial goods demonstrate widespread trade connections. Indeed, inhabitants of Pueblo Viejo Malacatancito may have controlled mano and metate trade, as do the modern residents of Santa Ana Malacatan.

The mixture of features here suggests mixed cultural influences. Since Pueblo Viejo is within the municipal boundaries of Santa Ana Malacatan, a Mam community, its pre-Hispanic residents probably were Mam as well. The site exhibits Early- and some Late-phase Rio Negro Basin traits, while maintaining a highly distinctive configuration of five temples. Apparently Sacapulas was an early center of cultural influence in the Rio Negro headwater region of the highlands during the Early phase and probably during the Early Postclassic Period as well. The Mam at Pueblo Viejo Malacatancito may thus have incorporated elements of Quiche culture from a Sacapulas power center, or, conceivably, may have had Sacapulas Quiche overlords. In fact, the unusual occurrence of at least five temples in one plaza implies that the local pantheon comprised many deities, perhaps a feature of frontier populations (Sloane 1974), as a population intermediate between distinct cultural systems might maintain temples to principal deities of both cultural systems. More specifically, the presence of settlements like Pueblo Viejo may be a result of a conquered population's adding the conqueror's deities to its pantheon.

Ethnohistory

The central Quiche subjugated the eastern Mam in the Malacatancito area in the same campaign as the Sacapulas Quiche, suggesting the possibility of some association between the vanquished groups (e.g., Xpantzay III).

In the account of the Spanish conquest of the eastern Mam, led by Gonzalo de Alvarado in 1525, a settlement named Malacatan is mentioned (see Fuentes y Guzman 1932–33). The account describes the routing of a second large Mam army that arrived from Malacatan on a battlefield before another Mam settlement, Mazatenango, supposedly three kilometers from Zaculeu (Woodbury and Trik 1953:14). After defeating the Malacatan warriors, Gonzalo de Alvarado marched unopposed into their settlement, which must have been a substantial march south of Mazatenango. Fuentes y Guzman has passed on an account describing the entrance of Malacatan as having a ditch and wall of earth and timber. This fits Pueblo Viejo's relatively open entrance, which still has "moats." However, before Pueblo Viejo Malacatancito is identified with the settlement Malacatan conquered by Alvarado, the *caserío* Xetenam, about fifteen kilometers east of the cabecera Malacatancito, should first be investigated for Late Postclassic ruins.

Pueblo Viejo Sipacapa

The municipality of Sipacapa is about twenty kilometers northwest of Malacatancito in the department of San Marcos. The east-

ernmost spur of San Marcos, borders on the departments of Huehuetenango and Quezaltenango and lies barely ten kilometers from
the western departmental boundary of Totonicapan. The site is in
the *aldea* Pueblo Viejo, some four to eight kilometers southwest of
the cabecera Sipacapa. My description is based on Shook's (n.d.)
visit of October 26, 1946.

This small community is inhabited by Quiche speakers although
it is almost entirely surrounded by Mam speakers. Furthermore,
the Quiche spoken at Sipacapa differs to such a degree from other
Quiche dialects that Campbell (1971:379) has proposed the possibility of a distinct language, Sipacapeño. Sipacapeño displays archaic linguistic forms, as well as a substantial borrowing from Mam
(Campbell 1971:377–80), although it is most closely related to the
Sacapulas Quiche dialect. David Fox (1973) contends that Quiche
speakers first inhabited Sipacapa during the colonial period, and
that the original language there most probably was Mam.

Topography and Ecology

Sipacapa is situated on a high ridgetop surrounded by cliffs and
terraces, that projects as a spur from the Sierra Madre. Accessible
from its northeast side, Pueblo Viejo overlooks the Rio Cuilco,
which eventually drains west to Chiapas.

At 2,800 meters elevation, Pueblo Viejo as well as the entire
region is definitely within *tierra fria*. Shook comments that the
surrounding hills are badly eroded and agricultural productivity is
low. Simmons, Tarano, and Pinto (1959:210) concur that soils are of
the relatively infertile central altiplano type.

Settlement Description

Civic architecture, quite well preserved, consists of five structures in a linear alignment oriented 77°East–257°West. Two
structures seem to be temples, rising four and five meters
respectively (Fig. 24). Attached to the highest temple, which has
three inset terraces, is a short rectangular flanking structure.
Although the site is well preserved, no altars were observed
between the temples. The two temples and flanking structure
are placed on a square elevated platform. The remaining two
constructions are fairly low rectangular structures. Masonry is

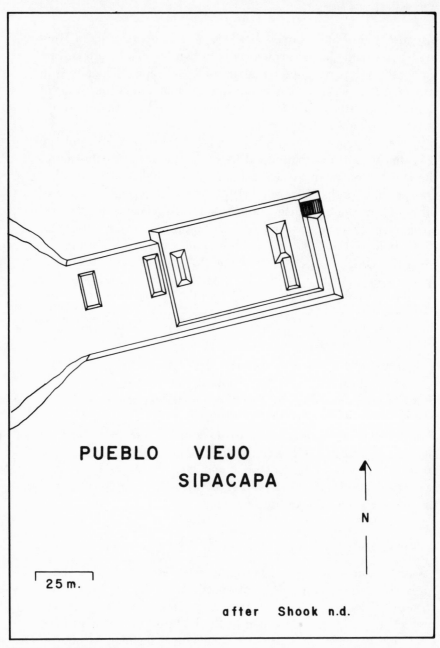

PUEBLO VIEJO
SIPACAPA

N

25 m.

after Shook n.d.

FIG. 24   Pueblo Viejo Sipacapa

generally of shaped slabs, although some dressed blocks are apparent in Shook's illustration of the main temple's outer facade. Apparently plaster was not used. (Shook's map lacks a scale or base measurements, although height dimensions are provided.)

Artifacts

There were few surface sherds and no obsidian. Shook did locate a pottery dump on the east slope of the side, but unfortunately he does not describe the ceramics.

Architecture and Settlement Pattern Interpretations

Pueblo Viejo Sipacapa appears to have been a small civic nucleus for a scattered population in the rugged uplands of the Sierra Madre. The region may be virtually incapable of supporting anything but a small, dispersed population as it does today by means of sectorial fallowing horticulture.

Although ceramic dating is lacking, Pueblo Viejo Sipacapa is apparently Late Postclassic, to judge from its excellent preservation and characteristic Late Postclassic topographic situation—a defensive ridgetop site with cliff sides and terraces.

Pueblo Viejo Huitan

There is a ridgetop site, known locally as Pueblo Viejo, just above the small *aldea* Rio Blanco and about six kilometers west of Huitan in the Department of San Marcos (IGN, Cuilco Map 1). In order to avoid confusion with several other highland sites also known as Rio Blanco, I decided to call this one Huitan. A small group from the Quiche Project briefly visited Pueblo Viejo in July 1971 (Marqusee, personal communication). The site comprised several badly mutilated mounds, lacking shaped stones. The mounds are strung along a narrow ridgetop. The steep ridge sides rise 60–80 meters above the surrounding countryside. Nearby, the Rio Blanco feeds into the west-draining Rio Cuilco. The rugged *tierra fria* habitat is characterized by poor soils and a widely scattered population. Pueblo Viejo Huitan lies just a few kilometers inside the department boundary, which also marks the Mam-Quiche linguistic division. In all likelihood, then, Pueblo Viejo was a Mam center.

Tuitenam

Tuitenam, also known as Xoltenam, is situated high above the Mam-speaking San Miguel Ixtahuacan in the department of San Marcos. San Miguel is about fifteen kilometers northwest of Sipacapa and also shares a border with the department of Huehuetenango. Shook (n.d.) surveyed the site in 1946.

Topography and Ecology

Tuitenam occupies a high terraced ridgetop mountain spur projecting from the Sierra Madre. At 2,500 meters elevation, the San Miguel area is also well within the limits of *tierra fria*. Soil in the region is the rather poor quality central altiplano kind (Simmons, Tarano, and Pinto 1959:209).

Settlement Description

Tuitenam closely resembles Pueblo Viejo Sipacapa. Briefly, it consists of five structures in linear pattern oriented 60°NE– 240°SW. Two temples, one at each end of the alignment, face each other. The three structures between these two temples are either low rectangular platforms or altars. "The principal pyramidal temple occupies the highest point of the ridge which has been terraced" (Shook n.d.). This temple and an associated altar occupy a square elevated platform. Shook does not mention construction material.

Architecture and Settlement Pattern Interpretations

As ready pointed out, Tuitenam shares a common settlement pattern with Pueblo Viejo Sipacapa. In fact, both sites are on narrow roughly east-west ridgetop spurs, with steep, terraced slopes, projecting out from the Sierra Madre. Moreover, the principal temple within each configuration rests on an elevated square platform, the highest point within each site. The two temples at Pueblo Viejo Sipacapa and Tuitenam, in addition, face each other; the temples at Sipacapa are next to each other, however, whereas those at Tuitenam occupy opposite ends of the plaza. The poorly preserved ruins at Pueblo Viejo Huitan also appear to have a linear ridgetop. In summary, Tuitenam, Pueblo Viejo Sipacapa, and perhaps Pueblo Viejo Huitan are similar enough to be considered manifestations of the same Mam culture. If this was the case, then Quiche speakers in Sipacapa may postdate the initial construction of Pueblo Viejo Sipacapa.

Ethnohistory

The preconquest Mam community of San Miguel Ixtahuacan has been identified by Brasseur de Bourbourg as Bamac (Carmack n.d.a:22), and as Zakehoj, based on oral tradition (Shook n.d.:291). There is some indication that the Mam here, during the Late phase, paid tribute to the Quiche (Fuentes y Guzmán 1932–33: 34–59 in Carmack n.d.a:34). Also, according to Fuentes y Guzmán, the Mam of San Miguel Ixtahuacan aided their besieged compatriots at Zaculeu during the Spanish conquest.

Zaculeu

The ruins of Zaculeu, four kilometers west of the city of Huehuetenango, have been a major tourist attraction since restoration by Woodbury and Trik (1953). Dutton and Hobbs (1943), Recinos (1954), and A. L. Smith (1955) commented on the ruins prior to their restoration. The site was occupied from the Early Classic Period until 1525, when Gonzalo de Alvarado, the brother of the leader of the conquistadores in Guatemala, Pedro de Alvarado, conquered it. There are architectural remains of earlier periods, but my discussion will be limited to those structures which show Late Postclassic construction. Therefore in the site map of Zaculeu (Fig. 25) structures used during the Late Postclassic Period are fully illustrated, whereas structures from earlier times not modified for use during the last aboriginal period are simply shown in outline.

Topography and Ecology

The ruins cover a flat plateau in the broad Huehuetenango Basin. Three of its sides are formed by 40-meter-high cliff-faced barrancas. The Spanish conquistadores reported that the open side was spanned by a massive wall.

At about 1,900 meters elevation, the basin floor is firmly *tierra templada*. Soils in this level area are some of the more productive of the otherwise fairly poor altiplano types (Simmons, Tarano, and Pinto 1959:119).

Huehuetenango's market traditionally has been an important agricultural redistribution center for such produce as maize and potatoes. It is also seen as a pivotal exhange center in the north-south network from the lowlands to the Cuchumatanes (McBryde 1945:77, 126; C. Smith 1972).

Zaculeu overlooks the Rio Selegua, which runs directly north-west, becoming the Rio Chiapas in Mexico, and eventually drains into the Rio Grijalva and the Gulf of Mexico.

Settlement Description

Most of the Late Postclassic civic architecture is oriented within several degrees of a line running 302°NW and 122°SE. Out of 43 civic structures at the site, at least 17 were built or modified during the Late Postclassic Period, as evidenced by Late Postclassic ceramics within often successive building phases.

The principal Late Postclassic temple, situated on the eastern edge of the civic precinct and oriented northwest, has one long flanking structure attached to each side (Fig. 25). This temple was first laid out in the Early Postclassic Period and went through twelve successive building phases before its superstructure was toppled by the Spanish. There is a single broad stairway on the temple front, and one narrow stairway on each of the two sides. Each of the stairways has similarly proportioned balustrades, with wide-angled *taluds* approximately twice as long as the *tableros*. The superstructure contains two principal rooms connected by a narrow passageway. The circular chamber on the back side was first constructed during the Early Postclassic Period. Two red-painted columns once stood in the entrance of the front room. Both rectangular flanking structures have a single room, with a bench against the back and side walls, an altar against the center back wall, and round pillars across the entrance. There are equal-sized single-room altars, both with 302° orientation, in the court in front of the temple and just northeast of the temple. One has double stairs and the other a single stairway, although both have similar styled *talud-tablero* balustrades.

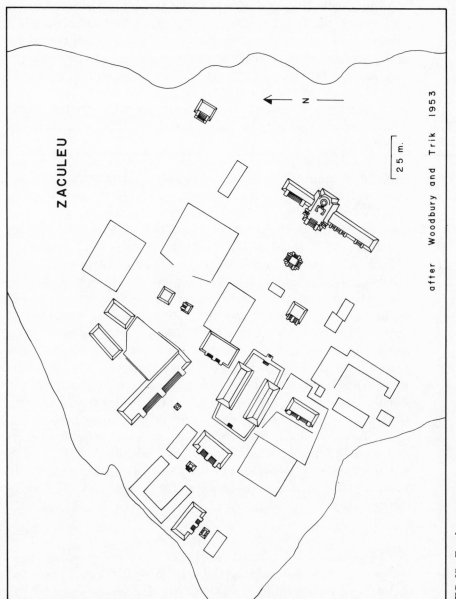

ZACULEU

N

25 m.

after Woodbury and Trik 1953

FIG. 25   Zaculeu

An unusually large and wide I-shaped sunken ball court occupied the center of the Late Postclassic civic configuration. It has the steep playing walls with a vertical overhung molding that are typical for sites within the political orbit of the Central Quiche. The ball court may have been built during Early Postclassic times (see Smith 1961:117).

In the Classic Period plaza to the north are two Late Postclassic altars, which are aligned with the large earlier pyramidal structures.

The northwest portion of the civic complex consists almost entirely of Late Postclassic architecture. Structures here are grouped into three semienclosed groups. The first enclosed group is formed by the long structure, a short rectangular structure, and the north side of the ball court, with an altar in its center. The long structure, like the flanking structures already described, consists of a single room with a bench against the back and side walls. Both the long structure and short rectangular structure have double stairways with *talud-tablero* balustrades. Indeed, with the exception of one flanking structure, all rectangular platforms at Zaculeu have double stairways. A second semienclosed group consists of an identical short rectangular structure, with an altar in the center of the court facing a U-shaped structure. Except for the short rectangular one, these structures are covered with grass. Finally, on the northwest perimeter of the site, two short rectangular structures face each other, with an altar between them.

The Late Postclassic masonry at Zaculeu is said to be superior to that of earlier times (Woodbury and Trik 1953:43, 287). It consists of slabs shaped by pecking, but not the dressed blocks with fully smooth sides characteristic of some Late-phase Central Quiche construction.

Artifacts

A wealth of artifactual material was unearthed at multi-phased Zaculeu, including within burial contexts. The reader is referred to Woodbury and Trik's (1953) detailed account. However, I will briefly describe Late Postclassic ceramics and projectile points.

The predominant Late Postclassic ceramic types, totaling over 1,200 sherds, are white-on-red, white-on-brown, monochrome red, monochrome brown, a dull paint polychrome, and ladle censers with molded decoration (Wauchope 1970:125–31). Micaceous ware apparently did not extend as far west as Zaculeu. Significantly, Fortress white-on-red amounted to only about one percent of the Late Postclassic sample, which is surprisingly low when compared to Quiche sites (see Wauchope 1970:101). The dull paint polychrome, which also occurs in excavated contexts at Utatlan, uses motifs reminiscent of the bright paint Chinautla polychrome.

All projectile points recovered are Postclassic in date. Late Postclassic points are leaf shaped (Woodbury and Trik 1953:225) as at Pueblo Viejo Malacatancito. Early Postclassic points, displaying a variety of shapes, are classified as primarily "tapering-stemmed" and "expanding-stemmed" points. Significantly, a rare variety of the "expanding-stemmed" (Woodbury and Trik 1953: Fig. 124 *c,d*) types also is characteristic of Chichen Itza and Tula.

Architecture and Settlement Pattern Interpretations

The investigators of Zaculeu did not look specifically for house mounds or examine the extent of the settlement (Woodbury and Trik 1953:25). Their work was thus directed entirely to monumental architecture on the fortified plateau. The Spanish did report a sizable residential settlement outside this plateau, seemingly where Huehuetenango sprawls today (Woodbury and Trik 1953:15). Given the size of Zaculeu's plateau in addition to the adjoining residential area, the nucleated settlement may have been substantial indeed.

Zaculeu shares some features of its general arrangement, as well as features of architectural style, with the Central Quiche. To begin with, its main temple faces west. The last facade of this temple resembles the first level of the Temple of Awilix at Utatlan, with broad, abruptly angled *talud-tablero* balustrades, the single front-stairway balustrades, and the side balustrades. A similar-styled temple at Iximche (Chapter 5, below) also has a superstructure with two chambers and two pillars in the front entrance. The temple's two unequal-sized rectangular flanking structures are like those adjoining the Temple of Awilix at Utatlan. The long structure, finally, lies on the north side of configuration and faces south. The form and architectural features of the long structure, flanking structures, and altars are similar to corresponding types in Greater Utatlan. Although apparently first laid out during the Early Postclassic Period, the last phase of the northwest-southeast-facing ball court is similar in size and style to Quiche ball courts. The generally lower and less well preserved structures on the west end of the Late Postclassic configuration, in and around the U-shaped structure, may pertain to an elite residential complex.

The Late Postclassic arrangement at Zaculeu, however, is unlike that of any Quichean site. Specifically, rather than the typical rectilinear enclosed civic plaza, there is a continuum of structures, either built or modified for use during the Late Postclassic Period, running southeast to northwest. Within this continuum are at least four separate small court groups of structures forming individual units, such as the two pairs of parallel short rectangular structures, closely spaced, with an altar between them. Such small, apparently self-contained groups differ from building groups so far known for Quiche civic complexes. Short rectangular structures in Quiche patterns, for example, tend to be on plaza sides. In addition, the round structure of Zaculeu is on the temple, rather than in the main court. There is just one temple, rather than two, and significantly, it lacks inset terraces. Inset terraces on a temple's core occur seemingly without exception in the highlands. Terraces occur even at Mam Pueblo Viejo Sipacapa, with a distinct linear pattern. One might hypothesize that the terraces were missed in the restoration of the temple, but it was one of the best-preserved structures (Woodbury and Trik 1953:40).

In sum, the pattern at Zaculeu has some spatial relationships in common with the Central Quiche, but overall it is quite distinct. Its northwest-running continuum of structures may reflect Mam linear civic structuring (as at Pueblo Viejo Sipacapa, Tuitenam, Pueblo Viejo Huitan). Zaculeu may have therefore incorporated a degree of Quiche spatial ordering into a basically Mam pattern. As the multiple building phases suggest, the basic elements of this "Mam" linear continuum were laid out in the Early Postclassic Period, if not before. The temple and ball court were first built during the Early Postclassic Period; the distinctly Quichean flanking structures and long structure and the last front and side facade of the temple are Late Postclassic additions. The ball court, however, with an associated altar, brings to mind the "open end a" courts of the culturally related Ixil. Its I-shape may prove to have been a later altera-

tion. The unique circular antechamber of the temple dates from the
Early Postclassic Period. While this round posterior room does not
occur elsewhere in the highlands, it is known in Mexico (Pollock
1936), particularly the Early Postclassic construction at Cempoala on
the Veracruz Gulf Coast. Interestingly, the Rio Selegua (Grijalva),
which Zaculeu overlooks, leads to the Veracruz coast. In sum, Zaculeu may have been a Mam community, perhaps exercising some
control over smaller Mam communities, that fell under influence
from the "Mexicanized" Gulf Coast during the Early Postclassic Period. Similarly, Zaculeu exhibits architectural influence arising from
control by the Central Quiche during the Late Postclassic Period.
Limited Quiche influence is also seen in ceramics; the hallmark of
the Quiche, Fortress white-on-red, totals a minuscule proportion of
the Late Postclassic sample.

Ethnohistory

The *Popol Vuh* (1950:221) states quite clearly that the Central
Quiche under Quicab conquered "the towns of the peoples of
Zaculeu" (see Xpantzay III 1957:145).

"At the time of this Quiche conquest, according to Villacorta, the
name of the site became Zaculeu, a Quiche term meaning 'white
earth,' whereas it had previously been known by the Mam name
Chinabajul" (Woodbury and Trik 1953:10). The Quiche maintained
control over the Zaculeu Mam until the Spanish conquest. "This is
corroborated by the fact that the Mam from that area (led by Caibil
Balam) came to the assistance of the Quiche in the defense of
Gumarcaah (Utatlan)" (Carmack n.d.a:43). According to Fuentes y
Guzmán (1932–33) the broad residential ward outside the fortifications of the elite center of Zaculeu was itself fortified with a
moat wall.

The native documents do not indicate whether there were
actually central Quiche lords dwelling at Zaculeu, although
Fuentes y Guzmán writes that Quiche princes were sent to rule the
Mam (cf. Miles 1954a:742). Looking at archaeological remains, the
small percentage of ceramics shared with Utatlan, such as Fortress white-on-red and dull point polychrome, suggest contact of
some sort with the Central Quiche. Considering Central Quiche
architectural styles at Zaculeu, I suspect that there was a small

entourage of Central Quiche overlords there, among a Mam population. On the other hand, side-notched "arrow" projectile points would be expected if there was Late-phase Central Quiche military presence.

Pueblo Viejo, El Caballero, Tenam

There is an additional site on the first hilltop south of Zaculeu, called Cerro Pueblo Viejo. The site has steep 140-meter-high slopes. As far as I know, no archaeologist has yet investigated here (IGN, Huehuetenango).

The next prominent hilltop farther south, six kilometers southeast of Zaculeu, called El Caballero, also contains Late Postclassic ruins. Carmack (personal communication) briefly visited here in 1970. The hilltop rises sharply 100 meters in elevation.

According to Gonzalo de Alvarado's account of the campaign against the Mam, there was a settlement called Mazatenango near present-day San Lorenzo. San Lorenzo is at the foot of El Caballero, some six kilometers southeast of Zaculeu, which suggests an association between El Cabellero and the community known in Nahuatl as Mazatenango.

There is yet another small hilltop site, Tenam, a few kilometers northwest of Zaculeu. Tenam, shown on the Tulane Map of the Maya Area, should not be confused with Smith's (1955) Xetenam (Wauchope 1970:124). Smith recovered no ceramics at Xetenam; there is a small collection from Tenam in the Museo Nacional de Arqueología y Etnología.

Xetenam

Xetenam is about three kilometers northeast of Zaculeu, equidistant from Zaculeu and the cabecera Chiantla (Map 1). In 1945 Smith briefly visited the site, measured the ball court, and hastily sketched mounds located within the plaza.

Topography and Ecology

The ruins lie on a ridgetop, surrounded by steep 100-meter slopes. No artificial fortifications, such as terraces or moats, were noted.

The broad Huehuetenango Basin begins at the southern foot of

Xetenam. Only two kilometers to the north, the Cuchumatanes escarpment rises abruptly 1,300 meters.

Settlement Description

Civic architecture at Xetenam consists of an enclosed plaza of rectangular platforms, with an altar in its center, an I-shaped ball court, and a U-shaped structure just north of the ball court. The plaza also features three equal-sized platforms in a row facing east (Fig. 26). These may once have been low triple temples. At the time of Smith's visit, however, none of the structures was over 2.5 meters high. Masonry was of rough slabs covered with plaster; its preservation was poor.

Artifacts

No ceramics were recovered.

Architecture and Settlement Pattern Interpretations

Inasmuch as Smith did not examine the remainder of the ridgetop it is not possible to discern the possible settlement size.

Like the Quiche sites, Xetenam also has an enclosed plaza. Its ball court is oriented basically north-south rather than the east-west characteristic of Quiche sites. Structures at Xetenam are small compared with Quiche structures, although comparable to those at Quiche "ward" sites. Certain similarities in civic patterning and structure size between Xetenam and Pueblo Viejo Malacatancito will be discussed below. Finally, the U-shaped structure on the northern terminus of Xetenam's civic complex is reminiscent of the U-shaped structure on the northwestern periphery of Zaculeu.

Considering its proximity to Zaculeu, Xetenam may have been a component in a nucleated settlement centered around Zaculeu. The Spanish reported a large residential settlement in the open land between Xetenam and Zaculeu. The sites that surround Zaculeu— Tenam (3 km northwest of Zaculeu), Cerro Pueblo Viejo (3 km southeast), and El Caballero (6 km southeast)—also occupy the hilltops closest to Zaculeu, which lies on the plain. Perhaps these sites were settlements with defensive functions, particularly blocking access to the apparently open residential settlement on the plain, like the fortified plazas (e.g., Resguardo) outside the elite centers of Greater Utatlan.

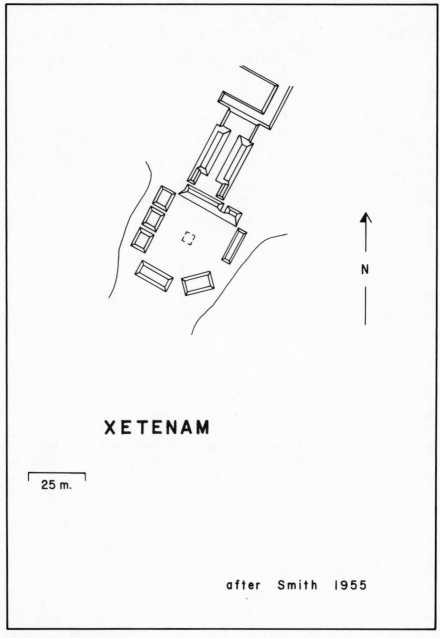

XETENAM

N

25 m.

after   Smith   1955

FIG. 26   Xetenam

Ethnohistory

Inasmuch as Zaculeu was under Quiche suzerainty for about a century, it seems reasonable to imagine that the probable satellite sites of Xetenam, Tenam, Cerro Pueblo Viejo, and El Caballero were too. Five (possibly six) Mam settlements grouped together in sixteenth-century native documents—Tzitzol, Halic, Tabahal, Bahnay, and Choxa naj (perhaps the same as Behnay and Coha) (Xpantzay II 1957:141–45; C'oyoi 1973:318; Xajil 1953:93; Carmack n.d.a:20)—were conquered by the Quiche at the same time as Zaculeu. The site of Coha may lie within the minuscule Mam municipality of Cojala in the department of Quezaltenango. Tzitzol is associated with ethnohistoric references to Zaculeu (Brasseur de Bourbourg 1861:cclxiv, in Carmack n.d.a:20). These four or five settlements may pertain to the four as yet unidentified Mam sites ringing Zaculeu. In addition, there may also be a site at Pueblo Viejo on the Rio Selegua just above San Sebastian Huehuetenango, about seven kilometers northwest of Zaculeu.

Intermontane Region

A number of sites are clustered on the bluffs overlooking the interconnected Totonicapan-Quezaltenango basins and the valleys of Nahuala and Santa Catarina Ixtahuacan. This area lies between two major avenues to the piedmont and lowlands—the Rio Nahualate passage on the east and the Rio Samala on the west. Mountain ranges border the area to the north and south. To the south is the recent volcanic axis with still active volcanos. The rich soil in these basins results from volcanic deposition. In fact, volcanos loom above the horizon at several of the sites. The north boundary for this intermontane area is the Old Cordillera or Continental Divide Range, paralleling the new volcanic axis. The first settlement to be examined, Sija, is the central site among the group (Map 8).

Sija

Sija is situated on top of an eroded volcanic neck jutting 150 meters above the Pan American Highway, about eleven kilometers by road west of Nahuala. This also is the summit of the Continental

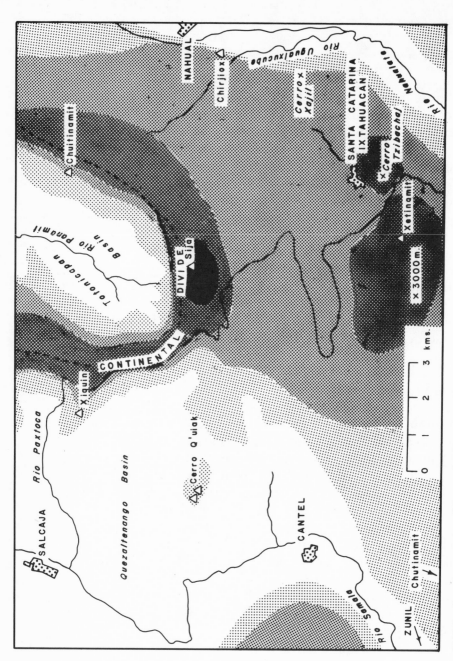

MAP 8   Quezaltenango Area (Western Quiche and Mam)

Divide Range, separating the Nahuala Valley from the Quezaltenango Basin. Inhabitants of the region speak the same Quiche dialect found around Utatlan (Campbell 1971:120).

Topography and Ecology

The flat-topped volcanic mesa is shaped like a parallelogram (Fig. 27). The upper 50 meters or so on all sides are rock-faced cliff. Below the cliff, talus slopes descend at least 600 meters to the basin floor. The settlement is only accessible from two narrow entrances, breaching the cliff on its east and west sides. The east entrance has steps hewn out of bedrock. Just before the summit this passageway proceeds through three walls that span a small break in the cliff. The uppermost wall, situated on the edge of the mesatop, consists of huge boulders, many of which measure 2 and 3 meters across. It spans the entire east side of the site, although there are frequent spaces between the boulders. The other two walls fortifying the entrance comprise smaller pieces of lava rubble. The western periphery of the site also contains a wall running its entire length. The combined effect of the cliffs and walls is one of an almost impregnable fortress.

At 3,165 meters' elevation Sija is several hundred meters above the elevation limits for maize cultivation. Given its steep slopes, moreover, maize cultivation on any scale seems unlikely on all but the basin floor far below.

Sija's strategic location commands a view of the basins and valleys below on all four sides, including the cabeceras of Totonicapan, Nahuala, and Santa Catarina Ixtahuacan. At the foot of the range where Sija lies, to the east, is the Rio Nahualate, which has cut a straight channel to the piedmont and lowlands and is a major commerce route today as it was in pre-Hispanic times (McBryde 1945:82). Sija thus overlooks a main thoroughfare for exchange between the *tierra fria* highland zones and the milder lower regions. The Late Postclassic inhibitants of Sija may have been traders as are their descendants today, residing in Nahuala and Santa Catarina Ixtahuacan east and southeast, respectively. Exploiting the lava beds on the mountain slopes, Nahuala and Santa Catarina are the major producers of manos and metates in Guatemala. After Spanish takeover, the community of Sija was at first transferred to the site of Santa Catarina Ixtahuacan, which was

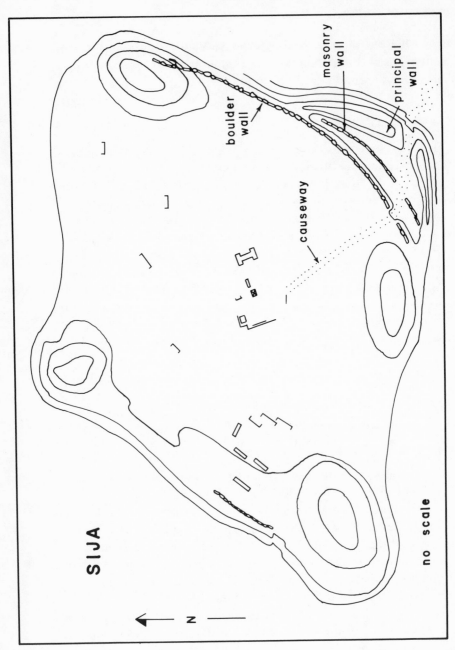

FIG. 27 Sija

called Santa Catarina Sija in the sixteenth-century Paxtoca document (in Carmack 1973). As an *aldea* of Santa Catarina, Nahuala seceded from the municipality formally in the nineteenth century (McBryde 1945:89). Community leaders of Nahuala still claim their *pueblo viejo* to be Santa Catarina—Sija in pre-Hispanic times.

Settlement Description

The large parallelogram-shaped mesatop is approximately one quarter of a square kilometer in area. Vegetation cover today consists of only a handful of scrub trees and tall grass. Curiously, the site displays further symmetry with a small knoll in each of its four corners. The two elevated corners on the east side have boulders set into their sides and were constructions of some sort. However, most of the architectural remains at the site are exceedingly poorly preserved. The remains of a civic plaza can just barely be distinguished in the direct center of the plateau, but the only structures that can be clearly identified are a sunken I-shaped ball court, oriented roughly north-south, the base of a temple, and several rectangular platforms. Foundation lines of dressed stone blocks also protrude through the grass. These structures are portrayed at a larger scale in Figure 27 than is the remainder of the mesatop. A straight sunken causeway leads directly from the main entrance of the site, through the walls, to the civic plaza. In many parts of the plateau, and especially on the west end of the mesa extending to the west wall, are masonry foundation lines at ground level, suggesting that much of the site contained buildings. They are most common on slight inclines where there has been some erosion. Sija must have been stripped of its monumental architecture at some point in the past, perhaps for the construction of some of the large post-Hispanic towns in the vicinity. In this regard, it should be noted that there are also abundant rock deposits for building materials on the slopes of surrounding hills.

Artifacts

We recovered a large ceramic sample, mostly from the slight rise near the west plateau edge. Interestingly, most of surface ceramics were rim sherds. Of a sample of 110 rim sherds, half are the thin double-groove red-slipped type. Also, a few of the narrow-mouthed globular-necked jar sherds seen at Utatlan are present. Most of the sherds are also thin walled and red slipped. Fortress white-on-red consists of white paint of thin composition on a orangish-red slip. A small proportion of sherds are unslipped micaceous ware. No projectile points were noted, although a number of short prismatic obsidian blades were recovered.

Architecture and Settlement Pattern Interpretations

Although architecture at Sija is almost entirely obscured, a few basic settlement pattern comparisons with Utatlan can be made. Sija and Utatlan are both located on flat-surfaced plateaus with clifflike barrancas; at both a straight sunken causeway leads to the civic complex in the center of the plateau; and the construction stone within the civic plaza is of finely dressed blocks. The only architecture worthy of comparison is the sunken I-shaped ballcourt at Sija. It differs from the ball courts within Greater Utatlan, however, in being oriented roughly north-south, and seems to be considerably smaller.

Sija and Utatlan differ in a number of notable topographic features. First, Sija is situated on one of the highest peaks in the volcanic basin region, towering over 600 meters above surrounding milpa lands. By contrast, Utatlan is in open country with milpa on neighboring plateaus of the same elevation. Sija also has the uncommon features of a series of masonry walls and small constructed "knolls" in each of its four corners. Finally, the mesatop at Sija is just about twice the size of that at Utatlan, although it is not possible from its obscured remains to tell whether it was covered with structures.

Although Sija seems to have more pronounced fortifications, with its mountaintop location and walls, it apparently was a "plateau" *tinamit* like Utatlan. Since ceramic types at Sija are the same as at Late-phase Greater Utatlan, and they are the same kind of settlements, we may infer that there was a cultural affinity between Sija and the Central Quiche of Greater Utatlan.

Ethnohistory

Sija is mentioned in a number of sixteenth-century Quichean documents as a loyal ally of the Central Quiche at a fairly early date in the Late phase. Specifically, after the death of the Quiche ruler Gucumatz, around the third decade of the fifteenth century, a feast was held at Utatlan and "Siha" was listed among the allies of the Central Quiche (Totonicapan 1953:188). The eight Tz'alam C'oxtun of Siha also are mentioned as allies in their conquest of the coast under Quicab (Totonicapan 1953:191; Nihaib I 1957:74,77), and as battling the Spanish on the plains of Quezaltenango a little over a half-century later (C'oyoi 1973:278–80).

Chirijox

This small site is situated on a barranca edge above the Pan American Highway, at the point where the Rio Ugualxucube crosses under the road, about a kilometer from the western entry road to the cabecera of Nahuala (Map 8).

Chirijox lies on the east edge of a flat shelf that is also the bottommost slope of the Old Cordillera, which Sija tops. Chirijox is situated a steep 80 meters above the valley floor. However, it does not have the vertical cliffs seen at many low sites.

At about 2,600 meters' elevation, Chirijox and the surrounding valley are definitely *tierra fria*. The Rio Nahualate runs parallel to the Rio Ugualxucube not more than half a kilometer from Chirijox. As previously remarked, the Rio Nahualate is a major trade route between the highlands and lowlands.

Chirijox's civic architecture consists of just three earth mounds that do not fit the classification of the enclosed plazas or the linear pattern (Fig. 28). Additional structures may once have existed where a soccer field is now situated, adjacent to the southern mound. There are no signs of masonry, although a few small rough stones protrude from the mounds.

Milperos piled abundant ceramics at the barranca edge, next to the mounds. Many sherds exhibit distinctive varieties of incising combined with modeled handles. Wavy-line and punctate incision occur sometimes with double and triple "straight strand" modeled handles. The punctate and wavy-line incision type and circular indentations a centimeter wide are the most frequent designs. The rim profiles, especially a thick out-flaring lip, are characteristic of the Early Postclassic Period and Early-phase Late Postclassic.

The settlement pattern of Chirijox is unlike that of any Post-

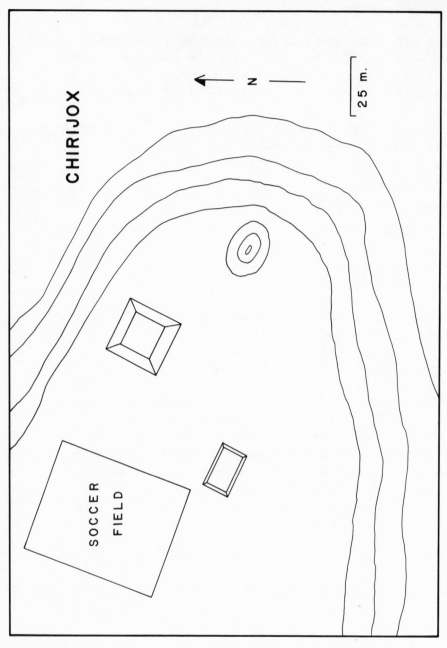

CHIRIJOX

N

25 m.

SOCCER FIELD

FIG. 28   Chirijox

classic site so far described, although it may have resembled Panajxit in the Quiche Basin. Its ceramics and the apparent earth composition of its mounds are similar to the "linear altar mound" sites. The ceramics are particularly analogous to ceramic types found in the Quiche Basin (e.g., at Cojonob and Semeja). Chirijox may thus have been a center for inhabitants of the Nahuala Valley prior to expansion of the Central Quiche.

Chuitinamit-Totonicapan

Along the west edge of the Old Cordillera, overlooking the post-Hispanic cabecera of Totonicapan 700 meters below, is a place known within the municipality as Chuitinamit. At about 3,000 meters' elevation, Chuitinamit overlooks Sija, about four kilometers in a straight line to the southeast (Maps 1,8). At nearly the same elevation, Chuitinamit and Sija are also the highest points in the region. Like Sija, Chuitinamit is continually shrouded in mist. There is scrub vegetation, and only wheat is cultivated in the vicinity today.

Chuitinamit also resembles Sija in the sparsity of discernible settlement remains, although numerous piles of uncut lava stone were scattered about. The only clearly identifiable archaeological remains are a single obsidian blade and a nondescript sherd, both recovered from recently turned earth, next to a modern grave. Given its similarity to conditions at nearby Sija, where settlement remains are hardly distinguishable, we may infer that Chuitinamit experienced the same obscuring process. Any attempt at delineating the settlement pattern would require extensive digging.

From documentary references there are two names for the pre-Hispanic community above Totonicapan: Chuvi-Miquina ("over or above hot water springs") (Recinos 1950:221 n.; Carmack n.d.a:23) and Tzibachaj. Chuitinamit, which is literally 700 meters directly above the hot springs of Totonicapan, apparently was the site for Chuvi-Miquina or Tzibachaj. The *Titulo C'oyoi* (1973:302) describes Tzibachaj as "above Mik'ina." And with the same topographic situation as the sizable Sija, a location like Chuitinamit is not out of the question for a major settlement like Chuvi-Miquina, even though surface remains are negligible. No other late Postclassic ruins are known within the municipality of Totonicapan, although the modern town itself is situated on a

defensible plateau surrounded by steep, often vertical barrancas
(cf. Carmack n.d.a:23). Furthermore, the hot springs are located at
the foot of this plateau, and thus also below the cabecera.

Xetinamit

In the fairly rugged country immediately south of the Old
Cordillera, two kilometers southeast of the cabecera Santa Catarina
Ixtahuacan and six kilometers in a line south of Sija, is the site of
Xetinamit (Map 8). Carmack visited Xetinamit briefly in 1970
(personal communication).

At 2,340 meters, Xetinamit is situated on a shelf midway up a
mountain, the summit of which is 3,000 meters in elevation. Both
the east side of Xetinamit, dropping 200 meters to the Rio Tejen,
and its west side, rising to the summit of the mountain, are quite
steep. The settlement is further fortified with terraces set into its
slopes. The Rio Tejen is a primary tributary of the Rio Nahualate,
which it joins two kilometers southeast of the site (Map 8).

Remains at Xetinamit are poorly preserved. However, four civic
structures in an enclosed plaza are relatively intact. Several
features can be made out on a temple facing east, notably double
stairways bordered by *talud-tablero* balustrades, and construction
with dressed stone blocks. Architectural features with "Mexican"
forms, such as *talud-tablero* balustrades and an enclosed plaza,
suggest that Xetinamit was a Late-phase Quichean settlement.

Directly across the Rio Tejen from Xetinamit is the promontory
Cerro Tzibachaj (IGN, Santa Catarina Ixtahuacan). To reiterate,
a Quiche settlement by the same name is mentioned ethnohistorically (C'oyoi 1973:327; Totonicapan 1953:191–92) and is associated
with Totonicapan.

Quiak

In the center of the broad Quezaltenango Basin is a high hill
known as Cerro Quiak (Map 8). It is the only hill in an otherwise
flat, almost treeless plain and can be seen from any direction up to
about four kilometers away.

Topography and Ecology

The hilltop at Quiak is a long narrow ridge, about one kilometer
long. Its width varies from about 20 meters to 100 meters. The

widest point, near the eastern extreme of the ridgetop, lacks signs
of settlement. The sides of the hill are quite steep, and the site can,
in fact, only be approached from the northeastern extremity of the
ridge, the furthest point from the pre-Hispanic settlement. On the
west side of the ridge—also its highest point—are vertical terraces
built of huge boulders, 2 and 3 meters high (Fig. 29). Here the
sides rise 160 meters above the basin floor, whereas slopes on the
remainder of the ridge are about 100 meters high.

Cerro Quiak is situated adjacent to two key resources: the rich
basin soil and the broad Rio Samala. The soil, of recent volcanic
origin (Simmons, Tarano, and Pinto 1959:147; West 1964a:77), is
rich and well watered, and receives replenishment both from
volcanic ejecta (the nearby volcano Santa Maria has erupted several
times in this century) and from hill wash (mud and alluvium) from
the steep mountains that surround it. Indeed, rich soils in the basin
have been estimated to be as deep as 300 meters (West 1964a:77).
The basin floor, at 2,400 meters' elevation, is definitely *tierra fria*
but, nevertheless, is considered one of the most productive
agricultural regions of the highlands.

The Rio Samala meanders across the broad plain only two
kilometers west of Cerro Quiak. The Samala passage has long been
a principal route between the highland and lowland regions. The
numerous towns strung along it today, such as Quezaltenango and
Cantel on the edge of the highlands and Zunil and San Martin
Zapotitlan along their descent, attest to its importance. Large
mounds just outside Salcaja, not far northwest of Quiak along
the river, also indicate that this area was well settled prior to
Postclassic times.

Settlement Description

Civic architecture is present only on the more elevated west half
of the ridgetop. The ridgetop as well as the mounds run northwest
and southeast. The civic architecture, which occurs in two groups,
is poorly preserved. Figure 29 portrays the two groups of civic
architecture but does not include the long, narrow area connecting
them. In the east group three earthen structures can be made out
in a line; what appears to be a fourth is off to the south side.
This group is separated from the remainder of the ridge by
30-meter-steep dropoffs on its east and west sides. A fairly heavy

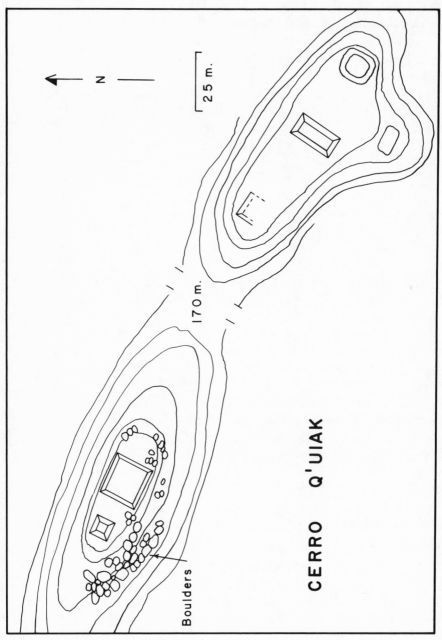

N

25 m.

170 m.

Boulders

CERRO Q'UIAK

FIG. 29   Cerro Q'uiak

concentration of surface ceramics occurs outside this group on the same level, which has been exposed by cultivation of the soil.

A second group occupies the westernmost crest of the ridgetop, rising 70 meters above the first group. The summit here is short and exceedingly narrow. Only two structures are visible, but, given the restricted space, not more than one additional structure could ever have existed in this spot. A small temple, facing southeast and 20 meters high, is centered on a broad platform 1 meter high. Uncut stone is visible in the sides of the platform. Within the past few decades five carved pre-Hispanic stelae have been arranged in a semicircle on the platform.

Artifacts

The ceramics are characterized by a variety of incised ceramic designs, including bands, triangles, and short parallel lines in various numbered clusters, which sometimes occur in a panel of alternating horizontal and vertical groups. The distinctive wavy-line-and-punctate type is also present. Quiak thus seems to have been occupied primarily in the Early phase, if not before, during the Early Postclassic Period.

Architecture and Settlement Pattern Interpretations

Ceramic concentrations adjacent to the east civic group suggest perhaps a small resident population. An absence of Late-phase ceramics implies occupation prior to Central Quiche expansion into the basin. Several of the distinctive incised ceramic types are the same as those at Chirijox, and suggest comtemporaneity.

A linear civic pattern, with earth structures either without masonry or with stelae also contrasts with the enclosed Quiche plazas. However, it is reminiscent of the Early-phase ridgetop sites like Cojonob in the Quiche Basin and Xabaj-Sajcabaja (see A. L. Smith 1955).

Ethnohistory

While delineating their boundaries in the Quezaltenango Basin, the C'oyoi Sakcorowach branch of the Quiche, who wrote the *Titulo C'oyoi*, mention Quiak several times as an important basin landmark (C'oyoi 1973:299, 300, 305). The description of the ridge is significant: "a fortress, a large structure is located on top of Q'uiak, the structure of the Sakiulew people" (C'oyoi 1973:300). This is a direct reference to the builders of Quiak as Mam, apparently tied in some manner to Zaculeu. Quiak is not mentioned as being inhabited by Quiche after the Mam were driven out, which fits the lack of Quiche archaeological remains. Thus the linear settlement pattern and the presence of stelae and certain incised ceramic types can be shown to belong to Mam in the basin, probably as late as the thirteenth or fourteenth centuries.

Chuitinamit-Zunil

Chuitinamit is situated about ten kilometers south of the cabecera Zunil and about a kilometer and a half south of the aldea La Estancia de la Cruz. It is on a mountain rising above the east bank of the Rio Samala. Chuitinamit is also known as Pueblo Viejo in the Quiche-speaking municipality of Zunil.

Chuitinamit occupies a shelf near the mountain summit, which, at 2,100 meters' elevation, is 400 meters above the gorge cut by the Rio Samala. The settlement is centrally placed at the pass between the volcanos Santa Maria, on the west side of the Rio Samala, and Santo Tomas and Zunil, on its east side. In effect, the thoroughfare between the highlands and piedmont must have passed below this site along the pass, as is the case today.

There is a dramatic change in vegetation only several hundred meters north of Chuitinamit from piedmont to highland flora. Fruit trees native to the region (e.g., zapotes; see McBryde 1945:146) can be seen near dwellings along the sparsely settled Samala trail. Not far up the valley on the more rocky hillslopes of the volcano are numerous outlets for steam and sulfur gases.

We arrived at the ruins just before dark and did not have time to investigate them thoroughly or collect sherds. Except for the south end, exposed by milpa, most of the shelf is engulfed by dense tropical vegetation; the structures we did identify were also covered in vegetation. We could make out a temple and flanking structure forming one plaza side; a low long structure forming the west side; and a short rectangular structure on part of the east side. The buildings of this semienclosed plaza are oriented 37° east of north (Fig. 30). In the milpa, beginning where the standing

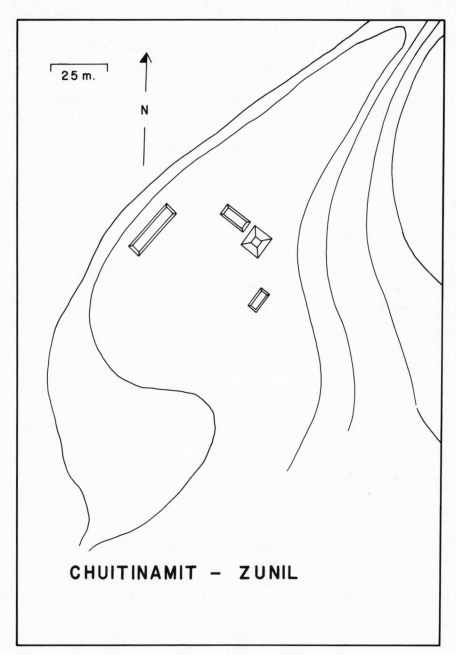

25 m.

N

CHUITINAMIT – ZUNIL

FIG. 30   Chuitinamit-Zunil

architecture ends, are piles of stone, suggesting that there probably were structures that since have been destroyed by cultivation
practices.

The few standing buildings bear some resemblance to Central
Quiche building types (such as the long structure) and their spatial
relationships (e.g., a temple and flanking structure sharing one
plaza side, with a long structure on its adjacent side); masonry of
cut stone is also a Quiche characteristic. However, the small size
and north-south orientation of the buildings differ from the
Quiche, and such hallmarks of the Central Quiche as two temples
and a ball court are lacking. On the other hand, there is little at
Chuitinamit to suggest construction by the Mam, who controlled
the Samala Pass prior to Quiche expansion. The small size of
Chuitinamit, as well as its small structures, which are roughly
comparable in size to some of the ward centers of the Quiche
Basin, suggest a provincial Quiche (Western Quiche?) center of
some sort.

Xelajuh

None of the Late-phase elite communities, most notably Xelajuh, known from ethnohistory to have been situated within the
strategic southern portion of the Quezaltenango Basin (Carmack
n.d.a:23–24) have yet been located. According to Alvarado (1924),
who entered Xelajuh, and from native chronicles (Nijaib II 1957;
C'oyoi 1973), Xelajuh was the principal center for the rich, heavily
populated Quezaltenango Basin. Xelajuh was taken from the Mam
and colonized by all the major Central Quiche lineages (Carmack
n.d.a:22).

Shook (n.d.) briefly searched the rugged heights above present-
day Quezaltenango without success. Carmack (personal communication) has inquired locally over the years for its whereabouts, also
without success. Unfortunately, Alvarado mentions its general location only as above the Samala Pass. Considering the extreme
topographic locations of nearby Sija and Chuitinamit-Totonicapan,
perhaps Xelajuh, on the bellicose Mam border to the west, was also
defensively situated in the lofty mountains. There is, in fact, a high
rugged range extending from volcano Santa Maria north ten
kilometers, running west of modern Quezaltenango.

We examined Xepach, a ridgetop on the lower slopes of Santa

Maria, on the extreme southern arm of the Quezaltenango Basin. Approximately 160 meters above the basin floor we noted occasional sherds and obsidian on the slopes, but we did not locate ruins. Since the slopes continued sharply up, there might be a site still farther up.

Piedmont and Coast

The Central Quiche eventually colonized the Samala passage, as well as the piedmont and some of the Pacific Coast (Carmack n.d.a). Not far below Chuitinamit-Zunil, a major Quiche settlement, Xetulul, was also located along the Rio Samala. This was the first Quiche settlement encountered by Alvarado in his conquest of Guatemala. He mentions (1924:54–56) that Xetulul (Zapotitlan) was near the riverbank and had wide streets and a large market. According to Carmack (n.d.a:26), "The Zapotitlan document clearly reveals that the ruling line of Zapotitlan was a branch of the Cawec lineage" of the Nima Quiche division at Utatlan. We spent two days in July 1973 searching for Xetulul, but found only the first Spanish settlement on the east bank of the Rio Samala. Since much stone was utilized in the colonial settlement, further investigation here may reveal an underlying or nearby Quiche town.

Farther west along the coast, near the general location of Ayutla, the westernmost Quiche settlement and western boundary of the Quiche state (Carmack n.d.a:25, 36, 43), on the present Mexican border, small samples of Late Postclassic ceramics have been reported (e.g., Coe and Flannery 1967). A large site in this area, Los Limones, along the west bank of the Rio Narango, has features that hint at a Late Postclassic date. Its main temple is five meters high, with inset terraces, covered with lime plaster, arranged in a plaza (Shook 1965:186, n.d.). In fact, Miles (1965b:279) considers Los Limones, along with nearby Abaj Takalik, to be Late Postclassic.

Conclusions

Several topographic patterns visible among the the nineteen sites reviewed above can provide a frame of reference for the interaction of Mam and Quiche groups. First, the sites dating from the early part of the Late Postclassic Period, Chirijox and Quiak, occupy fairly low topographic positions. Ceramics and documents suggest that these two sites were abandoned at least by the time of Quiche control of the southwestern highlands. At the beginning of the confrontation between Mam and Quiche populations, the Old Cordillera or Continental Divide separated the Western Quiche, in the relatively infertile hilly middle country (the Momostenango area), from the Mam, in the rich volcanic basins around Quezaltenango and the Samala Pass. With the growth of the Western Quiche as part of the emergent conquest state, a push into the rich volcanic basin area and Samala passage—that is, in the opposite direction from the Quiche heartland—would seem a natural course of action. Settlements firmly within the Western Quiche hilly country—Pugertinamit, Tzakabala, and Ojertinamit—are on low ridgetops with sides rising around 80–100 meters, and generally about the same elevation as the surrounding landscape. Sites higher in elevation with respect to surrounding topography (i.e., more fortified) are located nearer the border with the Mam. Thus, Sija, Xetinamit, Chuitinamit-Totonicapan, and Pueblo Viejo Momostenango rise 600, 200, 700, and 200 meters respectively above surrounding countryside; each is also situated in the Old Cordillera. Again, this mountain range roughly delineates the Western Quiche boundary with the Mam prior to the Quiche expansion into the Quezaltenango Basin in the fifteenth century. Sija may also have been settled fairly early, perhaps before the expulsion of the Mam from the volcanic basins. Thus the extreme topographic situations of Sija and Chuitinamit-Totonicapan may also reflect their location near the meeting point of the two bellicose political systems. Some Mam sites occupied during the Late phase, such as Pueblo Viejo Sipacapa, Tuitenam, and Pueblo Viejo Malacatancito, manifest lofty locations, whereas Zaculeu, which is surrounded by relatively low barrancas, may have been defended by the small hilltop sites ringing it.

The locations of the two remaining Late-phase Quiche sites, Chuitinamit-Zunil and Xetinamit, contrast with those of Late-phase Quiche sites generally, which are situated either on defensive plateaus or on mountaintops. Interestingly, Xetinamit and Chuitinamit-Zunil were small, single-plaza civic centers, which overlooked the commercially strategic Nahualate and Samala passes respectively. Both are situated on shelves below the peaks of the mountain.

In discussing Western Quiche and Mam sites, we have noted differences in landscape configuration and soil fertility for the hilly country and volcanic basin regions. Except for small ethnic enclaves (e.g., Cojala), after Quiche expansion the Mam retained only the less fertile areas to the west (San Marcos) and the northwest (much of Huehuetenango). The different ethnic areas are connected to some degree by different drainage systems. Thus, the Western Quiche hilly country drains northeast into the Negro-Chixoy river system, whereas the hilly Mam country drains northwest into the Chiapas-Grijalva. Along this system, the three Mam centers of Pueblo Viejo Sipacapa, Tuitenam, and Pueblo Viejo Huitan are situated on a north-south geographic line within a few kilometers of the Western Quiche ethnic border. The volcanic basins which were first controlled by the Mam and later colonized by the Quiche, drain to the south coast. A notable exception to this phenomenon of cultural and political influence coincident with river networks is the Malacatancito area of the Mam. The Rio El Aguacate, which Pueblo Viejo Malacatancito overlooks, is a primary headwater river of the Rio Negro. But the pre-Hispanic Mam population at Pueblo Viejo seem to have been highly influenced by their Quiche neighbors, especially the Rio Negro groups. Outside Malacatancito, the four primary headwater rivers of the Rio Negro drain from Quiche territory in Momostenango. Briefly, Pugertinamit is on the Rio Sacmequena-Pacaranat, Pueblo Viejo Momostenango overlooks the Rio Pologua, and both Tzakabala and Ojertinamit are on the Rio Sajcoclaj (Map 1).

A symbiotic relationship existing today between the relatively infertile *tierra fria* agricultural region of Momostenango and the slightly milder and more productive Quiche Basin may extend back into pre-Hispanic times. Today the Momostenango-Chiquimula area supplies Quiche with lime and pottery; Quiche supplies maize to Momostenango (McBryde 1945). The Sija area may also have supplied other Quiche regions with manos and metates as it does today. However, the movement of commodities such as these within the Quiche conquest state, perhaps as tribute, can only be generally inferred at this point. Central Quiche tribute lists are not known, as they are for the better documented conquest system of the Aztec.

The sites presented in this chapter exhibit two fundamentally different concepts of settlement patterning: (1) civic architecture arranged in a straight line and (2) architecture forming a rectangular enclosure. Quiak, Pueblo Viejo Sipacapa, Tuitenam, and Pueblo Viejo Huitan exhibit linear patterns. The three structures at Chirijox are offset from one another, thus fitting neither the linear nor the enclosed pattern type. There does not seem to be much consistency in orientations of linear sites. Quiak, Chirijox, and Zaculeu run northwest-southeast, Tuitenam runs northeast to southwest, and Pueblo Viejo Sipacapa is oriented 13° off an east-west alignment. With the exceptions of Zaculeu and Chirijox, however, these alignments closely follow their narrow ridgetops. Again, except for Zaculeu, no linear sites have ball courts.

Quiak and Chirijox share settlement pattern traits and ceramic types with early linear-configuration sites in the Quiche Basin area, such as Cojonob, Panajxit I, and Semeja. Since these latter sites, as well as Quiak, date prior to Quiche ascendancy (see Carmack, Fox, and Stewart 1975), perhaps they reveal a settlement pattern of the pre-Epi-Toltec autochthonous horizon. Moreover, west of these sites in the Sierra Madre, the large Early Postclassic Mam center of Tajumulco is also comprised of three mounds in a linear pattern (see Dutton and Hobbs 1943: Map IV).

We know from the C'oyoi document that Quiak was a Mam center occupied into the Early phase of the Late Postclassic Period. Pueblo Viejo Sipacapa, Tuitenam, and Pueblo Viejo Huitan were also Mam centers, although they probably were inhabited until the Spanish conquest. We can thus infer that the Mam at Pueblo Viejo Sipacapa, Tuitenam, and Pueblo Viejo Huitan continued traditional concepts of spatial organization. They reflect none of the Mexican cultural influence expressed by such architectural forms as long structures, I-shaped ball courts, and enclosed plazas. Moreover, the Mam perpetuated the conservative use of stelae—at least during the Early phase at Quiak—that was well established during the preceding Early Postclassic Period (cf. Tajumulco). As already pointed out, Zaculeu incorporates elements of both linear and enclosed patterns. However, Zaculeu also probably came under Mexican derived influences in the Early Postclassic Period, as well as Epi-Toltec Quiche influence during the Late Postclassic.

Linear sites seem to reflect less complex sociocultural organization, or communities with fewer administrative parts, than those using enclosed plazas. Linear sites are comprised largely of temples and altars, and occasionally short rectangular platforms. Few structure types implies few administrative institutions. The Quiche, in contrast, used numerous structure types that regularly occur in each enclosed civic configuration, suggesting more institutional parts. Moreover, these same structures occur in the same spatial relationships at sites in widely separated regions (e.g., Utatlan, Sacapulas, Aguacatan), thereby implying similar institutions that were probably an integral part of Quiche state organization. With different patterns which seem to reflect more of a religious or ceremonial function for their centers, the Mam apparently did not have anywhere near the degree of political centralization of the Quiche. Another inference from settlement patterning: the open nature of the linear pattern suggests a less rigid separation of administrators from the citizenry, compared to the inward-facing, tightly spaced structures of the enclosed plaza. The predominance of temples and altars at linear pattern sites suggests that they may have already been truly ceremonial or temple centers.

The enclosed plaza sites of Tzakabala, Pueblo Viejo Malaca- tancito, Xetinamit, Chuitinamit-Zunil, and Xetenam share a number of settlement features as well as differences. First, each site's structures are significantly smaller than corresponding structure types in Greater Utatlan. Quiche temples from sites outside this region—except for temples at Pacot, Xolpacol, and Comitancillo in Sacapulas—are at least twice as long on a side as temples from the above sites. Temple-base measurements at Tzakabala, Pueblo Viejo Malacatancito, and Chuitinamit-Zunil are virtually identical. These are also equal to the temple structure at Xetenam and are close to what remains of a temple at Sija. Temple orientations are fairly consistent as well. The only temple at Sija, and the temples at Tzakabala and Chuitinamit-Zunil, face roughly south. The triple temples at Pueblo Viejo Malacatancito and the triple structures at Xetenam face just south of east. However, I-shaped ball courts at Xetenam and Sija are roughly north-south, whereas the ball court at Pueblo Viejo Malacatancito is more east-west. Central Quiche sites, in general, have east-west ori- ented ball courts. The Mam at Pueblo Viejo Malacatancito, Zacu- leu, and Xetenam apparently were heavily influenced by the

Quichean groups bordering them to the east. Quiche influence at Malacatancito may originate at Sacapulas, although the evidence is far from conclusive. This influence stands out in contrast to the earlier linear Mam pattern and that still used in the peripheral western Mam territory which the Quiche apparently did not settle (e.g., Pueblo Viejo Sipacapa, Tuitenam, Pueblo Viejo Huitan).

If the Mam used Quichean structure types at their enclosed plaza sites, although in different spatial relationships within the plaza, it follows that these Mam structures housed generally similar kinds of institutions. A greater degree of governmental complexity is suggested by the larger numbers of structure types in the Mam enclosed plaza sites compared to linear pattern sites. The known Mam enclosed pattern sites occur along borders with the Quiche, such as at Pueblo Viejo Malacatancito and in the Huehuetenango Basin. More complex Mam communities may have evolved in these adjacent areas in response to the rapid growth of the expansive Quiche state. An extended settlement, for example, grew around the civic nucleus at Zaculeu, with additional settlement components of the residential ward at Chinabajul or Tzitzol, and perhaps hilltop military installations at Tenam, Cerro Pueblo Viejo, El Caballero, Tenam, and possibly Pueblo Viejo San Sebastian Huehuetenango ringing the area. Interestingly, Zaculeu may also have elite residential structures, such as palaces, seen at nucleated elite communities like Greater Utatlan or Iximche, the Late-phase Cakchiquel capital. Alternatively, there is good ethnohistoric and archaeological evidence that Central Quiche administrators actually dwelt at Zaculeu. By so doing, they may have directly stimulated the structuring of a regional capital, or administrative community, along the lines of Greater Utatlan. Zaculeu, especially with the nearby hilltop centers, was clearly the largest of the Mam elite communities in their northern area, although the earlier Mam community near Xelajuh may have exercised some control over the southern Mam area, the broad Quezaltenango Basin (cf. Carmack n.d.a). Nevertheless, Zaculeu apparently maintained a dominant position in political relationships with the Quiak community in the Quezaltenango Basin and San Miguel Ixtahuacan in the Sierra Madre to the west. However, Zaculeu was geographically central to the northern, hilly Mam territory, but not the southern basin area. Thus, by controlling Zaculeu, the Central Quiche were apparently able to administer much of the northern

Mam territory while directly colonizing their southern territory. Moreover, given the Early Postclassic Mexican overlay of a Mam pattern, control of the Mam through Zaculeu by an outside group may have been accomplished earlier as well.

From the foregoing settlement pattern comparison, no clear-cut ethnic pattern emerges other than the linear-enclosed pattern dichotomy. That is, no precise line can be drawn separating Mam from Western Quiche settlement patterns here. On the other hand, this combined hilly-country-volcanic-basin area exhibits limited overlap of settlement pattern features. For example, there is uniformity in structure size at Mam and Quiche sites. As a whole, then, this region stands in contrast to others, such as the Quiche Basin or Sacapulas. In this regard, Sija and Chuitinamit-Zunil, with documented allegiance to the Central Quiche, manifest settlement features such as structure sizes, north-south orientation, and topographic situation, that contrast with those of Greater Utatlan. In size and orientation, in fact, Sija's scant architectural remains are more like those of Mam Xetenam.

The Eastern Mam and Western Quiche may have developed in close association as frontier populations over the duration of the Late Postclassic Period. The culturally hybrid region comprising the interconnected southwestern volcanic basins became the most important of the Quiche provinces, from the height of the Quiche expansion in the mid fifteenth century to the Spanish conquest. Known to the Quiche as Otzoya, this region soon surpassed the Quiche Basin heartland itself in population, with such urban communities as Xelajuh, Totonicapan, Sija, and Momostenango. Political power also shifted to this region in the later years of the Quiche state, as reflected in the large fighting force raised here to combat the Spanish in 1524. A culturally hybridized region eventually eclipsing the political and innovative center of a state system appears to present a test case of Service's (1971, 1975) generalization about the evolutionary potential of subject provinces with cultural "hybrid vigor."

5

CAKCHIQUEL

The Cakchiquel were a vital part of the Quiche state from its inception in the fourteenth century until about A.D. 1470. At this date, the Cakchiquel successfully threw off Quiche suzerainty, foreshadowing the imminent fragmentation of the Quiche state (see Carmack 1968, n.d.a). As subjects of the Quiche, they served as military conscripts in the various campaigns of expansion, first under Gucumatz to the north and east, and then under Quicab in the western highlands and Pacific lowlands (see Xpantzay I–III 1957). Prior to their independence, the Cakchiquel inhabited the mountains of Chichicastenango, southeast of Greater Utatlan, which, in effect, formed a southern wall of the Quiche Basin. But about 1470, after much of the territorial base of the Quiche had shifted to the southwestern volcanic basins (Quezaltenango and Totonicapan), the Cakchiquel departed the Chichicastenango area, relocating on the western edge of the broad Chimaltenango volcanic basin.

The Cakchiquel initiated their own conquest system, which soon rivaled that of the Quiche themselves, and clearly were on the ascendancy when the Spanish abruptly terminated their expansion (cf. Carmack n.d.a.; Fox 1977). Their strength is attested by the repeated unsuccessful attempts of the Quiche to reconquer them; once they completely routed the Quiche and sacrificed their rulers (Xajil 1953:101–3, 109, 113–15; Carmack n.d.a:32–33). Early in their expansion the Cakchiquel subjugated the Akahal of the *tierra caliente-templada* Rio Motagua drainage to the east. Soon thereafter, they conquered much of the piedmont east of the Quiche holdings (Carmack n.d.a:28–29), and in the highlands were in the process of conquering various Pokoman communities when the Spanish arrived (Xajil 1953:99).

Today the Cakchiquel language is divided into western, eastern, and piedmont dialects, which conform to pre-Hispanic political boundaries (Campbell 1971:115, 1976:3,7). The differentiation of Cakchiquel from Tzutuhil, to which it is most closely related, and from Quiche (see Mayers 1966) may stem from political grouping during the Late Postclassic Period. The eastern dialect of Cakchiquel corresponds to the pre-Hispanic Akahal region; it is spoken today in such communities as San Martín Jilotepeque, San Juan Sacatepequez, and San Raimundo. According to Campbell (1976:7), "The Western Cakchiquel area corresponds to the other Cakchiquels, who were earlier Quiche allies and later of the 'kingdom' of Tecpan-Guatemala (Iximiche)," which relates to the modern municipalities of Tecpan, Patzun, Comalapa, Poaquil, Patzicia, Solola, and so on.

Geographically, both the Western and Eastern groups of the Cakchiquel occupied a huge central portion of the highlands, totaling about 3,000 square kilometers; they also held an additional 1,000 square kilometers on the piedmont. This chapter, however, will deal only with the highlands, since no civic centers are yet known for the Cakchiquel-controlled piedmont (cf. Parsons 1969; Borhegyi 1950).

Three broad environmental zones can be distinguished in the areas occupied by the Cakchiquel in the highlands: a high plateau zone, the low Rio Motagua Basin, and the north bank of Lake Atitlan. The Late Postclassic civic centers along Lake Atitlan— namely Ajchel and Tecpan Zolola—have not yet been located or surveyed, so this area will not be discussed further. The plateau area, by far the largest of the three zones, was probably the most populous in pre-Hispanic times, as it is today. It was an eastern province within the Quiche state (Carmack n.d.a:31), and later became the heartland of the Cakchiquel conquest state. Boundaries of the plateau zone, the Cakchiquel territorial base around the Chimaltenango Basin, are set forth in the Xpantzay I (1957:125–27) document. This rolling tableland ranges from 2,000 to 2,500 meters in elevation and is firmly *tierra fria*. Within a 5-by-20-kilometer strip of this rich land today are situated the population centers of Patzicia, Zaragoza, Chimaltenango, San Andrés Itzapa, Paramos, San Miguel Morazan, and Sumpongo. Judging from the immense earlier sites in this area, like Los Cerritos–Tecpan and Chimaltenango, it has been heavily populated since the Preclassic Period. The remaining Cakchiquel-held lands descend in various directions from this high plateau, except for some of the Pokoman communities to the east around the Valley of Guatemala, which were subjugated in late pre-Hispanic times. North of the plateau begins the steady drop to the Rio Motagua Basin, to the west is the Lake Atitlan basin, and to the south lies the piedmont. The Continental Divide separates the northern part of the plateau and the Rio Motagua Basin.

The Rio Motagua runs east-west the length of the Cakchiquel-speaking territory. Its headwater streams in the Chichicastenango Mountains lie at the foot of the earliest Western Cakchiquel centers. To the east, the Rio Motagua flows through the heart of the Akahal territory. Farther east, the Pokoman communities controlled by the Cakchiquel also overlook principal tributaries of the Motagua.

I will begin the discussion of Cakchiquel settlement remains with Iximche, capital of the Cakchiquel after they became independent of the Central Quiche. As an elite group who, when they dwelled at Chichicastenango, lived on the periphery of the Central Quiche heartland, the Western Cakchiquel apparently were heavily influenced by the Central Quiche in sociocultural organization, which is reflected in the settlement patterning and architectural style of Iximche. In some regards, then, the Cakchiquel at Iximche resemble other groups who departed the Quiche heartland in the fifteenth century to settle new territories. The remaining Western Cakchiquel civic centers in this chapter are arranged in reverse chronological order, with the youngest sites first.

Western Cakchiquel

Iximche

As the Contact Period Cakchiquel capital and the first Spanish capital, Iximche has long been of interest to archaeologists and has attracted numerous visitors through the centuries, among them

Francisco Antonio de Fuentes y Guzmán, John Lloyd Stephens, and Alfred P. Maudslay. The Swiss-born archaeologist Jorge Guillemin has been excavating and restoring Iximche since 1959. At this writing about two-thirds of the ruins have been restored.

Topography and Ecology

Iximche occupies a level, elongated plateau, nearly a kilometer and a half long and varying from 200 to 400 meters wide. Three plateau sides are sheer cliffs dropping 100 meters to the Rio Tzaragmajya.

The site, occupying an intermediate position between several broad ecozones, is itself situated in the northwest corner of the large Chimaltenango Plateau. Although these tablelands are for the most part *tierra fria*, with elevations near Iximche between 2,200 and 2,300 meters, they produce a maize surplus (McBryde 1945:75). The region's fertility, however, is occasionally impeded by frost. The Xajil document (1953:101–2) describes a widespread famine brought on by heavy frosts. Counterbalancing this cool habitat are the low warm habitats of the piedmont to the south and the Rio Motagua Basin to the north. Significantly, the Rio Tzaragmajya, which runs through Iximche, is a principal tributary of the Rio Madre Vieja, a major pass to the Pacific piedmont (Map 9). About 500 meters west of the Tzaragmajya at Iximche is another major river, the Xaja, which has cut a second major pass (the Xaja-Coyolate) to the piedmont. Some five kilometers north of Iximche begins the Rio Xecubal-Quisaya, a major tributary of the Rio Motagua running northeast to the Atlantic Ocean. Its location puts Iximche almost on the Continental Divide.

The market at Tecpan, where the post-Hispanic community formed after Iximche was abandoned, has long been important for interregional exchange. Pottery and lime, perhaps the most significant trade commodities produced around Iximche, come from the *aldea* Santa Apolonia, five kilometers north of Iximche (McBryde 1945: 47, 73, Map 15). Tecpan supplies lime to the Atitlan and Chimaltenango plateau regions.

Settlement Description

The settlement of Iximche is divided approximately in half; a southeastern portion comprised mostly monumental architec-

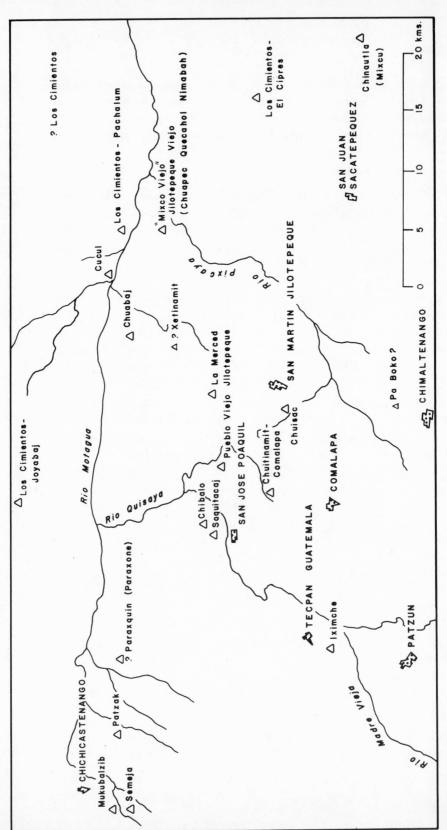

MAP 9 Cakchiquel Area

ture and a northwestern section had mostly low structures and may have been a residential zone. This latter zone has only surface occupational debris today, although it has been trenched by Guillemin. A moat and two massive bulwark structures separate the halves. The moat was originally a little less than 10 meters deep (Guillemin 1967:26). The civic zone appears to be further divided into three approximately equal-sized units (Fig. 31). However, only the first two-thirds of the monumental architecture, nearest the site's entrance, has been cleaned enough to distinguish architectural styles. Masonry is largely of dressed stone blocks covered with lime plaster. Occasionally Guillemin has come across painted murals on temples, altars, and a palace. In excavation, the last building stage, for the most part, has been removed, exposing an earlier, well-preserved facade.

Beyond an open court inside the civic precinct's northern moat and fortification structures is a large civic plaza (Fig. 31A). Two nearly identical temples face each other from opposite plaza sides, oriented 10° north of west and 30° southeast, respectively. The north plaza side is spanned by a long substructure supporting three rooms. Each room had benches against the back and side walls and contained notable amounts of domestic pottery. A southeast-northwest-oriented I-shaped sunken ball court forms a south plaza side. There is a short rectangular structure east of the ball court and two such structures behind the east-facing temple, which may have functioned as flanking structures. The plaza court contains two altars and two low square platforms. Adjoining plaza A is a large, single-story multiroom square palace with an adjacent court complex (Fig. 31B). "It consists of four residences facing onto a rectangular patio with a masonry altar-platform in its center. The interiors of these elaborate houses have built in benches along the walls and, additionally, fireplaces sunk into the room floors" (Guillemin 1967:31). The court adjacent to the palace has three short rectangular structures and what may be a small temple. An interesting low circular structure occupies the center of the court. Taken together, plaza A and palace complex B are separated from groups of civic architecture to the east by a trench and a thick masonry wall that spans the width of the plateau.

The next civic group east, plaza C and an adjoining palace complex, is remarkably similar to the group comprising plaza A and palace complex B. In fact, the spatial positioning of the plaza

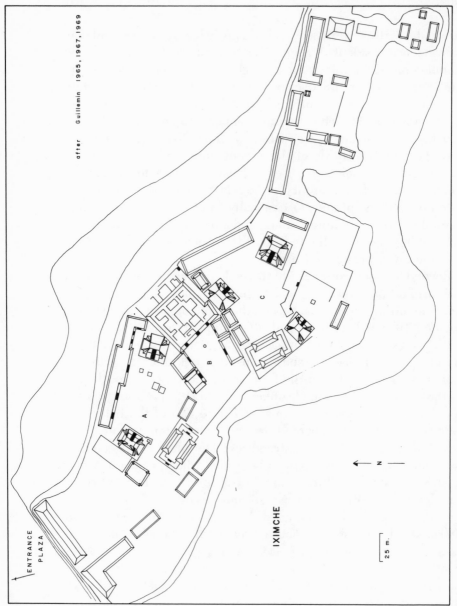

ENTRANCE
PLAZA

A

B

C

IXIMCHE

N

25 m.

FIG. 31 Iximche

structures with respect to one another is virtually the same, except that the three short rectangular structures are all on the west side of plaza C. Also, the plaza configuration is more northwest-southeast in orientation than in plaza A, owing to the land contours of the plaza. The two temples on opposite plaza sides are oriented 298°W and 142°SE. The adjacent palace complex was not yet excavated when I last visited Iximche in 1973. However, a small enclosed court can be made out next to the palace, consisting of a temple (oriented 135°SE) and what probably are short rectangular structures on the north and south court sides.

As of 1973, the remainder of the plateau was just being cleared of brush. However, a third civic plaza exists on the east end of the plateau, in addition, perhaps, to smaller groups.

About 100 meters west of Iximche's west entrance, along the plateau edge, is an elevated group of structures that is not shown in Figure 31 or Guillemin's site maps (1965, 1967, 1969). Just east of this group is a passageway, some 10 meters wide, to the river 100 meters below. This elevated civic cluster comprises a broad square platform between 25 and 30 meters on a side, and an adjoining narrow court with several poorly preserved structures. A small temple, oriented west, faces a rectangular structure on the opposite plaza side. About 35 meters west of this elevated group is a second massive bulwark construction, stretching from the edge of the barranca at least 50 meters across the plateau.

The extent of settlement outside Iximche's principal plateau has not yet been fully reported. In briefly walking the plateaus ringing Iximche, I noted moderate concentrations of ceramics and obsidian on the edges of the nearest plateaus, suggesting occupation. In the narrow zone immediately ringing Iximche are a number of small, steep hills, which may also have contained construction.

Artifacts

Over the years of excavation, Guillemin has recovered a wealth of artifacts including—to name just a few items—ceramic statuary, modeled incensaries, carved jade, and intricately worked gold jewelry. However, a detailed description of ceramics and obsidian has not yet been published. Guillemin (1965:30) briefly lists Iximche's main ceramic types as micaceous ware, Chinautla polychrome, and Fortress white-on-red. In Wauchope's (1970: 224–30) small surface sample, gathered in 1947, the overwhelming majority of sherds—80 percent—are monochrome red and tan. Chinautla polychrome amounted to a minuscule 1 percent of the sample.

Architecture and Settlement Pattern Interpretations

As pointed out above, Iximche is physically segmented into an elite precinct with monumental architecture, and what may be residential or other activity areas of less elite social strata on the two broad terraces just north of the civic zone (Fig. 31), and on the edges of the different plateaus surrounding Iximche. These settlement areas correspond well to Fuentes y Guzmán's map, made sometime before 1690 (in Guillemin 1965, 1967). Briefly, he shows single houses densely packed on the western half of the plateau and what would be terraces north and south of the civic precinct. He also shows two long walls, corresponding to the two massive bulwark constructions. Apparently on the opposite sides of the barrancas surrounding Iximche are small hills called *atalayas*, or fortified lookouts. These correspond in location to the small hills described above. One of these hilltop installations is shown near the entrance to the site in about the same position as the elevated civic group with the large square platform. Considering its location next to the principal causeway and the passageway to the river below, and its large square structure, suggesting an elite residence, this elevated civic group may have been a greeting station. Alternatively, its elevation and location between the fortifications of the bulwark structure and the barranca edge may indicate military functions.

The two parts into which the civic precinct is divided by a thick wall and trench may have been the domains of the two Cakchiquel ruling groups, the Zotzil and Xahil (Guillemin 1967:28). Excavated materials from the palace such as charred corn cobs, weaving instruments, cooking utensils, and copper needles reflect domestic activities; administrative activities are suggested by such items as council benches, nonutilitarian ceramic containers, and ceramic statuary. We may infer that ruling kin groups dwelt here. Excavation of long structures also has revealed evidence of domestic activities, particularly food preparation and consumption. Nonetheless,

benches, an altar, incensarios, and the like suggest ritual and administrative activities. Insofar as long structures form an integral part of
the civic plaza, which was controlled by kin-based social divisions—
the Xahil and the Zotzil—these structures may have been loci for the
chiefly lineages. Along this line of reasoning, Carmack (personal
communication) likens long structures to modern clan houses,
whose walls, significantly, are also lined with long benches.

There are settlement pattern and architectural resemblances
between Iximche and Utatlan. First, looking at locations with
respect to surrounding topography, each is situated near the
western periphery of an expanse of rolling tableland. Second,
both sites occupy flat mesas, with cliff-faced sides rising about
100 meters. Their civic precincts cover areas of about the same
size. Iximche, however, lacks separate elite centers on separate
plateaus, like Chisalin and Ismachi (Guillemin 1969:28). Within
the civic precinct both Iximche and Utatlan appear to have two
major palace complexes. At Iximche each is paired with a civic
plaza whereas at Utatlan both share the only civic plaza. At
Utatlan, moreover, the palace complexes are separated by an
"alley" not unlike the wall and trench in the same position at
Iximche (Stewart 1973). Finally, the excavated palaces at Utatlan
and Iximche are quite similar. Both are large, square, single-story
buildings, with a number of rooms and sunken patios, murals on
adobe walls, and circular plaster pilas. There are resemblances
between the elevated greeting plaza at Iximche and the elevated
civic group of Pakaman at Utatlan. Each has a large, square
platform on a small court arrangement, with a small temple on the
east plaza side and a rectangular structure on the west plaza side
(see Fox 1977). Pakaman, however, is nearly a full kilometer from
Utatlan, whereas the "greeting plaza" at Iximche is about 100
meters in front of the principal ruins. The organization of the two
excavated plazas at Iximche shares the following features with the
main plaza at Utatlan: two temples on opposite sides, facing
roughly east and west; a roughly east-west running I-shaped ball
court constituting the south side of the plaza; a causeway, entering
and leaving the plaza, alongside the ball court; a long structure
spanning the plaza's north side; and two low platforms in the plaza
center. Furthermore, Iximche's plaza floors have three plaster
layers, like Utatlan's plaza floor. This is intriguing, since Iximche
was in existence for only about fifty years, while Utatlan was

occupied for at least 120 years. There are differences between
Iximche and Utatlan in their flanking short rectangular structures,
building orientations differ, and there is no round structure in the
civic plazas at Iximche.

The architectural style of the temples at Iximche exhibits strong
similarities to those at Utatlan. Each has a single broad front
stairway, bordered by wide *talud-tablero* balustrades, which are
similarly proportioned. There are similarly proportioned balustrades on the sides, and four inset terraces on the core. The
west-facing temple in plaza C, however, has a second level set back
from the principal substructure. Nonetheless, the main-level substructure is virtually identical to the three other temples. The
second level has double stairways flanked by *talud-tablero* balustrades, leading to a typical single-room superstructure (see Guillemin 1969:29). Its two levels, each with *talud-tablero* balustrades,
brings to mind the west-facing temple at Utatlan (Awilix). Utatlan's
east-facing temple (Tohil), on the other hand, with stairways on
three sides and a generally steeper sloping facade, differs from the
temples at Iximche.

The slightly different orientations of the east- and west-facing
temples in plazas A and C, perhaps not unlike the slight variance
in orientation between corresponding temples at Utatlan and
Chisalin, seem to indicate that general orientations, notably east
and west, were of basic significance, whereas the slight variations
may be related to distinctions between the groups who occupied
the plazas, or possibly to other factors.

Ethnohistory

The Xajil (1953:97–99) and Tamub (1957:49) documents clearly
record the Cakchiquel departure from Chiavar to Yximche in about
1470. The name *Iximche* may derive from the locally common
ramon tree (Guillemin 1967:25). In the detailed Cakchiquel history
of political events recorded in the Xajil document, certain parts of
Iximche are occasionally mentioned. There are a number of
references to Zotzil and Xahil rulers dwelling within the city. A
third, less powerful group, the Tukuches, also are said to have
dwelt at Iximche prior to their unsuccessful revolt in around 1490
(Xajil 1953:108–9). They may have inhabited the peripheral eastern
portion of the site, beyond plaza C. In any case, the narration of

their actual revolt mentions a deep moat and a bridge near the entrance to the city (Xajil 1953:108). The Xajil document (1953:121) further claims that 2,000 Cakchiquel warriors were provided Alvarado from inside the city. Based on this reference, Carmack (n.d.c:16) calculates the population of the community of Iximche as at least 10,000 residents.

Patzak

The ruins of Patzak are located in the *cantón* Chontala, five kilometers due east of Chichicastenango (Map 9).

Topography and Ecology

The site covers a small (400 by 200 meter) plateau connected by a narrow land bridge to a considsrably larger plateau. The slopes of the plateau drop nearly vertically 100 meters on its west side and well over 300 meters on its east and north sides. At the foot of the site is the Rio Chipaca, which joins the Rio Motagua a little over a kilometer to the north.

The terrain of this region is part of a gradual decline from the eroded mountain range to the south toward the Quiche Basin and Motagua River to the north. At 2,100 meters elevation, Patzak is located between the *tierra fria* habitat of the higher ground to the south and the milder Quiche Basin, beginning only four kilometers to the north. In the surrounding area, cultivation is only practiced on the few small plateau tops in an otherwise rugged and heavily wooded terrain; in fact, there is only one square kilometer of cultivable plateau land adjacent to Patzak. Consequently, the region is relatively sparsely populated today. From Patzak, Santa Cruz del Quiche can be clearly seen, and thus in pre-Hispanic times the temples of Utatlan must also have been visible.

Settlement Description

Though poorly preserved, architecture is evident over much of the plateau. The adjoining plateau also has low terraces, which at other sites often contain house platforms, and a moderate deposition of occupational debris.

Patzak's narrow land-bridge entrance is fortified by two moats about 40 meters apart. Just inside the outer moat is a low wall.

Bordering the second moat and running the width of the plateau is a massive bulwark construction nearly 10 meters high. Spanning the distance between the two moats, immediately south of the causeway, is an elevated area whose structures are beyond recognition.

Three civic plazas, oriented about ten degrees north of west, exist in the center of the plateau (Fig. 32). The southernmost of these, sharing a leveled low ridge with modern farm houses, is in such bad condition that all that can be made out is a temple and flanking structure facing west, and a long structure facing south. At the foot of this hill are two completely enclosed square plazas. Both plaza floors are built up about one meter in height. The plaza in the center has twin temples on a single platform facing west; a single temple on the opposite plaza side faces east. The rectangular platforms are unusually high. No ball court was discernible, although what may have been a ball court range forms a southwest plaza corner (Fig. 32). No clearly discernible temples were evident within the nearly leveled building remains in the third plaza.

The northernmost part of the plateau rests on a slight slope, terminating in two projecting spurs (Fig. 32). Two almost completely mutilated groups of what was once monumental architecture, several broad terraces, and additional foundations of mutilated structures can be detected in this area.

Artifacts

Ceramics at Patzak are largely the thin-walled and red-slipped types (e.g., double-groove rim), typical of the Late phase. In addition, we recovered a "bat" tripod effigy foot and several small side-notched obsidian arrow projectile points.

Architecture and Settlement Pattern Interpretations

The size of the plateau of Patzak in addition to a portion of the adjoining plateau with archaeological remains indicates a settlement of significance. However, its location in the midst of an agriculturally poor area suggests secondary importance for the wider region, especially since the Late-phase power center Utatlan, a close neighbor, is situated in the midst of productive lands of the Quiche Basin.

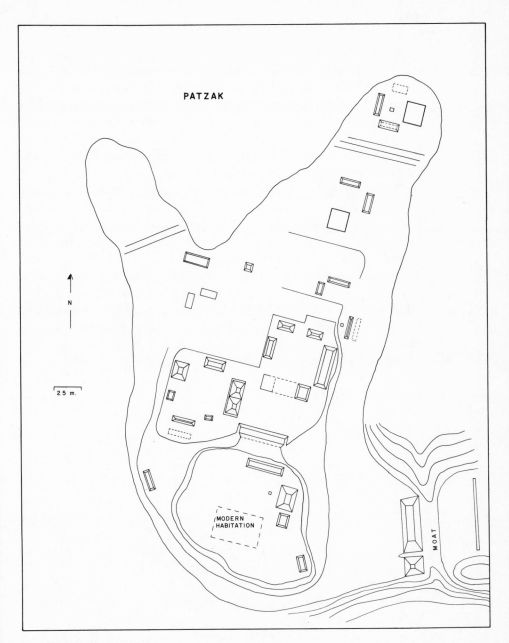

PATZAK

N

25 m.

MODERN
HABITATION

MOAT

FIG. 32   Patzak

Interestingly for a Late-phase site so close to Utatlan, most settlement features at Patzak differ from those associated with the Central Quiche. The site does share some general features with Greater Utatlan, notably its location on a plateau surrounded by cliffs; its elevated entrance plaza (like those at Pakaman or Resguardo); its rectilinear enclosed plazas; its east-west orientation; the presence of temples on the east and west sides of the plaza and dressed stone masonry.

The southernmost plaza, furthermore, has a west-facing single temple with a flanking structure, and a perpendicularly positioned long structure facing south. Except for this last item, Patzak's similarities to Utatlan are those that generally typify the Late phase of Quichean elite communities throughout the Guatemalan Highlands. However, the ceramic types at Patzak are also found at Greater Utatlan. Features that stand in contrast to Utatlan, on the other hand, are more specific, such as the presence of a massive bulwark wall, twin temples, and tall rectangular platforms, and the absence of a long structure in the central plaza. Structures at Patzak are significantly smaller than Contact Period structures at Greater Utatlan, while they are larger than structural remains at nearby Chujuyub.

Ethnohistory

The intermediate Late Postclassic Cakchiquel center Chiavar is thought to have been located near Chichicastenango (Recinos and Goetz 1953:91 n.; Edmonson 1971:235; Carmack n.d.a:21). The Xajil (1953:96–98) and Tamub (1957:47–49) documents further imply that Chiavar was in the vicinity of Utatlan. Patzak is just east of Chichicastenango and within view of Utatlan. Finally, Chiavar was "reached by following the bends of the river" from the eastern highlands (Xajil 1953:89). Patzak is situated on a main headwater river of the Rio Motagua. The Motagua itself is a short distance north of Patzak (Maps 1, 9).

The major Cakchiquel documents (e.g., Xajil 1953:91, 93; Xpantzay II and III 1957:147, 161) say that the Cakchiquel arrived at Chiavar Tzupitakah during the expansion of the Quiche, thought to have begun in the early fifteenth century. We know that Chiavar was abruptly abandoned by the Cakchiquel around 1470 (Xajil 1953:98), although it may have continued to serve as a minor

Quiche ward. Ethnohistoric dating thus correlates well with the relative dating of archaeology, which places Patzak early in the Late phase of the Late Postclassic Period.

Semeja

Topography and Ecology

Semeja is situated one kilometer west of the Los Encuentros–Chichicastenango road, roughly three kilometers north of Los Encuentros (Map 9) and of the Continental Divide. The site consists of a high narrow ridgetop containing mounds, with occupational debris scattered adjacent to the foot of the ridge. The ridgetop is approximately 150 meters long. Its slopes are steep; access is only possible from the less precipitous south slope. They rise 200 meters above the Rio Pixabaj on the east and 140 meters above the Rio Semeja on the west. The rivers parallel each other for about five kilometers, coming together 12 kilometers from Semeja to form the Rio Motagua proper (Maps 1, 9). Semeja is over 2,500 meters in elevation, while surrounding ridges tower to 2,800 meters. The region is firmly *tierra fria*. Cultivation is limited to small hillslope patches, with pine forest covering much of the landscape. The hamlet called Semeja today is located on a small shelf near the ruins. Owing to the exceedingly rugged terrain of the area, much of the local population is concentrated in this relatively level place.

Settlement Description

A linear pattern of three mounds stretches the entire length of the ridgetop, with a fourth low mound on a slightly lower north spur projecting from the center of the ridge (Fig. 33). Except for the easternmost structure, which is built of unworked stone, the other structures are simply earth mounds. A large temple, measuring 25 meters on a side, occupies the west end. The oddly shaped construction in the center, about 2 meters high, is now crisscrossed by several gullies and modern graves.

There is a heavy ceramic deposition on a lower ridge level some 50 meters below the mounds. The same ceramic types continue into the modern hamlet, about 200 meters from the ridgetop, indicating that this area was also inhabited in pre-Hispanic times.

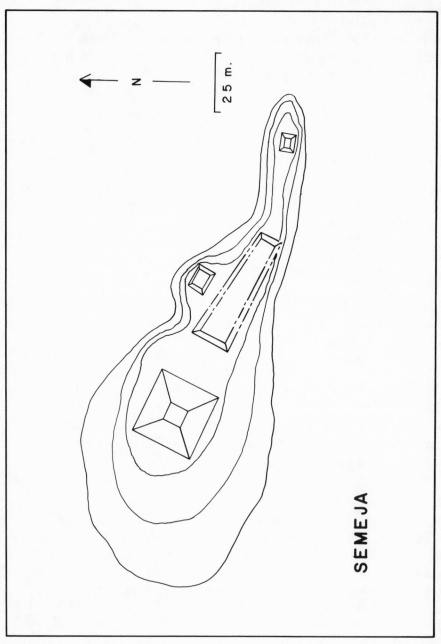

N

25 m.

SEMEJA

FIG. 33 Semeja

The long narrow building shown in Figure 33 between the temple and central structure may be a modern clan house. It is adobe, with benches against three walls and a shrine in the center of its east wall. There are also modern altars on the temple and the eastern structure.

Artifacts

Most decorated ceramics within our moderate-sized sample are unslipped, thin walled, and incised. Plastic decorative modes include varieties of rolled incising, such as slant-incised, slant-tooth incised, dash-line punctate handles, wavy-line incised, and double braid handles (see Fox 1975:199 for illustrations of these patterns). However, a few red-on-buff slipped and painted sherds were also noted. A number of Fortress white-on-red sherds, belonging to a single vessel, were noted on an altar atop the easternmost structure.

Settlement Pattern Interpretations

The linear pattern of three earthen mounds on a steep narrow ridgetop occurs throughout the highlands (at Quiak, Chirijox, Cojonob, Xabaj, and elsewhere) in the Early phase of the Late Postclassic Period. As discussed in earlier chapters, these sites appear to represent local populations prior to the mushrooming of Epi-Toltec sociopolitical systems that marks the beginning of the Late phase. This "local" linear pattern contrasts with the more Mexican-influenced enclosed patterns seen at contemporaneous sites in the Chujuyub area.

The heavy ceramic deposition below the ridge summit suggests a residential population. Within the civic precinct, the temple and altar occupying the east and west ends of the group probably had ideological functions for the local community. Their east and west locations and orientations may have pertained to the sun's daily movement, which was fundamental to many Mesoamerican religions. Perhaps the elongated structure in the center of the linear group functioned like the similar-sized meeting house standing next to it. An absence of stone suggests adobe or wood as the probable construction material.

The next ridgetop north of Semeja, separated from it by the Rio

Semeja, is known as Mucubaltzib. Semeja and Mucubaltzib are often grouped together (along with other sites) in early documentary accounts. However, we could not distinguish ruins at Mucubaltzib, which was covered with forest, in our brief survey there in 1971.

Ethnohistory

Semeja is referred to as Cimajijay or Zimahihay in the Xajil document (Carmack, Fox, and Stewart 1975). Two descriptive references (Xajil 1953:83, 87) seem to match local physiography. Zimahihay, according to the Xajil document (1953:87) is reached by following the bends of the Rio Motagua; on either side of Semeja are headwater streams of the Rio Motagua. Second, the document (Xajil 1953:83) describes annihilating the enemy deep in the mountainous forests at Zimahihay, which describes local ecology.

Cimajijay is listed as one of the first Cakchiquel centers in the highlands, along with Mukubal Sib Bitol Amak, Paraxone, Pantzic, Quejil, and Chi K'ojom. Rather than exhibiting the Mexican-influenced settlement remains we would expect of an early immigrant group from the Gulf Coast, Semeja has a linear pattern and ceramics characteristic of local highland peoples. Thus it would seem to have been a local community that fell under Cakchiquel control, as the above reference indicates. Perhaps the first Cakchiquel were fewer in numbers than some of the other groups, and were absorbed by an already established highland community. Lacking women, according to the Xajil document, they may even have settled among the local population. There is also the possibility that in fact the local warriors were annihilated, as the ethnohistoric reference suggests, and the Cakchiquel immigrants established themselves as rulers at this civic center with remnants of the former community.

Chuitinamit-Comalapa

The mountaintop site Chuitinamit is almost equidistant between the cabeceras San José Poaquil and Comalapa on the nearly impassable automobile road (Maps 1, 9). It overlooks the *aldea* Patzaj in the municipality of Comalapa.

Chuitinamit occupies much of a mountain summit which is

connected to the remainder of the mountain by a narrow neck of land. Its slopes descend steeply on all sides, although not as cliffs. The site commands a panoramic view to the west and north toward the Motagua Basin. At the base of the mountain the Rio Canacya winds around till it feeds into the Motagua, some twenty kilometers away. The surrounding region is rugged, precluding all but limited cultivation on steep hillslopes. The only exception is a small intermontane valley of probably no more than one square kilometer of relatively level terrain at Patzaj, just east of Chuitinamit.

Unfortunately, almost all monumental architecture has been destroyed. In recent years the municipality removed all monumental architecture except a badly mauled rectangular platform, so that the building stone could be used in construction of a nearby bridge. It is clear, however, that the area that once contained the civic structures is small, with space for little more than one Late-phase-sized civic plaza.

Most of the handful of sherds recovered were unslipped. Diagnostic sherds included three red-slipped, three micaceous ware, and one thin-walled cream-slipped ceramic fragment. We also recovered one tapering-base obsidian lance point.

A Late-phase Cakchiquel settlement in the mountains near Comalapa, named Chij-Xot, was conquered by the Spaniards in 1527 (Xajil 1953:126). Since inhabitants questioned in the western part of Comalapa, as well as the municipal officials, knew only of Chuitinamit, it seems likely to have been Chij-Xot.

Eastern Cakchiquel

Chimaltenango

Wauchope (1970:220–24) analyzed a collection of Late-phase ceramics stored in the National Museum marked *Chimaltenango.* The ceramics are largely of the cream- or white-slipped "bright paint" style that is common at Eastern Cakchiquel (Akahal) and Pokoman sites. Ximénez and Fuentes y Guzmán identify the precontact community in the Chimaltenango area as Pa Boko or Pokob. Also, the Chahoma (1956:15) document confirms the location of Chua Poc here. It apparently was a boundary between the Akahal Cakchiquel and the Western Cakchiquel (Ximénez

1929–31; Carmack n.d.a:22). Judging from the apparent lack of the red-slipped ceramics that are characteristic of the Western Cakchiquel, in addition to the ethnohistoric references, Chimaltenango seems to have been an Akahal settlement.

Pueblo Viejo Jilotepeque

The site known locally as Pueblo Viejo within the municipality of San Martín Jilotepeque is 9 kilometers northwest of the cabecera San Martín and 6 kilometers directly east of San José Poaquil. It occupies a narrow spur projecting north as part of the gradual descent toward the Motagua Basin. Pueblo Viejo also sits on an ecological boundary, separating the fertile, rolling *tierra templada finca* lands from the hotter and more arid timber lands that rapidly descend into the Motagua Basin proper. The same Rio Canacya that flows near Chuitinamit-Comalapa flows at the foot of Pueblo Viejo, entering the Rio Motagua 13 kilometers to the north (Map 9).

This narrow spur of land has cliff-faced sides rising between 100 and 120 meters on three sides; it is connected to a large tableland area (Finca El Molino) by a land bridge only a few meters wide that is further fortified by a moat hewn from the bedrock. The spur is just wide enough (about 200 meters on its north end) to accommodate several plazas in a row.

Regrettably, almost the entire civic center has been leveled. The site today is used for milpa cultivation. Only two isolated structures still stand, although rough shapes of other buildings can be distinguished. There apparently were two small civic plazas, back to back, near the spur's northern end. A larger third plaza occupied the tip of the spur, running roughly east-west.

Although architecture was destroyed, surface artifacts were abundant in the soil, freshly turned for cultivation. Of 65 sherds collected, 27 are thin walled micaceous ware. Slipped sherds include light orange (10), with one double-groove rim; dark red (15); and cream or white (13). Nine of the dark-red-slipped sherds have traces of white painted Fortess white-on-red motifs. The only painted cream-slipped sherd has a black spiral motif.

Obsidian remains were more plentiful at Pueblo Viejo than at other sites discussed in this study. We found a multitude of cores, blades, large and small retouched flakes, and so forth. Most notable was the recovery of some 40 projectile points. They conform to three types; a long, narrow lanceolate leaf-shaped point (7–10 x 2–2½ cm); side-notched arrow points (3.5–4.5 x 1.3–1.7 cm) and small, thin rectangular arrow points with indented bases (3.5–4 x 1–1.5 cm). We also recovered two fragmented stone celts and one broken earspool.

The size of the site alone suggests that Pueblo Viejo Jilotepeque was an important Late-phase settlement. The linear or "back-to-back" arrangement of the civic groups is like that at Iximche. The poor preservation, however, prohibits comparison with settlement patterns of the Central Quiche.

An important Contact Period Cakchiquel settlement, Holom Balam, was located north of Iximche in the vicinity of Chij Xot (Chuitinamit-Comalapa). This fits the general location of Pueblo Viejo Jilotepeque (Xajil 1953:126). Moreover, since perhaps three of the four *parcialidades* of Jilotepeque may have dwelled at Jilotepeque Viejo or Chuapec Quecahel Nimabah (the *Titulo Jilotepeque* cited in Carmack 1975, see below), perhaps the fourth *parcialidad* dwelled at contemporaneous Pueblo Viejo Jilotepeque. Chi Holom was known to have been a major Akahal settlement prior to the conquest (Xajil 1953:104). The Xajil document further suggests some association of Western Cakchiquel leaders with this elite community. The presence of Western Cakchiquel at Pueblo Viejo Jilotepeque may explain its similarity in settlement structuring and ceramics to Iximche, while lying within Akahal San Martín Jilotepeque.

Chuisac

Topography and Ecology

Chuisac, two kilometers west of San Martín Jilotepeque, is separated from the latter by a single plateau (Map 9). The site contains two concentrations of civic architecture 700 meters apart—a lower plateau group known as Chuisac Bajo and a ridge-top group, Chuisac Alto—situated at the east and west ends, respectively, of two broad plateaus joined by a fairly narrow point of land (Fig. 34). These three-sided plateaus are surrounded by a single barranca system with steep 80–120 meter sides. Although they are parts of a single landform, both plateau groups are quite

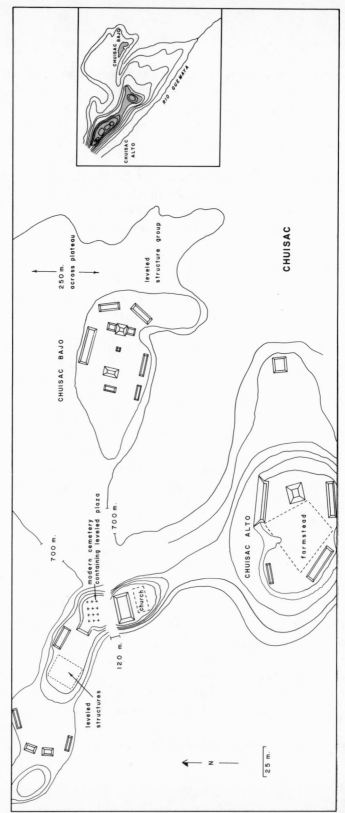

FIG. 34 Chuisac

large. Chuisac Bajo, which is essentially level, measures some 800 by 300 meters (Fig. 34). Chuisac Alto's plateau is larger, approximately one and one-half kilometers long and tapering in width from 400 meters in the south to about 50 meters in the north. The monumental architecture at Chuisac Alto lies along the ridgetop, which rises 50 meters above the plateau and forms the northern portion of this landform as well as its highest point. The Rio Quemaya runs along the west foot of Chuisac, joining the Rio Pixcaya, a main tributary of the Rio Motagua, about five kilometers distant.

A basinlike area of rolling fertile land, which is under milpa cultivation, surrounds Chuisac for about a hundred square kilometers. Varying from 1,200 to 1,900 meters' elevation, it is firmly *tierra templada*. Several nearby early open-valley sites (e.g., Varituc, El Molino) testify to the longstanding importance of this area. The bountiful obsidian outcrops are also a strategic resource here. Immediately east of Chuisac is a major obsidian deposit, with large obsidian boulders.

Settlement Description

A single plaza can be made out at Chuisac Bajo, occupying a slight elevation on the western edge of the plateau. A second civic group, too far mutilated for the recognition of specific structures, lies immediately east on the southernmost tip of the plateau (Fig. 34). Briefly, the intact plaza comprises a small temple with two flanking structures, oriented 292° west; a second temple facing east from the opposite plaza side; an altar equidistant between them; and six rectangular platforms. A two-meter-high long structure forms the plaza's north side, while its south side is formed by two low platforms. Behind the west-facing temple are high, intermediate-sized rectangular platforms at offset angles. The structures now are earth mounds covered with grass. However, numerous pumice fragments and several dressed pumice blocks lying about suggest that they were built with dressed stone masonry.

There are two separate civic clusters on the ridgetop of Chuisac Alto: an acropolis and on the remainder of the ridgetop, a series of rectilinear plazas. The ridgetop's southern end is in the form of a knob, rising about 15 meters above the next portion of the ridge. At the top of this leveled knob is the acropolis plaza. A modern farmstead occupies most of the center of the civic plaza. A temple facing 255° west occupies one end of an enclosed plaza, and its other sides are formed by rectangular platforms ringing the edges of the leveled plaza floor. A high masonry terrace is set into the edge of the knob. Buildings are composed of both slab and dressed pumice blocks, laid in mud mortar and covered with plaster. Several broad terraces, perhaps once containing residences, exist on the west slope below the acropolis. Midway down its east slope is a spur containing another civic plaza, which is now largely destroyed, with farm buildings between the few remaining pre-Hispanic structures. A narrow neck connects the acropolis to the remainder of the ridgetop.

This neck ends with an abrupt 15-meter climb and a slight widening of the ridge. At this point are found a modern church and a large earth mound. The mound, stretching nearly across the width of the ridge, may have restricted access to the remaining ridgetop civic groups, and thus have been defensive in function. Local residents reported that several thin gold objects and a finely worked stone knife were unearthed in this structure. Beyond this mound for a distance of 80 meters the ridge again narrows to about 10 meters wide, at which point it widens to accommodate a civic plaza which is now covered by a cemetery. Pre-Hispanic structures within the cemetery could not be typed. A second badly destroyed group lies immediately to the north (Fig. 34). To the west, down a slight decline, is the final enclosed plaza, with four distinguishable earth structures—twin temples at offset angles facing east, and rectangular platforms on the north and south sides of the plaza. As this is the widest point on the ridgetop proper, it may have been the principal civic plaza within this complex.

Artifacts

A sample of 33 sherds, collected entirely at Chuisac Alto, shows Early-phase modes. One diagnostic thick-walled micaceous sherd has both the distinctive outward-flaring lip and a row of the evenly spaced centimeter-long oval indentations characteristic of the Early Postclassic and the Early phase of the Late Postclassic Period. White, red, or black painted motifs are composed of horizontal, vertical, or intersecting horizontal and vertical bands. White bands are also outlined in black, and bands are incised in panels. Except for the cream-slipped sherds and micaceous ware, the sherds decorated by "plastic" methods are reminiscent of Chuitinamit-Atitlan. Finally, a small ceramic stylized serpent-jaguar was noted.

The ridgetop and slopes were heavily littered with obsidian cores, blades, and particularly obsidian debitage. Two large ovate bifacial tools, made by percussion flaking, were noted, as were four similar-sized (5.5–6 x 3 cm) broad, flat-based projectile points. No small side-notched or basal-indented points, characteristic of the Late phase, were noted.

Architecture and Settlement Pattern Interpretations

The habitable area at Chuisac totals well over one square kilometer, which indicates that Chuisac was an elite community of considerable importance in the Akahal region. Its division into two plateaus connected by a narrow point of land may correspond to social division. They recall similar-sized plateaus at Greater Utatlan, such as Ismachi or Chisalin on adjoining plateaus. The ridge's further segmentation into an acropolis complex and ridgetop group, separated by a narrow neck, terrace, and a bulwark structure, also suggests the presence of more than one social group.

There is some settlement pattern conformity between Chuisac Bajo and the Central Quiche. They share the presence of two temples facing each other from the east and west sides of the plaza; the west-facing temple associated with two flanking structures; and the long structure forming the north side of the plaza; as well as the enclosed, rectilinear plaza arrangement and the plateau location. Moreover, the offset rectangular platforms behind the west-facing temple are comparable to plaza A at Iximche, although differing from Greater Utatlan. Structure sizes at Chuisac Bajo are significantly smaller than at Iximche or Utatlan. Since no ceramics were found at Chuisac Bajo, its construction date cannot be confirmed, although stylistically, its settlement remains suggest a Late-phase date.

Chuisac Alto contrasts considerably in topographic location and plaza pattern with Chuisac Bajo. Its acropolis and ridgetop locations are Early-phase features (cf. Chuitinamit-Atitlan, Chamac, Chutinamit-Sacapulas). Linear arrangements of several small

plazas with correspondingly small-sized structures on steep ridgetops are reminiscent of the Chujuyub sites of Oquin and Cruzche.
Twin temples may occur within this assemblage and would also
date from the Early phase, but they are in poor condition, about
one meter high and composed solely of earth, making their identification tentative.

The acropolis differs in settlement pattern from the ridgetop
group, and its structures are larger and better preserved. A hole in
the temple shows its early slab contruction under later construction
of dressed stone blocks. The acropolis and the ridgetop belong to
different Late Postclassic time periods, but proximity would
suggest that the acropolis is contemporary with the remainder of
the ridgetop and was simply a main plaza like those at Chuitinamit-Atitlan and Chutinamit-Sacapulas. Unlike the latter acropolis
sites, however, its west-facing temple is in an intermediate position
between the plaza side and center. Nonetheless, as at other acropolis sites, there are numeorus broad terraces along its slopes. In
overall arrangement Chuisac Alto and Bajo parallel the relationship
of Chuitinamit-Atitlan and nearby Xikomuk (see Lothrop [1933]).
For example, Chuisac Alto's acropolis, like Chuitinamit, is high
and about 700 meters from the plateau complex. Moreover, the
two acropolises differ dramatically in plaza pattern from the plateau
groups. Chuisac Bajo, like Xikomuk, is situated on a broad, level
plateau with a civic configuration not unlike those of Greater
Utatlan (cf. Lothrop 1933: diagram of Xikomuk). As noted above,
ceramics at Chuitinamit-Atitlan are quite similar to those from
Chuisac.

Ethnohistory

Chuisac is firmly within Akahal territory, as delineated in the
Titulo Chahoma. In giving directions to the pre-Hispanic Akahal
settlements, the *Titulo Chahoma* (1956:15) describes the location
of a site called Ahquemaya that may be the same as Chuisac.
According to this document, it is reached by following the Rio
Pixcaya upstream. At the juncture with the road to Chimaltenango,
one proceeds up a primary tributary leading to Chuisac. The river
flowing past Chuisac today is called the Rio Quemaya, and thus
supports Chuisac's identification in the *Titulo Chahoma*. Chuisac's
identification is further supported by location in the *Titulo*

Chahoma of the nearby landmarks of Parituc (Chuisac is in the *aldea* Varituc) and the mountain Sarima (IGN, Tecpan-Guatemala). Ahquemaya is also associated with a second settlement, Chiratjamut (Chahoma 1956:15). Chuisac's two parts may correspond to these two names. Alternatively, the separation of Chuisac Alto into an acropolis group and a group of rectilinear plazas may correspond to these two divisions, or to occupation by the Central Quiche or Western Cakchiquel.

The Xajil document (1953:80) mentions that the Akahal "dawned" by themselves, far away from the other Cakchiquel groups. Chuisac, a sizable Early-phase settlement, would appear to have been the first Akahal center. An early Akahal capital, Ochal, is mentioned often in the Cakchiquel documents. An area just east of Chuisac today is still known as Ochal. Indeed, Ochal is described in the Xajil document (1953:89) as having a mild climate, as does the area around Chuisac, and as "divided"; Chuisac is segregated into several distinct parts. Since the Western Cakchiquel were said to have been at Ochal among the Akahal (Xajil 1953:89), the several rectilinear plazas at Chuisac Alto may have been built by the Western Cakchiquel during the Early phase, Chuisac Bajo during the Late phase.

Jilotepeque Viejo ("Mixco Viejo")

The large, well-known site known incorrectly as Mixcu, hence "Mixco Viejo," is situated in the northeastern corner of Cakchiquel-speaking San Martín Jilotepeque (Maps 1, 9). The site was apparently misnamed first by Fuentes y Guzmán, who visited it in the seventeenth century, and the misnomer has continued to this day. It has subsequently been renamed Jilotepeque Viejo (Carmack 1975), since it was the principal Akahal community at Spanish contact from which the municipality of San Martín was formed (Chahoma 1956). Karl Sapper and Ledyard Smith have made maps of the ruins. Beginning work in 1954, a French team under Henri Lehmann had restored almost the entire site by 1973, and consequently it has become a major tourist attraction.

Topography and Ecology

The ruins of Jilotepeque Viejo are strung along a fairly narrow plateau top. Its cliff-faced sides are steep, rising 80 or 90 meters from the surrounding ravines. One kilometer east of the site is the large river, the Pixcaya, which rushes to the broad Rio Motagua, two kilometers to the north.

Between 800 and 900 meters in elevation, the elite center occupies an arid *tierra caliente* habitat. This is the lowest center known in the highlands. Cultivation in the immediate environs is restricted to the banks of the Rio Motagua and some of the nearby mesatops. The highlands rise abruptly above the Rio Motagua's north bank and less than 10 kilometers to the south. From these steep basin walls Jilotepeque Viejo can be distinctly seen in its eroded basin floor.

Settlement Description

There are more than 90 structures in 12 groups, ranging from large civic plazas to groups of two or three structures (Smith 1955; Navarrete 1962:7). There is, we should note, some discrepancy in building orientations between Smith's (1955) and Lehmann's (1968) maps. My drawing (Fig. 35) follows Smith's diagram of the entire site, while building orientations presented below are taken from Lehmann's larger-scale maps. The four principal plazas are elevated at intervals in a line along the curved plateau top (Fig. 35). Construction is almost entirely of cut and shaped schistose slabs. Except for plaza C, few of the building surfaces today show signs of plaster (cf. Smith 1965:64).

Group A is the northernmost civic plaza, nearest the Rio Motagua. It consists of a temple in the center surrounded by four intermediate-sized rectangular platforms situated so that they follow the contours of the leveled plateau surface. The plaza's entrance is delineated on the east by an I-shaped ball court aligned just 2° off the north-south magnetic axis. On its west flank is a long structure, nearly equal in length to the ball court (fig. 35). The temple is oriented 230° west, with double stairways, a single-room superstructure, straight *talud* balustrades (no *tablero*), and four inset terraces rising against its core. The ball court's playing walls have vertical upper moldings, with inset, nearly vertical lower playing walls. The intermediate-sized rectangular platforms have pronounced *talud-tablero* balustrades and an indented wall overhung by a molding along the back and side walls. A depression

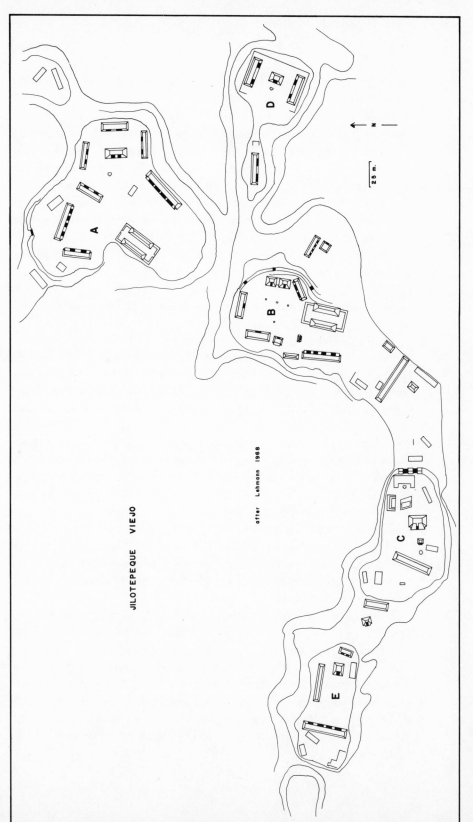

JILOTEPEQUE VIEJO

after Lehmann 1968

N

25 m.

A

B

C

D

E

FIG. 35   Jilotepeque Viejo

about 50 meters long separates plaza A from the next civic group along the plateau.

Plaza B is situated on a nearly circular elevation ringed by a 4-meter-high retaining masonry terrace. Three sets of stairways lead here from plazas A, D, and C2, respectively. Plaza B has twin temples on the east side, oriented just off the west cardinal point (272°); a single temple oriented toward the east cardinal point (93°); three intermediate-sized rectangular platforms; and an entrance bordered by a ball court oriented 2° off north-south and an equal-sized long structure (Fig. 35). The twin temples, sharing a single platform, have straight *talud* balustrades (no *tablero*) and five inset terraces. The I-shaped sunken ball court has typically Quichean *talud-tablero* playing walls coated with plaster. A finely carved slab ball-court marker was recovered here, depicting a human face protruding from the open mouth of a highly stylized serpent (Guillemin 1958:22; Lehmann 1968:52).

Plaza C is the highest point at Jilotepeque Viejo. It is set off from civic groups farther east along the plateau by a massive masonry terrace, rising about six or seven meters, with two broad *talud-tablero* balustraded stairways. The plaza arrangement consists of a temple facing toward the west cardinal point (267°), a long structure opposite it, and two altars in the center of the court. Both the temple and the long structure have thick plaster surfaces. The temple shows two building phases—an early facade with double stairways bordered by three pronounced *talud-tablero* balustrades, and what is apparently the last front, with a single broad stairway and straight *talud* balustrades (i.e., lacking a *tablero*).

Plaza E, separated from plaza C by a trench, is similar in layout to plaza C. It also has a temple facing west, a long structure on its east side, and short rectangular platforms on its north and south sides.

Terraces below the monumental architectural groups exhibit "an abundance of sherds, broken manos and metates, obsidian points and flake blades, stone axes, and flint chips [which] indicate that this may have been a living area where houses of perishable materials once stood" (Smith 1955:63–64). In contrast to these seemingly single-room house structures, Navarrete (1962:7) briefly makes note of a single large, square elite residential structure, with 70-meter sides, apparently in front of a plaza, but does not give its exact location.

Artifacts

The sizable ceramic collection assembled by the French, totaling over 4,000 sherds, is described by Navarrete (1962), and summarized by Wauchope (1970:220–21). The ceramic types and frequencies are as follows: micaceous ware (27.6 percent), "thick sandy" ware (29.4 percent), Chinautla polychrome (18.7 percent), "fine sandy" ware (11.3 percent), red slip (4 percent), white-on-red (2.3 percent), red-on-bay (2.1 percent), red-on-white (1.3 percent), and so forth (Navarrete 1962:9). Ceramics from Jilotepeque Viejo are further distinguished by

> (a) the white-outlined red-on-tan style of polychrome, which is distinct from other polychrome styles; (b) the large number of recurring polychrome design motifs; (c) the many variations of the serpent motif. (Wauchope 1970:220)

In fact, the serpent motif is common here on white-on-red, red-on-white, and Chinautla polychrome types, suggesting a local origin for them all. This open-mouthed, highly conventionalized serpent (cf. Navarrete 1962: Fig. 16) is also seen in the sculptured ball-court marker, although lacking a human face between its jaws. The Fortress white-on-red, with curvilinear motifs, and the lack of the early panel-incised wares suggest that Jilotepeque Viejo was a Late-phase settlement. The low percentage of red-slipped ceramics in general, contrasting with Western Cakchiquel and Quiche sites, suggests that not many ceramics were actually imported from the Cakchiquel at Iximche, or from the Central Quiche at Greater Utatlan before Cakchiquel independence. Finally, the large amount of micaceous ware here and in the general area leads Navarrete (1962:27) to believe that this type was also produced locally.

Architecture and Settlement Pattern Interpretations

Jilotepeque Viejo was a large Late-phase elite community, spread over at least two-thirds of a square kilometer, and about one kilometer in length. House platforms packed between civic groups and heavy occupational debris on the terraces further indicate a substantial population. Plaza B may have been a locus for the principal group within this center, since it is located near the site's geographic center, it has stairways or entrances leading from groups bordering it on all sides, and it has the largest plaza with the most structures.

Based on plaza patterns, two groups can be distinguished among the principal plazas: plazas A and B on the east end and plazas C and E on the west end. The first two plazas have many more structures and are enclosed. Moreover, both have the twin temple and the temple with twin stairways. Plaza A has four intermediate-sized rectangular platforms; plaza B has three. In both, the I-shaped ball court and long structure border either side of the plaza's entrance, and the ball courts share exact north-south orientation. Both plazas have curved, elevated floors, and both show an apparently sparse use of plaster (except in the ball court in plaza B). On the other hand, plaza A's temple is in the center of the court, while temples within Plaza B are on the sides of the plaza. By comparison, plazas C and E both comprise a temple facing a long structure, and a short low rectangular platform on the plaza's south side. Both plazas also lie on roughly rectangular elevated platforms, contrasting with the more circular platforms of plazas A and B. It is noteworthy, moreover, that the temple in plaza C has full *talud-tablero* balustrades in an earlier building phase and perhaps the last one, reminiscent of Iximche as well as Greater Utatlan.

The dichotomy in plaza patterns and architectural styles suggests strong intracommunity differences. Insofar as the four principal civic plazas of the twelve or so civic groups are physically isolated from each other by elevated masonry platforms, moats, and depressions, they may represent autonomous sociopolitical divisions within the elite community. The settlement may represent a regional capital comprised of allied social groups. However, Navarrete's statement concerning the occurrence of only one palacelike structure suggests that rulers came from just one of these groups. The remaining residential structures at the site appear to be small, single-room houses (see Lehmann 1968:41, illustration of house structures).

Differences from the Central Quiche in architectural style and settlement patterning are so pronounced as to suggest little influence from the Quiche Basin. For example, Jilotepeque Viejo's largest plazas (A and B) are elevated and more circular in their enclosure, tending to follow the plateau's contours, unlike the typically Central Quiche enclosed rectilinear plazas. All the temples—except those in plazas C and E—have double front stairways and five inset terraces (i.e., tiers). The two I-shaped ball courts are oriented north-south, rather than tending toward the east-west cardinal points. With its 12 civic groups and four main plazas, Jilotepeque Viejo further differs from Quiche sites, which generally have one or two main civic plazas. We may infer that the nature of social organization in these two regions was probably different. Jilotepeque Viejo, however, is as large as Late-phase Quiche communities, and also is situated on a low, cliff-faced plateau.

Yet there is notable correspondence in architectural style and settlement patterning between plazas C and E and the Late-phase Central Quiche and the Iximche Cakchiquel. These plazas are, for example, basically rectilinear, the structures have heavy plaster coats, and the single temples, on the east plaza side facing west, have abrupt *talud-tablero* balustrades on the earlier building phase. With a long structure opposite a west-facing temple on an elevated platform, these plazas resemble both the military or "greeting" plaza just outside Iximche and Pakaman at Greater Utatlan. As an alternative hypothesis, perhaps these two plazas represented militaristic administrators from Iximche. This hypothesis correlates with political domination known from ethnohistory.

Ethnohistory

Such Cakchiquel chronicles as the Chahoma (1956), Xajil (1953), and Xpantzay (1957) documents refer to the Cakchiquel inhabitants of this general region as the Akahal. Late-phase Mixcu was a Pokoman settlement (Xajil 1953:99, 110) as is modern Mixco. Carmack (1975) has brought to light colonial records that describe Late-phase Mixcu's location as the same as the ruins of Chinautla, which, briefly, are 30 kilometers in a line southeast of Jilotepeque Viejo, but only about 10 kilometers east of post-Hispanic Mixco (Carmack and Fox n.d). Jilotepeque Viejo is identified as Chaupec Quecahol Nimaabah.

The Chahoma document (1956:15) gives the general location of Jilotepeque Viejo as Chaupec Quecahol Nimaabah, along the Rio Pixcaya. It is thus located a short distance upstream from two other

settlements near the Rio Motagua (possibly Cucul and Los Cimientos; see Map 9). The Chahoma document contends that the
next settlement upstream, Ruyaalxqueh, is situated where the next
two tributary rivers enter the main channel of the Rio Pixcaya.
Accordingly, eight kilometers above Jilotepeque Viejo two rivers
join the Rio Pixcaya, one of which still carries the name Ryualpat
(IGN, San Juan Sacatepequez). Incidentally, this last settlement may
also be the Akahal settlement known as Ralabal Iq (Xajil 1953:106).
Chuapec Quecahol Nimaabah is evidently situated between these
topographic landmarks, where Jilotepeque Viejo is today.

Chuapec Quecahol Nimaabah was established early in the Late
phase (Xajil 1953:89) as an Akahal center. Like much of the Akahal
territory, however, it, came under the yoke of Iximche in the latter
part of the Late Phase (Xajil 1953:104–6).

Cucul

Topography and Ecology

Cucul is three kilometers as the crow flies, or a six-kilometer
walk, from the *aldea* of Pachalum, Joyabaj (Map 9). The site is
located on a high ridgetop rising a steep 200 meters above the
Motagua and 100 meters above the El Anono River. The ridgetop
is nearly one kilometer long, but only 40 meters across at its widest
point.

Varying from 900 to 1,100 meters in elevation, lands bordering
Cucul to the north are firmly *tierra caliente*. Citrus fruits, mangos,
and bananas, as well as maize, are primary crops in this area. An
immense unfortified site, halfway to Pachalum, attests to the area's
favorable conditions as well as its prior existence as a population
center. The resources of the Rio Motagua are available on Cucul's
south side.

On the hill rising north from Cucul are large marble boulders,
indicative that lime could have been produced here. In the Rio El
Anono's bed, at the foot of the site, are boulders of greenstone
similar to that used in the small greenstone celts. Within 10
kilometers northwest of the site are also large deposits of this
green durable rock. Cucul may have been a focal point in the
procurement of this material for the celts ubiquitous in southern
Mesoamerica. This little-known region of Baja Verapaz is also

thought to have contained pre-Hispanic jade and serpentine deposits (Foshag 1957).

Settlement Description

Settlement remains, stretching the length of the narrow ridge-top, are separated into two zones—an elevated civic precinct covering the north end of the ridgetop, and low, poorly preserved platforms, probably residential structures, covering the ridgetop's longer southern part. The point of separation between these two zones is marked by a narrowing of the ridgetop and two successive moats spanning its narrow (15-meter) width. Immediately beyond this point is a steep 40-meter ascent to the civic precinct, where the monumental public architecture is concentrated. Masonry here is almost entirely of shaped schistose slabs.

Beyond a massive bulwark structure, the first structure encountered on the elevation is a small court where the causeway enters from the Rio El Anono below (Fig. 36). To the north of this court are two civic plaza groups. The southern plaza has a temple on its south side, oriented about 330°NW, an altar in the center, and two intermediate-sized rectangular structures. The second plaza comprises a northwest-facing temple in the center, completely enclosed by four rectangular platforms. The temple has a single broad stairway flanked by slightly overhanging *talud-tablero* playing walls with "benches" extending into the playing alley. A short distance beyond the ball court is another moat, marking the site's north entrance.

Artifacts

Most sherds from our small sample are thick walled and unslipped; 15, however, have red slip, and 7 are thin-walled micaceous ware. Three sherds are a polychrome type with a broad, dark red painted zone covering a white slip and white designs outlined in black. There is also one mold-made sherd, like those seen at Utatlan and Zaculeu (e.g., Wauchope 1970:116). However, none of the sherds more typical of the Quiche or Iximche Cakchiquel, such as Fortress white-on-red and double-groove rims, were seen at Cucul. Several obsidian blades and one broken greenstone celt were also collected.

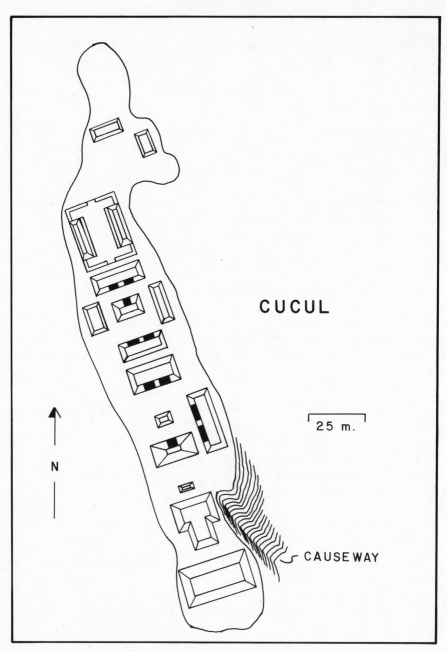

CUCUL

25 m.

N

CAUSEWAY

FIG. 36 Cucul

Architecture and Settlement Pattern Interpretations

There are notable differences in plaza arrangements between Cucul and Utatlan and Iximche. At Cucul the temple is in the center of the plaza and lacks inset terraces. The angle of *talud-tablero* balustrades is different at Cucul, as is the north-south orientation of the temple and the ball court. Moreover, structures at Cucul are significantly smaller than their counterparts at Iximche and Utatlan. The temple's balustrades are considerably closer in angle and proportions to those at Jilotepeque Viejo, which lacks the *tablero* altogether.

The high ridgetop topography of Cucul differs from that of most highland Late-phase Quichean sites, which are usually located either on cliff-ringed plateaus or on lofty mountaintops. However, its well preserved structures and polychrome ceramics suggest a Late-phase date, although earlier construction is a distinct possibility.

Los Cimientos-Pachalum

Topography and Ecology

Los Cimientos can be reached by a two-and-one-half-kilometer walk from Pachalum, Baja Verapaz, or by fording the Rio Motagua, just above Jilotepeque Viejo, and climbing the 500-meter escarpment rising from the river's north bank to the ruins. From its south side, Los Cimientos is situated on a pinnacle 500 meters straight up from the Rio Motagua. Fifteen-meter-high cliffs top this lofty massif on the site's south and east sides. On the north side, however, begins rolling tableland at about the same elevation as Los Cimientos. The site rises slightly above this plain, separated from it by a small barranca and several masonry terraces. The Rio Motagua Basin can be said to terminate with this sudden climb to between 1,200 and 1,300 meters elevation, and the *tierra templada* highland habitat once again resumes.

Settlement Description

The site consists of two levels: a large main plaza on a lower level and a small hilltop group, 40 meters above the first level (Fig. 37). Unfortunately, we only had time to survey the main

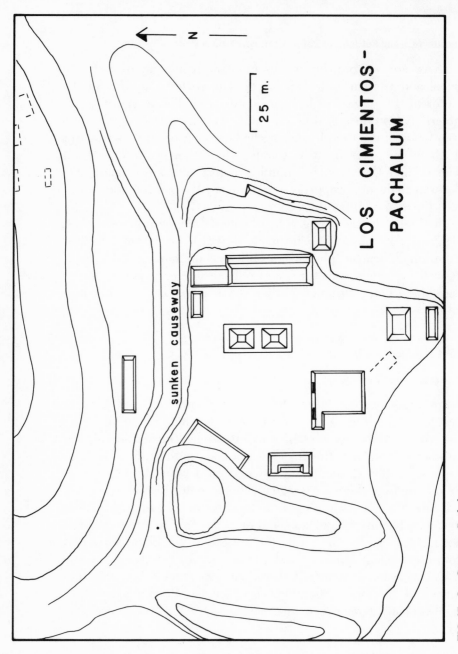

FIG. 37 Los Cimientos-Pachalum

plaza. Our guide said that there is a mound on the small hilltop, and the IGN topographic map shows the hilltop within the site.

The main plaza is in very bad condition. Most of the structures are little more than piles of rubble, although a few are well enough preserved to reveal stairways and *talud-tablero* balustrades. The structures are situated around small rock cliffs, between one and four meters high, that interlace the site. Several platforms integrate large boulders and natural rock outcrops with slab masonry facing. As at neighboring sites, masonry is primarily shaped schistose slabs, although a number of dressed pumice and limestone blocks are strewn about the site.

Most of the structures within the plaza are oriented to the cardinal points. The twin temples, on a single platform in the center of the plaza, are oriented directly east-west. The remaining structures, which form the plaza sides, are various-sized rectangular platforms. A straight sunken causeway with rock outcrop walls enters the main plaza from the adjacent tableland. What may be small temples are set off from the main plaza on the site's south edge.

Artifacts

A few micaceous ware sherds and one small obsidian arrow projectile point were noted.

Architecture and Settlement Pattern Interpretations

The extent of the ruins delineated by our survey and shown on the government topographic map indicates that Los Cimientos was a fairly sizable settlement. It is far smaller, however, than neighboring Jilotepeque Viejo. The few artifacts suggest a Late-phase occupation, although Early-phase construction is a distinct possibility. Indeed, the spatial relationship of the hilltop plaza, with a temple in the center, to the lower group that we surveyed is reminiscent of the Early-phase acropolis sites in the warm riverine basins throughout the highlands. Since some of the site was not surveyed, and since the remains were in such poor condition, architectural comparisons are far from conclusive. However, a few observations are possible. In addition to similarity with other Akahal sites, which will be discussed in the conclusions of this chapter, Los Cimientos manifests a number of settlement pattern features common to Pokoman sites, such as twin temples in the center of the plaza; plaza sides comprised solely of rectangular platforms; east-west orientation; and the absence of a ball court.

Located high above the Motagua Basin yet level with the adjacent tableland, Los Cimientos simultaneously has a riverine habitat, like the acropolis sites; a mountaintop situation, like some Pokoman sites; and a plateau location, like many Late-phase Quichean sites. It also occupies the highest topographic position on the north rim of the Motagua Basin. From Los Cimientos, Jilotepeque Viejo can be clearly seen on the basin floor below, as can Cucul, about two and a half kilometers upriver. Though these three sites are close, they may have had different adjacent agricultural tracts, reminiscent of the closely spaced Sacapulas centers. Los Cimientos is adjacent to the high *tierra templada* tablelands, Cucul lies near the confluence of three low river valleys, and Jilotepeque Viejo seems to dominate the basin floor and the fertile lands on the banks of the Motagua and Pixcaya rivers, on the west side of the Motagua Basin.

Ethnohistory

Although Los Cimientos resembles Pokoman sites, it lies near the Akahal Cakchiquel heartland. Two Akahal settlements, Choy Chichijalcat and Xalcat Sacmychao-Sacruachiachocom, are named in the Chahoma (1956:17) document as existing near the confluence of the Motagua and Pixcaya rivers. Los Cimientos and Cucul are in this general area. In addition, Carmack (personal communication) has data indicating that Los Cimientos was the pre-Hispanic center for San Juan Sacatepequez.

Los Cimientos–El Ciprés

Los Cimientos is a small site in the *aldea* El Ciprés of San Raymundo (Maps 1, 9). Shook (n.d.:279 24, 1952:13) surveyed it in 1941. The site diagram (Fig. 38) is drawn after Shook's map, which, regrettably, includes no scale. I tried unsuccessfully to locate the site in 1973, but the town and road have been relocated since Shook's visit, and none of the residents of El Cipres to whom I talked knew of it.

Shook shows one plaza group on a leveled hilltop containing

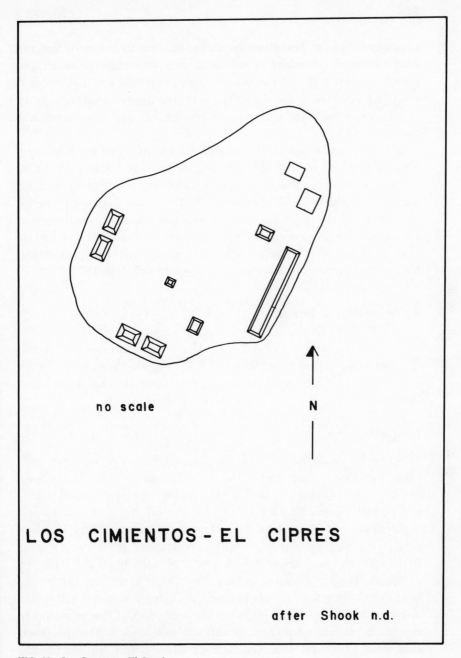

no scale

N

LOS CIMIENTOS - EL CIPRES

after Shook n.d.

FIG. 38   Los Cimientos-El Ciprés

masonry terraces. The ruins comprise at least 10 mounds, varying from two to five meters in height. The plaza exhibits the unique feature of two sets of twin temples, on perpendicular plaza sides, oriented southeast and northeast respectively. Masonry is of shaped schistose slabs and dressed pumice blocks, covered with "a poor lime plaster."

Los Cimientos is near the Akahal Cakchiquel-Pokoman border. The Cakchiquel stronghold Jilotepeque Viejo is situated about 20 kilometers due northwest of Los Cimientos, and Pokoman Chinautla Viejo (Mixcu) is 13 kilometers to the south. Judging from the placement of the twin temples on the plaza side, Los Cimientos seems to have been an Akahal site. Nearby Chuarrancho, which is also an *aldea* of San Raymundo, was apparently the Late-phase Cakchiquel center of Chibatany (Kelsey and Osborne 1939:273).

Early Postclassic Period

We located and surveyed four Early Postclassic sites in the Eastern Cakchiquel area, which I will describe briefly to survey cultural developments immediately preceding the Late Postclassic Period.

La Merced

Seven kilometers north of San Martín Jilotepeque, in a lush *tierra templada* zone above the Motagua Basin, this potentially defensive low ridgetop site (Map 9) consists of two enclosed plazas at opposite ends of the ridge, separated by a narrow neck approximately 100 meters long. The westernmost plaza has five structures: two intermediate-sized rectangular platforms, a long structure, and an unusual high, oval temple together form an irregular-shaped plaza around an altar in the center of the plaza. The only other known occurrence of a high oval temple is at Xolchun-Sacapulas. The plaza on the east end of the ridgetop is rectilinear and oriented east-west. Its east and west sides each consist of a temple. A rectangular structure forms the south side and its north side consists of a sunken rectangular ball court, oriented east-west. In the center of the ball court we unearthed a large slab sculpture depicting a human face protruding from a serpent's mouth. This appears to be in the same style as the sculpture unearthed in the ball court at Jilotepeque Viejo—a fine-featured human face and a flat, highly conventionalized serpent head. Ceramics recovered at La Merced fall into two broad categories—an unslipped orange paste ware and a thin-walled, cream-slipped, unpainted ware.

Chuabaj

Located on a high mountaintop fifteen kilometers north of San Martín, the huge site of Chuabaj (Map 9) overlooks the Rio Motagua 700 meters below and a kilometer and a half north. Worked obsidian and some ceramics litter sections of its two-square-kilometer area. Its architecture has been leveled, with the exception of a badly mutilated long structure and temple, suggesting a "Mexican" plaza pattern of some sort.

Saquitacaj

This potentially defensive hilltop site is about four kilometers north of San Jose Poaquil. Its structures now are low earth mounds, forming a rectangular plaza with a temple in the center. A sculpture of the familiar "human face in a serpent's jaw" was reported by both the town officials and the residents of Saquitacaj to be from the site. It now sits in front of the *alcaldia* in the cabecera of San Jose Poaquil.

Chibalo

Just 500 meters north across the ravine from Saquitacaj is this second single-plaza hilltop site; their proximity suggests that both may once have been part of the same community. The hilltop is elongated, surrounded by steep slopes and, on one side, a high cliff. Its rectangular plaza is perfectly symmetrical, with two equal-sized temples facing each other from' the north and south sides, and two equal-sized long structures forming the east and west sides, all with orientations just off the cardinal points.

Additional Sculpture

Two other "serpent mouth–human face" sculptures are known in the area occupied by the Eastern Cakchiquel during the Late Postclassic Period. A large serpent with a squared head and tenoned body is set into cement in the central plaza of the cabecera Comalapa today. Its human face is realistically portrayed, while the serpent, which is covered with scales (or feathers), is highly conventionalized. This piece was unearthed in the canton Tasbalaj, which reportedly does not have mounds. A squared "serpent mouth–human face" sculpture is also known from Patzun (Miles 1965a:270, Fig. 19c), but its specific provenience is not given.

At Guaytan, at least 60 kilometers down the Rio Motagua from the Cakchiquel border, another "serpent mouth–human face" sculpture was unearthed in a ball court (Smith and Kidder 1943: Fig. 60). Guaytan's civic precinct is on a low terraced hilltop, in a side valley 2 kilometers north of the Rio Motogua.

Conclusions

Every site considered in this chapter (except Iximche) overlooks the Motagua River or one of its tributaries. The presence of the Motagua in the midst of Cakchiquel territory unified these eastern Quichean peoples from early times, and they developed in close interaction with each other. The documents tell of strong ties between the early Cakchiquel along the headwaters of the Motagua, near Chichicastenango, and the early Akahal and Rabinal Quiche within the river's eastern drainage. The three tributary systems of the Motagua—the Rio Pixcaya, the Rio Canacya, and the Chichicastenango headwater streams—were the focal points for settlement and development of three Cakchiquel groups. The Akahal settlements were strung out along the Pixcaya; the earliest Western Cakchiquel centers were located along the headwaters of the Motagua. The Canacya seems to have been a frontier more or less between the Western Cakchiquel and the Akahal. It should be kept in mind, nonetheless, that the Cakchiquel, at a later time, also came to control considerable territory on the north bank of Lake Atitlan and on the Pacific piedmont. Iximche, the Late-phase Western Cakchiquel capital, was only five kilometers south of the headwaters of the Canacya.

The location of Iximche a short distance south of the Motagua watershed reflects the Late-phase expansion of Cakchiquel territorial holdings to the south to include the Chimaltenango Plateau and the piedmont and northern Atitlan lands, as well as their traditional base along the Rio Motagua. Iximche is thus strategically situated in the center of the preconquest Cakchiquel state, on two river passes to the piedmont and near the Continental Divide. Located near such ecologically diverse regions as the *tierra fria* plateau country, the immense highland lake, and channels to the warm piedmont and Motogua lands, it is ideally situated to direct a conquest-state economy.

The large number of Akahal sites along the Rio Pixcaya (see Chahoma 1956) may be related to the abundant resources along the river, notably the obsidian deposits. Late Postclassic as well as Early Postclassic sites here have extremely heavy deposition of worked obsidian. Moreover, on the north side of the Motagua, opposite the mouth of the Pixcaya, are deposits of greenstone, marble, limestone, jade, and serpentine, as well as a region suitable for feather procurement.

The cultural affinities reflected in similarity of settlement patterning are borne out by known historic relationships. For example, ties can be discerned between Jilotepeque Viejo and Patzak (Chiavar) as well as between Patzak and Iximche, that correlate with movements described in the Xajil and Xpantzay documents.

The main plazas at Patzak and Jilotepeque Viejo share a number of features of spatial organization. They have similar-size twin temples, both on single platforms, and built in a similar style, lacking side stairways or balustrades (in contrast, for example, to buildings at Comitancillo). Both have twin temples on the plaza side facing west and a single temple on the side facing east. Both have slightly elevated plazas in the geographic center of site. Finally, the next plaza south at both sites is elevated and more typically Quichean, with long structure and temple in a perpendicular west-oriented relationship.

Patzak, however, lacks Jilotepeque Viejo's ball court–long structure unit. Moreover, plazas at Patzak are close together, like plazas at Central Quiche sites, while those at Jilotepeque Viejo are physically segregated from one another. Although the Xajil document (1953:89) mentions a move of some Cakchiquel rulers from the Akahal region, the architectural similarity between Patzak and Jilotepeque Viejo may reflect sociocultural relationships between the Western Cakchiquel and the Akahal that predate the construction of Late-phase Jilotepeque Viejo.

There are general settlement pattern similarities between Patzak and the last Cakchiquel capital, Iximche. Both have three principal civic plazas, with civic groups clustered adjacent to each other. Plazas at both sites are rectilinear, and there is a close approximation in orientation between plaza A at Iximche and Patzak's main plaza. There are two large bulwark structures and two moats at the entrance to each site, as well as a "greeting plaza." At both, large residential areas are found on the same level as the civic precinct, rather than on lower terraces. However, the configurations of civic architecture at Iximche seem to be modeled directly after Utatlan, whereas Patzak resembles Akahal Jilotepeque as well as the Central Quiche center. Such discrepancies as Patzak's smaller structures and overall size, about half that of Iximche, probably reflect their occupation at different times. The Xajil document (1953:97–100) vividly narrates the movement of the Western Cakchiquel from Chiavar (Patzak) to Iximche. The similarities between the central plaza at Patzak and Akahal settlement features as seen at Jilotepeque Viejo, may reflect a subordinate early political relationship of the Western Cakchiquel, which is alluded to in the ethnohistoric documents.

Although Cakchiquel settlement patterning is characterized by regional and temporal diversity, some basic organizational themes are constant. For example, at the only sites with ball courts—Iximche, Jilotepeque Viejo, and Cucul—the plaza's entrance first passes by the ball court. More notably, Cakchiquel sites examined here, with the exception of the two easternmost sites, Los Cimientos–Pachalum and Los Cimientos–El Ciprés, exhibit linear arrangement of civic plazas and other groups of monumental architecture. That is, at Iximche, Jilotepeque Viejo, Cucul, and Chuisac, Pueblo Viejo Jilotepeque, and Patzak, specific civic groups are organized so that one follows another in a line. Interestingly Semeja, the earliest Western Cakchiquel center thus far surveyed, has a linear plaza pattern. If the several rectilinear plazas in a line at Chuisac Alto prove to have been built by the Early-phase Western Cakchiquel, there would be significant correspondence with their last center, Iximche, which also exemplifies this pattern.

Cakchiquel civic groups arranged in a line are often physically set apart from one another. Akahal Chuisac and Jilotepeque Viejo, for example, have plazas separated by moats, terraces, and bulwark structures. Excavation at Iximche also revealed walls and trenches between civic groups. More widely spaced civic plazas at Jilotepeque Viejo and Chuisac, with more pronounced intrasettlement fortifications, suggest that the Akahal may have been a looser alliance of kin groups constituting an elite community than various groups dwelling at Iximche, Patzak, or Pueblo Viejo Jilotepeque, for example. More compact spatial organization at Iximche and Patzak, in turn, may reflect more centralized sociocultural systems. The primary intrasettlement fortifications at Iximche and Patzak, the two large moats and two large walls, separate the respective residential areas of the nobility and the less elite social strata. Spatial organization in Akahal sites suggests that competition between kin groups, each occupying a separate plaza, was more acute; whereas at Iximche social cleavage may have developed more along class lines. This pattern recalls the revolt of the warrior class at Utatlan (Xajil 1953:94–97), which precipitated the Cakchiquel move from Patzak to Iximche. Kin-based social divisions, nonetheless, were still the foundation of Cakchiquel society at Iximche. The Xajil document (1953:106–9) records the expulsion of the Tukuches by the Xajil and Zotzil from Iximche.

In comparison with the Central Quiche at Greater Utatlan, the Cakchiquel at Iximche exhibit a more centralized settlement configuration, perhaps reflecting a later construction date and thus perhaps a more militarily oriented sociocultural system. The three Cakchiquel confederates, the Zotzil, the Xajil, and the Tukuche, were grouped on one plateau, whereas the three Central Quiche confederates, the Nima Quiche, the Tamub, and the Ilocab, occupied three neighboring although entirely separate plateaus. (This also may reflect the larger elite communities within Greater Utatlan. The Quiche confederates apparently did once reside on the single plateau of Ismachi, prior to their dispersal onto separate plateaus.)

In comparison with their neighbors, notably the Quiche and the Akahal, the Western Cakchiquel cultural identity seems to have evolved less distinctly over time. The early Western Cakchiquel center Semeja exhibits the same architecture, settlement patterning, and ceramics that characterize the local, pre-Epi-Toltec population. The Western Cakchiquel intermediate-phase capital, Patzak, reflects Akahal and Epi-Toltec settlement features, while their last capital, Iximche, is a replication of Utatlan in some respects. Moreover, the large amounts of red-slipped ceramics at Patzak and Iximche are reminiscent of Utatlan, in contrast to the largely cream-slipped and micaceous wares of Akahal sites. The Western Cakchiquel were originally wedged between the early power centers of the Quiche and Akahal and achieved sociocultural independence only after the move to Iximche and the subsequent submission of the Akahal (see Xajil 1953:104; Xpantzay II 1957:149).

Judging from settlement pattern changes during the Late Post-classic Period, the Western Cakchiquel absorbed a great deal of Central Quiche culture. The first Western Cakchiquel settlements, such as Semeja and Mukulbalzip, suggest a noncentralized local highland community organization. In contrast, the intermediate center, Patzak, which was firmly tied to the Quiche conquest state, manifests such features of centralization (i.e. militarization) as several groups residing within a single elite center, cliff-faced plateau sides, moats, a bulwarklike construction, and an outside elevated plaza (perhaps for a military ward). These same traits are present in the last elite center, Iximche. The Western Cakchiquel seem to have utilized settlement features whose first occurrence within the Central Quiche communities coincides with the first militaristic expansion of the Quiche outside the Quiche Basin.

As long as they could draft the Western Cakchiquel as warriors, the Quiche were quite successful in their expansionistic campaigns, but when the Cakchiquel left the Quiche Basin periphery in the third quarter of the fifteenth century, the Quiche state began to crumble. The subsequent success of the Cakchiquel conquest state may be due in part to its use of elements of Quiche statecraft, as reflected, for example, in the resemblance of the governmental civic plazas at Iximche to those of Greater Utatlan. Indeed, the growth of this once-subject group supports Service's (1971, 1975) generalization concerning "hybridized" sociocultural systems that perfect the basis of success of their former rulers and eventually surpass them.

The Akahal seem to have had a distinct sociocultural identity, manifested in a different overall settlement pattern and architectural style from those of the Western Cakchiquel and Central Quiche. Akahal sites have twin temples along the plaza side (Jilotepeque Viejo, Chuisac, Los Cimientos–El Ciprés) or in the plaza center (Los Cimientos–Pachalum); temple balustrades lack a *tablero* (Jilotepeque Viejo). They often have several intermediate-sized rectangular platforms (Cucul, Jilotepeque Viejo plazas A and B, Los Cimientos–Pachalum, Chuisac). Some plazas are nonrectilinear or curvilinear (the Chuisac acropolis, Jilotepeque Viejo plazas A and B); some are rectilinear (Cucul, Los Cimientos-Pachalum, Jilotepeque Viejo E, Chuisac). Ball courts are oriented north-south at Cucul and Jilotepeque Viejo. Moats and terraces separate civic groups at Chuisac, Jilotepeque Viejo, and Los Cimientos–Pachalum.

In ceramics, Akahal sites are characterized by high percentages of cream-slipped and "bright paint" polychromes and micaceous ware. The open-mouthed serpent motif characteristic of Akahal ceramics is strikingly similar to the open-mouthed serpent depicted on the ballcourt sculpture at Jilotepeque Viejo, although it lacks a human face. The strength of the Akahal cultural identity is suggested by the fact that this symbol not only dominates local decorated ceramics but is also present on the only verified Late Postclassic sculpture in the region. Ethnohistorically, the Akahal are said to have "dawned" independently of the Western Cakchiquel and were considered as separate regional groups throughout the Late Postclassic Period.

Settlement pattern data at Los Cimientos–Pachalum and Cucul suggest that they were first built during the Early phase, if not a little before, and inhabited throughout the Late Postclassic Period. The ridgetop rectilinear pattern of Cucul is reminiscent of the back-to-back rectilinear plazas at Chuisac Alto, which may prove to be an early feature (cf. Chujuyub). Moreover, the hilltop plaza at Los Cimientos may prove to be similar to the acropolis plaza at Chuisac Alto. The close spatial positioning of Los Cimientos and Cucul is reminiscent of the Sacapulas sites inhabited during the Early phase. The possible acropolis plaza and a second plaza with twin temples at Los Cimientos is also comparable to Chutinamit-Sacapulas.

Among the Akahal sites, Chuisac and Jilotepeque Viejo seem to have the highest degree of settlement pattern similarity (see Akahal traits listed above). Moreover, they are clearly the largest sites in the region, both in area of settlement and number of civic groups. Both sites have at least four major civic plazas; Jilotepeque Viejo has a number of lesser groups as well, and Chuisac probably had some additional groups of monumental architecture. Their large size and internal heterogeneity probably indicate that these settlements were regional Akahal capitals at different times. Since Chuisac is essentially Early-phase in settlement features and Jilotepeque Viejo is Late-phase, we can identify Chuisac as the earlier Akahal capital (Ochal) and Jilotepeque Viejo as Chaupec Quecahol Nimaabah, the last one. The Xajil (1953:90) document clearly states that the Akahal abandoned Ochal for Nimcakah Pec (Jilotepeque Viejo).

The heavier fortification at Jilotepeque Viejo points to the growth of militaristic political systems during the span of the Late Postclassic Period, probably owing to threats from both the Quiche and the Western Cakchiquel. Situated along the Rio Pixcaya, Chuisac is located toward the northwestern edge of the Akahal heartland (Chahoma 1956); Jilotepeque Viejo tends more toward the southeastern edge of this central area. The move of the Akahal center is probably related to the growth of the Western Cakchiquel at Iximche, which is fairly close to Chuisac. The Xajil (1953:106) document narrates a dispute concerning the Cakchiquel encroachment on Akahal lands at about this time.

In addition to Akahal plazas, both Chuisac and Jilotepeque manifest "foreign" plazas. At Chuisac Bajo there is a civic plaza strongly reminiscent of both Utatlan and Iximche. The occurrence of an acropolis plaza and a plateau plaza of this design at Chuisac Alto brings to mind Tenam in the Aguacatan Valley. Since Chuisac is the earlier Akahal capital, abandoned about the time of the Cakchiquel expansion, it may have been occupied by the Central Quiche, who controlled the Akahal prior to Cakchiquel independence (see Carmack n.d.a:31). The elevated plazas C and E at Jilotepeque Viejo are similar in settlement patterning to the outside elevated "military" or "greeting" plaza at Iximche as well as to Pakaman at Greater Utatlan. Carmack (1975) reasons that these plazas at Jilotepeque Viejo were Western Cakchiquel loci after the Akahal were subjugated by the Western Cakchiquel late in pre-Hispanic times. Similar Cakchiquel plazas are also seen farther east at the centers of Chinautla Viejo (Mixcu) and Yampuc Viejo (Ayampuc). (Carmack and Fox n.d.; Fox 1977). The similarity in settlement patterning between these plazas and Pakaman, a significantly earlier Greater Utatlan settlement complex, also points to the utilization of conquest administrative organization by the Cakchiquel, following the success of the Quiche conquest system.

A number of Akahal-like traits occur at Early Postclassic sites (i.e., La Merced, Saquitacaj, Chibalo) within this same area. For example, La Merced exhibits an irregular-shaped plaza with intermediate-sized rectangular platforms, a rectilinear plaza, thin-walled cream-slipped ceramics, and the "serpent head–human face" ball-court sculpture. Closely spaced Saquitacaj and Chibalo are similar to La Merced's east plaza and use the "serpent head–human face" sculpture. In fact, the greatest concentration of these distinctive sculptures is in the region controlled by the Akahal during the Late Postclassic Period. Other highland examples are at Guaytan, Pantzac-Sajcabaja (Smith 1955:38), and Zacualpa (Lothrop 1936).

Physical remains, then, suggest that Akahal-like traits were well established in this eastern highland area during the Early Postclassic Period. Judging from the numerous, closely spaced Early Postclassic sites, this region was also heavily populated. Although the Akahal are said to have migrated into the highlands as part of the general Epi-Toltec movement (Tamub 1957:47), they may have established themselves firmly here during the Early Postclassic Period, as suggested by ceramics and settlement patterning at Chuisac Alto and possibly Los Cimientos–Pachalum, if not earlier. They may simply have been in the Rio Motagua drainage earlier than the documents indicate, but how much earlier remains an open question. They may also have mixed with an already established "Mexicanized" population (see, for example, La Merced), continuing some of its traditions. In either case, we learn from the Xpantzay III (1957:153–54) document that when the Western Cakchiquel first arrived in the highlands they obtained women from the Akahal, who were apparently already established.

Mexican influences in architectural remains at these eastern Motagua Early Postclassic sites include long structures, sunken ball courts, and oval temples. As pointed out in Chapter 3, these traits also appear for the first time along the ,Rio Negro (at Xolchun-Sacapulas, Pantzac-Sajcabaja, and Chalchintan) during the Early Postclassic Period and probably during the Late Classic (i.e., Epiclassic, see Ch. 7). The "serpent head–human face" sculpture also appears to be part of this complex. These Mexican-influenced sites are situated along Highland Guatemala's two principal rivers—the Motagua, draining into the Gulf of Honduras, and the Negro, flowing to the Gulf of Mexico. Not only are these "foreign" centers found along the principal watercourses, but they exist at key resource areas, notably the Sacapulas-Sajcabaja region, a major source of salt, and the Jilotepeque region, with access to obsidian, greenstone, and jade. The foreign settlement of the two *tierra caliente* river basins coincides in time with major Gulf Coast cultures, antecedent to the Putun merchant warriors. During later times the Putun had established trading centers at the mouths of the Negro and the Motagua (Chapman 1957; Thompson 1970). Significantly, the "serpent head–human face" sculpture occurs along the Gulf Coast in the Putun heartland (Berlin 1953:122). Little is known yet about Gulf Coast architecture except that the long structure was a common plaza feature (see Berlin 1956:Fig. 2; Andrews 1943: Fig. 1). The orange paste ceramics found at sites like La Merced may be related to Gulf Coast fine paste wares, notably fine orange ware (see Thompson 1943). There would seem, then, to be a cultural affinity between the Putun and the Late Postclassic Epi-Toltec Quichean peoples, who also originated along the Gulf Coast. Thus, similarity between Early Postclassic (and Epiclassic) remains along the Motagua and Negro rivers and the remains of Late Postclassic groups like the Akahal is not surprising, regardless of the dates of migration.

There were several parallel developments in Late Postclassic settlement pattern features in the ecologically similar Motagua and Negro areas. For example, the twin temple only occurs in these two drainages. In addition, except in the Atitlan Basin, Early-phase acropolis sites also occur only in the Motagua and Negro basins.

Akahal settlement features appear to also resemble Pokoman sites to the east. Pokoman shared with the Akahal such features as twin temples; temple balustrades lacking a *tablero;* the presence of numerous rectangular structures; and the indented side and rear wall architecture of rectangular structures and temples. Upon closer examination, however, some of these shared features are outweighed by differences. Pokoman twin temples, for example, are situated in the center of the plaza, rather than on its sides as at Akahal sites. While Pokoman temples have indented side and rear walls, Akahal temples have inset terraces, like the temples of other Quichean peoples. And Pokoman plaza sides, composed entirely of rectangular platforms, lack ball courts.

The resemblances between Akahal and Pokoman settlement patterning may have resulted from the interaction of the two groups as close neighbors along a frontier. Their development in close association may also have incorporated some Late Classic (Epiclassic) and Early Postclassic traditions in the eastern Motagua area (see La Merced and Guaytan). The documents, however, inform us that Akahal-Pokoman interaction included conflict, endemic at that time and place. The Pokoman culture, then, may have developed partly in reaction to Quichean expansionism. Five major Pokoman settlements were subjugated by the Western Cakchiquel about the time of their move from Chiavar to Iximche (Xajil 1953:99). This movement may well have produced displacement waves, forcing Akahal expansion into Pokoman territory. The Pokoman community Chi Holom was displaced by Akahal settlers about this time. Also about this time, the Xajil document (1953:106) tells of land disputes on the western Akahal border with the Tukuche. The Akahal were subsequently forced into submission by Iximche. The Western Cakchiquel, after conquering the Akahal, subjugated a number of Western Pokoman communities, such as Mixcu (Chinautla Viejo) and Ayampuc (Yampuc Viejo), as mentioned above. Expansion to the east along the Rio Motagua drainage may be seen as following a geographical line of least resistance—away from the Central Quiche. The Cakchiquel also pushed south, against the Tzutuhil of the Lake Atitlan region, as well as onto the piedmont.

6

EASTERN QUICHE

The Quiche speakers east of the Central Quiche region beyond the ward of Chinque (Ah Chinic ethnohistorically; see Tamub 1957:57) of Greater Utatlan are grouped together in this study as the Eastern Quiche. They are known ethnohistorically to have comprised several political groups, such as the Rabinal of the upland basins, the Agaab of the Rio Negro Basin proper, and the Chahoma in the southern part of the province, but their homogeneous settlement patterning and geographic proximity suggest a single regional ethnic group. They spoke a single dialect of Quiche known as Achi or Rabinal. The Rabinal-speaking communities today, directly descended from the area's pre-Hispanic elite communities, are Joyabaj, Cubulco, Rabinal, San Andrés Sajcabaja, and San Miguel Chicaj (Campbell 1971, 1976:3). The Eastern Quiche were allied with the Central Quiche fairly early in the Late Postclassic Period. Although the exact nature and origin of this political relationship are not yet known, the Eastern Quiche were a key provincial group within the Quiche state from its inception until its fragmentation. Sometime following Cakchiquel independence, the Rabinal rebelled against Central Quiche domination (see *Rabinal Achi* 1955). However, they were once again dominated from the outside when they were conquered by the rapidly expanding Cakchiquel shortly before the Spanish conquest (Xajil 1953:114).

The Eastern Quiche boundary with the Central Quiche was apparently pushed eastward by Central Quiche growth during the Late phase (see Fox 1977). This border area lies within the eastern Quiche Basin, which offers few natural barriers to contain regional populations. Archaeological and ethnohistoric analysis may be able to clarify this dynamic situation along the border area between the core area of a conquest state and a major province.

The northwestern Eastern Quiche border community at Sajcabaja, in the Rio Negro Basin proper, will not be analyzed in this study beyond the few following comments, since it is presently being investigated by the Mission Scientifique Française au Guatemala, under Alain Ichon, and I await their results. The Agaab center of Zahkabaha manifests both an acropolis plaza, Los Cimientos (see Smith 1955:41, Fig. 95), and a typical Late-phase Quiche complex, Patzac (see Smith 1955:40–41, Fig. 94). The acropolis may have been the locus for the Sajcabaja Quiche, whereas Patzac, directly across the barranca, has a rectilinear plaza (Group A) with settlement features strongly reminiscent of the Central Quiche. It is interesting to note that Ichon (1976) obtained radiocarbon dates in the 1100s from this site, which supports my contention that the acropolis sites existed during the Early Postclassic Period, before the collapse of Chichen Itza.

The Eastern Quiche region, stretching about 100 kilometers east of the Central Quiche core region, comprises a 2,500-square-kilometer rectangle, bordered on the north by the Rio Negro Basin and on the south by the rugged Sierra de Chuacus escarpment (Map 10). The eastern boundary coincides with the change in direction of the Rio Negro from due east to directly north, and with the western wall of the Sierra de las Minas, a short distance south of the bend in the Rio Negro. The high Sierra de Chuacus range also separates the Rio Negro and Rio Motagua watersheds (Map 10). With the exception of the modern cabeceras of Zacualpa and Joyabaj, both at the southern foot of the Sierra de Chuacus, the entire Eastern Quiche region lies within the Rio Negro drainage.

Farther east, beyond the fairly even north-south line of the Rio Negro and the Sierra de las Minas, begin the Pokoman and Kekchi speakers. The Akahal, discussed in Chapter 5, were directly south of and parallel to the Eastern Quiche in the Rio Motagua drainage, with approximately the same east-west boundaries.

The Rabinal territory has a gradual northward downgrade from

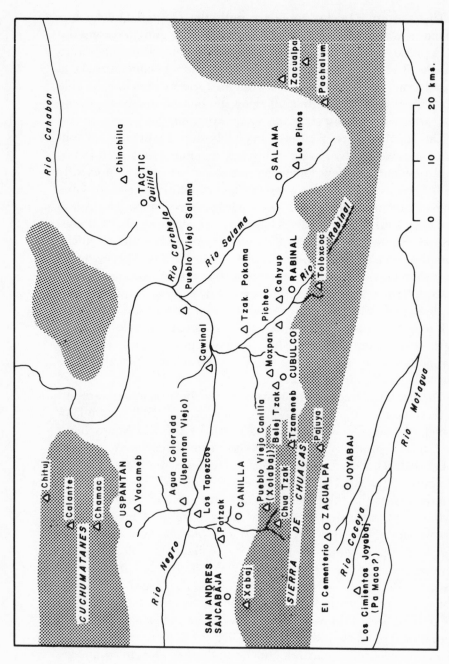

MAP 10   Eastern Quiche Area

the Sierra de Chuacus to the Rio Negro. Topography here is characteristically rugged, often intersected by steep barrancas. There is, however, a series of connected intermontane basins running east-west across the Rabinal territory, where the modern population centers of Cubulco, Rabinal, San Miguel Chicaj, and Salama are concentrated. These upland settlements contrast with the concentrations of population in the basin, at Sajcabaja and Sacapulas. Because the bedrock underlying the region is of an older crystalline "slab" structure (see Sapper 1891), Late Postclassic masonry construction is typically of schistose slabs.

Ranging in elevation from 1,000 to 1,900 meters, the region spans the *tierra templada* climatic spectrum in all but the hot and arid Rio Negro Basin floor, which, at 800 meters, dips well into *tierra caliente*. With the Sierra de Chuacus blocking the moist Pacific winds, the entire Eastern Quiche region is characteristically dry, though well-enough watered for dry-field agriculture. Today its large Indian population relies for the most part on the traditional staples of maize and beans (Sapper 1891; Teletor 1955). Moreover, the several documentary references to cloth products in this area indicate that cotton may have been an important cultigen in precontact times (C'oyoi 1973:290–91; *Rabinal Achi* 1955:19, 26).

I will discuss sites lying within the Eastern Quiche region beginning with those closest to the Central Quiche and moving east.

Western Area

El Cementerio

Within and adjacent to the cemetery at Zacualpa, 500 meters west of the cabecera, are two pre-Hispanic plazas, on the Chinique-Zacualpa road. The southern group was photographed by both Lothrop (1933:Fig. 70) and Wauchope (1948a:Plate 3).

Topography

The ruins, on the east edge of a flat plateau in open, rolling country between the cabeceras of Zacualpa and Joyabaj, are surrounded on three sides by sheer cliffs between 40 and 100 meters high. The southern end of the plateau narrows to a width of

100 meters and then connects with an immense adjoining plateau.

Lying at the southern foot of the Sierra de Chuacus, the site is near the northern limit of the Rio Motagua drainage. Below El Cementerio, the Rio La Vega runs past the large Early Postclassic ruins of Zacualpa, excavated by Wauchope (1948a), about three kilometers away, and eventually feeds into the Rio Motagua, some twenty kilometers to the southeast. A sizable shallow pond is just south of the site on the adjoining plateau.

Settlement Description

In addition to the two civic plazas, there are several small low mounds near the north edge of the site. All architecture is covered by grass and tall pines. Probably there were once more structures adjacent to the north plaza, but most traces have disappeared with the continual reshaping of the surface from burials over the years. Both of the relatively intact plazas are similar in structures and in size (Fig. 39), but they differ in orientation, with the north plaza oriented east-west, and the south plaza oriented a little off the north-south axis. The north plaza also has a flanking structure on one side of the temple.

Artifacts

A few red-slipped thin-walled sherds collected in a road near the south plaza suggest a Postclassic date, but we found none that allowed certain dating of the site as Early or Late Postclassic.

Architecture and Settlement Pattern Interpretation

Although dating is inconclusive, El Cementerio does share some settlement pattern features with the Early-phase Chujuyub sites, which begin only 17 kilometers to the northwest. Briefly, the plazas at El Cementerio exhibit similar-sized long structures, and temples in the same right-angled plaza configuration (cf. Cruzche). Moreover, they also resemble Chujuyub sites in having both east-west and north-south orientations. In contrast to the lofty ridgetop locations of the Chujuyub sites, however, El Cementerio is on a cliff-faced plateau in open country. In this critical settlement pattern feature, it resembles Late-phase Late Postclassic *tinamit* sites. However, El Cementerio is also comparable to Chibalo, which is also within the Rio Motagua drainage (Map 9). Chibalo

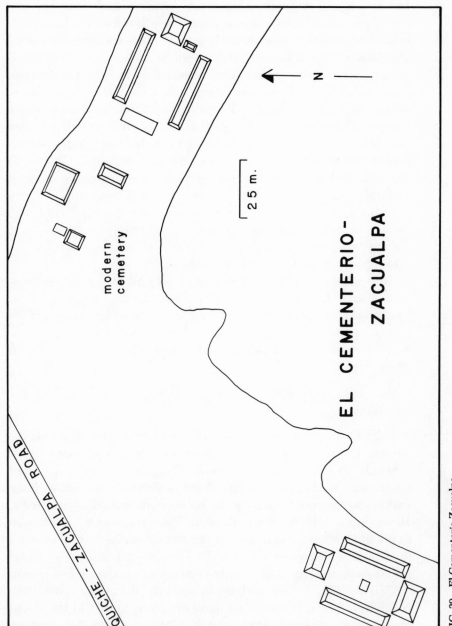

FIG. 39　El Cementerio-Zacualpa

has the same symmetrical pattern in size, configuration, and orientation as El Cementerio's north-south-oriented plaza. Chibala's few ceramics occur at Early-phase Late Postclassic sites (e.g., Oquin) as well as at Early Postclassic sites.

El Cementerio may thus have been an intermediate settlement between the Early Postclassic Mexicanized population in the large, nondefensive settlement of Zacualpa just three kilometers down the river, and the later Quiche horizon. It could thus have been settled at the same time as Chujuyub sites, but might represent an earlier group of culturally related peoples. As argued in Chapter 5, the Rio Motagua drainage was settled by Mexicanized groups, probably from the same Gulf Coast homeland, beginning perhaps in Terminal Classic times and continuing into the Early Postclassic. Since the warmer and presumably more attractive basins were already occupied, the last wave of Epi-Toltec peoples settled in the removed Sierra de Chuacus just to the north.

Alternatively, there is also a good possibility that El Cementerio was a Late-phase Late Postclassic Quiche *tinamit*, as its topographic situation suggests, but one whose architectural remains are not well enough preserved to be readily recognizable as such. We will have to await subsurface testing, however, to place it chronologically.

Ethnohistory

If El Cementerio is an Early-phase Quiche site, it should be mentioned in the sixteenth-century Quichean chronicles. It is centrally located among the early Quichean confederates—the Chujuyub Quiche, the Akahal, and the Rabinal—as well as lying within territory controlled by the Rabinal late in Late-phase times. However, the Early-phase Rabinal "dawning" center, Zameneb (Xajil 1953:80), is a mountaintop site not far northeast in the Sierra de Chuacus (Ximénez 1929–31:74–75; Carmack n.d.a:17). Ruins called Zameneb were apparently visited by Brasseur de Bourbourg (1857:125, 479, 505–6) and by informants of Teletor (1955:188). Numerous ostensibly early settlements are recorded in the documents (e.g., *Rabinal Achi* 1955:21, 30–34; *Titulo Totonicapan* 1953:180–83), but none that seems a likely candidate at this point for El Cementerio.

The Late-phase center in the Zacualpa area has long been

known to have been PaMaca (e.g., *Popol Vuh* 1950:221; *Rabinal Achi* 1955:33; Carmack 1973:204). There is a reportedly large, well-preserved hilltop fortress known as Los Cimientos–Joyabaj eight kilometers southwest of El Cementerio overlooking the same plain. Joyabaj's Late-phase center has been identified as Pueblo Viejo, about fifteen kilometers north of Zacualpa. Given the border position of Los Cimientos between the Rabinal and Akahal territories, fitting the ethnohistoric description of PaMaca, we may perhaps be able to establish an identity between the two (see Fox 1977). However, the site has not yet been surveyed. If El Cementerio proves to be Late phase in date, which seems less likely, it would be the overwhelming candidate for PaMaca, with the post-Hispanic community formed from PaMaca, Zacualpa, immediately bordering the site.

Pueblo Viejo–Canilla

Pueblo Viejo is most easily reached by following the Rio Cacuj four kilometers southeast of Canilla, then climbing a 1,000-meter-high mountain, which is an additional 4-kilometer journey (Map 10). Pueblo Viejo is also 16 kilometers directly north of Joyabaj, over the seemingly vertical Sierra de Chuacus. The ruins were first mapped in December 1972 by Alain Ichon of the Sajcabaja Project. For a more detailed description and interpretation of Pueblo Viejo, as well as a more complete site diagram, the reader is referred to Ichon (1975). The following data on Pueblo Viejo was compiled during our brief visit there in July 1973.

Topography and Ecology

The ruins are strung along a 450-meter-long tongue, projecting northwest from just below the mountain peak, rising about 1,000 meters above the Rio Cacuj on the west and the Rio Samam on the east. The spur is isolated by steep embankments 'and masonry terraces on all but its east side, where the causeway enters from the mountain crest (Fig. 40). In the deep gullies on the north and south sides of the spur are streams, formed in nearby springs, tumbling to the Rio Cacuj below. At 2,250 meters' elevation, the site commands a panoramic view of the rugged *tierra templada* northern slope of the Sierra de Chuacus. The arid *tierra caliente* Rio Negro Basin begins on the north foot of this same mountain.

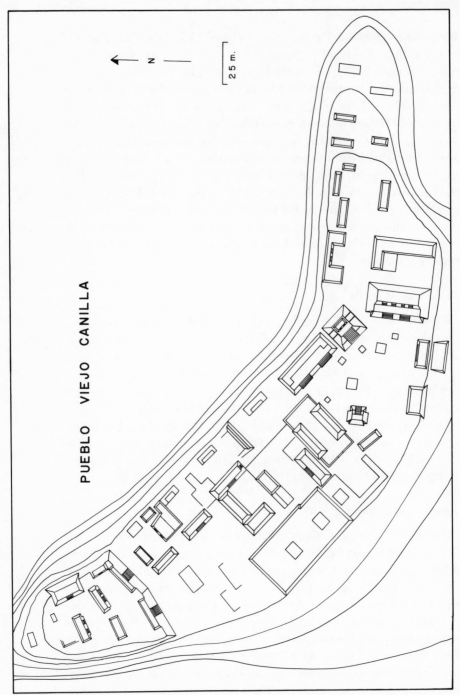

PUEBLO VIEJO CANILLA

N

25 m.

FIG. 40   Pueblo Viejo Canilla

Settlement Description

Pueblo Viejo's remarkably well-preserved architecture, showing stairways, benches, moldings, cornices, and more, was cleared by Ichon several months before our visit. The complete absence of surface ceramics and obsidian is due to this recent investigation. Masonry is largely of shaped igneous slabs, often still covered by patches of plaster.

Civic architecture falls into three groups; an eastern group along the site's entrance, the civic plaza, and a western, densely concentrated group (Fig. 40). A central causeway connects the various sections. The enclosed civic plaza comprises a southwest-facing temple, an east-facing temple, both on plaza sides, equal-sized long structures forming the north and east plaza sides, a sunken I-shaped ball court oriented northeast-southwest, and two short rectangular platforms forming a south side. In the center are at least six low square or rectangular platforms, aligned with the temples, long structures, and ball court. The high, large temple has two levels. The upper level, which supports a single-room superstructure, has three inset terraces and a double front stairway with *talud-tablero* balustrades. The lower or main level has four inset tiers and a single broad *talud-tablero* balustraded stairway. There is also a single stairway spanning the two levels on each of the two temple sides. The small temple has a single front stairway, bordered by *talud-tablero* balustrades and four inset terraces. The equal-sized long structures, with two broad front stairways each, bordered by *talud-tablero* balustrades, differ from one another in some respects. First, the long structure facing south is fairly low, with a single broad level containing a six-meter-wide bench against the back wall. In contrast, the long structure facing west has two high tiers, rising between two and three meters above the plaza surface. There is an equally long structure immediately behind this one, with free standing masonry walls on three sides of the superstructure.

West of the civic plaza are five smaller groups arranged around courts. The first of these, the "palace complex," borders the ball court in the civic plaza. Grouped on three sides of its slightly elevated court, it contains a main rectangular residential structure comprising a series of sunken patios, a high long structure, and a third structure with several levels. West of the palace complex are three successive court groups, each with one high rectangular structure, adjacent to the connecting "street," and at least two additional lower platforms. On the northwest tip of the spur, in contrast, are two sections containing only low, short rectangular platforms.

Architecture and Settlement Pattern Interpretation

Pueblo Viejo's civic architecture is aligned on two axes, 45° northeast by 225° southwest, and 98° east by 278° west. The four western court assemblages, including the "palace complex," seem to follow the northeast-southwest orientation. The large temple, flanking long structure, and ball court follow the northeast-southwest axis, while the small temple, perpendicular short rectangular structures, and the long structure opposite this temple follow the east alignment. There is thus a fundamental symmetry within the civic plaza, with each axis group containing one temple and a long structure. This two-part division is also evident in the court of the civic plaza, where the two equal-sized low square platforms ("skull racks") may be associated with the two temples.

The settlement seems to have two organizational axes, perhaps corresponding to two social groups. The four court-assemblage groups on the west side and the various groups on the east side may correspond to chiefly lineage groups, the foundation of Quichean social organization. Each of the west groups has a high long structure, which may have been the "big house" (*nim ha*) mentioned repeatedly in the *Popol Vuh* and *Rabinal Achi*. Appropriately, the palace complex, where the ruling lineage probably dwelled, lies closest to the civic plaza, the central focus of Quichean government. The elevated group at the northwest tip of the settlement, which does not conform in orientation or composition to the other sections of the site, could have housed social institutions apart from chiefly lineages.

Pueblo Viejo shares some notable architecture and settlement pattern features with Utatlan and Iximche. The southwest-facing temple at Pueblo Viejo, like the west-facing temple of Awilix at Utatlan, has two levels, a single broad *talud-tablero*-balustraded front stairway, and *talud-tablero* balustrades on its sides. Moreover, it has two stairways to the second level like the west-facing temple at Iximche. The similarities of these west-facing temples suggest that all three may represent the same deity, Awilix. Pueblo Viejo shares other settlement pattern features with Utatlan and Iximche. Its west-oriented flanking long structure, with two tiers, is similar in size to the structure in the same plaza position at Utatlan. As at Utatlan, an associated structure of equal length is immediately behind this flanking long structure, and there are two similar-sized low square platforms (skull racks or dance platforms?) in the plaza center. The palace complex is adjacent to the civic plaza. The palace, long structure, and other buildings enclose three sides of a court, as at plaza B at Iximche. A smaller temple is oriented east, like the Temple of Tohil at Utatlan, the ball court axis is close to that of the west-facing temple, and the small temple has four inset terraces. The two short rectangular structures on the plaza's south side may have functioned like similar-sized flanking structures within Greater Utatlan (i.e., at Chisalin and Resguardo), but they differ in that they are not adjacent to the temple. Finally, though Pueblo Viejo also has two temples on plaza sides, generally facing east and west, they are not directly opposite each other in a rectilinear plaza as at Utatlan.

There are notable settlement pattern discrepancies with Utatlan as well. Pueblo Viejo is located on a mountaintop spur, rather than a cliff-ringed, open-country plateau. The main temple and ball court are oriented northeast-southwest, there is no round structure, and long structures are considerably smaller at Pueblo Viejo. The east-facing temple is significantly smaller than temples within Greater Utatlan, and masonry is shaped slabs rather than dressed limestone and pumice blocks.

Plaza features at Pueblo Viejo may have had cosmological significance. For example, the 45°–225° axis is the median between north-south and east-west cardinal axes. Moreover, the seven inset terraces on the main temple's two tiers may correspond to the seven celestial levels. Thompson (1970:195) writes that

> the thirteen celestial layers were arranged as six steps ascending from the eastern horizon to the seventh, the zenith, whence six more steps led down to the western horizon. Similarly, four more steps led down from the western horizon to the nadir of the underworld, whence four more steps ascended to the eastern horizon. Thus there were really only seven celestial and five infernal layers.

Therefore, the highest temple and the ball court's sunken playing alley, aligned on the same axis, may reflect the sky-underworld dichotomy. Where observable, Quichean ball courts often have five steps leading to the sunken playing alley in the two stairways on the east and west ends (e.g., Iximche, Jilotepeque Viejo).

Ethnohistory

An 1814 land-dispute document locates Joyabaj's *pueblo viejo* at the ruins of Pueblo Viejo Canilla (Carmack, personal communication). The post-Hispanic municipality derives its name obviously from the precontact community known as Xoyabah (*Popol Vuh* 1971:239). Early in the Late Postclassic Period, Xoyabah was part of the Rabinal regional group known as the Chahoma (see Chahoma 1956:13–14), but during the Late phase was firmly tied to the Central Quiche. Thus, "according to Ximenez (1929:484), the Quiche border (Central Quiche) with the Rabinal of Tecocistlan was at Xoyabah" (Carmack n.d. a:41).

Chwa Tzak

Chwa Tzak is a small hilltop site in the *cantón* Chuchuca, eight kilometers north of Zacualpa, and about the same distance south of Canilla (Map 10). The hill is a northern pinnacle on a gradually ascending wide ridge. The ruins overlook this ridge, 60 meters below, to the south, with precipitous 600-meter slopes to the north, east, and west. Bordering on Chwa Tzak to the south, the north slope of the Sierra de Chuacus forms a 40-square kilometer area of rolling low hills, much of which is under cultivation.

The small hilltop plaza contains a temple (8 by 6 meters) facing 290° west, a perpendicularly aligned longer rectangular structure (15 by 5 meters) facing south, and a low, short rectangular structure (11 by 4 meters) opposite the temple. There are several small, low rectangular platforms adjacent to the plaza and on a terrace just below the plaza. The temple's construction of finely dressed limestone blocks and its west orientation, together with the longer structure facing south, are generally Quiche traits. No ceramics were recovered.

As a Late-phase single-plaza site of small structures on a low hilltop overlooking an expanse of rolling agricultural lands, Chwa

Tzak may have been an administrative ward center for a local rural population like those surrounding Greater Utatlan. The elite center Los Cimientos–Joyabaj (PaMaca?) is about seventeen kilometers to the southwest, whereas Pueblo Viejo Canilla (Xoyabaj) is only six kilometers northeast of Chwa Tzak. In fact, only the Rio Cacuj separates their respective 1,000- and 600-meter-high hilltops. Finally, Chwa Tzak's Quiche architectural style is consistent with the Quiche influence evident at Pueblo Viejo.

Eastern Area

Cawinal

The ruins variously known as Pueblo Viejo Cubulco, Rio Blanco, and Cawinal are situated along the Rio Blanco just north of its confluence with the Rio Negro (Maps 1, 10). The site can be reached by a 15-kilometer hike north of Cubulco, Baja Verapaz, following the Rio Chicruz until it joins the Rio Negro opposite the Rio Blanco. The ruins were known to several investigators, including Brasseur de Bourbourg (1857; see also Sonnerstern 1859), but I believe our 1973 survey was the first systematic investigation.

Topography and Ecology

The ruins are situated on both banks of the Rio Blanco, at least 10 meters above the river, for a distance of four kilometers. This unusual location is, nevertheless, defensive. Mountains on the west and east sides of the 300-meter-wide valley floor rise precipitously 200 and 600 meters, respectively, making access from above virtually impossible. The Rio Negro forms the southern terminus of the center; for most of the year the river is impassable (except for a modern cable suspension bridge). Just beyond the ruins to the north, the valley walls descend steeply to the river's edge, blocking access from this direction.

The Rio Negro Basin here, as elsewhere, supports mostly xerophytic vegetation, except at the river's edge, which is often lined with mango and other trees. Cultivation is restricted to the narrow plains. With so little arable land, the sparse population today must be greatly reduced from pre-Hispanic times. At about 800 meters' elevation, the basin floor is *tierra caliente*. Several of the side valleys with streams and rather dense tropical vegetation provide a suitable habitat for cultivation. Also, bees are kept in hollowed logs, placed in a row on elevated platforms, apparently a continuation of an aboriginal practice (see Carmack n.d.c).

In addition to the tropical microenvironments that result from the meeting of three river systems at Cawinal, there are notable mineral deposits in the immediate area. There is a large copper deposit on the southern border of Cawinal (IGN, Los Pajales), and serpentine deposits along the Rio Chicruz, a short distance south of Cawinal (Stewart, personal communication). The Nijaib II document (1957:111) also mentions that jade and "jewels" came from Cawinal.

Settlement Description

There are at least six groupings of civic architecture in "alcoves" alongside the Rio Blanco. These small pockets of level land are segmented by steep mountain slopes descending to the river, and are only connected by narrow paths cut into the steep hills. We surveyed eight civic plazas; there may be more north of the principal ruins, but we did not have the opportunity to investigate them. Four main plazas are grouped together on opposite banks, whose structures are many times larger than those at peripheral plazas. These four plazas are shown in Figure 41.

The main plazas are exceedingly well preserved, with plaster facades still largely intact. Indeed, according to Bancroft (1875:4:121), they were pronounced "by the Abbe Brasseur . . . the finest in Vera Paz." Masonry consists of finely worked limestone blocks as well as some shaped schistose slabs. We visited Cawinal during the peak of the rainy season, when the Rio Blanco is nearly impassable. We did not risk crossing with our survey equipment, and therefore the building orientations from the east bank groups should not be considered entirely accurate. However, I was informed by Russell Stewart, who visited Cawinal one year later, that there is only a 2° difference in orientation between the principal groups on the east and west banks.

The two "back-to-back" west bank main plazas differ only about 10° in their northwest-southeast orientation. Each plaza contains a

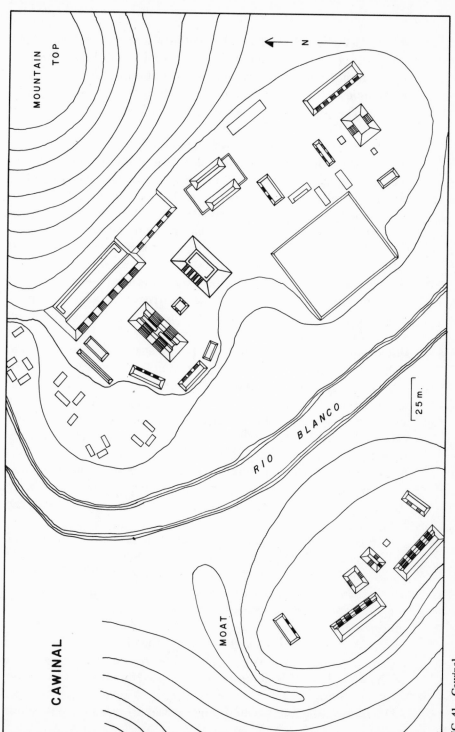

FIG. 41 Cawinal

temple facing a short rectangular platform with two stairways, and a long structure, perpendicular to the temple, with four stairways. Both temples have stairways on their front and rear facades, and the temple in the southern plaza has a third stairway—an unusual feature. The plazas occupy a low elevation bordered on the north by a steep, 15-meter-wide moat.

The civic plazas, a palace complex, and a residential sector are clustered on the east bank. Cawinal's largest plaza is here, with a "double" temple in the plaza center, surrounded by two inter-mediate-sized rectangular platforms. The double temple has two superstructures on a single-substructure temple base. There are two low, short rectangular platforms on the north and west sides of the plaza, an immense long structure spanning the east side, and an unusual templelike structure forming a south side. The double temple has two broad stairways on its east and west sides, five inset terraces, and two superstructures, whose masonry walls are partially standing. The huge templelike structure on the south plaza side has four front stairways, four inset terraces, and a single-room superstructure with a bench against its back and side walls. The long structure with six stairways, and its southern extension with four stairways, totals over 90 meters in length. Its recessed second tier on the main long structure supports a single-room superstructure with a long bench against the back and side walls. Just beyond a masonry wall north of the plaza is a large sector containing dozens of low, short masonry residential platforms (e.g., 8 x 3 meters), completely exposed and grouped in threes and fours around small square courts. This highly concentrated zone extends to the river and continues 100–200 meters northeast of the civic precinct.

The southern half of the east bank's civic precinct, containing a ball court and what appears to be a large elite residential structure and a smaller civic plaza, is oriented several degrees farther to the south than the principal civic plaza. The ball court occupies an intermediate position between the principal civic plaza and the elite residential structure and smaller civic plaza. Red paint is still observable on the west range of this northwest-southeast-oriented I-shaped sunken ball court. The elite residential structure, a labyrinth of low walls, foundations, and sunken patios, is built on a gradual decline.

The remaining four isolated single plazas are situated south along the Rio Blanco. Each has only one temple and one or more small rectangular structures with two stairways, which are considerably smaller than structures within the four main plazas. An interesting small (5 x 3 meters) residential structure, situated on the west bank between two peripheral civic plazas, has free-standing masonry walls.

Artifacts

Our small ceramic sample, collected in one area south of the west bank main plazas, produced sherds characterized by red to red-orange slip, with some mica temper in the paste. The Late phase is represented by Fortress white-on-red, and by red-slipped thin-walled sherds generally. The Early phase can be seen in the red-slipped geometrically carved ware found at the acropolis sites (e.g., Chuitinamit-Atitlan, Chutinamit-Sacapulas) characterized by straight-line incised motifs, often painted white, in a single panel around the vessel. In addition, we found one fragment of moldware, seen at Late-phase Quiche sites, and several distinctive orange-red "wavy line" incised sherds. The "wavy line" style persists today in the Cubulco-Rabinal area.

Early-phase red-slipped geometrically carved ware predates Fortress white-on-red in some Quiche regions, so perhaps the earlier ware was ancestral to the later. The change from rigid straight-line geometric motifs to curvilinear motifs over time seems natural, as the application technique changed from the pressure movement of incision to the more fluid motion of painting. However, heavy white paint lines on red slip occur at the early Central Quiche sites, which are probably later in time than the acropolis sites. Thus, this heavy line "white-on-red" may be intermediate in form as well as time between the carved ware and Fortress white-on-red.

Architecture and Settlement Pattern Interpretations

Cawinal's unusual river valley location is partially due, no doubt, to the need for water in an otherwise arid environment. Secure in their defensive side valley off the Rio Negro proper, the population occupied six or so alcoves totaling about one square kilometer in area. Judging from the intact residential area north of the principal civic plaza, the settlement seems to have been densely packed. The settlement here is roughly comparable in size to the four

Sacapulas centers (Chutinamit, Chutixtiox, Xolpacol, and Pacot) together. However, its valley floor location is more reminiscent of the Early Postclassic civic centers like Pantzac-Sajcabaja and Chalchitan upstream in the Rio Negro Basin.

Certain features within the site suggest possible lines of social cleavage. The large size of the structures within the tightly grouped main plazas, including perhaps a palace, indicates that this was the administrative nucleus. Interestingly, there is a slight orientation difference between the two plazas on the east bank, and between the two plazas on the west bank, which suggests, perhaps, a four-part societal division. The three smaller plazas are roughly equal in size and composition. Each has a single temple, with front and rear stairways, flanked by a long structure and facing an intermediate-sized structure with two stairways. The largest civic plaza is divided into "halves"—that is, it comprises two temples, two intermediate-sized rectangular platforms, two short rectangular platforms, and a single long structure with two parts— suggesting a dualistic ruling organization. However, the four-part division of plazas can be grouped into two larger units, perhaps indicating moieties. There is a stylistic difference between the east and west bank plazas, with six stairways on the long structures in the two east bank plazas and four stairways on corresponding west bank structures. And, obviously, they are physically separated by the river.

The remaining plazas, south of the quadripartite civic precinct, seem to represent less central sectors of society. For example, they could correspond to peripheral allied groups, or perhaps such emerging classes as artisans or warriors. In this respect, the two small plazas on Cawinal's south border, situated on high bluffs overlooking the confluence of the Blanco and Negro rivers, and thus fortified, may have been "military" plazas like those evident at Iximche and other Quichean centers. The wall separating the sector of small residences from the civic precinct on the east bank suggests a class separation between the elite civic precinct and the inhabitants of the small houses.

While overall architectural style at Cawinal contrasts markedly with that of the Central Quiche, there are several basic spatial organization themes held in common. The right-angled relationship between temples and long structures, and the position of the palace complex, adjacent to both the main plaza and the ball court, resembles Utatlan. The two temples within Cawinal's principal plaza are comparable in size to Utatlan's temples, the largest such structures in the highlands. The size of the temples at Cawinal may have been the result of long occupation and periodic refacing. The west bank main group at Cawinal also shares certain features with the Early-phase Chujuyub sites. Like Chitinamit, for example, the west bank has "back-to-back" plazas, with temples at the plaza "head." Structure sizes, notably of long structures, are also comparable (cf. Cruzche).

There are significant stylistic and settlement pattern discrepancies between the principal civic plazas at Cawinal and Utatlan. Cawinal's has a temple in the court's center, a double temple, stairways on opposite front and rear temple sides, a double temple with five inset terraces, a high long structure with numerous stairways, a large *tablero* over a small inset *talud* on rectangular platforms, a ball court peripheral to the main plaza and oriented northwest-southeast, and altars with stairways on their front and rear sides. Both the Early- and Late-phase Central Quiche nucleated settlements were divided into three topographically distinct centers. In contrast, Cawinal is divided into four basic parts. We may infer from these differences that the Quiche speakers of Cawinal were largely independent of direct Central Quiche influence.

Ethnohistory

Cawinal's identification is secure, since a mountain rising above this site is still called Cerro Cauinal (IGN, Los Pajales). According to the *Popol Vuh* (1971:221), there were five associated communities—Chi Q'ix, Chi Chaq, Humeta Ha, Kuluba, and Kavinal—which Recinos, Goetz, and Morley (1950:211 n.) believe were simple divisions of the same larger community. These may correspond to the five civic clusters on both sides of the Rio Blanco, or possibly to the quadripartite division of the main civic precinct. Chi-Quix, distinguished from the other sections in the *Popol Vuh* (1950:211), may have been removed from the others.

Numerous sixteenth-century Quichean chronicles refer to relocation of some Central Quiche to Cawinal, after they abandoned Hacawitz (Chitinamit-Chujuyub). We are told that the Quiche built houses of limestone at Humeta and Culba-Cavinal (Totonicapan 1953:183; C'oyoi 1973:289). Under the Agaab rulers of Cawinal, to whom the Quiche gave their daughters (*Popol Vuh* 1971:221), the Quiche tell of "hardships" (Totonicapan 1963:182–93, C'oyoi 1973:290–91). Carmack (personal communication) argues that the move to Cawinal by some Central Quiche simply reflects an alliance of these early confederates, apparently with Cawinal maintaining a superior position in the relationship. Finally, during the mid-fifteenth-century Central Quiche expansion, this political relationship was reversed, for the Quiche required tribute payments from the Agaab at Cawinal (Nijaib II 1957:111; Carmack n.d.a:37).

Belej Tzak and Moxpan

About a kilometer north of Cubulco is a hilltop site called Belej Tzak (Sonnerstern 1859; IGN Cubulco) (Maps 1, 10). The ruins occupy the summit and several terraces of a 100-meter-high hill, with moderately steep slopes, surrounded by a small, basinlike area of rich *tierra templada* milpa land, totaling about 25 square kilometers.

Its small, ridge-shaped summit contains at least three low rectangular platforms, each about 30 meters long. No ceramics were recovered, but its hilltop location and shaped schistose slab masonry suggest a Late Postclassic date.

Two kilometers northeast of Belej Tzak is a similar hilltop site called Moxpan (IGN, Cubulco). It also has moderately steep, terraced hillslopes, rising between 80 and 100 meters, but it occupies a ridgelike spur descending from a higher mountain which forms a rim above the small Cubulco Basin. Moxpan's summit, like Belej Tzak, features two low rectangular platforms perpendicular to each other. A small temple, apparently standing alone, is situated on a narrow lower level, just below the summit. In addition, there are small, low rectangular "house" foundations along the upper terraces.

Belej Tzak and Moxpan were probably ward centers controlled by the Agaab of Cawinal, or the Rabinal in the next valley east. The *Rabinal Achi* (1955:18, 101, 106, 107) mentions a settlement called Beleche Qoxtun, thought to be near the Rabinal Plain; the Cubulco Plain is separated from the Rabinal Plain by just three kilometers of low hills. The Xajil document reports that a settlement known as Beleh Cuihay was subjugated by the Central Quiche during the mid fifteenth century (Xajil 1953:93).

Cahyup

Cahyup is just two kilometers north of Rabinal (Map 10). These well-known ruins have been variously called "Cakyu, Cakhay, Cajyup, Cakjaj, Kak-Yu, and Rabinal" (Smith 1955:44). My drawing follows Smith's (1955: Figs. 98–108) highly detailed site diagrams. We visited the site briefly in 1971.

Topography and Ecology

The ruins occupy both a steep hilltop, 260 meters above the Rabinal Basin, and a lower level, approximately 60 meters below the summit. In addition, a single round structure on top of a conical peak one kilometer to the northeast is connected to the main mountain by a narrow "saddle." The slopes of Cahyup are quite steep, with many masonry terraces near their tops.

Cahyup overlooks the Rio Rabinal, which empties into the Rio Negro some 20 kilometers to the northwest. At 900–1,000 meters elevation, the level Rabinal Basin floor, totaling about 50 square kilometers, borders on both the *tierra caliente* and the *tierra templada* ecological zones.

Settlement Description

Of the eight distinct groups of structures, five can be considered civic plazas. Two peripheral groups contain only a temple and long structure each, and will not be described further. The remaining "group" is actually a single five-tiered round structure on the peak to the northeast. Of the five civic plazas, three occupy the principal mountain's summit; the remaining two occupy separate elevations near the beginning of the saddle, about 60 meters below the summit. My site diagram (Fig. 42) shortens the distance between the summit and saddle groups. For their true topographic relationships see Smith (1955: Fig. 98). Preservation at Cahyup is excellent, with many exposed masonry surfaces. Masonry consists largely of thin shaped schistose slabs.

Similar architecture is found in all the civic plazas. All the rectangular platforms have stairways on four sides and one stairway on each of the two small sides. Moreover, each of the superstructures has square pillars in its entrance. Balustrades on the rectangular platforms are typified by a heavy *tablero* over a small inset *talud*.

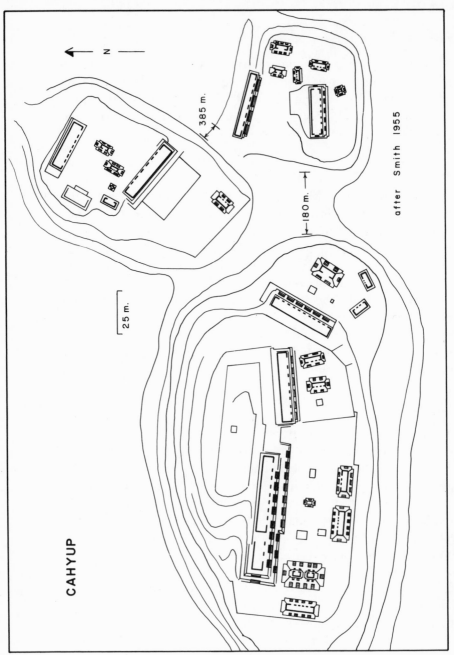

FIG. 42 Cahyup

The main plaza occupies about half the leveled summit and is slightly higher than the two other civic plazas on the summit. It consists of a double temple within the court, and four rectangular platforms forming plaza sides. The plaza is oriented 100°E–280°W, with the temple facing east. The double temple has two tiers, with four stairways on the front and rear sides leading to identical superstructures. The three smaller rectangular platforms, forming the west and south plaza sides, are comparatively high for such structures at Quichean sites. The huge long structure, nearly 100 meters long, has two high tiers, with six stairways on its front facade and three stairways on what seems to be a recessed northern extension. Immediately north of the long structure and slightly above it is a series of patios and wall foundations that may be an elite residential complex.

The remaining two summit plazas are similarly laid out. Each contains a temple in the center, with two stairways on the front and back; a long structure on the north plaza side with six stairways, forming a right angle with the temple; and a short rectangular structure with two stairways on the front and back sides. The central plaza is oriented just 2° off the east-west cardinal points (92°–272°), while the east plaza is aligned 125°–305°.

Interestingly, both the two lower-level groups contain two temples; two long structures generally with four stairways; and at least two short rectangular structures.

Artifacts

Wauchope (1970:205–9) types Smith's ceramic sample largely as white-on-red, white-on-brown (14.3 percent), monochrome (37.1 percent), and mica ware (34.3 percent). Significantly, only one "polychrome" sherd was reported. The ceramics thus point to a Late-phase Quiche community, with little ceramic influence from the Akahal region to the south. We noted a few obsidian projectile points, including both large and small side-notched types.

Architecture and Settlement Pattern Interpretation

Inhabitable space on the hilltop, terraces, and saddle, totaling about a third of a square kilometer, indicates that Cahyup was a medium-sized Late-phase civic center. Cahyup may have controlled the southern half of the Rabinal Basin, which it overlooks.

While there is strong stylistic homogeneity at Cahyup, suggesting construction by one culture, there is some variation in arrangement, suggesting distinct social units, which were probably ranked lineages. Civic architecture is divided into an upper, summit group, and a lower, saddle group. Also conforming to this division, long structures within the summit group have six stairways, while those within the lower group, except for one such building with five stairways, have four front stairways. Although each of the plazas is oriented roughly east-west, they differ slightly in orientation, suggesting connections with different social groups. The temple in the main civic plaza is oriented east, whereas the temples in other plazas face generally west. The main plaza, the highest at Cahyup, is also distinguished by its possible adjacent elite residential complex. As a locus possibly for the ruling lineage, the main plaza is set apart from the other plazas, which share arrangement and orientation features.

Cahyup shares little in specific settlement patterning with the Central Quiche. A hilltop site in a low *tierra templada* basin, rather than a plateau site in the more elevated highlands, it has at least five plazas on one mountain, rather than a single plaza surrounded by densely concentrated multiroom structures. In contrast to Central Quiche settlement patterning, it has a temple in the center of the court, a double temple, and three inset temple terraces, rather than four. The orientation of the largest temple is east. There are stairways on four sides of rectangular platforms, numerous stairways on rectangular substructures, and a heavy *tablero* over a slight *talud* on rectangular platforms. There is no ball court. Interestingly, ball courts are often absent at Pokoman sites, and Cahyup was a frontier settlement near the once fluctuating Quiche-Pokoman border. The single short rectangular platform behind the temple in the main plaza occurs throughout the Rio Negro region (for example, at Los Ciemientos–Sajcabaja and Chutixtiox-Sacapulas).

The location of the round structure on the peak to the northeast overlooking the civic precinct is also a point of contrast with Utatlan, for a similar-sized round structure at Utatlan is situated in the center of the main plaza. However, Fuentes y Guzmán reports a round masonry structure on a high hill overlooking Iximche to the west. At Tula, the legendary starting point of the Quichean peoples, there is a large round structure standing alone several kilometers north of the main civic precinct (Acosta 1958). Round structures spatially removed from the main civic precinct may have been a civic component of Epi-Toltec spatial ordering (cf. Pollock 1936).

Ethnohistory

Cahyup still carries its precontact name—Cakyug or Cakhay as specified by Brasseur de Bourbourg (1947:99–104). It has also been referred to as Cakyug-Zilic-Cakocaonic-Tepecanic (*Rabinal Achi* 1955:19), suggesting a four-part confederated settlement.

The earliest ethnohistoric reference to Cahyup is made during the expulsion of the Pokoman from the Rabinal Valley around the mid 1300s (Xajil 1953:67). As an earlier Pokoman center, Cahyup seems to have been occupied by Rabinal Quiche about this time. Documentary evidence suggests that the Central Quiche were allied with the Rabinal Quiche from early in the Late Postclassic Period and controlled them for much of the duration of the Quiche state. Chicakyug is listed under Central Quiche suzerainty in the mid 1400s (Xajil 1953:93), when the Rabinal paid tributes of precious metals and stones as well as finely embroidered cloths (*Rabinal Achi* 1955:19, 26). Late in Late-phase times the Rabinal expelled Central Quiche administrators (the Cawek lineage of the Nima Quiche; see the *Rabinal Achi*). Their independence was short, however, for Cahyup was conquered by the increasingly more powerful Cakchiquel in 1517 (Xajil 1953:114).

Tzak Pokoma

The well-known ruins variously called Chuitinamit (Roys, in Smith 1955), Los Cimientos (IGN, Cubulco), the "Ruins near Rabinal" (Maudslay 1899–1902), and Tzak Pokoma (Brasseur de Bourbourg 1947; Sonnerstern 1859) are situated eight kilometers northeast of Rabinal (Maps 1, 10). To avoid confusion with the several sites called Chuitinamit in this study, I will use Brasseur's name, Tzak Pokoma. Each of the above investigators provides some architectural description, but only Smith (1955:48–53, Figs. 109–125) provides a detailed site diagram as well as a highly detailed description of its 44 civic buildings. I have not visited the ruins.

Topography and Ecology

The ruins are strung along a narrow ridgetop 1.4 kilometers long, forming a northern rim of the Rabinal Basin. Masonry terraces are also found on the upper slopes. Near the eastern end of the ridge are two high parallel masonry walls (Smith 1955:49, Fig. 109 a, b; Maudslay 1899–1902:2:25). At the foot of the ridge on the north and south sides are streams that feed into the Rio Rabinal, 3 kilometers to the west.

Settlement Description

Tzak Pokoma has eight groups of civic architecture on slightly varying levels and at widely spaced intervals along the narrow ridgetop. Seven of these contain plaza arrangements; group G, on the western extreme of the site, has only two structures, and thus will not be considered a plaza (see Smith 1955: Fig. 109). The two largest plazas at the site, groups C and H, both contain ball courts and are situated in the center of the ridge; thus they are considered "main plazas." Two plazas (groups B, A in Smith 1955: Fig. 109) east of main plaza C, and three plazas (groups D, E, F) are west of plaza H. My diagram (Fig. 43) shows only the two main plazas and the first west plaza. Preservation is quite good, with shaped schistose slab masonry covered with plaster (Maudslay 1899-1902:2:27; Smith 1955:49).

Plaza C is roughly triangular shaped. Its sides comprise four short rectangular platforms, a long structure on the north side, and an l-shaped sunken ball court aligned along the cardinal north-south axis (0°N–180°S). A double temple in the center of the court forms a right angle with both the long structure and a short rectangular structure. The double temple has two levels, with three inset terraces on the first level and two inset terraces on the second recessed level; three stairways span both levels on the front and rear sides. The long structure has two levels and six stairways on its front.

The second main plaza, H, has a temple in the center, an l-shaped ball court oriented 30°N–210°S behind the temple, two short rectangular structures with two stairways each on their front

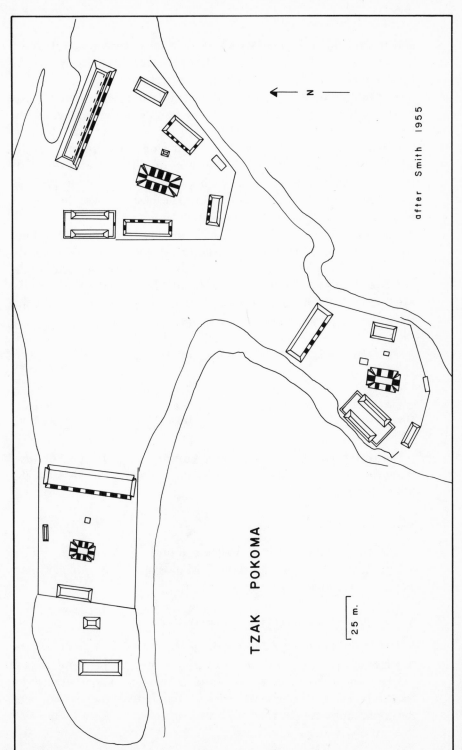

N

after Smith 1955

TZAK POKOMA

25 m.

FIG. 43 Tzak Pokoma

and rear sides, and a long structure with four stairways on its front and rear sides. The single-room temple has two stairways on its front and rear sides, and just two inset terraces.

The remaining five plazas manifest similarities in structure types and orientation. Each plaza contains a temple in the center, a long structure, and one or two short rectangular platforms. Each temple has two stairways on the front and rear sides—except in plaza A, where the temple has a single stairway on all four sides—and all have superstructure entrances facing east. The temple in plaza B has superstructure entrances on both the east and west sides and two altars within the single-room superstructure.

Each long structure faces south or southwest and has four stairways, except for the long structure in plaza D, which has six stairways. Except for main plaza C, the characteristic right-angle spatial relationship between temple and long structure does not exist at Tzak Pokoma. Temple and long structure orientations for the seven plazas are shown in Table 3.

TABLE 3. Temple and long structure orientations at Tzak Pokoma

Plaza	A	B	C	D	E	F	H
Temple	90°E	94°E	104°E	84°E	64°E	119°E	104°E
Long structure	246°SW	246°SW	188°S	226°SW	180°S	221°S	225°SW

On terraces just below the ridge summit are at least 400 house platforms, averaging about three by eight meters (Smith 1955:49; Maudslay 1899–1902:2:25).

Artifacts

Except for a few stone artifacts found by Maudslay (1899–1902:2:27), Brasseur de Bourbourg, Maudslay, and Smith all report an absence of surface artifacts.

Architecture and Settlement Pattern Interpretations

The high elongated ridgetop situation of Tzak Pokoma suggests the Early phase. Indeed, the site may first have been inhabited early in the Late Postclassic Period by Pokoman, or perhaps in transitional times between the Early and Late phases. However, the topography recalls that of Late-phase Jilotepeque Viejo in the neighboring Akahal region, which is Late phase. Architectural style at Tzak Pokoma suggests a Late-phase date as well.

While a general homogeneity of architectural style and orientations suggests a uniform culture, slight settlement pattern differences may indicate social divisions within the settlement. First, all temples at the site are oriented east and all but one of the long structures face between the west and south cardinal points. Thus each plaza has a slightly different orientation, suggesting the presence of seven distinct social divisions. A notable exception is that the temples in both main plazas are oriented 104° east. Since both these plazas have a ball court, the same temple orientation, and are situated in the center of the ridge, they appear to balance one another, perhaps representing two primary groups, such as the highest ranking lineages within each of two moieties. The plazas on the east half of the ridge may have been associated with main plaza C and those to the west with main plaza H, which would suggest a dualistic organization. Main plaza C has a double temple, and is slightly larger and 10 meters higher in elevation than main plaza H; hence it may have been the locus for a higher ranked group.

The more than 400 small house platforms concentrated on the upper terraces provide a rare suggestion of resident population size at an Eastern Quiche center. In addition to these dwellings, there probably were residence sectors between the widely spaced civic groups on the ridgetop proper (cf. Jilotepeque Viejo). If all these potential dwellings were inhabited simultaneously, Tzak Pokoma could easily have had a population more than large enough to be considered "urban" (see Sanders 1962). As we have noted, ample water is available below the site, and could have been carried to the settlement according to the practice of the modern Quiche.

The site shows little settlement pattern similarity to Central Quichean sites. Obviously, the division into seven widely spaced civic plazas differs from the one civic plaza on each of three separate plateaus seen at Greater Utatlan. In addition, Tzak Pokoma lacks multiroom residences and has a temple in the plaza center, one temple in a plaza, a double temple, three or five terraces on a temple, temples facing east, stairways on four sides of platforms, a long structure with numerous stairways, and ball courts oriented north-south. Tzak Pokoma also largely lacks the right-angle relationship between the temples and long structures that is often characteristic of Quiche sites. Finally, the location of ball courts behind temples is unusual.

Ethnohistory

The ruins apparently were still called Tzak Pokoma, translated as "buildings of the Pokoman," when Brasseur de Bourbourg visited them in 1855. Miles (1957a:752) identifies Tzak Pokoma as the community of Nim Pokom overrun by the Rabinal around 1350. This would be roughly contemporaneous with the Central Quiche movement into the Quiche Basin, and these events may have been related. The conquest of the Rabinal Valley is recorded extensively in the native chronicles (i.e., *Rabinal Achi* 1955:20, 24; Xajil 1953:66–67, 93; Ximénez 1929:195; Carmack n.d.a:18).

Pichec

The small hilltop site of Pichec sits on the western rim of the Rabinal Basin, at the eastern edge of the foothills separating the Rabinal and Cubulco basins. Smith (1955:53–54, Fig. 126) made a map of the site in 1947, and we visited it briefly in 1971.

A temple and altar on the small summit are the only architectural remains at Pichec. The well-preserved temple, oriented 109° east, has two stairways each on the front and back, single stairways on the sides, and two inset terraces. It is built with shaped schistose slabs covered with plaster. There are a number of masonry terraces with house platforms on the upper hillslopes.

The hilltop centers of Tzak Pokoman and Cahyup, six kilometers northeast and due east respectively, can be made out from the lofty summit of Pichec. Pichec shares the same architectural style as these two centers, and it may have been a wardlike center with a small resident population controlled by one of them.

Pueblo Viejo Salama

Pueblo Viejo is situated near the confluence of the Rio Negro with the Salama and Carchela rivers (IGN, Tactic). I did not visit the ruins. However, Brasseur de Bourbourg visited a site he called Salama, which, considering the proximity of Pueblo Viejo to Cawinal and Salama (which he visited during the same period) seems likely to have been Pueblo Viejo.

Pueblo Viejo is situated just 10 kilometers downriver from the

Quiche center Cawinal. Within the short distance from Cawinal, the Rio Negro abruptly changes direction from east to north. Just above Pueblo Viejo the river rapidly descends to the lowlands. This is thus a strategic interchange, a gateway from the resource-laden highlands to the lowlands.

Taking into account language distribution and references in Ximénez, Carmack (n.d.a:41) argues that the Quiche political boundaries did not extend beyond the Salama Valley. Pueblo Viejo, situated near the Quiche boundary on the Rio Negro as well as the Rio Salama—which drains the rich Salama Valley from the south—may thus have been the Quiche border community of Tzalamha. If this identification is correct, the Quiche extended just far enough east to control the system of rich *tierra templada* basins (i.e., Rabinal, Salama) and the principal trade route to the lowlands.

Sometime between about 1440 and 1470, the Quiche also conquered the Pokoman and Yaqui town of Quilaha, east of the Rabinal Quiche (Nijaib II 1957:109; *Rabinal Achi* 1955:34; Carmack n.d.a:37). About ten kilometers directly east of Pueblo Viejo, the Rio Carchela, which Pueblo Viejo overlooks, is called the Rio Quilala. Probably, then, Quilaha was located just east of Pueblo Viejo, where the Pokoman (Pokomchi) ethnic group began. The Nijaib II (1957:105) document also states that the Itza of this same general Cahabon area paid tribute to the Quiche. Thus, perhaps the Yaqui and Itza are the same "Mexicanized" people. In the lowlands just north of this area, "Putun" communities were characterized by two ethnic populations living side by side (Thompson 1970; Hellmuth 1970). As a frontier between highland and lowland cultures, the Cahabon area may have been a point of highland-lowland exchange. However, at this point there is no concrete ethnohistoric evidence for trade other than some products probably from Verapaz, such as jade and Quetzal feathers, which were known to have reached Putun ports of trade on the mouth of the Rio Usumacinta-Negro (Borah and Cook 1963:143).

Los Pinos

On the hill called El Portezuelo, or Los Pinos, two kilometers southeast of Salama, is a fortified site (Maps 1, 10). The elongated hill, with steep slopes of 100 and 140 meters rising to two separate levels, stands near the center of the broad Salama Basin, which together with the adjoining valley at San Miguel Chicaj totals nearly 100 square kilometers.

Los Pinos contains two architectural groups: a plaza on a lower shelf, and a temple and wall on the summit of the hill. Among the earth mounds of the lower group can be distinguished a northwest-facing temple and several rectangular platforms. A broad stairway leads from this plaza to a path ascending the 40 meters to the summit. The leveled summit, completely enclosed by a high masonry wall, contains only a single east-west facing temple in its center. Although the temple is largely covered by grass, *talud-tablero* balustrades can be detected on its sides, and several monolithic stone columns protrude from its top. A series of masonry terraces immediately below the squared summit contain what may be small residence platforms and two rectangular civic platforms. No ceramics were recovered.

As a defensive hilltop site within the broad Salama Basin, Los Pinos appears to have been a small civic center, perhaps subsidiary to a larger center. Cahyup and Pueblo Viejo Salama are 20-some kilometers directly west and northwest, respectively, from Los Pinos. In the towering Sierra de las Minas range, forming an eastern wall of the Salama Basin beginning about 10 kilometers from Los Pinos, are three highly "Mexicanized" Late-phase sites (Pachalum, Zacualpa, and San Jose Apantes). Since they lie outside the bounds of this study, they will not be dealt with except to suggest they may pertain to Pokoman settlements (cf. Carmack and Fox n.d.). Although the cultural affiliation of Los Pinos cannot be determined from its physical remains, let us note that it lies in a relatively vulnerable position near this ethnic and political border.

Conclusions

The primary Eastern Quiche civic centers are situated either directly on the Rio Negro, or nearby on one of the main tributaries. Cawinal and Pueblo Viejo Salama are located at the confluence of three rivers within the Rio Negro Basin itself, whereas Pueblo Viejo Canilla, on the Rio Cacuj, and Tzak Pokoma and Cahyup, on the Rio Rabinal, are situated just beyond the basin. There is also a parallel distribution of what may be "ward" sites. Chwa Tzak, Belej Tzak, Moxpan, Pichec, and Los Pinos are located on terraced hilltops rising about 100–200 meters in a belt of fertile mid-land basins, running respectively west to east. The geographic positioning of civic centers in and about the Rio Negro Basin and the smaller "ward" sites in the upland areas implies that the major centers had sustaining territories extending back from the Rio Negro, crosscutting the arid *tierra caliente* and the fertile lower range *tierra templada* ecological zones. In any event, all of the Eastern Quiche centers, with the possible exception of PaMaca, which may prove to be Los Cimientos–Joyabaj, lie within the Rio Negro drainage.

Three of the four known Eastern Quiche civic centers, Cawinal, Tzak Pokoma, and Cahyup, display strong similarities in settlement organization and architectural styles, suggesting cultural affinity and ethnic similarity. As pointed out earlier, they are all situated along the Rio Rabinal, with Tzak Pokoma approximately equidistant from Cawinal and Cahyup. These sites all have a double temple with five inset terraces in the west center of the main plaza, and an immense long structure with two levels. The main-plaza long structures at Cahyup and Cawinal have recessed additions, and the main facades of all the main-plaza long structures have six front stairways and face southwest. The long structures outside of the main civic precincts often have four stairways. A heavy *tablero* over a small inset *talud* is found on rectangular structure balustrades. Ball courts are oriented north-south at Cawinal and Tzak Pokoma, and all three centers have five to eight civic plazas. These characteristics can be said to define the Late-phase Eastern Quiche settlement pattern and architectural style. At Cahyup and Tzak Pokoma there are stairways on all four sides of the various-sized temple and rectangular platforms, whereas at Cawinal there are stairways only on the front and rear sides of temples and on the front facades of rectangular platforms. Cawinal is further distinguished by a possible palace and a huge, unusual templelike structure (in addition to the double temple in the main plaza).

Pueblo Viejo Canilla, grouped in this chapter with the Eastern Quiche sites because of its geographical location, shares with Cawinal and Tzak Pokoma a high, two-tiered long structure, a north-south oriented ball court, and rectangular structure balustrades characterized by a heavy *tablero* over a small inset *talud*. Pueblo Viejo, however, differs dramatically from the other sites in having a single civic plaza, in the southwest orientation of its largest temple, in the location of the main temple on the side of the plaza, with four terraces on its first level. Its long structures have two stairways, and numerous multiroom residential units are grouped around courts. These features correspond to Central Quiche settlement pattern features. Thus archaeological remains corroborate ethnohistory, indicating strong cultural ties between the Central Quiche and the community at Xoyabah, which may even have been inhabited largely by Central Quiche. However, as a border community, Pueblo Viejo also shows some stylistic influence (such as the heavy *tablero* architectural form) from the Rabinal area as well as ethnohistoric identification with the Chahoma.

There appears to be direct Central Quiche influence in settlement remains at the Eastern Quiche border communities of Xoyabaj and Sajcabaja, but little at the three farther removed centers of Cawinal, Cahyup, and Tzak Pokoma. A Central Quiche–like complex at Patzac, immediately adjacent to an acropolis plaza (Los Cimientos–Sajcabaja), is reminiscent of what appear to be Central Quiche enclaves (i.e., Tenam, Zaculeu, Chuisac) established during the first generation of Quiche expansion, under Gucumatz. Xoyabaj, in the mountains just beyond the northeastern rim of the Quiche Basin, appears to have been a Central Quiche colony. Central Quiche influence in material remains at Cawinal, Cahyup, and Tzak Pokoma remains to be proven, although it is known from ethnohistory that there were Central Quiche lords at Cahyup. While Cahyup is spatially close to Cawinal and Tzak Pokoma, it does not exhibit characteristics that would distinguish it as a central "regional capital"; as well as sharing a remarkably homogenous architectural style, these three centers are all about the same size. All three also, curiously, manifest the double temple, which may indicate Central Quiche influence in the form of a Central Quiche conquest deity, such as Tohil, which faced east—as do the double temples—placed alongside a local Rabinal deity (Sloane 1974). Tohil was the patron deity of the Rabinal. On the other hand, the Pokoman, who first occupied Cahyup and Tzak Pokoma, made use of twin temples, which may have simply been incorporated in the modification of these centers after Rabinal takeover.

It is noteworthy that the Eastern Quiche centers are all divided into two parts. Cawinal, for example, is divided into east- and west-bank complexes of monumental architecture. Tzak Pokoma has an east and a west ridgetop group of civic plazas, and Cahyup has summit and "saddle" area civic groups. Even the possibly Early Postclassic or Late Postclassic site El Cementerio has two symmetrical civic plazas.

In addition to their similar architectural style, Cawinal, Tzak Pokoma, and Cahyup seem to have been similarly organized, although they do not have similar locations. Specifically, they contain eight, seven, and five civic plazas, respectively, that are more or less linearly arranged. This apparent cultural homogeneity of the Eastern Quiche contrasts with their ethnic identities as known from ethnohistory, for Cawinal was inhabited by Agaab, who were culturally related people extending west to Sacapulas (Carmack 1973), although comparison of architectural styles with Sacapulas does not reveal apparent cultural similarity. Cahyup and Tzak Pokoma were occupied by the Rabinal during the Late phase, although they may originally have been settled by Pokoman.

Tzak Pokoma and Cahyup seem to be still further related. In addition to their similar architectural style and settlement organization, they are both situated on the north rim of the Rabinal Basin. Their nearly identically styled double temples vary only 4° in orientation. It is conceivable that Cahyup and Tzak Pokoma were centers within a single community. Cahyup may have had an elite residential complex, which Tzak Pokoma lacks, and there are ball courts at Tzak Pokoma but not at Cahyup. There are numerous references in the *Rabinal Achi* (1955:17, 22, 50–51, 60) to the 12 jaguars and 12 eagles of Rabinal, which may have been military organizations, and the 12 chiefs of Rabinal, perhaps signifying social divisions. The 12 plazas at the two sites may correspond to 12 kin-based social units.

Excluding the main plazas at Cawinal, Cahyup, and Tzak Pokoma, most of the numerous other Eastern Quiche civic plazas comprise a temple, long structure, and a short rectangular structure. This fundamental triad unit may correspond to social units, perhaps chiefly lineages aggregated within each settlement. There are several cases of an additional temple and long structure unit adjoining a plaza, although apparently not aligned with the minimum triad unit (e.g., Cahyup D, E; Tzak Pokoma D). Insofar as these additional structures are attached to the often widely spaced plazas, they could represent lineages that split from the main lineage with time. Lineage fission is well documented in the early chronicles (Carmack 1974). Temple, long structure, and short rectangular structure units also occur in the outlying ward centers (such as Chwa Tzak), which may have administered agricultural communities composed of one or two kinship groups.

As noted earlier, Pueblo Viejo Canilla stands apart from the other Eastern Quiche settlements in basic organization as well as architectural style. It has just one civic plaza, surrounded by densely concentrated sectors of various-sized residences. Pueblo Viejo would thus seem to have had a more complexly evolved society, apparently with class-based residential zones (see Ichon 1975:97). There are at least five large residential courts within the civic center and a less exclusive residential zone on the surrounding terraces below. The various-sized elite residential courts contrast in structure types with the peripheral plazas at the other Eastern Quiche centers, although each has a long structure. The large overall size of buildings within these courts at Pueblo Viejo also contrasts with the uniformly small residential structures at Tzak Pokoma and Cawinal. The Eastern Quiche communities at Cawinal, Tzak Pokoma, and Cahyup seem, then, to have been less socially stratified, and thus less centralized. The single plaza at Pueblo Viejo, in contrast, integrates the respective axes of the east and west elite residential sectors, thereby bringing together into one centralized locus the disparate sections of Xoyabaj society. Interestingly, however, this single civic plaza comprises two triad (temple–long structure–short rectangular structure) units. Each of these units is united by right-angle spatial relationships on their respective axes.

The acutely defensive 1,000-meter-high mountaintop location of Pueblo Viejo also contrasts sharply with the other Eastern Quiche sites, particularly Cawinal and Pueblo Viejo Salama. This extreme topographic situation probably reflects the border location of Pueblo Viejo, which was the easternmost settlement of the Central Quiche. Since the Rabinal broke away from the Quiche state in late pre-Hispanic times, relations may have been tense with the Central Quiche rulers.

It is not possible to appraise change in fortifications, both natural and artificial, within the Eastern Quiche region during the span of the Late Postclassic Period, since Tzamaneb, the Early-phase Rabinal center, has not yet been surveyed. Apparently, however,

Cawinal, with its valley floor location, was inhabited during both phases. Moreover, Cahyup and Tzak Pokoma, occupied by the Pokoman first, may also have been occupied into the Early phase. In sum, although these three sites are well fortified in their respective valley floor, hilltop, and ridgetop locations, they do not exhibit the extreme mesatop plateau locations of some of the Late-phase Quichean centers like Utatlan or Iximche. Being situated toward the eastern periphery of the Late-phase Quichean interaction sphere, such communities may have felt less need for extreme fortifications than the capitals of conquest states.

The Eastern Quiche at Cawinal, Cahyup, and Tzak Pokoma are reminiscent of the Akahal in settlement patterning, with numerous widely spaced and generally linearly arranged plazas. However, intrasettlement divisions within the Eastern Quiche centers, such as moats, walls, and terraces, are not as pronounced as at Akahal centers, suggesting a slightly greater degree of political centralism than among the Akahal.

The Rabinal Quiche also share some settlement pattern and architectural features with the Akahal, such as temples in centers of courts, temples on side of court (Cawinal only), temples with two stairways on a side, slightly elevated plazas (Cahyup, Cawinal), long structures with numerous stairways (cf. Jilotepeque Viejo), heavy *tablero* over small inset *talud* on rectangular structure balustrades, I-shaped ball courts oriented north-south, and schistose masonry. The double temple of the Eastern Quiche may also have been functionally equivalent to the twin temple of the Akahal. And the arid *tierra caliente* Rio Motagua Basin is ecologically similar to the Rio Negro Basin.

Akahal sites, on the other hand, are more often characterized by temples on the sides of plazas, numerous intermediate-sized rectangular platforms in nonrectilinear configurations, long structures directly opposite temples, and long structures with two stairways. The difference in long structures, however, may simply have reflected Cakchiquel garrisons from Iximche among the Akahal. Moreover, Akahal temples only have stairways on their fronts.

The basic similarity between the Eastern Quiche and the Akahal seems to have been well established at an early date—prior to their incorporation first into the Central Quiche state system and the later inclusion of the Akahal and Rabinal within the Western Cakchiquel conquest system. In fact, the political climate seems to have been reversed during the Early phase, with the Rio Negro and Rio Motagua areas as the intial power centers. The sixteenth century chronicles state that the Central Quiche moved for some time to Cawinal and paid tribute, while the Western Cakchiquel dwelled among the Akahal (e.g., *Popol Vuh* 1950:211; Xajil 1953:72, 78–80, C'oyoi 1973:289–91). When power shifted from the eastern *tierra caliente* river basins to the western *tierra templada-fria* "plateau" basins of Ismachi-Utatlan and later Iximche, the Eastern Quiche and Akahal can be said to have had independent but related architectural styles. Moreover, the lack of Chinautla Polychrome in the Rabinal area indicates that these parallel architecture styles may have resulted from a common ancestry rather than from interwoven political and economic systems.

As pointed out in Chapter 3, the Rio Negro and Rio Motagua basins contained related Early Postclassic and probably Late Classic (Epiclassic) "Mexicanized" communities (Xolchun-Sacapulas, Pantzac-Sajcabaja, La Merced-Jilotepeque, and so on). Later both drainages also had the Early-phase Late Postclassic Period acropolis sites. Parallels between the double temple (two superstructures on one temple substructure), which occurs only in the Rabinal area, and the twin temple (two identical temple substructures on a low common base), which occurs only in the Rio Negro and Rio Motagua drainages, suggest a similar function and perhaps a common ancestry. Interestingly, both the twin temple and double temple are thought first to have appeared during the transition from Early to Late phases (ca. 1350), and thereby to represent parallel evolutionary forms.

To summarize, the Eastern Quiche area, encompassing the eastern Rio Negro drainage, manifests closely overlapping but independent architectural styles. Sharing a distinctive style in the Rabinal Quiche region, however, are peoples variously known as Agaab, Pokoman, and Rabinal at various points during the Late Postclassic Period. Their cultural homogeneity, reflected in archaeological remains, seems to outweigh their separate ethnohistoric sociocultural identities. Thus, the entire eastern Quichean area, spanning the Akahal and Eastern Quiche regions, can be viewed as a broad continuum of culturally related peoples. The early Pokoman and later Eastern Quiche of Tzak Pokoma can hardly be distinguished from neighboring Agaab centers, recalling the cultural intergradation of Akahal Jilotepeque Viejo (Chuapec

Quecahol Nimaabah) and Pokoman Chinautla (Mixcu) on the neighboring frontier to the south (Carmack and Fox n.d.). However, direct Central Quiche and Western Cakchiquel influence seen in distinctive architectural forms, such as those as Pueblo Viejo Canilla and Jilotepeque Viejo, respectively contrast with architectural forms of the local Eastern Quichean regional groups.

Some of the principal features of the Eastern Quiche architectural style can be seen as continuities from earlier times. Notably, the characteristic stairways on four sides of structures may have been an embellishment that persisted from the earlier acropolis centers. The use of stairways on four sides in Late-phase times was apparently stylistic, insofar as most superstructures only had entrances on one side. As pointed out in Chapter 3, main plaza temples of the Early-phase acropolis sites, located in the plaza centers, had this unusual feature of stairways on four sides, as did Early Postclassic sites in Yucatan (cf. Chichen Itza) as well as along the Gulf Coast. Moreover, Eastern Quiche main temples continued to occur in plaza centers through the Late phase. The central location of temples apparently was more pervasive than Central Quiche influences, which emphasized two temples on opposite plaza sides. In fact, the double or twin temple integrates the dualistic Epi-Toltec scheme of two temples. The double temples face east, the direction of Tojil, the patron deity of the Rabinal and the Central Quiche. Unlike arrangements in the Gulf Lowlands, however, the single temple in the center of Chichen Itza's main plaza is oriented east of north. The ball court there, however, as at Eastern Quiche and Akahal sites, is oriented more north-south, rather than the east-west characteristic of the Central Quiche.

7

CONCLUSIONS: PATTERNED CHANGE OF SETTLEMENTS

Postclassic Lowland to Highland Movements

The migration of the ancestors of the Quiche into the highlands in the early 1200s A.D. was simply the last of at least three separate lowland to highland movements during the Postclassic Period. Since the accuracy of both the highland and lowland Maya ethnohistoric chronicles becomes increasingly blurred as we proceed back in time from the Late phase, with historicity almost nonexistent for what would be the Early Postclassic Period, our understanding of earlier ties to the lowlands is based chiefly on archaeology. Within the climatically lowland Rio Negro and Rio Motagua basins are two pre–Late Postclassic horizons which also seem to be linked to the Gulf Coastal and Yucatecan lowlands.

The horizon exemplified by the acropolis sites occurred during the Early Postclassic Period, although the acropolis sites, for the most part, continued to be occupied during the Late Postclassic as well. They may have had some relationship with Chichen Itza, though its nature is as yet undetermined. During the latter part of the Early Postclassic Period (ca. A.D. 1000–1200), Toltec Chichen was the center of the clearly dominant political system in the lowlands of southern Mesoamerica.

Within the same territories as the acropolis sites, but earlier in time, are sites exhibiting Mexican as well as lowland Mayan settlement pattern features (e.g., Chalchitan in Aguacatan, Pantzac in Sajcabaja, La Merced in San Martín Jilotepeque). In this study I have called this preacropolis horizon Early Postclassic; it may prove to date from about A.D. 800 to 1000. However, we will have to await firmer dating as well as ceramic correlations from surface collections. (It is generally called Early Postclassic in archaeological reports.) I distinguish this apparently earlier horizon as the Epiclassic, following Jiménez Moreno (1966) and Webb (1973a, 1973b) for elsewhere in Mesoamerica. At this time, sites along the Gulf Coast and in the Guatemalan highlands first manifest what are generally considered Postclassic settlement features (Armillas 1951), such as fortification and some degree of urbanism.

During the Epiclassic Period new centers of cultural vitality, exemplified by newly emerged Postclassic features, arose along the physiographically homogeneous Gulf Coastal plain, an area geographically and culturally intermediate between the highland Mexican Classic Period centers (e.g., Teotihuacan, Cholula) and the Classic Period lowland Maya of the Peten and Yucatan (see Sabloff and Willey 1967; Thompson 1970; Webb 1973a, 1973b; Sabloff 1974, 1975; Ball 1974). During the Postclassic, the Gulf Coastal plain was characterized by overlapping resemblances in material culture between neighboring groups in a gradual grada-tion moving from Tajin in the west to the Rio Bec and Puuc areas in the east. It thus can be seen as a far-reaching transitional zone between the greater Mexican and Mayan culture areas, with con-siderable overlap and exchange between neighboring populations. In southern Tabasco, at about the geographic mid-point of this elongated region, a frontier can be seen to have separated the Mayan and Mexican areas. On the eastern side of this frontier, several centuries later, the Chontal Maya were characterized as having a hybrid Mexicanized-Mayan culture (Scholes and Roys 1968; Roys 1966; Thompson 1970). Apparently dating from the beginning of the Epiclassic Period, a number of Gulf Coast groups had economic systems in which trade figured prominently. This frontier served as a transshipment locus for goods moved between the Mexican highlands and lowlands and the Mayan highlands and lowlands (Chapman 1957; Thompson 1970; Sabloff 1975; cf. Sabloff and Rathje 1975).

The result is a kind of overlapping chain, each link of which—highlands (Mexican) to central Gulf Coast (Veracruz),

central Gulf Coast to Tabasco-Campeche, Tabasco-Campeche
to Puuc, Tabasco-Campeche to Guatemalan highlands—is
closely similar to a corresponding stage in a major Gulf
Coast–Yucatecan highland Guatemalan trade network which
we know existed at the time of the Spanish conquest. (Webb
1973a:10)

Beginning in the Epiclassic, the Gulf Coastal groups expanded
with a kind of sociocultural "hybrid vigor," probably motivated by
the acquisition of goods for internal growth, commercial exchange,
and simply territorial expansion (Thompson 1970; Rathje 1973;
Webb 1973a, 1973b; Sabloff 1973, 1974). As more research is
conducted, it is becoming increasingly clear that this expansion
had militaristic as well as economic underpinnings. As an example
of Epiclassic Gulf Coast expansion, the Cotzumalhuapa-Pipil
movement into the rich cacao-producing piedmont of Guatemala
has long been thought to have originated on the Veracruz Gulf
Coast around Tajin (Thompson 1943; Borhegyi 1965; Sabloff and
Willey 1967; Parsons 1969). Recent studies also suggest that the
Classic Maya in the Peten, who may have depended upon long-
distance trade, were choked and eventually overrun by Gulf Coast
groups (Rathje 1973, 1975; Sidrys 1976; Sabloff 1974, 1975).
  There is evidence for parallel Gulf Coast movements into the
rich Rio Negro and Rio Motagua valleys of the highlands, which
may correspond in time to the demise of the large Classic Period
center, Kaminaljuyu. Indeed, sites with patterns reminiscent of
the Kaminaljuyu area in these river basins (e.g., La Lagunita, in
Sajacabaja, which dates from the Postclassic [Smith 1955:37], and
the Preclassic [Ichon, personal communication]) tend to be replaced by what may be Gulf Coast patterns (e.g., Pantzac, Chalchitan), with some similarity to the Puuc region in the lowlands (cf.
Uxmal), and probably other Gulf Coast regions (e.g., Putun). The
collapse of Teotihuacan in Mexico, which was related in some
manner to Kaminaljuyu (Kidder, Jennings, and Shook 1946), also
has been related to the rise of militarily expansive groups (e.g., at
Tula and Xochicalco) on its periphery, reminiscent of the Gulf
Coast groups on the periphery of the lowland Classic centers (cf.
Service 1975). In any event, the resources of the highland Guatemalan river basins—salt, gems, copper, and manos and metates in
and around Sacapulas, and obsidian, feathers, jade, and serpentine

in the Motagua region—may have been fed into far-reaching commercial networks controlled by Gulf Coast groups (see Carmack 1968:60; Thompson 1970). In this regard, large Mexicanized-Mayan sites (e.g., Xolchun, Pantzac, Chalchitan, Guaytan) at key resource nodes in the western Rio Negro Basin and the Rio Motagua Basin were probably established by Gulf Coast peoples during the Epiclassic Period.

Architectural forms in Epiclassic, Early Postclassic (i.e., acropolis horizon), and Late Postclassic highland sites demonstrate relationships with Epiclassic lowland sites. Perhaps, for example, an antecedent form of the Late Postclassic twin temple was the twin-spired temple seen throughout Epiclassic Tabasco and Campeche (e.g., Str. 1 at Xpuhil, Rio Bec [Pollock 1965:426] and El Chile, Usumacinta area [Maler 1903:96–98]). A similar "triple temple," Temple I at Becan (R. E. W. Adams 1974:106) in the Rio Bec area, has stairways on all four sides of each spire, reminiscent of the central pyramidal temple and rectangular platforms, with stairways on all four sides, at the highland acropolis sites (e.g., Chutixtiox). Moreover, the appearance of twin and triple temples along the Gulf Coast may be related to the contemporaneous development of "twin pyramids," also with stairways on all four sides, on the periphery of Tikal (see W. R. Coe 1970:77–78, 82–87). The unusual Epiclassic elliptical temples at Xolchun and La Merced correspond in design to the elliptical temple at Uxmal, in the Yucatan peninsula just north of the Gulf Plain (see Marquina 1964:768–73). Finally, the small round temple, defined as "Mexican" architecture by A. L. Smith (1955), which occurs at Late Postclassic Quichean sites, is also associated with the Tabasco Gulf Coast invasion of Seibal (Sabloff and Willey 1967:376). With the eventual domination of the Yucatan peninsula by Mexicanized groups, round structures are also present at Chichen Itza, Mayapan, and Tulum. The Mexicanized architecture of the Late Postclassic Quichean groups can be argued, then, to derive ultimately from the Epiclassic Mexican-Mayan frontier on the Gulf Coast.

Along the Gulf Coast, variants of geometric art styles first developed during the Epiclassic, ranging from the distinctive Tajin-Huastec to the Puuc styles on the west and east extremes, respectively. As examples, the Rio Bec and Chenes-Puuc architectural styles in northern Campeche exhibit a mixture of Mexican and Maya motifs (Ball 1974:86–87), underlining the hybrid nature of

Gulf Coast cultures beginning in the Epiclassic. Prior to Toltec domination in the Mexican highlands and the Yucatan, a "Mixteca-Puebla" art style rapidly moved from its Highland Mexican point of origin, around Cholula and Tlaxcala, throughout the Gulf Coast region (Nicholson 1960; Webb 1973a).

Centered at Tula, the Toltec slowly filled the pan-Mesoamerican power vacuum left by the collapse of Teotihuacan. This gradual takeover may be seen as marking the end of the Epiclassic. Commencing in the tenth century, the Toltec may eventually have pulled the various individual sociocultural enclaves along the Veracruz-Tabasco-Campeche coast within their sphere of control, although this is far from clear (Thompson 1970:10–25; Roys 1966; Sabloff and Rathje 1975). Not unlike Teotihuacan's southern Mesoamerican center at Kaminaljuyu, a second center of Toltec influence arose at Chichen Itza, in the distant Maya area. Its location just beyond the eastern terminus of the Gulf Coastal region, rather than in the highlands, may reflect the importance of the newly emerged Gulf Coast commerce. The Toltec, however, may also have exerted influence in the resource-laden highlands along the already established network of the Usumacinta and Negro rivers established during the Epiclassic Period. With time, tertiary centers may have been established under Toltec influence in the principal highland river basins. As argued in Chapters 3 and 5, in fact, these acropolis sites correspond in some settlement pattern features to Chichen Itza itself. However, it is not yet possible to be certain whether the acropolis centers were built by new emigrés from the Gulf-Yucatan area or by Mexicanized groups already established in these same highland basins from earlier Epiclassic movements.

The collapse of the Toltec centers at Chichen Itza and Tula, like that of Teotihuacan and Kaminaljuyu before them, set displacement waves of peoples in motion. At this time a final immigration brought the "upland" Quichean groups—the Central Quiche, Rabinal Quiche, Western Cakchiquel, and perhaps Western Quiche—to the highlands from the Gulf Coast. They built sites that exhibit general Mexican traits (*talud-tablero* balustrades, four inset terraces on temples), rather than the specific Toltec or Puuc traits (such as the central pyramid with four separate stairways) seen at Chichen Itza. However, this wave was close enough chronologically to the movement into the highlands of the peoples who built the earlier acropolis centers so that the native documents seem to consider them as one movement. There may have been only a generation between the fall of Chichen Itza and the arrival of the ancestors of the Central Quiche, which Carmack (n.d.a) calculates at approximately A.D. 1250.

This last migration into the highlands, reflecting the collapse of Chichen Itza and perhaps the reassertion of local Gulf Coast sociocultural systems (if the Toltec were ever politically dominant in the first place) exhibits some continuity with Epiclassic settlement patterning. For example, both Epiclassic Guaytan (see Smith and Kidder 1943:Fig. 3a) and the first Central Quiche center, Chitinamit (Fig. 8), manifest the same highly unusual combined structure of a temple protruding from a ball-court range. Indeed, the triangular settlement configuration of the first three Central Quiche centers, Chitinamit, Cruzche, and Oquin, is much like the three central Cotzumalhuapan sites, Bilbao, El Baul, and El Castillo, which are also situated on elevated rectangular platforms with rectilinear plazas following each other in a line (see Shook 1965; Parsons 1969).

Late-phase Quichean centers also reveal some settlement pattern parallels with contemporaneous Yucatecan sites located just beyond the Gulf Coast, perhaps reflecting a related cultural heritage. For example, "flanking structures," a Central Quiche hallmark, also can be seen at the Epi-Toltec lowland centers of Mayapan and Dzibilchaltun. A double temple, with two superstructures on one substructure and five inset terraces, diagnostic of the Late-phase Eastern Quiche centers, also occurs at Dzibilchaltun (Andrews 1960:257). At Mayapan, moreover, Proskouriakoff (Pollock et al. 1962) isolated the same triad unit—a temple, long structure, and short rectangular structure (an "oratory")—noted in Chapter 6, but present within all Quichean groups. On the other hand, the principal lowland Late Postclassic centers reveal notable differences from Quichean patterns as well: Mayapan, Dzilbilchaltun, Tulum, and Topoxte all lack a ball court, seemingly a basic Epi-Toltec settlement component.

Regionalism

Regionalism describes the tendencies of highland populations to maintain ethnic continuity, even after inclusion within conquest state systems like that of the Quiche or the Spanish. Such ethnicity is evident in the distinctive settlement patterns of each regional group, which are defined in the conclusions of Chapters 2 through 6. Linguistic patterns also vary with regional groupings, and each group is generally known today by its language (Quiche, Cakchiquel, Pokoman, Mam, and so on).

Environmental circumscription, whereby each group was bounded by topographic barriers such as mountain ranges, while also in a sense united by a generally homogeneous habitat and a common river system, has segmented the highland populations into interacting units. With Late Postclassic civic centers overlooking the principal tributaries of a single river within a regional territory, the river valleys served as communication channels cutting through rugged landscape. The Quiche-speaking groups—the Central Quiche, Sacapulas Quiche, Eastern Quiche and Western Quiche, in addition to the Aguacatec and Uspantec—all lie within the Rio Negro drainage. Both the Eastern and Western Cakchiquel occupy the Rio Motagua drainage, flowing east. The scattered Ixil centers overlook rivers flowing north that eventually come together to form the Rio Lacantun. Underscoring regional segmentation according to river systems, the Mam speakers were separated along the Continental Divide into two principal groupings: the Northern (and Western) Mam along the Selegua and Cuilco arteries of the Rio Chiapas, flowing northwest, eventually to the Atlantic, and the Southern Mam, prior to displacement by the Quiche, overlooking the Rio Samala meandering through the volcanic basins before rapidly tumbling to the Pacific piedmont and coast.

The distinctive settlement patterns and architectural styles of each of the regional groups midway through the Late Postclassic Period, when they were brought within the Quiche state, can be seen as a synthesis of various population movements into the geographically bounded regions up to that time. Two categories of regional groupings stand out, corresponding to two separate cultural traditions and two broad ecozones: the acropolis regional groups of the warm ecozones, and the upland Epi-Toltec-derived regional groups of the cool ecozones. Comprising the first category are the Sacapulas Quiche, Aguacatec, Eastern Quiche (including the Agaab), Uspantec, Akahal Cakchiquel, and Tzutuhil, who occupied the *tierra caliente* river basins and lower range (i.e., below 1,500 meters elevation) *tierra templada* small midland basins. (Again, it has not been fully discerned whether the Tzutuhil came under Quiche domination at this point, although they certainly were independent of the Quiche during the latter part of the Late phase.) A second category comprises the Central Quiche, the Western Quiche, the Rabinal of the Eastern Quiche, and the Western Cakchiquel, who occupied large-sized *tierra fria* and upper-range *tierra templada* basins.

The acropolis regional groups also, in various instances, manifest the Late Postclassic twin-temple or double-temple patterns, which, as argued in Chapters 3 and 6, were outgrowths of the acropolis pattern and may coincide in time with Quiche political domination. The acropolis pattern itself seems to relate to Chichen Itza during the Early Postclassic Period. To a lesser degree, it also shows some continuity with Epiclassic sites, as seen, for example, in corbeled arched tombs within the principal temple at Xolpacol and Chalchitan. Within the arid river basins, agriculture is restricted to the narrow river floodplains, and is dependent on proximity to the water table, or direct irrigation. Populations tied to the valley floor niches were further circumscribed by nearly vertical valley walls, such as the Cuchumatantes Massif, rising as high as 1,000 meters as the northern rim of the Rio Negro Basin. Thus, from the Epiclassic Period on, migratory groups apparently joined already established peoples within circumscribed territories. Different settlement patterns for civic centers during the span of the Postclassic in basins containing interregionally valuable resources (e.g., obsidian, greenstone) may simply reflect the rise and fall of lowland political systems, but with a continuity of local communities.

As a case in point, the Postclassic sequence of sites at Aguacatan exhibits different settlement patterns for the Epiclassic through the Late Postclassic (i.e., Chalchitan, Huitchun, and Tenam, including the acropolis and Quiche plazas), but also a continuity in orientations to the cardinal points (cf. also Xolchun and Pacot in Sacapulas both of which are oriented 284°W–104°E). The Eastern Quiche architectural style of stairways on all four sides of rectangular buildings appears to be a continuity from the Early Postclassic Period.

The three successive civic centers within the Akahal territory of San Martín Jilotepeque also indicate continuity in elite social organization for the duration of the Postclassic. A circular pattern on an elevated platform of long structures surrounding a single temple, which is situated in an intermediate position between the plaza center and edge, is evident at Epiclassic La Merced, Early Postclassic and Early-phase Late Postclassic Chuisac Alto, and Late-phase Jilotepeque Viejo. Architectural differences may prove to indicate links to the lowlands, for the Epiclassic temple is elliptical, not unlike that of El Adivinio at contemporaneous Uxmal, whereas the Early Postclassic temple might be compared to the Castillo at Chichen Itza. The duration of the Akahal community is also suggested by the persistence of fine paste cream-slipped ceramics (Chinautla Polychrome) from the Epiclassic to the contact period, and the human face–serpent sculpture.

Within our second category, the upland Quichean regional groups were descended from the Epi-Toltec migration following the demise of Chichen Itza. They thereby represented a separate tradition, characterized by rectilinear plazas. Upon entry into the highlands, they settled in the lofty Sierra de Chuacus, far removed from the well-established acropolis communities. The Central Quiche were grouped together in the Chujuyub area, the Western Quiche built Tzakabala, and the Rabinal were at Tzamaneb—all mountain enclaves overlooking the southern fringe of the Rio Negro watershed, and thus sharing a river system as well as a common habitat (Map 1). These "dawning centers," as they were known ethnohistorically, were close to one another; the Central Quiche, the ethnohistorically undefined Quiche group at Xabaj-Sakiribal in Sajcabaja, and the Rabinal inhabited a section of mountains no more than 30 kilometers long in a direct line. Outside this immediate zone, but in a related habitat, the early Western Cakchiquel were situated in the neighboring Chichcastenango Mountains at Semeja, Mukulbalzib, and Paraxone, overlooking the western fringe of the Rio Motagua drainage.

Rather than joining already established communities, as hypothesized for earlier migrations into the river basins, the Epi-Toltec ancestors of the Central Quiche built small civic centers modeled after those they knew on the Gulf Coast (see, for example, Pozas de Ventura, Andrews 1943).The Cakchiquel, who apparently were subordinate to the Epi-Toltec Quiche from the outset (Fox 1977), must have been so insignificant in actual numbers that they were absorbed by an already established non-Mexicanized community (cf. Semeja), or took over the civic center and women of a defeated local community. However, when the autochthonous peoples of the rich upland basins, such as the Vukamak of the Quiche Basin, were finally subjugated, the Quiche and Cakchiquel built their new centers of Ismachi and Patzak with a settlement pattern apparently uninfluenced by local highland groups. The Epi-Toltec Rabinal, however, seem to have been an upland group that adopted elements of a firmly rooted local acropolis pattern when they moved from their mountaintop center, Tzamaneb, into a lower ecozone and took over already existing Pokoman centers. It is noteworthy that the Pokoman sites taken over at this time by the Rabinal shared major elements of settlement patterning with the Rabinal (i.e., both groups were Mexican influenced). In the upland basins, then, local communities were directly incorporated into the more pluralistic Epi-Toltec derived systems, largely as peasants. As a final point of contrast with the more topographically circumscribed acropolis groups tied to specialized agricultural systems, the vast upland basins of Quezaltenango and Chimaltenango were characterized by the more generalized rainfall-based dry-field agriculture (Fox 1977).

A third category, comprising non-Quichean ethnic groups like the Ixil and Western Mam (e.g., Pueblo Viejo Sipacapa), had regional settlement patterns of long antiquity in the highlands. These appear to have been largely uninfluenced both by movements of Mexicanized lowland groups into the highlands during the Epiclassic and Early Postclassic periods and by later political domination by the Quiche. The conservative Ixil "open-end *a*" civic center pattern remained essentially unchanged from the Late Classic and perhaps the Early Classic, that is, a period of nine to twelve centuries. However, the Ixil may have been influenced by the lowland Maya during the Classic Period. The Western Mam's linear altar mound pattern dates from the Early Postclassic Period, if not earlier. Both regions are mountainous with relatively infertile soils, supporting a scattered population. Apparently lacking in resources of interregional interest, they appear to have been bypassed by Postclassic lowland-to-highland movements, except for larger centers like Tajumulco, which may have figured in the procurement network of the widely traded Tojil Plumbate ceramics.

A homogeneous culture shared by various communities within a region, as indicated by settlement pattern and architectural style, may have been the binding element in the emergence of regional polities, such as those known for the Cakchiquel, Rabinal, and Aguacatec after their break from the Quiche state late in pre-Hispanic times. The Rabinal, for example, had at least three major civic centers with a remarkably homogeneous architectural style (Tzak Pokoma, Cahyup, and Cawinal), as well as a number of others mentioned in the *Rabinal Achi*. Other culturally distinctive regional groups, such as the Ixil, did not form separate polities, but nevertheless maintained ethnic identity within the Quiche and Spanish systems. In overview, thus, the various regional groupings comprised fundamental population units. They may have been brought into a single centralized state system, like that of the Quiche, but they reappeared, following the same ethnic and territorial lines of cleavage, when the larger political system dissolved.

Centralism

Centralism refers to change in the components of a system as a result of domination by a single component. In this case, in the late 1300s and the 1400s, the Central Quiche welded such regional-ethnic groups as the Sacapulas Quiche, Aguacatec, Ixil, Mam, Uspantec, Agaab, Rabinal, Akahal, and Cakchiquel, as well as several piedmont and coastal groups, into a conquest state that endured, after the loss of several groups, until the Spanish conquest in 1524. The dynamic relationship between dominant and subordinate groups, involving processes of conquest, control, and tribute flow, caused change in each of the regional components, including the Central Quiche.

Formation of a Quiche City-State: A Base for Expansion

Ethnohistoric and archaeological sources agree that the Vuka-mak of the Quiche Basin, just below the Early-phase Chujuyub mountain fortresses, were the first highland peoples to be brought within the Epi-Toltec-derived conquest system. At this point, the descendants of the Epi-Toltec immigrants had been in the high-lands for several generations. Upon relocation in the basin in the mid 1300s, a century later, the Epi-Toltec victors and the defeated

Quiche-speaking Vukamak came to form a single regional-ethnic group. As the conquest state first took shape, the Vukamak communities, peasant agriculturalists in outlying districts, constituted one social stratum, and the Epi-Toltec descendants became an urbanized ruling stratum, first at Ismachi but soon occupying the surrounding plateaus of Greater Utatlan. The Vukamak descendants apparently continued to occupy their former territories, although their civic centers (e.g., Pakaja-Lemoa) were abandoned. Overseeing the rural districts were small administrative ward centers of Greater Utatlan. Of the more than thirty such wards mentioned ethnohistorically (Nijaib I 1957:71–73; Nijaib II 1957:105; Tamub 1957:55–61, C'oyoi 1973:302), all of the six that were surveyed archaeologically, Cakolquiej (Cakolqueh), Panajxit (Nacxit), Ilotenango, Chuila, Xesic, and Chicabracan (Cakbrakan), were situated near large Early Postclassic Vukamak centers. Such spatial proximity suggests that the Quiche wards were simply substituted for the earlier civic centers as loci for local leaders or Quiche administrators (Fox 1977). Carmack (1974) suggests that the vanquished Vukamak lineages became Quiche vassals. These outlying districts provided foodstuffs to the urban dwellers. As functionaries of a militarily expansive system, the increasingly powerful Central Quiche warlords were thus freed from subsistence activities to direct their attention to further conquests (see Boserup 1965:74–75).

Acculturation is generally a two-way process. By abducting local women for wives upon settling in the highlands (cf. Xajil 1953:77, 82; *Popol Vuh* 1950:194–96), and later marrying into defeated leading Vukamak lineages upon moving into the Quiche Basin, the Epi-Toltec became Quiche speakers and eventually what we may consider a Mayan ethnic group, the Central Quiche. As we have seen, the loss of identity as separate political entities was more complete for the former Vukamak communities. Judging from archaeological data alone, the Vukamak lost their monumental architectural tradition as well as their decorated ceramic styles, such as the polychrome red and brown on orange, and the bichrome red on orange (see Carmack, Fox and Stewart 1975:112). Interestingly, the occurrence of the local highland ware, characterized by wavy line incision, at the Early-phase Chujuyub centers and Vukamak basin sites correlates with the taking of local women as wives, and disappears with the full emergence of the Central

Quiche regional sociocultural system. The Epi-Toltec-derived governmental organization of the victors, exemplified by Mexican architectural forms and spatial arrangements, persisted and evolved within the urban center of Greater Utatlan.

Evolutionary Processes of State Emergence: The Change from Early to Late Phases

The move onto the plains of the Quiche Basin and the formation of the city-state corresponds to the transition from the Early to the Late phase evident in archaeological remains. At this time the other Epi-Toltec upland groups shifted their territorial bases from small enclaves high in the Sierra de Chuacus to comparatively large plateau sites in fertile *tierra templada* basins. Roughly contemporaneously with the Quiche move from Chujuyub to Ismachi, the Cakchiquel abandoned their small mountaintop sites (Semeja, Mukubalzib, Paraxone) for the large plateau center Patzak (Chiavar), bordering the Quiche Basin to the south, and the Rabinal moved from Tzamaneb to the Pokoman-built-centers of Cahyup (Cakyug) and Tzak Pokoma (Nim Pokom) in the center of the Rabinal Basin.

Surface survey reveals a change in the actual weapons of war corresponding in time to the emergence of the conquest state. The Early-phase atlatl dart, characterized by leaf-shaped and tapering-base projectile points, was replaced by the bow and arrow, characterized by small side-notched and indented-base projectile points.

In ceramics, Fortress white on red became the most prevalent decorated ware, along with red-slipped ceramics without the white painted designs, at civic centers dominated by the Central Quiche. Apparently developed from a "heavy white line on thick red slipped ware" prototype of the Early-phase Chujuyub sites, Fortress white on red is thought to have been a regional variant of the widespread Mixteca-Puebla art style, which again points to the Mexican underpinnings of the Quiche conquest system (Carmack and Larmer 1971; Marqusee 1974).

As we would expect, profound changes in Central Quiche sociocultural organization occurred with the formation of the conquest state. One change in governmental-ideological organization is manifest in the appearance of two temples in the civic plaza at

Ismachi, double temples at the Rabinal centers, and twin temples as well as a single temple in the central plaza at Cakchiquel Patzak. The Early-phase Chujuyub *tinamit* had two civic plazas each, seemingly reflecting moietal social organization, rather than the single plaza at Ismachi with two temples. Sloane (1974) argues that twin temples reflect the adoption of a Quiche deity alongside the patron deity of the local community. Indeed, all Quichean Early-phase plazas seem to have a single temple, including the Quiche shrine sites of Awilix and Tohil, and Cakchiquel Semeja. A single centrally situated temple, as at the Chujuyub shrine sites or the acropolis sites, may prove to be linked in inspiration to the Toltec (cf. Chichen Itza). However, a single temple on a plaza side is a common Gulf Coastal Yucatecan feature (cf. Epiclassic Uxmal). With the emergence of the Quiche state, Tohil, a god of warfare, may have replaced Hacawitz, who apparently had merchant characteristics reminiscent of the Gulf Coast, as the principal Quiche deity. The sixteenth-century documents, however, claim that the principal Quiche deity prior to their arrival in the Guatemalan highlands was Tohil (e.g., *Popol Vuh* 1950:179).

Covariation of Centralism and Geography

A generation or two after consolidating the Quiche heartland, the Central Quiche and their "allies," the Western Cakchiquel and Rabinal, embarked on a series of expansionistic campaigns. The earliest thrusts outside the Quiche Basin were led by the ruler Gucumatz, beginning in the late 1300s or early 1400s. They were largely to the north and east, bringing within the Quiche tributary system the Sacapulas Quiche, Aguacatec, Uspantec, some of the Northern Mam, and apparently the Ixil and Akahal. The second series of expansionistic campaigns was led by Gucumatz's son, Quicab, whom the Quiche often considered their greatest general and ruler. He brought within the conquest system the Western Quiche and Southern Mam of the southwestern volcanic basins of Totonicapan and Quezaltenango and the adjacent piedmont and coastal groups.

Greater Utatlan is situated in the geographic center of the Quiche state at its maximum extent. It lies near the headwaters of the Rio Negro and Rio Motagua, which eventually drain into the Atlantic Ocean, as well as near the headwaters of the Rio Salama, which drains into the Pacific (Map 11; Edmonson 1971:xvi). These three rivers flow through most of the provinces of the Quiche state: the Rio Negro flows to the north and east, linking the Sacapulas Quiche, Aguacatec, Uspantec, and Eastern Quiche; the Rio Motagua leads to the Cakchiquel and Akahal; and the Rio Salama flows through the southwestern basins of the Western Quiche and Southern Mam. A sixteenth-century native pictorial shows Chwa Tz'ak (Pueblo Viejo Momostenango) directly linked to Utatlan by a river (see Carmack 1973:12, 62). Chronologically, Quiche expansion can be seen as following these communication lines, first along the Negro and Motagua rivers, and later along the Salama.

Direct centralistic influence, as gauged by Central Quiche architectural forms, does not occur, with the exceptions of Vicaveval, Zaculeu, and perhaps Xikumuk, beyond the limits of these river systems (Map 11). The Ixil in general and the Western Mam (Pueblo Viejo Sipacapa, Tuitenam, and Pueblo Viejo Huitan) lie outside these river systems and show little Quiche influence.

Moving outward from the Central Quiche heartland, we can trace concentric rings of Central Quiche settlement pattern features denoting degrees of centralistic influence. The civic centers closest in settlement patterning and architectural style to Utatlan, irrespective of mechanism of transmittal, are Sija, Pueblo Viejo Canilla, Patzak-Sajcabaja, Tenam-Aguacatan, Xikumuk, and Iximche, which are nearly the same distance in different directions from the Central Quiche capital (Map 11, Ring C). Moving farther out (Ring D), Chuisac, Vicaveval, Zaculeu, and Chuitinamit-Zunil, which manifest Central Quiche as well as local influence, are virtually equidistant from Greater Utatlan. Among the Eastern Quiche beyond Pueblo Viejo Canilla, Central Quiche political domination is known from ethnohistory, but is absent in settlement remains, at least at the level of surface survey. The Rabinal centers manifest only a general cultural affinity, as would be expected from their common Epi-Toltec cultural heritage with the Central Quiche. Also on the edge of this last ring, the Early-phase Uspantec center, Chamac, does not seem to manifest Quiche influence in settlement patterning, but it may have been abandoned after Quiche subjugation in the beginning of the Late phase. Beyond this last ring, Central Quiche influence cannot be discerned, although political domination was known for the Western Mam and Ixil.

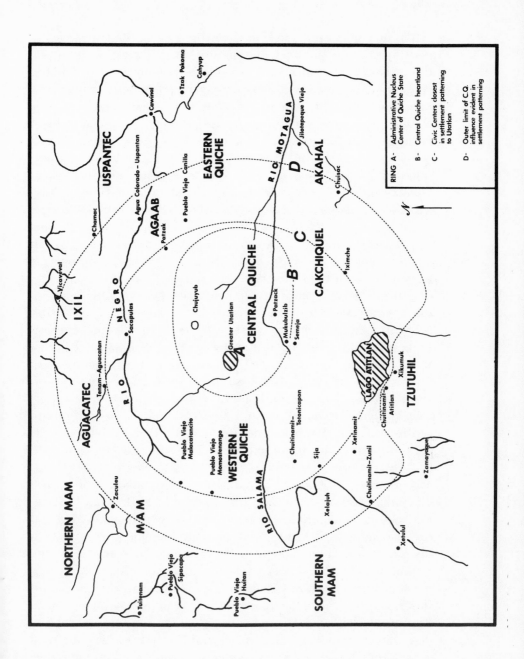

RING A- Administrative Nucleus
Center of Quiche State

B- Central Quiche heartland

C- Civic Centers closest
in settlement patterning
to Utatlan

D- Outer limit of C.Q.
influence evident in
settlement patterning

We may generalize, therefore, in the case of the Quiche state, that degrees of political domination and vectors of expansion (i.e., along communication lines of rivers) seem to be related to geographic distance within the rugged highlands. Furthermore, in a conquest state where integration is maintained by force, settlement pattern variables reflecting direct control and indirect influence are directly proportional to geographic distance from the state's center. Supporting this proposition, the once-subject regional groups most successful in becoming independent of Quiche control were the Rabinal, on the state's eastern extremity, and the Aguacatec, on its northwestern border. The Cakchiquel could only effectively divest themselves of Quiche rule by moving from Patzak, near the Central Quiche heartland, to Iximche. When Quiche armies did eventually lay siege to Iximche, they became logistically overextended and were soundly defeated.

Farther east and south respectively, beyond the state's borders, the Tzutuhil and Pokoman were not under direct Quiche control, but were occasionally in conflict with them. To reiterate, there is some possibility that the Tzutuhil were briefly subjugated during the earliest Quiche expansion, but they were clearly independent during most of the Late phase, if not all of it. Both groups manifested relatively independent sociocultural systems, as reflected in settlement patterning and ceramics. The Tzutuhil continued their acropolis complex, in addition to the "carved" ceramic tradition, uninterrupted from the Early phase and probably before. The Pokoman, like the Rio Negro Basin groups and other Rio Motagua drainage groups, developed twin temples. Since the Pokoman were beyond the borders of the Quiche state, but seemingly experienced pressures from Quiche expansion and displacement at the hands of the Rabinal, the emergence of a twin temple among them may also be related to the growth of the conquest state. A number of Pokoman communities were subjugated by the Western Cakchiquel late in pre-Hispanic times, but this postdates the appearance of the twin temple (Fox 1977). Except at Pokoman centers conquered by the Western Cakchiquel (e.g., Chinautla Viejo; see Carmack and Fox n.d.), which might be considered Quiche centralistic influence transmitted through their "cultural offspring" (the Cakchiquel), the ceramic markers of Central Quiche influence, notably Fortress white on red, appear to be minimal at Pokoman sites.

The general Quichean affinity of the Pokoman, as well as of some Mam communities, can be seen within the context of a frontier situation. There is a gradual gradation of Quichean settlement patterning in general in an east-west-running midsection of the highlands, moving outward from the Quiche heartland. To the west of the Quiche, there is notable overlap between the Western Quiche (e.g., Xetinamit) and the Mam (e.g., Pueblo Viejo Malacatancito). To the east, there is overlap among the Rabinal, Akahal, and Pokoman both in social organization, with each elite community having maintained a number of civic plazas for respective kin-based social divisions, and in architectural style, which ultimately derives from acropolis traditions.

Natural and Social Environment of Early Expansion: Ecological Symbiosis.

The acropolis groups conquered during the first wave of Central Quiche expansion are thought to have dominated power relations during the Early phase, perhaps as a legacy from Toltec Chichen Itza. The Zaculeu Mam can be included with the acropolis groups, since Zaculeu was continuously occupied by a "Mexicanized" community at least from the Early Postclassic Period. Some ethnohistoric documents, written by the Quiche and Cakchiquel well after power relationships with the acropolis groups had been reversed, suggest that the acropolis groups maintained a superior position. The Quiche are said to have recognized the political stature of the Cawinal community in the Rio Negro Basin (C'oyoi 1973:290–91), as the Western Cakchiquel recognized that of the Akahal in the Rio Motagua Basin (Xajil 1953:80). Quichean political history, however, was probably revised occasionally, especially upon changes of rulers and the like, as was true of the Aztec, also of Epi-Toltec heritage. Our knowledge of the political defeats of the Central Quiche, such as the coup against the Quiche, comes not from Quiche texts, but from those of their rivals. Thus it is not surprising that there is little direct reference to the Early-phase acropolis communities, especially at such an early date for Quichean historiography. We may infer from the large size of the acropolis centers and from their proximity to strategic resources (salt at Sacapulas, obsidian near Chuisac), that the acropolis groups held considerable power vis-à-vis other highland groups, notably the upland Epi-Toltec on their small peripheral mountaintop enclaves.

Prior to their thrusts to the north and east, the Central Quiche territorial base comprised the rather ecologically homogeneous *tierra templada* uplands. Upon subjugation of the acropolis groups, the Central Quiche effected an ecological symbiosis with the warm river-basin habitats by demanding tribute in precious gems and metals, feathers, and *tierra caliente* produce, all of which were lacking in the uplands. Rather than a true two-way symbiotic relationship (for a general application of this principle see Sanders 1956, 1962), however, the movements of materials were essentially one-way.

Settlement pattern data indicate that the Central Quiche administrative enclaves were located in habitats similar to that of the Quiche homeland. Tenam-Aguacatan, Chuisac, and Zaculeu are situated in upper-range *tierra templada* basins scarred by barrancas, none differing more than 150 meters in elevation from the Quiche Basin. The immediate environs of these communities are characterized by the same dry-field agriculture as the Quiche Basin.

The location of the Central Quiche administrative enclaves may also have been related to the social exigencies of the environment. Two of the administrative enclaves at regional capitals, Zaculeu and Chuisac, were near the west and east state borders, respectively. This relates to the outermost ring of Quiche influence (Map 11, D). While situated closer to the Central Quiche, Tenam overlooked the strategic northwestern entrance to the Rio Negro Basin, which, as we have seen, was the principal link between the northern provinces. This also was near the juncture of the Mam, Ixil, and Sacapultec regional boundaries. Such enclaves may have been "relay stations" of Quiche authority, for, as noted earlier, control decreases as distance from the center increases (cf. Balandier 1970:142). Provinces between these enclaves, such as Sacapulas, were accessible directly from the center, Greater Utatlan, or from an enclave on its opposite side, such as Tenam. Sacapulas was also directly linked to the Central Quiche heartland by a thirty-kilometer-long corridor. Similarly, on this outer ring of Quiche influence, the small fortified center of Vicaveval, in the midst of the Ixil region, may have been a Quiche administrative outpost.

The shift in power relations between the long established "warm-basin" groups and the upland Quiche may be seen in terms of growth potential in their respective habitats. Rio Negro Basin sites as well as some Akahal communities within the Rio Motagua Basin are situated on bluffs overlooking the small river valley floor tracts of arable land circumscribed by steep, arid basin walls. Population growth was thus restricted. The acropolis groups were adapted to river valley floor cultivation, dependent upon proximity to the river. This specialized adaptation is also evident in the longevity of these sites. The acropolis centers of the river basins (including Chuitinamit in the Lake Atitlan Basin) are the only civic centers, with the exception of Zaculeu, to span the entire Late Postclassic Period, from the collapse of Chichen Itza to the Spanish conquest (Fox 1977). In contrast, the generalized cultivation system of dry-field agriculture was practiced in the vast upland basins, with rich volcanic soils; these were many times larger than the narrow river basins. One or two generations after relocation in the upland basins, the Central Quiche and their allies, the Cakchiquel and Rabinal, who also occupied upland basins, embarked on their conquest of the acropolis groups. The niche of the upland Quiche and allies had a long-run competitive edge, for greater populations could field larger armies.

Growth of the Center: Urbanism

As the administrative nucleus of the Quiche state, the elite community of the Central Quiche grew both in overall complexity and in size, increasing perhaps fortyfold, at least partially as a result of Quiche control over territories of ecological and ethnic diversity. In size, the three Chujuyub civic centers that made up the earlier nuclear community together total about one tenth of a square kilometer in habitable space. Ismachi, the intermediate center, is a quarter of a square kilometer (with Culbut, half a sq km), whereas Greater Utatlan was at least four square kilometers on seven contiguous plateaus. The documents clearly state that Ismachi was outgrown in just one generation (*Popol Vuh* 1950:212–15; Totonicapan 1953:83), when the Quiche expanded from the one plateau of Ismachi to the neighboring plateaus at the time of Gucumatz's conquests. It should also be kept in mind that additional population growth within the nuclear community was diverted into colonizing newly acquired territories, especially in the mid fifteenth century (see below).

The maintenance of a conquest-tributary system required permanent new social categories within Greater Utatlan, such as administrators to oversee the multitude of tasks necessary for the coordination of large, multiethnic populations, a military to maintain control of subject groups, and artisans to fashion exotic raw material tribute into sumptuary symbols for office and class distinction (Carmack 1968:77, 1974, n.d.b). Correlating with the increase in governmental offices mentioned ethnohistorically is the increase in building types surrounding the civic plaza at Utatlan, which do not occur at the Chujuyub centers. Also, beyond the two social classes, the urban elite and the peasants, that existed at inception of the Quiche city-state a half-century earlier, several newly emerged social classes can be distinguished within Greater Utatlan at this time, such as the elite, the military, and the artisans. These distinct classes are thought to be spatially represented by concentric rings of occupation within the city. The elite (that is, the Nima Quiche, Tamub, and Ilocab) divisions were located in the center of the city on three closely spaced although separate plateaus, Utatlan, Ismachi, and Chisalin, respectively. The military were thought to occupy areas on the periphery of the elite sectors, perhaps Resguardo or Pakaman before Utatlan, the entrance plaza at Chisalin, and, if the Ilocab did in fact dwell at Ilotenango prior to their unsuccessful coup, the plaza of Chicoculjip at the entrance to Pakaja-Ilotenango. According to Weeks's (1975) excavations, artisans, such as metalworkers, were also situated outside the elite centers near the military (at least in the case of Resguardo). There also remains the possibility that some metalworkers were linked to the military in the manufacture of axes or other armaments. Beyond the urban core were some thirty rural wards overseeing the peasant class of the city-state. It should be pointed out that while Greater Utatlan was sectioned apparently along class lines, ranked lineages still remained the principal mechanism of organization, which is typical of newly evolved states (Carmack 1974; cf. Miles 1957b:241–43; R. M. Adams 1966:165; Balandier 1970:140; Harner 1970:69; Service 1975:xii).

Judging from the immense size and central location (adjacent to the civic plaza) of the three places thus far identified within Utatlan, several leading lineages stood at the apex of the conquest-tributary system (see Wallace 1977). However, it has not yet been determined whether tribute was in fact redistributed throughout the palace lineages. Since Quiche administrative enclaves in the widely spaced provinces, such as those at Tenam, Zaculeu, and Chuisac, were apparently modeled after the elite centers within Greater Utatlan, it may be reasoned that they were occupied by Quiche elite, corroborating ethnohistory. In addition to overseeing the interest of the Quiche rulers (i.e., the ruling lineages who supported the actual rulers), such faraway enclaves may have siphoned off potential rivals from within the royal lineages, functioning as security against conspiracy or insurrection. For example, the Quiche military leader during the Spanish conquest, Tecum Umam, resided at the provincial center in Totonicapan, a considerable distance from the Quiche Ajpop (ruler) at Utatlan (C'oyoi 1973:302; for other examples, see Nijaib I 1957:101–3). Tecum was apparently slated to succeed to the throne at a later time.

The transplanting of Quiche aristocrats to outlying provinces seems to have taken on characteristics of private estates for scions of leading lineages, perhaps in reward for military service, but in concept not unlike that known for the Aztec (R. M. Adams 1966:118–19; Soustelle 1970:81), or feudal Europe. Thus, for example, the Nijaib nobleman Izquin of the Nima Quiche, who distinguished himself in numerous campaigns under Quicab, personally came to reign over several newly subject communities among the Western Quiche (Nijaib I–II 1957). Izquin maintained several palaces within this province and extracted tribute in both foodstuffs and luxury materials (Carmack 1970:93–94; Carmack et al. 1972:14–19).

Centralistic Expansion and Environmental Similarity

A series of expansionistic campaigns southwest of the Quiche heartland under the ruler and general Quicab in the mid fifteenth century brought the territorial holdings of the Quiche state to their maximum extent. This also completed a geographical circle of subject territories surrounding the Central Quiche (Map 11). In the historical perspective, Quicab simply picked up where his father, Gucumatz, left off when the latter was killed in battle by the Mam (Totonicapan 1953:187–88; Xpantzay II 1957:141; Xpantzay III 1957:163; Carmack n.d.a). Quicab next moved against the Mam of the Quezaltenango Basin, the Samala Pass, and the piedmont and coast, as well as the neighboring Western Quiche (i.e. Momostenango, Totonicapan, Chiquimula) (*Popol Vuh* 1950:221; C'oyoi 1973:291, 197; Nijaib I 1957:74–76; Xpantzay II 1957:141–45).

The Momostenango hilly country and the Totonicapan and Quezaltenango basins colonized by the Central Quiche relate to the second and third concentric rings of Quiche influence evident in settlement patterning (Map 11, C,D). Unfortunately, these areas exhibit perhaps the least well preserved settlement remains in the highlands, which do not lend themselves to architectural comparison. Nevertheless, direct Central Quiche influence is seen at Sija, which appears to have been laid out much like a Central Quiche elite center with a single central civic plaza, and at the considerably smaller Chuitinamit Zunil on the Samala Pass. Architecture at these two apparently different kinds of centers (i.e., large upland center versus small river-pass/piedmont center), curiously, is similar sized and may prove to share characteristics of orientation. While monumental architecture is scant in this region, the large areal extent evident by "occupational debris" corroborates ethnohistoric testimony that large urbanized Quiche colonies existed at Sija, Pueblo Viejo Momostenango (Chwa Tz'ak), Chuitinamit-Totonicapan (Chuvi-Miquina), and Xelajuh (the pre-Hispanic Quezaltenango). The native chronicles further indicate that each of these communities was colonized by members of the major lineages of Greater Utatlan (Carmack n.d.a:23–24). Thus the polycentric lineage organization of Greater Utatlan was transplanted in some measure. There may, however, have been distinct spheres of colonial holdings, for at Momostenango the Nijaib division of the Nima Quiche and the Ilocab tended to dominate, while at Totonicapan the Nijaib dominated exclusively and at Xelajuh the Tamub were prominent.

These large colonies occupied *tierra fria* habitats, although characterized by dry-field agriculture not unlike that of the milder Quiche Basin. But the slightly cooler conditions of the Quezaltenango and Totonicapan basins were more than compensated for by their rich volcanic soils, which allowed cultivation (cf. West 1964a:74; Stevens 1964:306). The ecology of this region was symbiotically linked with the piedmont in a manner reminiscent of the linkage between the Quiche Basin and the environmentally lowlandlike Rio Negro and Rio Motagua basins discussed earlier.

The conquest and colonization of such basins of habitat generally similar to the Quiche homeland may be linked to the rapid population growth and interior crowding of the Quiche Basin, which is well recorded ethnohistorically (Fox 1977; e.g., Tamub 1957:49–53). Indeed, a passage in the *Titulo C'oyoi* (1973:298) specifically describes Quiche armies conquering the Quezaltenango Basin for the stated purpose of procuring milpa lands. Thus, population growth and military expansionism seem to be interrelated outward-directed forces, with surplus population diverted into armies and colonies.

Beyond the volcanic basins to the southwest were the piedmont and coastal provinces, which, again, are virtually unknown archaeologically. Nonetheless, Chuitinamit-Zuil occupied an upper-range *tierra caliente* habitat along the Samala Pass, and therefore may be considered a piedmont Quiche site. Its small size in comparison to the upland urban centers (cf. Sija) seemingly reflects the differences in productivity between the upland dry-field farming and the mixed cultivation niche of piedmont communities, which comprised arboriculture (zapotes, manos, avocados), cacao, and maize farming. The difference in size may prove to relate to the piedmont towns yet to be located, such as Xetulul (see Alvarado's [1924] description) and Samayac.

As we have seen, the Quiche colonies established in the southwestern basins during the reign of Quicab soon grew into urban communities that might eventually have overshadowed Greater Utatlan, if the Spanish had not cut short their growth. Today, the modern descendants of the large Quiche centers here, such as Quezaltenango, San Miguel Totonicapan, and Santiago Momostenango, are at least comparable in size to Santa Cruz del Quiche and San Pedro Jocopilas, descendants of Greater Utatlan. At the apex of the Quiche state, at any rate, much of the territorial base shifted from the Quiche Basin toward the heavily populated southwestern basins (see Carmack n.d.a:22–25, 43). Thus this outer ring of earlier Quiche influence in a sense surpassed the political center of the state, thereby supporting Service's (1971, 1975) generalization about the growth potential of geographically removed provinces. This shift in territorial base to the southwest was followed shortly by successful revolt of the Aguacatec and Rabinal provinces, on the geographical perimeter of the Quiche state opposite the southwestern basins. The revolt of the Cakchiquel also indicates a centrifugal movement of power to the southeastern periphery.

The revolt of the Cakchiquel, one of the original allies of the Central Quiche, from Patzak and the subsequent fragmentation of the Quiche state can be seen as a continuation of the developmental processes of the conquest system traced in the southwestern basins. Briefly, about A.D. 1470, following Quiche expansion to the southwest, the Cakchiquel moved about sixty kilometers (in a straight line; in travel, it is easily two or three times the distance) southeast of Utatlan (Patzak is within sight of Utatlan) to Iximche, sufficiently distant for them to establish an independent and rival political system. Seemingly as part of the fissioning process from the well-populated heartland region, the move from the southern rim of the Quiche Basin at Patzak to Ixmiche on the western edge of the broad Chimaltenango Basin parallels the Quiche move into the southwestern basins in some respects. Like the upland Quezaltenango and Totonicapan basins, the Chimaltenango Basin has fertile volcanic soils supporting dry-field, generalized agriculture, and is firmly within the cool *tierra fria* climatic zone. However, also like the southwestern basins, it is susceptible to occasional frost. Indeed, ethnohistory relates an interesting case underscoring the symbiotic relationship between this upland basin and the adjacent *tierra caliente* piedmont. The Cakchiquel were saved from being starved back into submission by the Quiche, following crop failure brought on by frost, by importing maize directly from their piedmont lands (Xajil 1953:101–2).

The strong resemblance in settlement patterning and architectural style between Iximche and Utatlan is coincident with the first geographic concentric ring (Map 11,C). Iximche is thus more or less equidistant from the southwestern basins (i.e., Sija) and Utatlan, only it is in the opposite direction from the Quiche heartland. However, it is yet to be resolved whether this resemblance is due to a common Epi-Toltec heritage with the Central Quiche or whether it is from strong Central Quiche influence when the Cakchiquel were a subordinate "ally" and dwelt at Patzak within the shadow of the Central Quiche. Early-phase Paraxone has not yet been appraised, although the Cakchiquel seem to have been fully within the rectilinear-plaza tradition from the Gulf Coast, judging from their intermediate center, Patzak (which compares well with Ismachi, the contemporaneous Quiche center). There is also a possibility that the string of small rectilinear plazas along the ridgetop at Chuisac Alto was built by the Cakchiquel. In this regard, there is some Akahal influence (e.g., twin temples) at Patzak. Considering the second hypothesis to account for similarity with Utatlan, the more successful governmental and ideological organization of the Central Quiche may have been instituted at Iximche after the Cakchiquel became thoroughly familiar with it as a ward (Patzak) on the periphery of the Quiche heartland. The continuity in orientations between Patzak and Iximche supports both hypotheses.

General Dimensions of Centralistic Change

Fortifications

In addition to the presence of Quiche architecture, another index of centralistic influence from the center of the conquest state to its regional components is the increase of fortifications in settlement patterning after political interaction with the Central Quiche. Increased fortification may be seen in changes from less fortified to more fortified natural locations and by the construction of artificial fortifications, such as moats, masonry terraces, and walls. However, without excavation, which was beyond the research design of this study, it was not possible to discern when fortifications were constructed at continuously occupied sites (e.g., the moats and masonry terraces at the Sacapulas sites, the moat and bulwark construction at Tenam-Aguacatan, the wall at Zaculeu mentioned by the Spanish conquistadores).

Increased fortifications among regional groups at the time of expansion of the conquest state correlate directly with concentric rings of Central Quiche influence evident in settlement patterning. In fact, it may be postulated that as geographic proximity to the center of a conquest state increases, so does the amount of fortification.

In the geographic center itself (Map 11,B), the newly arrived Epi-Toltec ancestors of the Quiche, who brought with them the foundations of conquest statecraft, chose fortified locations high in the Sierra de Chuacus. The Chujuyub *tinamit* sites, Hacawitz, Amaktan, and Uquincat, are situated on still more removed mountaintops. These were considerably more fortified than other highland sites during the Early Postclassic Period. When the Central Quiche began their outward expansion, marking the beginning of the Late phase, they relocated on the vertical cliff-faced plateaus of Greater Utatlan, which were accessible only through the entrances. The conquistador Pedro de Alvarado (1924), who was keenly sensitive to fortifications, made note of the movable bridge leading into Utatlan.

Within the first concentric ring of Quiche influence (Map 11, C) are perhaps the most heavily fortified sites, in addition of course to Greater Utatlan. Perhaps the most dramatic change in natural defenses is evident among the Western Quiche. During the Early phase they occupied centers like Tzakabala, situated on an 80-meter-high ridgetop, but during the Late phase their main centers were situated on such naturally fortified eminences as the cliff-ringed volcanic necks of Sija and Chuitinamit-Totonicapan, which rise respectively 600 and 700 meters (cf. also Pueblo Viejo Momostenango). The selection of such extreme situations at the beginning of the Late phase and of Quiche expansion may reflect location of the Western Quiche along the Mam border at this time, prior to the Quiche thrust into the southwestern basins. Situated along the Quiche border, with the Rabinal and Agaab to the east, Pueblo Viejo Canilla also sits atop a high mountain, rising 1,000 meters. It is the highest site with respect to surrounding topography known in the highlands. Also within this first concentric ring of Quiche influence, the Western Cakchiquel changed locations from their Early-phase ridgetop centers of Semeja and Mukubal-zib, high in the Chichicastenango Mountains, to the cliff-ringed plateau sites of Patzak and Iximche. The Uspantec apparently abandoned their Early-phase center, Chamac, after subjugation by the Central Quiche, and relocated on the Rio Negro proper. Within this first geographic ring of conquest interaction, only the Sacapulas communities did not change locations.

Beyond the perimeter of Central Quiche influence discernible in settlement patterning, the Western Mam, Ixil, and Tzutuhil apparently continued in the same locations throughout the Late Postclassic Period. Situated at the almost impregnable fortress of Chuitinamit, with three sides on Lake Atitlan, connected to the mainland only along the slope of the volcano San Pedro, the Tzutuhil were able to withstand repeated pressure by the Quiche and Cakchiquel, but not the Spanish (Xajil 1953; Alvarado 1924). Also beyond the last ring of Central Quiche influence, the Eastern Quiche sites of Cawinal, Tzak Pokoma, and Cahyup were more or less continuously occupied for much of the Late Postclassic Period, although the Rabinal displaced the Pokoman at the latter two sites at the beginning of the Late phase. Also beyond this ring, the Akahal followed the relocational pattern more typical of communities closer to the center of political interaction, when they moved from ridgetop Chuisac to the cliff-ringed plateau of Jilotepeque Viejo. However, this move can be seen as related to the growth and pressure of the Cakchiquel at Iximche (Fox 1977; Carmack and Fox n.d.), so that in this case the geographic center of centralistic influence (i.e. Iximche) was farther east, putting Jilotepeque Viejo within the first concentric ring from Iximche.

Urbanism and Centralism

As hypothesized in Chapter 1, the increase in militaristic political interaction between communities seems related to increased urbanization. Supporting this, the growth of urban communities correlates with the concentric rings model of Quiche influence. However, since settlement data are insufficient to warrant population estimates, the usual measure of urbanism, I will rely on the characteristic of occupational specialization. That is, it can be inferred from ethnohistory and settlement remains that most of the city-dwelling population at the better known Quiche elite communities was engaged in nonagricultural pursuits, and that their subsistence needs were furnished by peasants in the surrounding countryside (see Sanders 1962:38; Crumley 1976:67). The growth of the largest urban community in the highlands, Greater Utatlan, at the geographic center of the Quiche state, has been delineated above. The next closest urban centers in size are also those closest geographically to the center of the state and thus those where militaristic political interaction was most intense. These urban centers, with the exception of Zaculeu and Xelajuh, lie within the closest concentric ring of Quiche influence (Map 11, C). Iximche of the Cakchiquel and the Tzutuhil community around Chuitinamit-Atitlan (including Xikumuk and Chukumuk) are clearly the largest of the surveyed urban sites, besides Greater Utatlan. Like Greater Utatlan, both were capitals of conquest states. There were sizable urban communities as well at Sija, Pueblo Viejo Momostenango, Tenam-Aguacatan, and Pueblo Viejo Canilla. Also within this first concentric ring, the cluster of civic centers at Sacapulas may relate to a nucleated community of sorts. But the individuality of each of these centers in settlement patterning does not suggest that they were confederates within a single urban community, as was the case for the three Central Quiche confederates at Greater Utatlan or the three Cakchiquel confederates at Iximche.

Beyond the limit of Central Quiche influence evident in settlement remains, the three Eastern Quiche communities of Cawinal, Tzak Pokoma, and Cahyup are fairly large, comparable to the other large Eastern Quichean communities of this frontier, such as the Akahal at Jilotepeque Viejo and the Pokoman at Chinautla Viejo (Carmack and Fox n.d.). The least urbanized centers in the highlands lie north and west of the limit of Quiche influence, in rather infertile mountain ranges. The small, widely scattered civic centers of such groups as the Ixil, Kekchi, Pokomchi, and Western Mam, each with just a few buildings apparently religious in function (temples, altars, ball courts), may actually have been ceremonial centers. The Spaniards were able to conquer the more urbanized upland groups rapidly in 1524 (see Alvarado 1924), but it took them several decades to subdue the less centralized regional groups located in the relatively inaccessible departments of Alta Verapaz and the northern part of Quiche (see Las Casas 1958). These groups may have been too distant and insufficiently lucrative in resources to warrant more direct Central Quiche or Spanish control.

We have seen, in the case of the growth of the Greater Utatlan urban community, that as the size of the community increases, so will the governmental mechanism for the integration of the more numerous parts (see White 1975:90). As part of this process, the various kin groups of a community will lose ultimate governing power to just a few leading lineages. The government of a ranked lineage community becomes stratified itself with increased centralism, as fewer people have access to ultimate authority. Urban communities in close geographical and thereby interactional proximity to the Central Quiche manifested more centralized governments. We may see this among the Central Quiche themselves after the inception of the conquest state, when the two civic plazas that characterized each of the three Chujuyub civic centers, probably reflecting a moietal community organization, were synthesized into a single plaza at the three elite centers within Greater Utatlan. Correspondingly, the urban communities within the first concentric ring of Quiche influence manifest a single civic plaza (e.g., Sija, Pueblo Viejo Canilla) or two civic plazas, perhaps reflecting Central Quiche administrative enclaves among subject regional groups (such as at Tenam-Aguacatan or Patzak-Sajcabaja). Beyond Central Quiche influence, in settlement remains to the east, the various large Quichean communities of the Rabinal, Akahal, or Pokoman contrast dramatically in community organization with the more centralized urban communities closer to the Central Quiche, by manifesting from five to eight civic plazas within a single community. Numerous plazas bespeak a less centralized governmental organization, with a number of contending, relatively autonomous kin groups, whose individuality is reflected in separate civic plazas segmented by walls, terraces, and moats.

A trend toward increased integration is also evident in proximics within the Central Quiche and Cakchiquel communities during the span of the Late Postclassic Period. Thus, the Early-phase governmental loci at Hacawitz, Uquin cat, and Amak tan are between two and three kilometers apart. The Late-phase elite centers within Greater Utatlan are only a few hundred meters apart. Similarly, the Early-phase Cakchiquel centers were situated on separate mountaintops in Chichicastenango, whereas the three civic plazas at their intermediate center, Patzak, and last center, Iximche, suggest that the three Cakchiquel confederates were situated on a single plateau. Indeed, at Iximche, the last Quichean center to be built and perhaps reflecting still greater governmental integration, the three civic plazas and adjoining elite residential complexes of the three confederates are closer yet, separated only by narrow, walled ditches, just a few meters wide, in comparison to the barrancas separating the three Central Quiche confederates at Greater Utatlan.

The restriction of access to power and authority and the increase in centralism are also manifest in ethnohistory. The documents clearly show, for example, when both the Central Quiche and the Cakchiquel embarked on their separate expansionistic trajectories, roughly one century apart, a reduction from three to two principal confederates each. The Nima Quiche and Tamub dominated the Quiche state, at the expense of the Ilocab, whereas the Tukuches were expelled by the Zotzil and Xajil confederates from Iximche. In processual development, the coup attempt of the Tukuches parallels that of the Ilocab more than a half-century earlier.

Concomitant with the centralization of power into fewer kin

groups was the growth of distinct social classes. As a middle-sec-tor social group, the military apparently were situated on the periphery of urban communities, as at Resguardo and Pakaman, in front of Utatlan, discussed earlier. This peripheral location reflects not only social distance from the elite lineages at the geographical center of the community, but the protective functions of the military as well (Fox 1976). Several of the larger and more thoroughly surveyed sites, such as Iximche, Chuitinamit-Atitlan, and Zaculeu, are encircled by a number of hilltop outposts, seemingly serving as a protective umbrella by military wards (for Iximche, see the map of Fuentes y Guzmán detailing "atalyas"; Zaculeu is surrouned by Xetenam, Tenam, El Caballero, and Cerro Pueblo Viejo). The Tzutuhil capital, Chuitinamit, exhibits a more linear distribution of outlying sites, following the shoreline of Lake Atitlan and the slopes of the volcanos. Its military installa-tions and additional settlement components (e.g., Xikumuk and Chukumuk) lie along elevated portions of the shoreline (Lothrop 1933; Orellana n.d.).

Territorial Organization

Central place theory has some application in examining degrees of Quiche influence in particular communities. Generally, we have referred to such communities as regional capitals. As we have seen, such Quiche influence is evident both in actual Central Quiche architecture, and in general trends, such as urbanism and in-creased fortifications. An examination of the distribution of civic centers manifesting greater degrees of Quiche influence reveals that within most regions one community is clearly paramount. Examples are Zaculeu for the Northern Mam, Tenam for the Aguacatec, and Chuisac, as well as Jilotepeque Viejo later, for the Akahal. Ethnohistory suggests that Xelajuh was a regional capital for the Southern Mam during the Early phase, and for the Quiche after their expansion into the Quezaltenango Basin. The *Rabinal Achi* indicates that Central Quiche administrators were stationed at Cahyup, one of several comparable Eastern Quiche centers, in the middle of the Rabinal Basin.

Central place theory describes a hierarchy of central places within a bounded system that are linked to a single supreme city, such as Greater Utatlan, at the system's geographic center. In a conquest-state system where the flow of tribute seems to have been essentially one-way (toward the central places), such civic centers served as collection depots for the main central place, Greater Utatlan. A lesser flow, however, effecting a kind of redistribution of luxury tribute, appears to have moved from various regions to Greater Utatlan and then out again to different regional central places. As a hypothetical case awaiting verification in the archaeological record, for example, jade was procured in the eastern provinces (e.g., Verapaz) of the Quiche state, but it would have found its way along this network to the rapidly expanding Quiche colonies in the southwestern volcanic basins, where it was used by the elite in sumptuary goods.

A generalization broadly consistent with central place theory is that the regional capitals tend to be situated on natural communication arteries (e.g., river valleys) as well as near ecological boundaries, thereby serving as focal points for exchange between difference ecozones (see Sanders 1962; Hardoy 1973:xviii). For example, both Zaculeu and its post-Hispanic descendant, Huehuetenango, seem to have functioned as exchange points between the hilly *tierra templada* countryside of the Northern Mam region and the *tierra fria* Cuchumatanes. Xelajuh was known to lie at the top of the Samala Pass connecting the rich *tierra fria* Quezaltenango Basin with the lush *tierra caliente* piedmont, as was Sija for the Nahualate pass to the piedmont from the Totonicapan Basin. Although outside the Quiche state proper, Iximche, as the central place for the Cakchiquel state, and Chuitinamit-Atitlan, for the Tzutuhil state, exemplify similar characteristics. Iximche is centrally situated, near the Continental Divide, between rivers draining north to the *tierra caliente* Rio Motagua lands and those draining to the piedmont. Chuitinamit-Atitlan overlooks the rich plains surrounding Lake Atitlan as well as the pass to the nearby Tzutuhil piedmont holdings.

In addition to proximity to various ecozones, each of the regional capitals seems to have controlled fairly large tracts of good farming land, capable of supporting large non-food-producing populations by dry-field agriculture. Of the regional capitals, only Chutinamit-Sacapulas seems not to have been situated near a broad-based sustaining area. Chuitinamit, moreover, seems to lack the Central Quiche influence in settlement patterning evident at the regional capitals surrounded by good farming lands.

In the closing decades of the pre-Hispanic period, political events known from ethnohistory attain greater significance when seen within the broad ecological framework utilized in this study of the growth and decline of the Quiche state. Specifically, the ecologically diverse regions, when grouped as single ecologically symbiotic systems, can be seen as territorial bases for the contending political entities that arose following fragmentation of the Quiche state. According to the historian Fuentes y Guzmán (1932–33; Carmack 1973, n.d.a), the half-century prior to the Spanish conquest saw a series of protracted wars between the Quiche, the newly independent Cakchiquel, the Tzutuhil, and the Pipil. With the exception of the Pipil of the piedmont, on whom there has been little research to date, each of these contending political systems had territory comprising both highlands and lowlands. The capital of each of these systems was situated in a broad upland basin directly linked to ecologically lowlandlike provinces. As we have seen, the Tzutuhil capital overlooked a pass linking the Lake Atitlan Basin with the piedmont by a walk of just a few hours. The Cakchiquel capital was equidistant between the lowland ecozones of the Rio Motagua Basin and the piedmont. The Cakchiquel were rapidly expanding into both upland and lowland regions toward the east when the Spanish cut short their growth. The Quiche maintained two principal territorial groupings: their heartland, the Quiche Basin, which was about a day's walk from the Rio Negro Basin of Sacapulas; and the southwestern volcanic basins linked to the piedmont. Late in the pre-Hispanic period, as we have seen, the Quiche power base shifted gradually to the southwestern basins, which, incidently were the first areas to be conquered by the Spaniards in the highlands. At the time of Spanish takeover, the Cakchiquel were clearly on the ascendancy with their continuous expansion to the east, in a direction opposite the Quiche. The vast Pokoman basins to the east, such as the Valley of Guatemala, were directly in the line of Cakchiquel expansion. Because of the pattern of Spanish conquest in Mesoamerica, it has been said that the conquistadores were masters of sensing the political strengths and weaknesses of competing native groups. In this atmosphere of protracted wars between the highland Maya states, the Spanish chose to side with the Cakchiquel, and established their first capital, Santiago de los Caballeros, at Iximche itself. On a higher level of sociocultural integration, the Spanish soon welded all of Mesoamerica together into a conquest state system that was not at all as unfamiliar to the Quiche or the Aztec as has generally been assumed.

REFERENCES

Acosta, Jorge R.
  1958 Interpretación de algunos de los datos obtenidos en Tula relativos a la época Tolteca. *Revista Mexicana de Estudios Antropológicos* 14:75–110
Adams, Richard E. W.
  1966 The Ceramic Chronology of the Southern Maya. Manuscript, University of Minnesota.
  1972 Maya Highland Prehistory: New Data and Implications. In *Studies in the Archaeology of Mexico and Guatemala*, ed. J. Graham, pp. 1–21. Contributions of the University of California, no. 16. Berkeley: Archaeological Research Facility.
  1974 *Preliminary Reports on Archaeological Investigations in the Rio Bec Area, Campeche, Mexico.* Middle American Research Institute, pub. 31. New Orleans: Tulane University.
Adams, Robert McC.
  1961 Changing Patterns of Territorial Organization in the Central Highlands of Chiapas, Mexico. *American Antiquity* 26:341–60.
  1966 *The Evolution of Urban Society.* Chicago: Aldine-Atherton.
Alvarado, Pedro de
  1924 *An Account of the Conquest of Guatemala in 1524.* New York: Cortés Society.
Andrews, E. Wyllys, IV
  1943 *The Archaeology of Southwestern Campeche.* Carnegie Institution of Washington, pub. 546. Contributions to American Anthropology and History, no. 40. Washington, D.C.: Carnegie Institution of Washington.
  1960 Excavations at Dzibilchaltun, Northwestern Yucatan, Mexico. *Proceedings of the American Philosophical Society* 104:254–65.
Armillas, Pedro
  1951 Mesoamerican Fortifications. *Antiquity* 25:77–86.
Balandier, Georges
  1970 *Political Anthropology.* New York: Pantheon Books.
Ball, Joseph W.
  1974 A Coordinate Approach to Northern Maya Prehistory: A.D. 700–1200. *American Antiquity* 39:85–93.
Bancroft, Hubert H.
  1875 *The Native Races of the Pacific States of North America.* 5 vols. New York: Appleton and Co.
Becquelin, Pierre
  1966 Informe preliminar sobre las excavaciones en Acul. *Antropología e Historia de Guatemala* 18:11–22.
  1969 Archéologie de la Région de Nébaj. *Mémoires de L'Institut d'Ethnologie*, no. 2. Paris: Musée de L'Homme.
Berlin, Heinrich
  1953 *Archaeological Reconnaissance in Tabasco.* Current Reports vol. 1, no. 7. Washington, D.C.: Carnegie Institution of Washington.
  1956 *Late Pottery Horizons of Tabasco, Mexico.* Carnegie Institution of Washington, pub. 606, contribution 59. Washington, D.C.: Carnegie Institution of Washington.

Berry, Brian J. L.

1967   *Geography of Market Centers and Retail Distribution.* Englewood Cliffs: Prentice-Hall.

Borah, Woodrow, and Sherburne F. Cook

1963   *The Aboriginal Population of Central Mexico on the Eve of the Spanish Conquest.* Ibero-Americana, no. 45. Berkeley and Los Angeles: University of California Press.

Borhegyi, Stephen F. de

1950   Estudio arqueológico en la falda norte del Volcán de Agua. *Antropología e Historia de Guatemala* 2:3–22.

1956   Settlement Patterns in the Guatemalan Highlands: Past and Present. In *Prehistoric Settlement Patterns in the New World,* ed. G. R. Willey, pp. 101–6. Viking Fund Publications in Anthropology, no. 23. New York: Wenner-Gren Foundation.

1965   Archaeological Synthesis of the Guatemalan Highlands. In *Archaeology of Southern Mesoamerica,* ed. G. R. Willey, pp. 3–58. Handbook of Middle American Indians, vol. 2. Austin: University of Texas Press.

Boserup, Ester

1965   *The Conditions of Agricultural Growth.* Chicago: Aldine.

Brasseur de Bourbourg, Charles Etienne

1857   *Histoire des Nations Civilisées du Méxique et de l'Amérique Centrale.* 4 vols. Paris.

1861   *Popol Vuh. Le Livre Sacré et les mythes de l'antiquité américaine (avec les livres héroiques et historiques des Quichés).* Paris: A. Bertrand.

1947   Antigüedades Guatemaltecas. *Anales de la Sociedad de Geografía e Historia de Guatemala* 22:99–104.

Brundage, Burr Cartwright

1975   *Two Earths, Two Heavens: An Essay Contrasting the Aztecs and the Incas.* Albuquerque, University of New Mexico Press.

Bullard, William R.

1970   Topoxte: A Postclassic Maya Site in Peten, Guatemala. In *Maya Archaeology,* ed., W. R. Bullard, pp. 245–307. Papers of the Peabody Museum of Archaeology and Ethnology, vol. 61. Cambridge, Mass.: Harvard University.

Burkitt, Robert

1930   Explorations in the Highlands of Western Guatemala. *The Museum Journal* (Museum of the University of Pennsylvania) 21:41–72.

Butler, Mary

1959   Spanish Contact at Chipal. *Festband Franz Termer. Mitteilungen aus dem Museum für Völkerkunde in Hamburg* 25:28–35.

Campbell, Lyle R.

1971   Historical Linguistics and Quichean Linguistic Prehistory. Ph.D. diss., University of California, Los Angeles.

1976   Quichean Prehistory: Linguistic Contributions. Paper presented at the Conference on Prehispanic Quichean Cultures, Albany, State University of New York.

Carmack, Robert M.

1966   La perpetuación del clan patrilineal en Totonicapán. *Antropología e Historia de Guatemala* 18:43–60.

1967   Análisis histórico-sociológico de un antiguo título Quiché. *Antropología e Historia de Guatemala* 19:3–13.

1968   Toltec Influence on the Postclassic Culture History of Highland Guatemala. In *Archaeological Studies in Middle America,* pp. 42–92. Middle American Research Institute, pub. 26. New Orleans: Tulane University.

1970   A Social History of the Guatemalan Indian. In *Stranger in Our Midst: Guided Culture Change in Highland Guatemala,* ed. P. T. Furst and K. B. Reed, pp. 75–153. Los Angeles: Center for Latin American Studies, University of California.

1971 Ethnography and Ethnohistory: Their Application in Middle American Studies. *Ethnohistory* 18:127–45.

1973 *Quichean Civilization*. Berkeley: University of California Press.

1974 La Estratifación Quicheana Prehispánica. Paper presented at the 41st meeting of the International Congress of Americanists, Mexico City.

1975 La verdadera identificación de Mixco Viejo. *Anales de la Sociedad de Geografía e Historia de Guatemala*. (in press)

n.d.a. *Quichean Political History*. Manuscript, State University of New York, Albany.

n.d.b. Political Geography and Settlement Patterns of Utatlan According to the Ethnohistoric Sources. Manuscript, State University of New York, Albany.

n.d.c. Quichean Prehispanic Ecology. Manuscript, State University of New York, Albany.

n.d.d. Prehispanic Quiche Historiography. Manuscript to be published by *Revista Mexicana de Estudios Antropológicos*.

Carmack, Robert M., Thomas Forhan, Steven Marqusee, Florence Sloane, Russell Stewart, and Jeff Thelen

1972 La pre y proto-historia de Santiago Momostenango. *Guatemala Indígena* 7:5–21.

Carmack, Robert M., and John W. Fox

n.d. Chinautla prehispánico. *Obras Públicas de Guatemala*. (in press)

Carmack, Robert M., John W. Fox, and Russell E. Stewart

1975 La formación del reino Quiché. Instituto de Antropología e Historia, Especial no. 7. Guatemala: Ministry of Education.

Carmack, Robert M., and Lynn Larmer

1971 Quichean Art: A Mixteca- Puebla Variant. *Katunob* 7:12–35.

Carneiro, Robert L.

1970 A Theory of the Origin of the State. *Science* 169:733–38.

Caso, Alfonso

1966 El culto al sol: notas a la interpretación de W. Lehmann. *Sociedad Mexicana de Antropología* 1:177–90.

Chahoma (1555)

1956 Títulos indígenas de tierras, trans. M. Crespo. *Antropología e Historia de Guatemala* 8:10–15.

Chapman, Anne M.

1957 Port of Trade Enclaves in Aztec and Maya Civilizations. In *Trade and Market in the Early Empires*, ed. K Polanyi, C. M. Arensberg, and H. W. Pearson, pp. 114–53. Glencoe, Ill.: Free Press.

Christaller, Walter

1966 *Central Places in Southern Germany*, trans. C. W. Baskin. Englewood Cliffs: Prentice-Hall.

Coe, Michael D., and Kent V. Flannery

1967 *Early Cultures and Human Ecology in South Coastal Guatemala*. Smithsonian Contributions to Anthropology, vol. 3. Washington, D.C.: Smithsonian Press.

Coe, William R.

1970 *Tikal, A Handbook of the Maya Ruins*. University of Pennsylvania. Philadelphia: University Museum.

Colby, Benjamin N.

1976 The Anomalous Ixil—Bypassed by the Postclassic? *American Antiquity* 41:74–80.

Colby, Benjamin N., and Pierre L. Van Den Berghe

1969 *Ixil Country: A Plural Society in Highland Guatemala*. Berkeley: University of California.

C'oyoi (ca. 1550–1570)

1973 "Título C'oyoi" in Carmack 1973:265–345.

Crumley, Carole L.
1976 Toward a Locational Definition of State Systems of Settlement. *American Anthropologist* 78:59–73.

Daly, César
1857 Note pouvant servir à l'exploration des anciens monuments du Méxique. In *Archives de la Commission Scientifique du Méxique*, vol. I, pp. 146–61. Paris.

Díaz del Castillo, Bernal
1908–1916 True History of the Conquest of New Spain. Trans. A. P. Maudslay. 5 vols. London: Hakluyt Society.

Dutton, Bertha P., and Hulda R. Hobbs
1943 *Excavations at Tajumulco, Guatemala.* Monographs of the School of American Research, no. 9. Santa Fe, New Mexico: School of American Research and Museum of New Mexico.

Edmonson, Munro S.
1971 *The Book of Counsel: The Popol Vuh of the Quiche Maya of Guatemala.* Middle American Research Institute, pub. 35. New Orleans: Tulane University.

Ekholm, Gordon F.
1944 Excavations at Tampico and Panuco in the Huasteca, Mexico. *American Museum of Natural History, Anthropological Papers*, vol. 38, pp. 321–509.

Feldman, Lawrence
n.d. Archaeology at Beleh. Occasional Papers in Anthropology, Department of Anthropology. University Park: The Pennsylvania State University.

Foshag, William F.
1957 *Mineralogical Studies on Guatemalan Jade.* Smithsonian Miscellaneous Collection, no. 135. Washington, D.C.: Smithsonian Institution.

Fox, David
1973 Lecture presented to members of the Utatlan Project, Guatemala City, June 23.

Fox, John W.
1975 Centralism and Regionalism: Quiche Acculturation Processes in Settlement Patterning. An Archaeological and Ethnohistoric Study of Late Postclassic Highland Maya Ethnic Groups. Ph.D. diss. State University of New York, Albany.
1976 "A Model of Late Postclassic Highland Maya Urbanism," paper presented at the annual meeting of the Society for American Archaeology. St. Louis, Missouri.
1977 Quiche Expansion Processes. In *Archaeology and Ethnohistory of the Central Quiche*, ed. D. T. Wallace and R. M. Carmack, pp. 82–97. Albany: Institute for Mesoamerican Studies.

Fuentes y Guzmán, Francisco Antonio de
1932–33 *Recordación florida: Discurso historical y demonstración natural, material, militar y política del Reyno de Guatemala.* Biblioteca "Goathemala," Sociedad de Geografía e Historia de Guatemala, vols. 6–8. Guatemala: Tipografía Nacional.

Gage, Thomas
1958 *Thomas Gage's Travels in the New World*, ed. J. E. S. Thompson. Norman: University of Oklahoma Press.

Gorenstein, Shirley
1973 Tepexi el Viejo: A Postclassic Fortified Site in the Mixteca-Puebla Region of Mexico. *Transactions of the American Philosophical Society.* Vol. 63, Part 1. Philadelphia: American Philosophical Society.

Guillemin, Jorge F.
1958 La Pirámide B6 de Mixco Viejo, y el Sacrificatorio de Utatlán. *Antropología e Historia de Guatemala* 10:21–27.
1965 *Iximche, Capital del Antiguo Reino Cakchiquel.* Guatemala: Instituto de Antropología e Historia.

1967 The Ancient Cakchiquel Capital of Iximche. *Expedition* 9:22–35.
1969 Exploration du Groupe C d'Iximché (Guatemala). *Bulletin de la Société Suisse des Americanistes* 33:23–33.

Haggett, Peter
1966 *Locational Analysis in Human Geography.* New York: St. Martin's Press.

Hall, A. D., and R. E. Fagen
1956 Definition of System. *General Systems* 1:18–28.

Hardoy, Jorge E.
1973 *Pre-Columbian Cities.* New York: Walker and Co.

Harner, M. J.
1970 Population Pressure and the Social Evolution of Agriculturists. *Southwestern Journal of Anthropology* 26:67–86.

Hellmuth, Nicholas M.
1970 The Chorti-Lacandon of Dolores (Sac Balam) Chiapas 1695-1712. Manuscript, Guatemala City.

Hole, Frank, and Robert F. Heizer
1973 *An Introduction to Prehistoric Archeology.* Third Edition. New York: Holt, Rinehart and Winston.

Ichon, Alain
1975 *Organisation d'un Centre Quiche Protohistorique: Pueblo-Viejo-Chichaj.* La Mission Scientifique Française au Guatemala. Paris: Ministère des Affaires Etrangères.
n.d. Campagne de Fouilles 1972–1973. Manuscript, Paris.

IGN
n.d. Instituto Geográfico Nacional, topographic maps, scale 1:50,000. Avenida las Americas, Guatemala.

Jiménez Moreno, Wigberto
1966 Mesoamerica Before the Toltecs. In *Ancient Oaxaca,* ed. J. Paddock, pp. 1–82. Stanford: Stanford University Press.

Kaplan, David
1960 The Law of Cultural Dominance. In *Evolution and Culture,* ed. M. D. Sahlins and E. R. Service, pp. 69–92. Ann Arbor: University of Michigan Press.

Kelsey, Vera, and Lilly de Jongh Osborne
1939 *Four Keys to Guatemala.* New York: Funk and Wagnalls.

Kidder, Alfred V., J. D. Jennings, and Edwin M. Shook
1946 *Excavations at Kaminaljuyu, Guatemala.* Carnegie Institution of Washington, pub. 561. Washington, D.C.: Carnegie Institution of Washington.

Kubler, George
1958 The Design of Space in Maya Architecture. *Universidad Nacional Autónoma México, Miscelleanea Paul Rivet* 1:515–31.
1961 Chichen Itza y Tula. *Estudios de Cultura Maya* 1:47–80.

La Farge, Oliver, and Douglas Byers
1931 *The Year Bearer's People: A Detailed Study of the Daily Life and Ceremonies of the Jalealteca Indians of Guatemala.* Middle American Research Institute, pub. 3. New Orleans: Tulane University.

Landa, Diego de
1941 *Landa's Relación de las Cosas de Yucatán* (1566). Translated and with notes by A. M. Tozzer. Papers of Peabody Museum of Archaeology and Ethnology, vol. 13. Cambridge, Mass.: Harvard University.

Las Casas, Bartolomé de
1958 *Apologética historia de las Indias.* Biblioteca de Autores Españoles, no. 106. Madrid: Ediciones Atlas.

Lehmann, Henri
1968 *Mixco Viejo: guía de las ruinas de la plaza fuerte Pocomam.* Guatemala: Tipografía Nacional.

Lothrop, Samuel K.
1933 *Atitlan: An Archaeological Study of the Ancient Remains on the Borders of Lake Atitlan, Guatemala.* Carnegie Institution of Washington, pub. 444. Washington, D.C.: Carnegie Institution of Washington.
1936 *Zacualpa: A Study of Ancient Quiche Artifacts.* Carnegie Institution of Washington, pub. 472. Washington, D.C.: Carnegie Institution of Washington.

Maler, Teobert
1903 *Researches in the Central Portion of the Usumatsintla Valley.* Memoirs of the Peabody Museum of Archaeology and Ethnography, vol. 2, no. 2. Cambridge, Mass.: Harvard University.

Margain, Carlos R.
1971 Pre-Columbian Architecture of Central Mexico. In *Archaeology of Northern Mesoamerica,* ed. G. F. Ekholm and I. Bernal, pp. 45–91. Handbook of Middle American Indians, vol. 10. Austin: University of Texas Press.

Marquina, Ignacio
1964 *Arquitectura prehispánica.* Memorias del Instituto Nacional de Antropología e Historia, no. 1. Mexico City: Instituto Nacional de Antropología e Historia.

Marqusee, Steven J.
1974 Mixteca-Puebla Trade and Styles in Guatemala. Paper presented at the 41st meeting of the International Congress of Americanists, Mexico.

Maruyama, Magoroh
1963 The Second Cybernetics: Deviation Mutual Causal Processes. *American Scientist* 51:164–79.

Maudslay, Alfred P.
1899–1902 *Archaeology, Biologia Centrali-Americana.* 5 vols. London: R. H. Porter.

Mayers, Marvin K.
1966 *Languages of Guatemala.* Juna Linguarum, Series Practica, no. 23. The Hague: Mouton.

McBryde, Felix Webster
1945 *Cultural and Historical Geography of Southwest Guatemala.* Smithsonian Institution, Institute of Social Anthropology, pub. 4. Washington, D.C.: Smithsonian Institution.

Michels, Joseph
1971 Lecture delivered at SUNY, Albany, April.

Miles, Suzanne W.
1957a The Sixteenth Century Pokom-Maya: A Documentary Analysis of Social Structure and Archaeological Setting. In *Transactions of the American Philosophical Society* 4:731–81.
1957b Maya Settlement Patterns: A Problem for Ethnology and Archaeology. *Southwestern Journal of Anthropology* 13:239–48.
1958 An Urban Type: Extended Boundary Towns. *Southwestern Journal of Anthropology* 14:339–51.
1965a Sculpture of the Guatemala-Chiapas Highlands and Pacific Slopes and Associated Hieroglyphs. In *Archaeology of Southern Mesoamerica,* ed. G. R. Willey, pp. 237–75. Handbook of Middle American Indians, vol. 2. Austin: University of Texas Press.
1965b Summary of Preconquest Ethnology of the Guatemala-Chiapas Highlands and Pacific Slopes. In *Archaeology of Southern Mesoamerica,* ed. G. R. Willey, pp. 276–87. Handbook of Middle American Indians, vol. 2. Austin: University of Texas Press.

Navarrete, Carlos
  1962 *La Cerámica de Mixco Viejo.* Cuadernos de Antropología, vol. 1. Guatemala: Universidad de San Carlos, Instituto de Investigaciones Históricas.
Nicholson, Henry B.
  1957 Topiltzin Quetzalcoatl of Tollan: A Problem in Mesoamerican Ethnohistory. Ph.D. diss. Harvard University.
  1960 The Mixteca-Puebla Concept in Mesoamerican Archaeology: A Re-examination. In *Men and Cultures: Selected Papers of the Fifth International Congress of Anthropological and Ethnological Sciences,* pp. 612–18. Philadelphia: University of Pennsylvania.
Nijaib I (ca. 1550–60)
  1957 Título de la Casa Ixquin-Nehaib, Señora del territorio de Otzoya. In Recinos (1957:71–94).
Nijaib II (1558)
  1957 Título Real de Don Francisco Izquin Nehaib. In Recinos (1957:96–117).
Nijaib III
  1973 In Carmack (1973:349–52).
Nijaib IV (1555)
  1973 In Carmack (1973:352–55).
Orellana, Sandra L.
  n.d. Ethnohistory and Archaeological Survey of the Tzutujil Maya. Manuscript, University of California, Los Angeles.
Parsons, Lee A.
  1969 *Bilbao, Guatemala.* Milwaukee Public Museum, Publications in Anthropology, no. 12. Milwaukee: Milwaukee Public Museum.
Plog, Fred T.
  1974 *The Study of Prehistoric Change.* New York: Academic Press.
Pollock, H. E. D.
  1936 *Round Structures of Aboriginal Middle America.* Carnegie Institution of Washington pub. 471. Washington, D.C.: Carnegie Institution of Washington.
  1965 Architecture of the Maya Lowlands. In *Archaeology of Southern Mesoamerica,* ed. G. R. Willey, pp. 378–440. Handbook of Middle American Indians, vol. 2. Austin: University of Texas Press.
  n.d. Field Notes for the Carnegie Institution of Washington. Deposited in the Peabody Museum of Archaeology and Ethnology, Harvard University, Cambridge, Mass.
Pollock, H. E. D., R. L. Roys, T. Proskouriakoff, and A. L. Smith
  1962 *Mayapan, Yucatan, Mexico.* Carnegie Institution of Washington, pub. 619. Washington, D.C.: Carnegie Institution of Washington.
Popol Vuh (ca. 1554–58)
  1950 see Recinos, Goetz, and Morley (1950) or Edmonson (1971).
Rabinal Achi
  1955 Teatro indígena prehispánico: Rabinal Achi. F. Monterde, ed. Biblioteca del Estudiante Universitario, no. 71. Mexico City: Universidad Nacional Autríoma.
Rathje, William L.
  1973 Classic Maya Development and Denouement: A Research Design. *In The Classic Maya Collapse,* ed. T. P. Culbert, pp. 405–54. Albuquerque: University of New Mexico Press, School of American Research Advanced Seminars Series.
  1975 The Last Tango in Mayapan: A Tentative Trajectory of Production-Distribution Systems. In *Ancient Civilization and Trade,* ed. J. A. Sabloff and C. C. Lamberg-Karlovsky, pp. 409–48. Albuquerque: University of New Mexico Press, School of American Research Advanced Seminar Series.
Recinos, Adrian
  1954 *Monografía del Departamento de Huehuetenango.* 2d ed. Colección Monografias, no. 2. Guatemala City: Editorial del Ministerio de Educación Pública.

1957   *Crónicas Indígenas de Guatemala.* Editorial Universitaria, vol. 20. Guatemala City: Imprenta Universitaria.

Recinos, Adrian, and Delia Goetz
1953   *The Annals of the Cakchiquels.* Civilization of the American Indian Series, no. 37. Norman: University of Oklahoma Press.

Recinos, Adrian, D. Goetz, and S. G. Morley
1950   *Popol Vuh: The Sacred Book of the Ancient Quiche Maya.* Civilization of the American Indian Series, no. 29. Norman: University of Oklahoma Press.

Remesal, Antonio de
1932   *Historia general de las indias occidentales y particular de la gobernación de Chiapa y Guatemala; escríbese juntamente los principals de la religión de nuestro glorioso padre Santo Domingo y de las demás religiones.* 2d. ed. Biblioteca "Goathemala" de la Sociedad de Geografía e Historia de Guatemala, vols. 4–5. Guatemala City: Tipografía Nacional.

Rivera Maestre, Miguel
1832   *Atlas guatemalteco en ocho cartas formadas y grabados en Guatemala de orden del jefe del Estado C. Dr. Mariano Galvez, año de 1832.* Guatemala.

Rowlands, M. J.
1972   Defense: A Factor in the Organization of Settlements. In *Man, Settlement and Urbanism,* ed. P. J. Ucko, R. Tringham, and G. W. Dimbleby, pp. 447–62. London: Gerald Duckworth.

Roys, Ralph
1966   Native Empires in Yucatan. *Revista Mexicana de Estudios Antropológicos* 20:153–77.

Sabloff, Jeremy A.
1973   Continuity and Disruption during the Terminal Classic Times at Seibal: Ceramic and Other Evidence. In *The Classic Maya Collapse,* ed. T. P. Culbert. Albuquerque: University of New Mexico Press, School of American Research Advanced Seminar Series.
1974   Old Myths, New Myths: The Role of Sea Traders in the Development of Ancient Maya Civilization. Paper presented at the Dumbarton Oaks Conference on The Cult of the Sea, Washington, D.C.
1975   The Rise of the Maya Merchant Class. *Scientific American* 233:72–82.

Sabloff, Jeremy A., and William L. Rathje
1975   Changing Pre-Columbian Commercial Systems. Peabody Museum Monographs no. 3. Cambridge, Mass.: Harvard University.

Sabloff, Jeremy A., and Gordon R. Willey
1967   The Collapse of Maya Civilization in the Southern Lowlands; A Consideration of History and Process. *Southwestern Journal of Anthropology* 23:311–36.

Sacapulas (1551)
1973   Título Sacapulas. See Carmack (1973:37–39, 355–59).

Sahlins, Marshall D., and Elman R. Service, eds.
1960   *Evolution and Culture.* Ann Arbor: University of Michigan Press.

Sanders, William T.
1956   The Central Symbiotic Region: A Study in Prehistoric Settlement Patterns. In *Prehistoric Settlement Patterns in the New World,* ed. G. R. Willey, pp. 115–27. Viking Fund Publications in Anthropology, no. 23. New York: Wenner-Gren Foundation.
1962   Culture Ecology of Nuclear Mesoamerica. *American Anthropologist* 164:34–43.
n.d.   Chiefdom to State: Political Evolution at Kaminaljuyu, Guatemala.

Sanders, William T., and Joseph W. Michels
1969   *The Pennsylvania State University Kaminaljuyu Project 1968 Season.* Department of Anthropology Occasional Papers in Anthropology, no. 2. University Park: Pennsylvania State University.

Sanders, William T., and Barbara J. Price
    1968 *Mesoamerica: the Evolution of a Civilization.* New York: Random House.
Santa Clara (1583)
    1957 Título del pueblo de Santa Clara la Laguna. In Recinos (1957:171–81).
Sapper, Karl
    1891 Die Verapaz und ihre Bewohner. *Das Ausland* 51:1011–16, 52:1034–36.
    1895 Altindianische Ansiedelungen in Guatemala und Chiapas. *Veröffentlichungen der Museum für Völkerkunde* 4:13–20.
    1896 The Old Indian Settlements and Architecture of Northern Central America. In *Annual Report of the Smithsonian Institution*, 1895, pp. 537–55.
Schiffer, Michael B.
    1976 *Behavioral Archeology.* New York: Academic Press.
Scholes, France V., and Ralph L. Roys
    1968 *The Maya Chontal Indians of Acalan-Tixchel.* Norman: University of Oklahoma Press.
Sedat, David W., and Robert J. Sharer
    1972 Archaeological Investigations in the Northern Maya Highlands: New Data on the Maya Preclassic. In *Studies in the Archaeology of Mexico and Guatemala*, ed. J. Graham, pp. 23–35. Contributions of the University of California, no. 16. Berkeley: Archaeological Research Facility.
Segraves, B. Abbott
    1974 Ecological Generalization and Structural Transformation of Sociocultural Systems. *American Anthropologist* 76:530–52.
Service, Elman R.
    1960 The Law of Evolutionary Potential. In *Evolution and Culture*, ed. M. Sahlins and E. Service, pp. 93–122. Ann Arbor: University of Michigan Press.
    1962 *Primitive Social Organization.* 2d ed. New York: Random House.
    1971 *Cultural Evolutionism.* New York: Holt, Rinehart and Winston.
    1975 *Origins of the State and Civilization.* New York: W. W. Norton & Co.
Sharer, Robert J.
    1974 The Prehistory of the Southeastern Maya Periphery. *Current Anthropology* 15:165–87.
Shook, Edwin M.
    1952 Lugares arqueológicos del altiplano meridional central de Guatemala. *Antropología e Historia de Guatemala* 4:3–40.
    1956 An Archaeological Reconnaissance in Chiapas, Mexico. In *New World Archaeological Foundation Publication 1*, pp. 20–37. Orinda, California.
    1965 Archaeological Survey of the Pacific Coast of Guatemala. In *Archaeology of Southern Mesoamerica*, ed. G. R. Willey, pp. 180–94. Handbook of Middle American Indians, vol. 2. Austin: University of Texas Press.
    n.d. Field Notes, 1942–48, for the Carnegie Institution of Washington. Deposited in the Peabody Museum of Archaeology and Ethnology, Harvard University, Cambridge, Mass.
Shook, Edwin M., and Tatiana Proskouriakoff
    1956 Settlement Patterns in Meso-America and the Sequence in the Guatemalan Highlands. In *Prehistoric Settlement Patterns in the New World*, ed. G. R. Willey, pp. 93–100. Viking Fund Publications in Anthropology, no. 23. New York: Wenner-Gren Foundation.
Sidrys, Raymond V.
    1976 Classic Maya Obsidian Trade. *American Antiquity* 41:449–64.
Simmons, Charles S., José Manuel Tarano T., and José Humberto Pinto Z.
    1959 *Clasificación de Reconocimiento de los Suelos de la República de Guatemala.* Guatemala City: Instituto Agropecuario Nacional, Ministerio de Agricultura.

314   REFERENCES

Sloane, Florence P.
1974   Ideology and the Frontier: A Hypothesis of a Quiche Innovation in Religion. Paper presented at the Thirty-ninth Annual Meeting of the Society for American Archaeology, Washington, D.C.

Sloane, Florence and Russell Stewart
n.d.   Archaeological Survey of the Momostenango Area. Manuscript, State University of New York, Albany.

Smith, A. Ledyard
1955   *Archaeological Reconnaissance in Central Guatemala.* Carnegie Institution of Washington. pub. 608. Washington, D.C.: Carnegie Institution of Washington.
1961   Types of Ball Courts in the Highlands of Guatemala. In *Essays in Pre-Columbian Art and Archaeology,* ed. S. K. Lothrop, pp. 100–125. Cambridge, Mass.
1965   Architecture of the Guatemalan Highlands. In *Archaeology of Southern Mesoamerican,* ed. G. R. Willey, pp. 76–94. Handbook of Middle American Indians, vol. 2. Austin: University of Texas Press.

Smith, A. Ledyard, and Alfred V. Kidder
1943   Explorations in the Motagua Valley, Guatemala. Carnegie Institution of Washington, pub. 546. *Contributions to American Anthropology and History,* no. 41. Washington, D.C.: Carnegie Institution of Washington.
1951   *Excavations at Nebaj, Guatemala.* Carnegie Institution of Washington, pub. 594. Washington, D.C.: Carnegie Institution of Washington.

Smith, Carol Anne
1972   The Domestic Marketing Systems in Western Guatemala: An Economic Locational and Cultural Analysis. Ph.D. diss., Stanford University.

Sonnenstern, Maximilian
1859   Mapa General de la República de Guatemala. Guatemala.

Soustelle, Jacques
1970   *Daily Life of the Aztecs.* Stanford: Stanford University Press.

Stephens, John L.
1841   *Incidents of Travel in Central America, Chiapas and Yucatan.* 2 vols. New York: Harper and Brothers.

Stevens, Rayfred L.
1964   The Soils of Middle America and Their Relation to Indian Peoples and Cultures. In *Natural Environment and Early Cultures,* ed. R. C. West, pp. 265–315. Handbook of Middle American Indians, vol. 1. Austin: University of Texas Press.

Stewart, Russell E.
1973   Excavations at Utatlan, Guatemala: A Progress Report. Paper presented at the Thirteenth Annual Northeastern Anthropological Meeting. Burlington, Vermont.
n.d.   The Post Classic in the Santa Cruz del Quiche Basin and Vicinity. Manuscript, State University of New York, Albany.

Swadesh, Morris
1960   Interrelaciones de las lenguas Mayas. *Anales de la Instituto Nacional de Antropología e Historia* 2:231–67.

Tamub (1580)
1957   Título Tamub, or Historia Quiche de Don Juan de Torres. In Recinos 1957:23–67.

Tax, Sol, and Robert Hinshaw
1969   The Maya of the Midwestern Highlands. In *Ethnology,* ed. E. Z. Vogt, pp. 69–100. Handbook of Middle American Indians, vol. 7. Austin: University of Texas Press.

Teletor, Celso Narciso
1955   *Apuntes para una Monografía de Rabinal (B.V.) y algo de nuestro Folklore.*

Coleccion Monografías, no. 3. Guatemala City: Editorial del Ministerio de Educación Pública.

Termer, Franz
1939 The Archaeology of Guatemala. A translation by E. W. Andrews of Zur Archäologie von Guatemala (1931), *Baessler Archiv* 14:167–91. Typewritten copy in the Peabody Museum Library, Cambridge, Mass.

Thompson, J. Eric S.
1943 A Trial Survey of the Southern Maya Area. *American Antiquity* 9:106–34.
1948 *An Archaeological Reconnaissance in the Cotzumalhuapa Region, Escuintla, Guatemala.* Carnegie Institution of Washington, pub. 574. Contributions to American Anthropology and History, no. 44. Washington, D.C.: Carnegie Institution of Washington.
1970 *Maya History and Religion.* Civilization of the American Indian Series, no. 99. Norman: University of Oklahoma Press.

Totonicapan
1953 *Title of the Lords of Totonicapan.* Translated by Delia Goetz from Dionisión José Chonay. Civilization of the American Indian Series, no. 37. Norman: University of Oklahoma Press.

Trigger, Bruce G.
1968 The Determinants of Settlement Patterns. In *Settlement Archaeology,* ed. K. C. Chang. Palo Alto: National Press Books.

Uchabaja (1600)
1973 Título Uchabaja. In Carmack (1973:369–71).

Villacorta C., José Antonio, and Carlos A. Villacorta
1930 Arqueología guatemalteca. Collección "Villacorta" de Historia Antiqua de Guatemala, vol. 2. Guatemala City: Tipografía Nacional.

Wallace, Dwight T.
1977 An Intra-Site Locational Analysis of Utatlan: The Structure of an Urban Site. In *Archaeology and Ethnohistory of the Central Quiche,* ed. D. T. Wallace and R. M. Carmack, pp. 20–54. Albany: Institute for Mesoamerican Studies.

Wauchope, Robert
1948a *Excavations at Zacualpa, Guatemala.* Middle American Research Institute, pub. 14. New Orleans: Tulane University.
1948b Utatlan, Iximche and the Maya Correlation Problem. *Central States Bulletin* 2:19.
1949 Las Edades de Utatlán e Iximché. *Antropología e Historia de Guatemala* 1:10–22.
1970 Protohistoric Pottery of the Guatemalan Highlands. In *Monographs and Papers in Maya Archaeology,* ed. W. R. Bullard, pp. 89–245. Papers of the Peabody Museum of Archaeology and Ethnology, vol. 61. Cambridge, Mass.: Harvard University.

Webb, Malcom C.
1973a The Significance of the "Epi-Classic" Period in Mesoamerican Prehistory. Paper presented at the Ninth International Congress of Anthropological and Ethnological Sciences, Chicago.
1973b The Peten Maya Decline Viewed in the Perspective of State Formation. In *The Classic Maya Collapse,* ed. T. P. Culbert, pp. 367–404. Albuquerque: University of New Mexico Press, School of American Research Advanced Seminar Series.

Weeks, John M.
1975 The Archaeology of Greater Utatlan: El Resguardo and Pakaman Excavations. M.A. thesis, State University of New York, Albany.

West, Robert C.
1964a Surface Configuration and Associated Geology. In *Natural Environment and Early Cultures,* ed. R. C. West, pp. 33–83. Handbook of Middle American Indians, vol. 1. Austin: University of Texas Press.

1964b The Natural Regions of Middle America. In *Natural Environment and Early Cultures*, ed. R. C. West, pp. 363–83. Handbook of Middle American Indians, vol. 1. Austin: University of Texas Press.

White, Leslie A.

1975   *The Concept of Cultural Systems.* New York: Columbia University Press.

Wolf, Eric R.

1959   *Sons of the Shaking Earth.* Chicago: University of Chicago Press.

Woodbury, Richard B., and Aubrey S. Trik

1953   *The Ruins of Zaculeu, Guatemala.* 2 vols. New York: United Fruit Co.

Xajil (1573–1604)

1953   Annals of the Cakchiquels (Memorial de Solola). See Recinos and Goetz 1953.

Ximénez, Francisco

1929–31 *Historia de la provincia de San Vicente de Chiapa y Guatemala de la Ordén de predicadores.* Biblioteca "Goathemala" de la Sociedad de Geografía e Historia de Guatemala, vols. 1–3. Guatemala City: Tipografía Nacional.

Xpantzay I (1550–60)

1957   Historia de los Xpantzay de Tecpan. In Recinos (1957:119–29).

Xpantzay II (1550–60)

1957   Guerras Comunes de Quiches y Cakchiqueles. In Recinos (1957:131–49).

Xpantzay III (1554)

1957   Testamento de los Xpantzay. In Recinos (1957:151–69).

INDEX

acculturation, 281–82
Achi. *See* Rabinal
acropolis pattern, 113–19, 123–24, 270, 274, 276, 277, 287–88
administrators, 290
Agaab, 249–50, 265
Aguacatan Valley, 100–101, 103, 109, 277; strategic value of, 112
Aguacatec provinces, revolt of, 293
Aguacatec sites: ceramics at, 105; location of, 101
Ahquemaya, 202–3
Akahal, 195–96, 197, 202–3, 209–10, 216, 218, 220, 221, 223, 224–27, 228–29, 267–68, 277–78, 287, 297
Aldea Lemoa, 62
altars: at Aguacatec sites, 103; in Cakchiquel area, 181, 199, 206, 211; in Chujuyub settlements, 47, 50; at Greater Utatlan, 23–24, 25, 29–32, 33–34; at Ixil sites, 96; at Pueblo Viejo Malacatancito, 134; at Sacapulas Quiche sites, 72, 76, 77, 82, 85; at Tuitenam, 142; at Zaculeu, 144, 146, 147–48
Alvarado, Gonzalo de, 138
Alvarado, Pedro de, 35, 39, 296
architecture: defined, 5; and ethnicity, 6–7; Maya influence on, 123; Mexican influence on, 3, 67, 123, 227–28
artifacts. *See* ceramics, obsidian artifacts
artisans, 38, 290
Awilix (god), 59, 63, 64, 68, 240–42; temple of, 37
Awilix (site), 51; ethnohistory of, 59

Balamiha, 106–7
ball courts: at Aguacatec sites, 103; in Cakchiquel area, 181, 204, 206, 211, 218, 222; in Chujuyub settlements, 47–50; in Eastern Quiche area, 239, 242, 246, 256, 263; at Greater Utatlan, 23, 25, 27, 29, 33, 37; at Ixil sites, 93, 96, 100; at Pueblo Viejo Malacatancito, 134; at Sacapulas Quiche sites, 74, 75, 77, 80, 82, 84, 85, 87, 88; at Sija, 157, 158; at Zaculeu, 146, 148
Bamac, 143

beekeeping, 58, 243
Belej Tzak, 250
Bijux, 96–100
Blanco, Rio, 102–3, 242
brick, 50, 67

Cacuj, Rio, 237
Cahyup, 264; artifacts of, 253; civic plazas of, 251–53; elite residential complex of, 253; ethnohistory of, 255; settlement pattern of, 253–55; topography of, 251
Caja San Pedro, 61
Cakchiquel, 255, 278–79, 282, 286, 296, 302; Central Quiche influence on, 224; conquest system of, 176–77; dialects of, 177; highland areas of, 177–78; as Quiche subjects, 176; revolt of, 293–94
Cakolquiej, 39
Cakyug, 255
Canacya, Rio, 195, 196
Canil, 81, 120
Carmack, Robert, xi, 19
carved ware, 117
caves: at Greater Utatlan, 24, 34; at Ixil sites, 96
Cawinal, 287; artifacts at, 247; civic plazas of, 244–47; ethnohistory of, 249–50; residential structures of, 246, 247; settlement pattern of, 247–49; topography of, 243–44
centralism, defined, 7–8, 280
centralization: in Cakchiquel area, 223; in Central Quiche area, 62; in Eastern Quiche area, 266; among Mam, 173; measurement of, 10–12; in Sacapulas Quiche sites, 111; and settlement patterns, 298–99
central-place theory, 11–12, 300–301
ceramics: at acropolis sites, 117; at Aguacatec sites, 105; in Cakchiquel area, 183–84, 188, 193, 195, 196, 200–201, 207, 211, 215, 219, 227, 228; Central Quiche, 282; Central Quiche influence in, 117–18; at Chirijox, 159, 161; in Chujuyub settlements, 53–55, 56, 67–68; of Eastern Quiche area, 234, 247, 253; Pokoman, 286; at Pueblo Viejo Malacatancito, 135; at Quiak,

317